CULTIVATING HUMANITY

Cultivating Humanity

A CLASSICAL DEFENSE OF REFORM
IN LIBERAL EDUCATION

Martha C. Nussbaum

HARVARD UNIVERSITY PRESS
Cambridge, Massachusetts
London, England

Library of Congress Cataloging-in-Publication Data
Nussbaum, Martha Craven, 1947–
Cultivating humanity : a classical defense of reform in liberal
education / Martha C. Nussbaum.
p.   cm.
Includes bibliographical references (p.   ) and index.
ISBN 0-674-17948-X (cloth)
ISBN 0-674-17949-8 (pbk)
1. Education, Humanistic—United States—Case studies.
2. Education, Higher—Social aspects—United States—Case studies.
3. Universities and colleges—United States—Sociological aspects—
Case studies.   4. Curriculum change—United States—Case studies.
I. Title.
LC1011.N87   1997
370.11′2—dc21   96-53190

For Rachel
"Aliquid et de tuo profer"

CONTENTS

This book began from many experiences stored up from twenty years of teaching at Harvard, Brown, and the University of Chicago and from travels to dozens of American campuses, both as a visiting lecturer and as a Phi Beta Kappa Visiting Professor. During the latter program I visited ten campuses for three days each, in each case teaching three or four undergraduate classes (in either philosophy or classics) as well as giving public lectures to students and faculty and holding many informal office hours. The Council for Philosophical Studies has a similar program, funded by a grant from the National Endowment for the Humanities, in which I regularly participate. The aim of both programs is to bring speakers to campuses that might otherwise be unable to afford such visits. As time went on, I found myself comparing what I had experienced with what I read in books about higher education; frequently I felt that the reports did not correctly represent the overall situation in our colleges and universities. I began to express this discontent in review pieces written for the *New York Review of Books* and the *New Republic.*

My own approach was, and is, philosophical. I intend to argue for a particular norm of citizenship and to make educational proposals in the light of that ideal. But philosophy should not be written in detachment from real life, and it is therefore important to me to ground my proposals in understanding of current developments in American colleges and universities. This experiential basis is all the more important since the general public may well have internalized a picture of these developments that is incomplete or even seriously misleading. It seems important, too, to stress the variety of American students and colleges, in order to make proposals that would not be too abstract to be useful. This project neither attempts nor requires a statistical survey; it will not furnish data about how many college English courses study Shakespeare or how many institutions teach

Bengali and Hindi. What is required, however, is a rich and variegated description of institutions of many different types whose efforts in the direction of curricular change can usefully exemplify, and ground, the philosophical proposals. Most books on higher education confine themselves to a few, usually famous and elite, institutions or to a few anecdotes drawn from others. My aim was to convey something of the feeling of life at institutions of a variety of types, in order to put the reader in a position to think clearly about the changes that are taking place.

In order to make my understanding of higher education in America more systematic and more focused for the book, I initially selected for close examination a "core" group of fifteen institutions chosen to represent different types of U.S. colleges and universities. I preferred campuses where I had spent some time. In each case I selected a single primary source, someone I knew and could trust. (Usually this meant that the person was in philosophy or classics or political theory.) This person, in all cases but one a faculty member, was invited to write a report on campus efforts to incorporate these new forms of education, to send me other names and printed materials, and to assist me or my research assistants on a visit to the campus. Inevitably, life did not proceed exactly according to plan. I received more detailed reports from some schools than from others; in some cases the original "informant" wrote nothing, but I met other people who filled the gap. In some cases other schools came to my attention with curricular initiatives so interesting that I shifted my original focus. The St. Lawrence program, for example, was unknown to me at the beginning of my work, although I had visited the campus. In all cases I sought out different points of view and talked to students as well as to faculty.

Throughout the project I have been immeasurably helped by four fine research assistants. Since they play a role in the book—especially the two who did many campus interviews—the reader should know something about them. Sam Houser, a graduate student in the Brown Classics Department (currently finishing a doctoral dissertation on Stoic political thought), gathered published materials, wrote dozens of letters of inquiry, and organized my files during the first six months of my work. Eric Klinenberg, who worked for me during 1993–94, just after receiving his B.A. in American Civilization from Brown, is currently in the Ph.D. program in sociology at the University of California at Berkeley. He visited Morehouse, Spelman, and Belmont as my representative, interviewing and gathering materials. It was not easy for a Jewish man raised in Chicago and educated at

Brown to go first to Belmont, a conservative Baptist school in Nashville, and the next day to Morehouse and Spelman, inspiring confidence in both places across barriers of religion, culture, and race. When I listen to the hours of interviews he taped I feel that, through intelligence and tact, he succeeded. In the spring and summer of 1994, Yasmin Dalisay worked for me, traveling to the University of California at Riverside, to Brigham Young, and to the University of Nevada at Reno. Yasmin's parents, both Filipino doctors, shortly after moving to the United States accepted job offers in Orem, Utah, near Provo, where Brigham Young is located. They had no previous knowledge of Mormonism. Yasmin grew up as a liberal mixed-culture foreigner in that highly conservative community. Her deep knowledge of Mormonism and her respect (albeit critical) for Mormon traditions made her able to conduct searching interviews there, as well as on campuses where most Brown students would have felt more at home. Yasmin graduated from Brown in 1996 with a philosophy major. In the final days of preparation of the manuscript, my research assistant was Ross Davies, a University of Chicago law student and 1996–97 editor-in-chief of the *University of Chicago Law Review;* in 1997–98 he will serve as a clerk with Judge Diane Wood of the U.S. Court of Appeals for the Seventh Circuit.

Throughout the process all interviewees were aware of the nature of my project; they consented to be interviewed, taped, and cited. A few student names used in the text are pseudonyms, though most are real.

I owe thanks to many individuals who have helped me in conceiving and writing the book, and in the first place to four marvelous editors. Robert Silvers of the *New York Review of Books,* by inviting me to review Allan Bloom's *The Closing of the American Mind* in 1987, started the whole thing; and Leon Wieseltier and Andrew Sullivan of the *New Republic* helped me along by working with me in 1992 on an article on controversies about gay studies. But I owe a special debt of gratitude to Joyce Seltzer of Harvard University Press. She suggested the project to me and has shepherded it through its development, always an exigent, meticulous, tough-minded critic.

For several years before I began work on this book, I found myself living and raising children in a multicultural and multinational family, whose origins were in India, Germany, Italy, and England. Through my own awareness of my ignorance, I learned to ask critical questions about the education I had received, which gave me no information about Hinduism and Islam, about Indian history, or, indeed, about the economic and social situation of the developing world in general. As I worked in a project on development ethics at the World Institute for Development Ethics Research in Helsinki, my awareness of ignorance grew deeper, and I am grateful to Lal Jayawardena and to all who worked with me at the Institute for their patience and support. But it is above all to the Sen family that I owe whatever I have been able to grasp in the area of world citizenship: to Indrani, Kabir, Tumpa, Picco, "Thamma," Babu—and, above all, to Amartya, whose imagination, compassion, and moral commitment are exemplary of what a "world citizen" can achieve.

I owe a palpable debt of gratitude to the hundreds of people who consented to be interviewed for this book or who sent me information, and especially to the campus "informants" who gave me detailed and comprehensive material. Some of these also sent comments on the manuscript, and I wish to thank Scott Abbott, Deborah Achtenberg, John Armstrong, Grant Cornwell, Marilyn Friedman, Ronnie Littlejohn, Walter Massey, Susan Moller Okin, Philip Quinn, Eve Stoddard, and Paul Weithman, and especially David Glidden for his detailed comments on the entire manuscript. Others who contributed very helpful comments include Lawrence Blum, Victor Caston, Thomas D'Andrea, Henry Louis Gates, Amy Meselson, Jean Porter, Witold Rabinowicz, Steven Strange, Candace Vogler, and Robert Gooding Williams. The University of Chicago Law School provides an atmosphere in which deep intellectual and political differences can be discussed with a truly Socratic civility and commitment to reason; I am grateful to my colleagues there for discussing and commenting on a project with parts of which some of them disagree deeply—and especially to Elizabeth Garrett, Dan Kahan, John Lott, Michael McConnell, Tracey Meares, Richard Posner, Mark Ramseyer, David Strauss, and Cass Sunstein.

Finally, I want to thank my many students at Harvard, Brown, and Chicago for all that I have learned about citizenship from teaching them, and for the great pleasure of arguing with them over the years.

But there is one student with whom I have argued more than any other, and with greater pleasure and pride. This is my daughter, Rachel Nussbaum. Wagnerite and market libertarian, Socratic arguer and Nietzschean romantic, she has disputed almost every claim in this book from some point of view within this complex identity—and has made my formulations sharper and more adequate.

Chicago
November 1996

... while we live, while we are among human beings,
let us cultivate our humanity.

Seneca, *On Anger*

The Old Education
and the Think-Academy

In Aristophanes' great comedy *The Clouds,* a young man, eager for the new learning, goes to a "Think-Academy" run by that strange, notorious figure, Socrates. A debate is staged for him, contrasting the merits of traditional education with those of the new discipline of Socratic argument. The spokesman for the Old Education is a tough old soldier. He favors a highly disciplined patriotic regimen, with lots of memorization and not much room for questioning. He loves to recall a time that may never have existed—a time when young people obeyed their parents and wanted nothing more than to die for their country, a time when teachers would teach that grand old song "Athena, glorious sacker of cities"—not the strange new songs of the present day. Study with me, he booms, and you will look like a real man—broad chest, small tongue, firm buttocks, small genitals (a plus in those days, symbolic of manly self-control).

His opponent is an arguer, a seductive man of words—Socrates seen through the distorting lens of Aristophanic conservatism. He promises the youth that he will learn to think critically about the social origins of apparently timeless moral norms, the distinction between convention and nature. He will learn to construct arguments on his own, heedless of authority. He won't do much marching. Study with me, he concludes, and you will look like a philosopher: you will have a big tongue, a sunken, narrow chest, soft buttocks, and big genitals (a minus in those days, symbolic of lack of self-restraint). Socrates' self-advertisement, of course, is being slyly scripted by the conservative opposition. The message? The New Education will subvert manly self-control, turn young people into sex-obsessed rebels, and destroy the city. The son soon goes home and produces a relativist argument that he should beat his father. The same angry father then takes a torch and burns down the Think-Academy. (It is not made clear whether the son is still inside.) Twenty-five years later, Socrates, on trial for corrupting the young, cited Aristophanes' play as a major source of prejudice against him.

In contemporary America as in ancient Athens, liberal education is changing. New topics have entered the liberal arts curricula of colleges and universities: the history and culture of non-Western peoples and of ethnic and racial minorities within the United States, the experiences and achievements of women, the history and concerns of lesbians and gay men. These changes have frequently been presented in popular journalism as highly threatening, both to traditional standards of academic excellence and to traditional norms of citizenship. Readers are given the picture of a monolithic, highly politicized elite who are attempting to enforce a "politically correct" view of human life, subverting traditional values and teaching students, in effect, to argue in favor of father-beating. Socratic questioning is still on trial. Our debates over the curriculum reveal the same nostalgia for a more obedient, more regimented time, the same suspiciousness of new and independent thinking, that find expression in Aristophanes' brilliant portrait.

This picture of today's campuses bears little resemblance to the daily reality of higher education in America, as faculty and students grapple with issues of human diversity. Sensationalistic descriptions of horrors may sometimes be more fun to read than nuanced accounts of responsible decision-making, but the latter are badly needed, since they represent the far more common reality. In order to evaluate the changes that are taking place in colleges and universities, we have to look more closely to see exactly what is changing, and why. What are faculty and students really doing, and how do newly fashionable issues about human diversity affect what they do? What sort of citizens are our colleges trying to produce, and how well are they succeeding in that task? To answer these questions, we need to look not only at one or two well-known institutions but at a wide range, representative of the variety that currently exists in American higher education: institutions public and private, religious and secular, large and small, rural and urban, four-year and university.

When we look in this way, we do see problems; and we do see tendencies that ought to be criticized. But on the whole, higher education in America is in a healthy state. Never before have there been so many talented and committed young faculty so broadly dispersed in institutions of so many different kinds, thinking about difficult issues connecting education with citizenship. The shortage of jobs in the humanities and social sciences has led to hardships; many have left the professions they love. But those who have stayed are intensely dedicated; furthermore, the ablest teachers and scholars are now no longer concentrated in a few elite schools. They are all over the country, reflecting about the mission of higher education, trying out strategies to enliven the thinking of the students who come their way. The real story of higher education in America is the story of the daily struggles of these men and women to reason well about urgent questions and to engage the hearts and minds of their students in that search.

At St. Lawrence University, a small liberal arts college in upstate New York, near the Canadian border, the snow is already two feet deep by early January. Cars make almost no sound rolling slowly over the packed white surface. But the campus is well plowed, even at Christmas. In a brightly lit seminar room young faculty, gathering despite the vacation, talk with excitement about their month long visit to Kenya to study African village life. Having shared the daily lives of ordinary men and women, having joined in local debates about nutrition, polygamy, AIDS, and much else, they are now incorporating the experience into their teaching—in courses in art history, philosophy, religion, women's studies. Planning eagerly for the following summer's trip to India, they are already meeting each week for an evening seminar on Indian culture and history. Group leaders Grant Cornwell from Philosophy and Eve Stoddard from English talk about how they teach students to think critically about cultural relativism, using careful philosophical questioning in the Socratic tradition to criticize the easy but ultimately (they argue) incoherent idea that toleration requires us not to criticize anyone else's way of life. Their students submit closely reasoned papers analyzing arguments for and against outsiders' taking a stand on the practice of female circumcision in Africa.

In Riverside, California, already at 8 A.M. a brown haze blankets the mountains and the orange groves. It is the first day of the summer session at the University of California campus, and the ethnically mixed student body, more than 40 percent minority, crowds the campus green. Richard Lowy, a young white instructor in Ethnic Studies, talks rapidly to my research assistant Yasmin Dalisay, herself a daughter of two Filipino doctors who immigrated to Orem, Utah. Lowy speaks in a low, gentle voice, peering through his thick glasses. He describes the difficulty of teaching about immigration, assimilation, and the political struggles of new minorities in a political climate saturated with sensationalism, mistrust, and appeals to irrational emotion. "Certainly there are some people who teach multiculturalism in a provocative way. I choose a more gentle approach. I try to tell everybody I'm not here to degrade you and I'm not here to condemn anybody for what your ancestors, relatives, or anybody did; I just try to explain what's going on, and I hope that the knowledge I present will begin to affect people, whereas the emotionalism of some people is what turns people off. I think that for people to be orienting their humanity only in political terms is too narrow, and I always tell people that you can either package your humanity in your politics or you can package your politics in your humanity, and if you're really a decent human being with the right attitude and the right heart and good faith toward people it will come out. So I try to put things in that kind of perspective."

In Reno the University of Nevada campus is a small enclave of red brick and manicured lawns in the middle of casino-land. Yasmin talks with Eric Chalmers, a senior health science major from Carson City, who describes himself as having "more bigoted ideas than some people at the university level." Chalmers, who has never heard of the recently introduced "diversity requirement," requiring new freshmen to take one course on a non-Western culture or on an ethnic or gender issue within the United States, applauds the trend to internationalizing, wishing he had had the opportunity to study Islam and the Middle East. But he criticizes a course on domestic violence taught by a "liberated woman professor" because it seemed to him "too demeaning to men." As the interview is drawing to an end, he laughs, remembering something. "Here's another interesting thing. In English 102 we had to write a letter putting ourselves in the shoes of a gay person, like breaking the news to our parents saying we were gay, and explaining our lifestyle to them. At the time, when I was a freshman, it seemed really off the wall to me, and it was kind of an uncomfortable assignment, but now, looking back on it, it seems as though I can understand why he would do something like that—because you come into contact with people like—you know, different types of people—all the time, and maybe it's an understanding of their belief system." He laughs nervously.

On a dark afternoon in February 1995, I go to my Cambridge, Massachusetts, health club. There is a young man behind the check-in desk whom

I haven't seen before—tall, beefy, red cheeked, in his late teens, wearing a red baseball cap and a bright purple sweatshirt with "Washington" in silver letters across the top and a glow-in-the-dark picture of the White House. He tells me his name is Billy. He is reading Plato's *Apology* and *Crito*. So you're reading Plato, I say. "Yeah. You like that stuff?" he asks, and his eyes light up. I tell him I like that stuff a lot, and I ask him about his class. It's at Bentley, a college in nearby Waltham, focused on business education. Who's the instructor? "I don't remember," he says, "She's foreign." The syllabus reads, "Dr. Krishna Mallick." Krishna Mallick, originally from Calcutta, has written some wonderful study questions about Socrates' mission of self-examination, his obedience to the laws of Athens, his willingness to die for the sake of the argument. Soon students will go on to use the techniques they have learned from Plato to stage debates about moral dilemmas of our time. Before I head for the Stairmaster, we talk for a while about why Socrates did not escape from prison when he had the chance, and it's plain that Krishna Mallick has produced real excitement. "You know, I really like this philosophy. Most courses, you have to remember lots of little facts, but in this one they want you to think and ask questions."

At the University of Chicago, a chain-link fence out back of the law school parking lot marks the line between the university campus and the impoverished black community that surrounds it. Black children sometimes climb over the fence or get round it by the driveway, but they are not allowed to stay long. On a May afternoon seventy students, one black, sit in a law school classroom discussing Richard Wright's *Native Son,* a novel set in that very part of Chicago in 1940. They talk about the "line" that Bigger Thomas thought of as the symbol of white hatred and black shame, and they argue intensely over Bigger's state of mind and the degree of his criminal responsibility. Since Justice Clarence Thomas has recently made a statement opposing mitigation in sentencing for blacks who trace their criminal tendencies to their deprived backgrounds, they ask whether Wright's novel supports or subverts Thomas' claims.

Scott Braithwaite, a young gay Mormon, recent graduate of Brigham Young University, gives a Sacrament meeting talk referring to the importance of including discussion of the history and variety of human sexuality in the liberal arts curriculum. This is currently a topic of intense controversy at BYU, and Braithwaite's talk is thick with references both to biblical texts and to Mormon scripture and history. "Ideally," he concludes, "we should love everyone. Yet it is often difficult to love someone unknown, or different from oneself."

As Richard Lowy justly remarks, it is easier in our culture to purvey an emotion-laden sensationalizing message than to tell, with accurate information and humanity and even humor, stories of people's real diversity and complexity. Individuals can all too easily be forgotten when we engage in political debate. This book will let the voices of these representative yet highly individual teachers and students be heard—in the hope that the reader will decide to "package his politics in his humanity," imagining the concrete situations of the teachers who are making curricular choices and thinking about the issues with flexibility and empathy, rather than making a political prejudgment about the faculty who are actually teaching in our universities.

Today's teachers are shaping future citizens in an age of cultural diversity and increasing internationalization. Our country is inescapably plural. As citizens we are frequently called upon to make decisions that require some understanding of racial and ethnic and religious groups in our nation, and of the situation of its women and its minorities in terms of sexual orientation. As citizens we are also increasingly called upon to understand how issues such as agriculture, human rights, ecology, even business and industry, are generating discussions that bring people together from many nations. This must happen more and more if our economy is to remain vital and effective solutions to pressing human problems are to be found. The new emphasis on "diversity" in college and university curricula is above all a way of grappling with the altered requirements of citizenship, an attempt to produce adults who can function as citizens not just of some local region or group but also, and more importantly, as citizens of a complex interlocking world.

When I arrived at Harvard in 1969, my fellow first-year graduate students and I were taken up to the roof of Widener Library by a well-known professor of classics. He told us how many Episcopal churches could be seen from that vantage point. As a Jew (in fact a convert from Episcopalian Christianity), I knew that my husband and I would have been forbidden to marry in Harvard's Memorial Church, which had just refused to accept a Jewish wedding. As a woman I could not eat in the main dining room of the faculty club, even as a member's guest. Only a few years before, a woman would

6

not have been able to use the undergraduate library. In 1972 I became the first female to hold the Junior Fellowship that relieved certain graduate students from teaching so that they could get on with their research. At that time I received a letter of congratulation from a prestigious classicist saying that it would be difficult to know what to call a female fellow, since "fellowess" was an awkward term. Perhaps the Greek language could solve the problem: since the masculine for "fellow" was *hetairos*, I could be called a *hetaira*. *Hetaira*, however, as I knew, is the ancient Greek word not for "fellowess" but for "courtesan."

In a setting in which such exclusions and such "jokes" were routine, is it any wonder that the academic study of women's history, of literature written by women, of the sociology and politics of gender—that all these perfectly normal and central topics were unavailable for serious study? They were just as unavailable as was (in most places) the serious academic study of Judaism, of African and of African-American cultures, of many other ethnic minorities, of many non-Western religions and cultures, of the variety and diversity of human sexuality. Exclusions of people and exclusions of their lives from the domain of knowledge went hand in hand. The exclusions seemed natural and apolitical; only the demand for inclusion seemed motivated by a "political agenda." From the rooftop of Widener, there were many people and many lives that my colleague could not see.

We are now trying to build an academy in which women, and members of religious and ethnic minorities, and lesbian and gay people, and people living in non-Western cultures can be seen and also heard, with respect and love, both as knowers and as objects of study, an academy in which to be a "fellowess" need not mean being called "courtesan," an academy in which the world will be seen to have many types of citizens and in which we can all learn to function as citizens of that entire world.

Inevitably there is pain and turmoil in these attempts to bring about change, and not all proposals for change are healthy ones. Some faculty pursue the diversification of the curriculum in a way that ultimately subverts the aims of citizenship, focusing on interest-group identity politics rather than on the need of all citizens for knowledge and understanding. Some, too, have become unjustly skeptical of rational argument, thinking of its abuses as if they were part of the essence of rationality itself. These errors and excesses, however, are neither ubiquitous nor uncontroverted. Instead of a monolithic "politically correct" orthodoxy, what I hear when I visit campuses are the voices of many diverse individual faculty, administrators, and students, confronting curricular issues with, for the most part, resourcefulness, intelligence, and good faith. This means confronting it locally, understanding the nature of one's students and the resources of one's own institution. Any single set of curricular proposals for citizenship indicts itself by its very singleness, since U.S. college students are an extraordinarily heterogeneous group. So the heroes and heroines of my book are the many thousands of instructors who are working with dedication on this task: instructors like Richard Lowy, Eve Stoddard, Grant Cornwell, and Krishna Mallick, each going to work in a concrete context to create a conception of citizenship for the future. They are thinking searchingly, disagreeing fruitfully, and coming up with concrete solutions that should command our respect even where we do not fully agree.

Our campuses are producing citizens, and this means that we must ask what a good citizen of the present day should be and should know. The present-day world is inescapably multicultural and multinational. Many of our most pressing problems require for their intelligent, cooperative solution a dialogue that brings together people from many different national and cultural and religious backgrounds. Even those issues that seem closest to home—issues, for example, about the structure of the family, the regulation of sexuality, the future of children—need to be approached with a broad historical and cross-cultural understanding. A graduate of a U.S. university or college ought to be the sort of citizen who can become an intelligent participant in debates involving these differences, whether professionally or simply as a voter, a juror, a friend.

When we ask about the relationship of a liberal education to citizenship, we are asking a question with a long history in the Western philosophical tradition. We are drawing on Socrates' concept of "the examined life," on Aristotle's notions of reflective citizenship, and above all on Greek and Roman Stoic notions of an education that is "liberal" in that it liberates the mind from the bondage of habit and custom, producing people who can function with sensitivity and alertness as citizens of the whole world. This is what Seneca means by the cultivation of humanity. The idea of the well-educated person as a "citizen of the world" has had a formative influence on Western thought about education: on David Hume and Adam Smith in the Scottish/English tradition, on Immanuel Kant in the continental Enlightenment tradition, on Thomas Paine and other Founding Fathers in the

American tradition. Understanding the classical roots of these ideas helps us to recover powerful arguments that have exercised a formative influence on our own democracy.

Our democracy, indeed, has based its institutions of higher learning on these ideals to a degree unparalleled in the world. In most nations students enter a university to pursue a single subject, and that is all they study. The idea of "liberal education"—a higher education that is a cultivation of the whole human being for the functions of citizenship and life generally—has been taken up most fully in the United States. This noble ideal, however, has not yet been fully realized in our colleges and universities. Some, while using the words "liberal education," subordinate the cultivation of the whole person to technical and vocational education. Even where education is ostensibly "liberal," it may not contain all that a citizen really needs to know. We should ask, then, how well our nation is really fulfilling a goal that it has chosen to make its own. What does the "cultivation of humanity" require?

The classical ideal of the "world citizen" can be understood in two ways, and "cultivation of humanity" along with it. The sterner, more exigent version is the ideal of a citizen whose *primary* loyalty is to human beings the world over, and whose national, local, and varied group loyalties are considered distinctly secondary. Its more relaxed version allows a variety of different views about what our priorities should be but says that, however we order our varied loyalties, we should still be sure that we recognize the worth of human life wherever it occurs and see ourselves as bound by common human abilities and problems to people who lie at a great distance from us. These two different versions have existed at least since ancient Rome, when statesman and philosopher Cicero softened the stern demands of Greek Stoicism for a Roman audience. Although I do sympathize with the sterner thesis, it is the more relaxed and inclusive thesis that will concern me here. What, then, does this inclusive conception ask us to learn?

Three capacities, above all, are essential to the cultivation of humanity in today's world. First is the capacity for critical examination of oneself and one's traditions—for living what, following Socrates, we may call "the examined life." This means a life that accepts no belief as authoritative simply because it has been handed down by tradition or become familiar through habit, a life that questions all beliefs and accepts only those that survive reason's demand for consistency and for justification. Training this capacity requires developing the capacity to reason logically, to test what one reads or says for consistency of reasoning, correctness of fact, and accuracy of judgment. Testing of this sort frequently produces challenges to tradition, as Socrates knew well when he defended himself against the charge of "corrupting the young." But he defended his activity on the grounds that democracy needs citizens who can think for themselves rather than simply deferring to authority, who can reason together about their choices rather than just trading claims and counterclaims. Like a gadfly on the back of a noble but sluggish horse, he said, he was waking democracy up so that it could conduct its business in a more reflective and reasonable way. Our democracy, like ancient Athens, is prone to hasty and sloppy reasoning, and to the substitution of invective for real deliberation. We need Socratic teaching to fulfill the promise of democratic citizenship.

Citizens who cultivate their humanity need, further, an ability to see themselves not simply as citizens of some local region or group but also, and above all, as human beings bound to all other human beings by ties of recognition and concern. The world around us is inescapably international. Issues from business to agriculture, from human rights to the relief of famine, call our imaginations to venture beyond narrow group loyalties and to consider the reality of distant lives. We very easily think of ourselves in group terms—as Americans first and foremost, as human beings second—or, even more narrowly, as Italian-Americans, or heterosexuals, or African-Americans first, Americans second, and human beings third if at all. We neglect needs and capacities that link us to fellow citizens who live at a distance or who look different from ourselves. This means that we are unaware of many prospects of communication and fellowship with them, and also of responsibilities we may have to them. We also sometimes err by neglect of differences, assuming that lives in distant places must be like ours and lacking curiosity about what they are really like. Cultivating our humanity in a complex, interlocking world involves understanding the ways in which common needs and aims are differently realized in different circumstances. This requires a great deal of knowledge that American college students rarely got in previous eras, knowledge of non-Western cultures, of minorities within their own, of differences of gender and sexuality.

But citizens cannot think well on the basis of factual knowledge alone. The third ability of the citizen, closely related to the first two, can be called the narrative imagination. This means the ability to think what it might be like to be in the shoes of a person different from oneself, to be an intelligent reader of that person's story, and to understand the emotions and wishes and desires that someone so placed might have. The narrative imagination is not uncritical, for we always bring ourselves and our own judgments to the encounter with another; and when we identify with a character in a novel, or with a distant person whose life story we imagine, we inevitably will not merely identify; we will also judge that story in the light of our own goals and aspirations. But the first step of understanding the world from the point of view of the other is essential to any responsible act of judgment, since we do not know what we are judging until we see the meaning of an action as the person intends it, the meaning of a speech as it expresses something of importance in the context of that person's history and social world. The third ability our students should attain is the ability to decipher such meanings through the use of the imagination.

Intelligent citizenship needs more than these three abilities. Scientific understanding is also of the first importance. My excuse for not dwelling on this aspect of a liberal education is that others are far better placed to describe it than I. The same is true of economics, which I shall approach only in its relationship to philosophy and political theory. I focus on the parts of a liberal education that have by now become associated with "the humanities" and to some extent "the social sciences": above all, then, on philosophy, political science, religious studies, history, anthropology, sociology, literature, art, music, and studies of language and culture. Nor do I describe everything in these areas that a good citizen should know. I focus on areas of current urgency and controversy. (Even within the areas of controversy I am selective, allowing the example of African-American studies to stand for more complex debates about ethnic studies generally. Issues of poverty and social class, which I have treated elsewhere, are treated selectively, within chapters organized along other lines.)

It was through ancient Greek and Roman arguments that I came upon these ideas in my own history. The Greek and Roman versions of these ideas are immensely valuable to us as we pursue these debates today, and I shall focus on that contribution. But ideas of this sort have many sources in many traditions. Closely related notions can be found in India, in Africa, in Latin America, and in China. One of the errors that a diverse education can dispel is the false belief that one's own tradition is the only one that is capable of self-criticism or universal aspiration.

Consider my examples of contemporary liberal education in the light of the three goals of world citizenship. The St. Lawrence program focuses on the second goal, that of producing students who are well informed about the lives of people different from themselves, and who can participate in debates about these lives with interest in the future of humanity. But the program leaders hold that any responsible teaching on the first issue must also be Socratic teaching, training logical abilities to think critically and to construct an argument. This training is built into the program, in the central role it gives to philosophy. Finally, the program's emphasis on travel develops imagination as well as factual knowledge. Living with people in Kenya expands one's ability to see the world from those people's point of view, and to approach new knowledge in a more empathetic spirit.

Richard Lowy's ethnic studies classes face an uphill battle: the tenacious loyalty of students to their group identities. He faces a classroom already politicized by these identities, and he must struggle to create a community of learning and dialogue within that situation. Like the St. Lawrence teachers, he emphasizes the importance of thinking of humanity in broader and more flexible terms than those dictated by ideological focusing on group loyalty; like them, he thinks of his goal as one of world citizenship and understanding. The Socratic logical abilities are less stressed in his approach, largely because of the nature of his discipline and subject matter. But imagination and empathy are clearly in evidence in the way in which he appeals to students to transcend their narrow sympathies.

Billy Tucker's philosophy class, by contrast, focuses on the Socratic ability to question and to justify, using this as the underpinning of a concept of citizenship. Krishna Mallick and Richard Lowy are pursuing related goals, each starting from a different disciplinary perspective: goals of broad understanding and respectful dialogue. But there is no doubt that the philosophical contribution to Tucker's education has been important to him as a citizen; it could not have been replaced by factual knowledge alone. Tucker is acquiring a new mode of approaching political debate, one that focuses on issues rather than on personalities, on reasoned analysis rather than on name-calling or sloganeering. He will need facts in order to make his arguments well, and the course stresses this requirement when it asks debaters to do research on their subjects. But the facts would not have produced a dialogue without the course's strong emphasis on Socratic argumentation, and without Mallick's ability to get students interested in such apparently boring phenomena as detecting fallacies and formalizing arguments.

Eric Chalmers' English class focused on the imagination, pursuing the goal of world citizenship through practice in narrative understanding. Chalmers resisted courses presented in what he took to be an ideological or politically partisan manner. But the invitation to present the world from the point of view of a person different from himself did engage him, producing a person who was still capable of critical judgment, but who probably will relate to gay people, as a health care worker, in a more knowledgeable and sympathetic manner.

Scott Braithwaite did not encounter such instruction. Indeed, his training at Brigham Young was constructed in deliberate opposition to all three of my goals. It has more in common with Aristophanes' portrait of the Old Education than with the Socratic approach of the world citizen. Braithwaite was not taught to think critically about his tradition; he was taught to internalize its teachings. In a sense, as a young Mormon in a highly international church, he was taught to interact with others from different parts of the world—but usually in the mode of proselytizing, and never with the thought that learning might move in both directions. Finally, as he reports, his education did not invite his fellow students to imagine or know someone like him, nor did it invite him to know himself. He argues that this failure of knowledge entails a failure in the kind of love his own religion asks all people to have for one another.

Law students at the University of Chicago will soon be influencing life in our country in many ways. A large proportion will soon clerk for judges and write judicial opinions. Others will be involved in public service projects; still others will move directly into work with firms in a variety of capacities. Most will at one or another time deal with the problem of race—as clerks researching cases on affirmative action and minority hiring, as lawyers representing minority clients. Most of these law students, like Wright's character Mary Dalton, have never been into a tenement such as those that still exist several blocks from their classroom. If they are going to become good citizens in their future roles, they need not only logical ability and knowledge, aspects of citizenship already amply stressed in their curriculum. They also need to be able to participate imaginatively in a life such as that of Bigger Thomas, seeing how aspiration and emotion are shaped by their social setting.

In five of six cases, then, nontraditional studies, studies that would not have been in the curriculum twenty-five years ago, are supplying essential ingredients for citizenship. Billy Tucker's class is the closest to one that might have been taught in the last generation, but even that class has a focus on citizenship and on issues of the day that would not have been characteristic of the philosophical academy a while back. The St. Lawrence program involves a radical reform of a curriculum formerly focused on Europe and North America. The emphasis on ethnic studies at Riverside is part of a complex transformation of that curriculum to incorporate a variety of approaches to human diversity. Eric Chalmers encountered an English assignment that would have been unknown in Reno, Nevada, until very recently, part of a diversity movement that still generates intense controversy on campus. Scott Braithwaite laments the absence of such changes in the BYU curriculum. The University of Chicago, like most major U.S. law schools, devotes more attention to issues of race in response to interests of students and faculty. Unlike many such efforts, Chicago's focuses on the humanistic imagination as well as on factual knowledge.

Our campuses educate our citizens. Becoming an educated citizen means learning a lot of facts and mastering techniques of reasoning. But it means something more. It means learning how to be a human being capable of love and imagination. We may continue to produce narrow citizens who have difficulty understanding people different from themselves, whose imaginations rarely venture beyond their local setting. It is all too easy for the moral imagination to become narrow in this way. Think of Charles Dickens' image of bad citizenship in *A Christmas Carol,* in his portrait of the ghost of Jacob Marley, who visits Scrooge to warn him of the dangers of a blunted imagination. Marley's ghost drags through all eternity a chain made of cash boxes, because in life his imagination never ventured outside the walls of his successful business to encounter the lives of the men and women around him, men and women of different social class and background. We produce all too many citizens who are like Marley's ghost, and like Scrooge before he walked out to see what the world around him contained. But we have the opportunity to do better, and now we are beginning to seize that opportunity. That is not "political correctness"; that is the cultivation of humanity.

CHAPTER ONE

Socratic Self-Examination

> If I tell you that this is the greatest good for a human being, to engage every day in arguments about virtue and the other things you have heard me talk about, examining both myself and others, and if I tell you that the unexamined life is not worth living for a human being, you will be even less likely to believe what I am saying. But that's the way it is, gentlemen, as I claim, though it's not easy to convince you of it.
>
> Socrates, in Plato, *Apology* 38A

The Old Education, in Aristophanes' portrait, acculturated young citizens to traditional values. They learned to internalize and to love their traditions, and they were discouraged from questioning them. As Aristophanes sees it, the most dangerous opponent of this Old Education is Socrates, whose questions subvert the authority of tradition, who recognizes no authority but that of reason, asking even the gods to give a reasoned account of their preferences and commands. Socrates' "Think-Academy" is depicted as a source of civic corruption, where young people learn to justify beating their parents. This fictional attack fed a real suspicion of the Socratic way of life. Athenian leaders, unsettled at the idea that young people would search for arguments to justify their beliefs rather than simply following parents and civic authorities, blamed Socrates for the cultural disharmony they sensed around them. Charged with corrupting the young, he eventually forfeited his life.

The ancient debate between Socrates and his enemies is of value for our present educational controversies. Like Socrates, our colleges and universities are being charged with corruption of the young. Seeing young people emerge from modern "Think-Academies" with many challenges to traditional thinking—about women, about race, about social justice, about patriotism—social conservatives of many kinds have suggested that these universities are homes for the corrupt thinking of a radical elite whose ultimate aim is the subversion of the social fabric.[1] Once again an education that promotes acculturation to the time-honored traditions of "Western Civilization" is being defended against a more Socratic education that insists on teaching students to think for themselves. At institutions of the most varied sorts, students are indeed asking questions and challenging the authority of tradition.

At Notre Dame University in South Bend, Indiana, students in a course on science and human values, taught by philosopher Philip Quinn, fulfill the institution's two-semester philosophy requirement. Quinn, a Catholic who left Brown University for Notre Dame because he wished to teach in a Catholic institution, sees the requirement as a way of getting even the most passive students to think for themselves and to argue for their beliefs. Most students in the class say that the philosophy requirement has made them better Catholics by forcing them to defend their choices with arguments. Several students dissent. Speaking for this group, Kevin Janicki, a tall, athletic blond man, says that philosophy has led him to question his Catholic faith by forcing him to notice how little rational argument is in evidence when the university administration handles issues relating to women and homosexuality. They ask you to take philosophy and ask questions, and then they ask you to obey authority and to ask no questions. He stands in the back of the crowded classroom puzzled.

At Belmont University, a Baptist institution in Nashville, Tennessee, I spend the day talking about ancient Greek ethics to a group of remarkably eager and well-informed students.[2] Then I go over to Professor Ginger Justus' house for an informal supper with philosophy majors. Justus, a gifted young philosophy teacher, greets the students warmly; her voice crackles with humor. As we all sit around on the floor eating, the students tell me of their decision to major in philosophy at a time when that department has recently won permission to separate itself from the religion department. They love what they are doing, they tell me, but many of their friends have dropped them. They are under strong parental pressure not to associate with them, since philosophy majors are thought to be tainted by "secular humanism."

At Brown University just before Christmas I meet with my three senior honors thesis advisees for 1995. Amy Meselson is writing about the Stoics and Aristotle on free will and determinism. She trudges in early to discuss the twenty single-spaced pages of meticulous textual analysis she has given me that morning. Nicole Li, a second-generation citizen of Chinese and British origins, is writing about women and revenge, connecting ancient Greek accounts with modern ethical and legal arguments. She brings me a new book on justifiable homicide, asking me to be sure to read it in the next two days (along with two others she gave me the week before) so that she can take them all home to Seattle for vacation. Liliana Garcés is writing about philosophical and religious arguments for and against abortion in her native country of Colombia, from which she emigrated to the United States at age twelve, speaking no English. (Her mother worked as a janitor to send her through parochial schools, and now works as a beautician.) A serene, lucid woman with a lightly accented voice (and a 4.0 average in philosophy), Liliana is about to return to Medellín to conduct interviews over the vacation. We go over her interview questions before discussing her law school application. Two of these three thesis topics would have been unknown in an American philosophy program even fifteen years ago. And yet those two are just as much in the ancient Greek tradition as the first one—like the writings of Seneca and Marcus Aurelius in the tradition of critical reflection stemming from Socrates, applying concepts from philosophy to the analysis and criticism of one's own culture.

At the Cambridge health club, Billy Tucker has received a good grade in his first philosophy test, about Socrates and his arguments. As we talk across the counter, he exudes pride and enthusiasm. He thought philosophy was for people in the Ivy League, and now he knows he can do it. Krishna Mallick has been asking them to use the techniques they learned in thinking about Socrates to analyze arguments in the newspaper. Tucker reports that he is detecting lots of fallacies. Next week they will stage a classroom debate about Dr. Kevorkian and the morality of his conduct. Tucker is surprised that he was asked to find arguments for a position that he does not hold.

Philosophical questioning arises wherever people are. These students are discovering that philosophy is not an abstract, remote discipline, but one that is woven, as Socrates' arguments were woven, into the fabric of their daily lives, their discussions of life and death, abortion and revenge, institutional justice and religion. Philosophy breaks out wherever people are encouraged to think for themselves, questioning in a Socratic way. For all these students, philosophy supplies something that formerly was lacking—an active control or grasp of questions, the ability to make distinctions, a style of interaction that does not rest on mere assertion and counterassertion—all of which they find important to their lives with themselves and one another.

In colleges and universities around the country, students are following Socrates, questioning their views to discover how far they survive the test of argument. Although Socratic procedures have been familiar for a long time in basic philosophy courses, philosophy is now reaching a far larger number of students than it did fifty years ago, students of all classes and backgrounds and religious origins. And philosophy, which at one time was taught as a remote and abstract discipline, is increasingly being linked to the analysis and criticism of current events and ideas. Instead of learning logical analysis in a vacuum, students now learn to dissect the arguments they find in newspapers, to argue about current controversies in medicine and law and sports, to think critically about the foundations of their political and even religious views.

To parents in contemporary America, as to parents in the time of Socrates, such developments can appear very unsettling. Argument seems like a cold strange invader into the habits of the home. The father in Aristophanes came home one day to encounter an argument in favor of father-beating. The parents of the philosophy majors at Belmont may encounter "secular humanism" at the end of the semester, where previously there had been traditional Christianity. Nicole Li's parents send her to Brown and find her making arguments in defense of women who take extralegal revenge against their abusers. The Socratic emphasis on reason seems not only subversive but also cold. To kind and affectionate people, it can seem insulting to demand an argument for some political belief they have long held and have taught to their children. It can appear that their cherished traditions must now undergo scrutiny from the point of view of an elite intellectual world that is strange to them. It is not surprising that the proliferation of "applied ethics" courses, and of philosophy generally, in our colleges and universities should alarm many parents.

Tradition is one foe of Socratic reason. But Socrates has other enemies as well. His values are assailed by the left as well as by the right. It is fashionable today in progressive intellectual circles to say that rational argument is a male Western device, in its very nature subversive of the equality of women and minorities and non-Western people. Socratic argument is suspected, here again, of being arrogant and elitist—but in this case the elitism is seen as that of a dominant Western intellectual tradition that has persistently marginalized outsiders. The very pretense that one is engaged in the disinterested pursuit of truth can be a handy screen for prejudice. Such critics would look askance at the thesis projects of Liliana Garcés and Nicole Li: as powerless, marginalized people, they are allowing themselves to be co-opted by the dominant liberal tradition when they devote their energies to rational argument in the Socratic tradition.

But Socrates' opponents on the left make the same error as do his conservative opponents, when they suppose that argument is subversive of democratic values. Socratic argument is not undemocratic. Nor is it subversive of the just claims of excluded people. In fact, as Socrates knew, it is essential to a strong democracy and to any lasting pursuit of justice. In order to foster a democracy that is reflective and deliberative, rather than simply a mar ketplace of competing interest groups, a democracy that genuinely takes thought for the common good, we must produce citizens who have the Socratic capacity to reason about their beliefs. It is not good for democracy when people vote on the basis of sentiments they have absorbed from talk-radio and have never questioned. This failure to think critically produces a democracy in which people talk at one another but never have a genuine dialogue. In such an atmosphere bad arguments pass for good arguments, and prejudice can all too easily masquerade as reason. To unmask prejudice and to secure justice, we need argument, an essential tool of civic freedom.

Liberal education in our colleges and universities is, and should be, Socratic, committed to the activation of each student's independent mind and to the production of a community that can genuinely reason together about a problem, not simply trade claims and counterclaims. Despite our allegiances to families and traditions, despite our diverse interests in correcting injustices to groups within our nation, we can and should reason together in a Socratic way, and our campuses should prepare us to do so. By looking at this goal of a community of reason as it emerges in the thought of Socrates and the Greek Stoics, we can show its dignity and its importance for democratic self-government. Connecting this idea to the teaching of philosophy in undergraduate courses of many sorts, we shall see that it is not Socratic education, but its absence, that would be fatal to the health of our society.

Socratic Inquiry

Greek philosophers before Socrates claimed to have authoritative knowledge of the topics on which they spoke. Parmenides' poem depicted the philosopher as an initiate who has received insight into the truth from a goddess who holds the keys of justice in her hands. From this vantage point he denounces the ordinary opinions of "mortals" as riddled through and through with error. Empedocles claimed special knowledge on the basis of his own long cycle of incarnations as "a boy, a girl, a bush, a bird, and a dumb sea fish." "Know well," he asserted, "that the truth is in what I say to you." Heraclitus compared his pithy aphorisms to the sayings of the Delphic oracle, implying that they contained a hidden wisdom that the listener must work to extract. Followers of Pythagoras thought of their teacher as a wonder-working sage, and formed communities bound by vows of silence to perpetuate his wisdom.

None of these teachers had a democratic idea of learning. For none was the truth something publicly available to all who can think;[3] for none was it the case that "everyone has something of his own to contribute to the truth."[4] Furthermore, the preferred subject matter of these thinkers was usually remote from the daily choices of a democratic citizenry—the creation of the cosmos, the number and nature of the elements, the relation between thought and being. For these reasons, such philosophical thinkers—who operated in Ionia and in southern Italy, not in Athens—did not have a close rapport with the developing Athenian democracy.

That democracy, however, had home-grown thinkers of other types, who supported better the emerging regime's desire for public evidence and public argument. Historians such as Herodotus gathered data about populations of many kinds in order to reflect about political values. Medical writers publicized facts about epidemics and about the structure of the body. Tragic poets depicted scenes of reasoning about central moral issues that imitated, and in turn shaped, the evolving culture of public debate in the democratic assembly. The distinctive contribution of Socrates was to bring sustained unrelenting philosophical argument to bear on these issues of communal concern—as Cicero later put it, bringing philosophy from the heavens down to earth.[5] His activity did not please everyone who encountered it.

Socrates walks up to a leading politician—a person who "seems knowing and clever to many people, and especially to himself."[6] He engages him in questioning about his alleged expertise, asking him no doubt, as Socrates does so often, for a coherent, contradiction-free account of some central legal and political concepts, concepts such as equality, justice, and law. The expert proves unable to answer Socrates' questions in a satisfactory way. Socrates professes surprise. He goes away, concluding that he is after all a little more knowing than this expert, since he at least knows how difficult the concepts are, and how much his own understanding of them stands in need of further clarification, whereas the expert lacks not only an adequate understanding of the concepts but also knowledge of his own inadequacy. Socrates concludes that he is a very useful figure for democratic government to have around—like a stinging gadfly on the back of a noble but sluggish horse.[7]

When intellectuals behave this way, the people they intend to benefit are not always happy. Socrates proposed that he should be given a salaried position for life at the city's expense. The citizens of Athens had a different idea. To people who are deeply immersed in practical affairs, especially in a democracy, the questioning intellectual—especially, perhaps, the philosopher—is always a slightly suspect character. Why is this person so detached? What is his field of empirical expertise? What gives him the right to walk up to people and question them, as if he had the right to tell them what was wrong with them? Today too, when our campuses "sting" students into rethinking their values, there is likely to be anxiety and resentment. It is very natural to feel that the faculty who are causes of this rethinking must be a self-appointed radical elite, detached from and insensitive to popular values.

Socrates said that the unexamined life is not worth living for a human being.[8] In other words, this life of questioning is not just somewhat useful; it is an indispensable part of a worthwhile life for any person and any citizen. What did he mean by this?

Most of the people Socrates encountered were living passive lives, lives in which, in the most important things, their actions and choices were dictated by conventional beliefs. These beliefs inhabited and shaped them, but they had never made them truly their own, because they had never really looked into them, asking whether there were other ways of doing things, and which ways were truly worthy of guiding them in their personal and political lives.[9] To this extent, they had not made their own selves fully their own. Many of their beliefs were no doubt true, and possibly noble; this Socrates acknowledges, when he holds that education progresses not through indoctrination from the teacher, but through a critical scrutiny of the pupil's own beliefs. When he compares democracy to a noble though sluggish horse, he implies that much of the material of conventional belief is on the right track. The real problem is the sluggishness of thought characteristic of these democratic citizens, their tendency to go through life without thinking about alternatives and reasons.

It is not surprising that they were this way, given the education they had had. Aristophanes' humorously nostalgic portrayal no doubt exaggerates: was there ever a time in any part of human history when young people asked no questions? But its very exaggeration shows the depth of a certain cultural ideal: that of the strong, manly young citizen who is quick to sing the old warlike songs and horrified by the thought of questioning or innovation. It is this sort of citizen whom Socrates intends to awaken.

We might wonder how such questioning can bring a practical benefit. When a skeptical culture looks at today's campuses from a distance, it is easy to judge that young people who question convention are rude and disrespectful, rootless and hedonistic. Their Socratic tendency to ask for reasons and arguments makes them insolent without making them wise. But if we look more closely at Plato's account of Socratic questioning, we will begin to understand how it could be beneficial to democracy; and we will begin to recognize some of those same benefits in our colleges and universities.

In the first book of Plato's *Republic,* Socrates and a group of his friends gather at the home of Cephalus, a wealthy elderly man. The dramatic setting chosen by Plato makes the reader vividly aware of problems of justice and right action. For the reader knows what the characters do not know—that some years after the peaceful scene of philosophical discussion depicted here, they will be embroiled on opposing sides in a violent political conflict that will result in death for three of them and risk of life for them all. A group of oligarchs known as the Thirty Tyrants will seize power in Athens, led by members of Plato's own family. Using slogans appealing to the notion of justice ("we must cleanse the city of the unjust"), they will set about en-riching themselves in any way they can, arranging political charges against wealthy citizens in order to seize their property. Plato intends his reader to recall a famous speech by the orator Lysias—a silent character in the *Republic,* brother of the prominent character Polemarchus—in which he de-scribes the brutal murder of his brother and his own narrow escape. So great was the greed of the new antidemocratic rulers, he exclaims, that they dragged Polemarchus' wife out into the courtyard and ripped the gold earrings out of her ears. And all the while they said that their motive was justice.[10]

Here, then, we have a calm philosophical conversation about justice, set against a background of intense practical urgency. Glaucon and Adeimantus, Plato's own half-brothers, represent the future oligarchic side; Polemarchus, Lysias, and the silent character Niceratus (later murdered) represent the endangered democracy. When these people begin to talk about moral questions, the reader is likely to feel that much is at stake, and may, as well, be skeptical of the role of calm debate in settling what is all too obviously a question of power. When Plato's character Thrasymachus bursts out that justice is merely "the advantage of the stronger," his cynicism about morality would express a concern already alive in Plato's readers. Isn't justice, as Lysias suggests, simply a word that people throw around as a screen for their greedy appetites? Socrates' modern left-wing opponents resemble Lysias and Thrasymachus. They would urge us to see all this talk of argument and reason as a screen for the silent operations of power. Socrates' job is to illustrate the contribution of rational examination, justifying it both to the lover of tradition and to the power-conscious skeptic.

One moment in this exchange shows vividly the benefit that Socrates' "gadfly" technique can bring to democracy. Cephalus, a pious and virtuous man, has spoken of his satisfaction in a life well and justly lived, and the clear conscience with which he faces his impending death. He mentions that his own prosperity has contributed to his morality—for he felt no pressure to cheat or steal, but was able to go through life telling the truth and paying back what he owed. Socrates now asks him whether that is the way he would define justice—as telling the truth and paying back what you owe. Cephalus' son Polemarchus shows enthusiasm for this definition, which is based on conventional poetic authorities—the sort of texts the traditional education asked young people to memorize and not to question. Cephalus himself, gently laughing at the zeal of philosophers, hands over the discussion to his son and goes off to attend to the sacrifices.

What difference does it make that we define our concepts reflectively? Why shouldn't we, like Cephalus, follow traditional practices without philosophical examination? Or why shouldn't we, like Thrasymachus, wake up to the reality that it is all power and dismiss the interest in argument as a way the powerful have of keeping the powerless in line? The dialogue that ensues gives us some answers to both questions. It turns out that the traditional conception of justice does not really prove adequate to guide Polemarchus in a variety of situations in which choice is called for. For example, it does not appear to give good guidance in a situation in which telling the truth and paying debts would result in a disaster. Socrates' example is that an insane person comes to you to ask for the return of a knife you have borrowed; you believe that he will use it to do harm, and you wonder what is the right and just thing to do. Such examples show that a morality that defines duties narrowly, without regard to their consequences, may be inadequate to guide us in a world in which the consequences of our acts matter, and matter greatly. It also indicates that our moral duties themselves are not always simple, and may, as in the case imagined, impose conflicting demands on the well-intentioned person who wishes both to behave honestly and to prevent harm to others. Morality, it seems, needs to recognize the existence of such conflicts and to learn to think well about them. We are, in addition, urged to think hard about the whole question of a morality based on rules and principles: can such a morality be adequate to the complex contingencies of life? Or must we cultivate, along with reverence for principle, moral faculties of discretion or discernment that can help us when we meet a difficult case that does not seem to be fully handled by the existing rule?

In this way, Socrates' inquiry opens up questions that are, and already were, of urgent importance for a culture committed to justice. These questions are still with us, when doctors try to decide how to balance patients' rights against patients' interests, asking what conduct justice requires; when judges try to decide when it is appropriate to use their own discretion in criminal sentencing or in constitutional or statutory interpretation, asking when the codified principle needs to be supplemented, extended, or even revised in the light of judgment about the complexities of a case. Should I, as a doctor, tell the truth to a terminally ill patient, even though such news, removing hope, will blight the remaining time this person has to live? Should I, as a judge, exercise discretion in the direction of leniency to do justice to the particular character of this criminal offender's history and conduct? A lawyer or doctor in the position of Cephalus—one who had never reflected about principles and their possible limits, one who had never attempted to systematize his or her intuitions about the just and the right—would be ill equipped to reach an adequate decision in such circumstances. He or she would no doubt make some decision; but it is unlikely that such decisions would be consistent and evenhanded, reflecting a well-considered policy about the practice of his or her profession. That is why medical schools and law schools are increasingly supplementing their technical education with courses in ethics that pose just such questions and show students how difficult, and how urgent, they are. Such courses, like Socrates, do not impose anything from outside: in that sense they are highly respectful of the content of traditional ethical beliefs. But they do demand reflective sorting-out and consistency; and they claim that in so doing they are bringing a practical benefit.

Socrates' dialogue with Polemarchus and its modern counterparts show us something else as well: that progress can be made through a reflection that seeks the common good. Sorting these issues out does make it possible to give a more precise and adequate analysis of a medical or legal dilemma. Such an analysis, in turn, can help powerless people defend their claims against those in power. Progress needs clarity; it needs concepts and arguments. Distinguishing patients' rights from patients' interests, for example, as reflection about Socrates' example helps us to do, proves crucial in organizing people to oppose the excessive control of a professional medical elite and to vindicate their autonomy.

Socrates questions generals about courage, friends about friendship, politicians about self-restraint, religious people about piety.[11] In every case he demands to know whether they can give good and coherent reasons for what they do, and in every case they prove to have been insufficiently reflective. Socrates shows them that the demand for reasons has a bearing on what they will actually choose. This demand now begins to seem not an idle luxury in the midst of struggles for power, but an urgent practical necessity, if political deliberation is ever to have a dignity and consistency that make it more than a marketplace of competing interests, that make it a genuine search for the common good. Or, as Socrates himself says, "Remember that it is no chance matter we are discussing, but how one should live."[12]

Isn't all this undemocratic? Isn't Socrates really saying that an intellectual elite should rule and that the ordinary person has no right making his or her own decisions? This question raises two distinct problems, one historical and one philosophical. Historically, it is very important to distinguish Socrates' own practice of argument from the philosophical views of Plato, who was certainly an elitist about reason, and openly hostile to democracy. It is not easy to draw this distinction, but it can be done: in some works, Plato represents Socrates as he was, and in others he advances his own ideas, using Socrates as a character. Other sources for the thought of the real-life Socrates help us make this distinction. The historical Socrates is committed to awakening each and every person to self-scrutiny. He relies on no sources of knowledge external to the beliefs of the citizens he encounters, and he regards democracy as the best of the available forms of government, though not above criticism.[13] Plato, by contrast, argues for the restriction of Socratic questioning to a small, elite group of citizens, who will eventually gain access to timeless metaphysical sources of knowledge; these few should rule over the many. It would be a bad thing to follow the example of Plato, concluding that most people cannot govern themselves. But to follow the example of the historical Socrates will help us fulfill our capacity for democratic self-government.

If, however, we follow the historical Socrates, can we really avoid becoming, in the end, philosophical followers of Plato? That is, if we make the demand that citizens scrutinize traditional authority through rational argument, does this inevitably lead to contempt for the people and the rule of an intellectual elite? The historical Socrates is plenty critical, sometimes downright contemptuous, of the citizens he meets. He doesn't think them competent to decide the big political questions that are before them, until they have satisfied his tough intellectual demands. What happens to those who flunk the test? Is he going to say that they should be ruled by people who have passed the test? The fear that antidemocratic political elitism will be the product of a Socratic college education underlies much of the unease about contemporary higher education. Both Socrates' conservative and his left-wing opponents have this fear—the former on behalf of traditions that may lose their authority, the latter on behalf of minority voices that may fail to be heard. It is important, then, to insist that Platonic elitism is not the necessary or even the likely result of allegiance to Socratic values.

Socrates—unlike Plato—holds that the capacities it takes to become a good reflective citizen are in all citizens, or at least all who are not in some unusual degree deprived of the ordinary ability to reason. Unlike Plato, who holds that a high level of mathematical and scientific expertise is required of the potential judge and legislator, Socrates, like the later Stoics, demands only the sort of moral capacity that ordinary people have and use in their daily conduct. What he asks is that this capacity be trained and sharpened so as to realize itself more fully. Nor did Socrates propose that democracy should be replaced by aristocracy or tyranny if people proved resistant to his demands. In fact, in prison just before the end of his life—an end brought about, it would seem, by the irrational behavior of the democracy—he continued to hold that democracy was the best form of government. He believed, it seems, that his demands needed to be met if that noble but sluggish horse would ever be able to realize its potential fully. But even in its semi-somnolent state it did better than the more repressive forms of government—perhaps because, more than other forms, it gave most respect to the powers of reasoning and moral judgment that reside in each and every citizen. It is perfectly obvious that the best educational system in the world will not make all our citizens rational in the Socratic way. The sources of irrationality in human life are many and profound. Thus, there is room in democracy for nonmajoritarian institutions, such as the judiciary. It also seems good that in our democracy, unlike many others, fundamental rights and liberties cannot be abridged by a majority vote. But rights belong to everyone, and this should mean that the development of reason belongs to everyone. The successful and stable self-realization of a democracy such as ours depends on our working as hard as possible to produce citizens who do examine tradition in the Socratic way. The successful integration of previously excluded groups as citizens with equal respect depends on realizing their capacities for rational autonomy and Socratic self-examination. Our institutions of higher education have a major role to play in this project.

The case for preferring democracy to other forms of government is weakened when one conceives of democratic choice as simply the clash of opposing interests. It is very much strengthened by conceiving of it in a more Socratic way, as the expression of a deliberative judgment about the overall good.[14] Socrates prefers democracy because democracy is noble, and he thinks it noble because it recognizes and respects powers of deliberation and choice that all citizens share. His case for democracy cannot easily be separated from his conception of what democratic choice is, and his respect for the moral faculties that are involved in these choices, if not for their current level of development. That is why education seems to him so urgently required in democracy. That is why it seems to him so irrational to turn the most important things over to people whom you then fail to educate. If your children were colts or calves, he says to a prominent citizen, you would make sure that you found a really high-quality trainer for them. Why, then, do you neglect the education of your children, turning it over in a haphazard manner to any slick operator who happens along?[15] These questions would not matter so much in an aristocracy—except for the elite. And they would not matter in a democracy either, if we really thought that democratic choice was and should be simply the clash of uninformed interests. It is because we share with Socrates a richer conception of democratic deliberation—one that the Founders derived from their own reading of ancient Greek sources—that we need to take Socrates' demand to heart.

Socratism and Liberal Education: The Stoics

Socrates depicted "the examined life" as a central educational goal for democracy. But he gave few indications of how this abstract ideal might be realized in formal educational programs. It is from the writings of the Greek and especially the Roman Stoics that we begin to see the curricular implications of Socrates' example. Stoicism began in the third century B.C. at Athens; it continued to exercise enormous influence, in both Greece and Rome, at least through the second century A.D.[16] Its leading participants included figures of enormous political influence—including Seneca, who was regent and tutor to the young emperor Nero, and thus effectively ruler of the Roman Empire during that time; and, later, the emperor Marcus Aurelius, who poignantly reasoned that, since it was possible to philosophize anywhere, it must also be possible to philosophize in a palace. Since these thinkers left copious writings behind, as Socrates did not, and since they were actively engaged in the design of educational and other institutions, we can learn a good deal from them about the practical realization of Socratic goals. It is from their writings that we derive our modern conception of liberal education—or, rather, two distinct ideas of liberal education, which they carefully distinguished but we sometimes do not.

The central task of education, argue the Stoics following Socrates, is to confront the passivity of the pupil, challenging the mind to take charge of its own thought. All too often, people's choices and statements are not their own. Words come out of their mouths, and actions are performed by their bodies, but what those words and actions express may be the voice of tradition or convention, the voice of the parent, of friends, of fashion. This is so because these people have never stopped to ask themselves what they really stand for, what they are willing to defend as themselves and their own. They are like instruments on which fashion and habit play their tunes, or like stage masks through which an actor's voice speaks. The Stoics hold, with Socrates, that this life is not worthy of the humanity in them, the capacities for thought and moral choice that they all possess.

According to the Stoics, critical argument leads to intellectual strength and freedom—by itself a remarkable transformation of the self, if the self has previously been lazy and sluggish—and also to a modification of the pupil's motives and desires. This initially surprising claim has cogency and political importance. Stoics observe that public life is frequently rendered irrational by the power of sentiments such as anger, fear, and envy. Such sentiments, however, are not simply biological urges: they have an intimate relation to thought. A person who gets angry at someone believes that the other person has willingly or culpably committed a serious offense. His anger depends on those beliefs. If he comes to believe that the alleged wrong-doer is really innocent, or that the so-called offense was really an accident, his angry emotion can be expected to be altered in consequence. Anger will also be transformed if the person changes his views about the importance of the wrong done, thinking it a trivial matter. Rational argument can't do anything about the things that other people do to us; Socratic inquiry cannot prevent me from being insulted or criticized. But it can make me think hard about the importance I assign to such slights, and the evidence on which I base my assignments of blame; and this itself affects the emotions.

Usually, the Stoics observe, the ideas involved in emotions such as fear and anger come from the habits and conventions of the surrounding society. Thus an average Roman male is likely to get very angry indeed if his host seats him in a low place at the dinner table.[17] Challenge the culture's obsession with these outward marks of status, and you have effectively challenged that person's basis for anger. If he really comes to believe that his place at table isn't worth worrying about, there will be a bit less anger around for society to channel. The Stoics claim that people who have conducted a critical examination of their beliefs about what matters will be better citizens— better in emotion as well as in thought.

Reason, in short, constructs the personality in a very deep way, shaping its motivations as well as its logic. Argument doesn't just provide students with reasons for doing thus and so; it also helps to make them more likely to act in certain ways, on the basis of certain motives. In this very deep way, it produces people who are responsible for themselves, people whose reasoning and emotion are under their own control.

It is difficult, in a traditional culture, to devise an education that promotes rational freedom. Seneca addresses this problem in his famous letter on liberal education. The letter is addressed to Seneca's friend and constant correspondent Lucilius, a middle-aged political man whose questions about various aspects of philosophy, and of life, serve Seneca as occasions to develop his own views in an intimate and particularized way, while engaging in the give-and-take of argument. Lucilius has asked for Seneca's opinion on the traditional "liberal studies," or *studia liberalia.* This was an education by acculturation to the time-honored values and practices of the Roman upper classes; it included grammar, music and poetry, some math and science, and the use of rhetoric in public life—all taught in a way that emphasized uncritical assimilation of tradition. The word *liberalis* in the traditional phrase meant "suited for the freeborn gentleman." Seneca begins his letter by announcing that he will call that understanding of the term into question. For the only kind of education that really deserves the name *liberalis,* or, as we might literally render it, "freelike," is one that makes its pupils free, able to take charge of their own thought and to conduct a critical examination of their society's norms and traditions. He then proceeds to examine this notion. Combining his discussion here with material taken from elsewhere in Stoic writings, we may extract five claims about Socratic education.

1. *Socratic education is for every human being.*   From the Socratic idea that the unexamined life is not worth living for a human being, together with their belief that a certain sort of critical and philosophy-infused education is both necessary and (if well done) sufficient for a Socratic examined life, the Stoics derive the conclusion that this sort of education is of essential importance for every human being. Since they also hold that it has prerequisites, such as literacy, basic logical and mathematical capability, and a good deal of knowledge about the world, they tend to think of this as a kind of higher education and to defend the view that higher education is an essential part of every human being's self-realization. Because of this focus on advanced or "higher" studies, we may draw on their insights to flesh out a picture of higher education in our own society, though we should not neglect the considerable differences between their era and our own.

Indeed, our own society has followed this Socratic/Stoic line more thoroughly than any other nation, attempting to construct a higher education that combines specialized preprofessional education with a liberal education shared by all students. The nations of Europe do not do this. Students in Europe enter university to study one subject, be it law or medicine or philosophy or history or chemistry or classics. There is no idea, in these curricula, of a core of common studies that is essential to the good life for each and every person.

The Greeks and Romans had a noble ideal, which they did not always fully realize in practice. Socrates announces that he questions everyone he meets—but it is only in his imagined picture of life in the underworld that he can question women. Later philosophers broadened the scope of "everyone," instructing women and even, in the case of the Roman Stoics, arguing for their equal education. The extension of education to women, and also to slaves and poor people, followed directly from the Socratic sense of education's importance for every human being—combined with the recognition of a simple fact, that these people are also human, worthy of respect and concern.[18]

Similarly in our own society, the noble ideal that Socratic education is for all has not been fully realized in practice. We must remember how many people were excluded from the benefits of higher education until very recently. Today our campuses are attempting to fulfill the original Socratic mission, really questioning *everyone,* recognizing *everyone's* humanity. The United States has a larger proportion of college-enrolled citizens than any other nation (although many other nations do more to subsidize higher education for qualified students). It is not surprising that this simple idea has generated many changes, and many demands for further change.

There is an intimate connection between the conception of what liberal education involves and the conclusion that it must be extended to all citizens alike. For if higher education were conceived of as the calling of a select few to a life of theoretical contemplation—as it is sometimes conceived, for example, in Plato—it would be impossible, as Plato in fact argues, to extend it broadly. We would have to search for an elite with special powers of mind, and only these should be admitted to the higher curriculum. Indeed, trying to admit all to this form of study would lead to large-scale social problems. For this contemplative life, as Plato imagines it, is not compatible with a daily active pursuit of political and familial duties. But then, who will there

31

be left to attend to the practical functions of life? Thus Plato's conception of contemplation entails political elitism in more than one way. The Socratic/Stoic conception, by contrast, supports and is supported by democracy. It is because higher education is the development of powers of practical reasoning that every citizen is believed to have that it can be universalized; and it is because it is intimately connected with citizenship and the family that its universalization does not threaten, but promises to strengthen, the democratic political community.[19]

2. *Socratic education should be suited to the pupil's circumstances and context.* If education is understood in the Socratic way, as an eliciting of the soul's own activity, it is natural to conclude, as Socrates concludes, that education must be very personal. It must be concerned with the actual situation of the pupil, with the current state of the pupil's knowledge and beliefs, with the obstacles between that pupil and the attainment of self-scrutiny and intellectual freedom. Socrates therefore questions people one by one. The Stoics, concerned with the broad extension of education to all, are not always able to do this. But they insist that individualized instruction is always, in principle, the goal. Education, they say, is to the soul what the medical art is to the body. As doctors do well only if they are sufficiently sensitive to their patients' actual conditions and symptoms, so too with the teacher. This they show in practice in many ways; these include refusing to recommend a universal curriculum, and writing philosophical works exemplifying Socratic attentiveness to the particular situation of the student.

In recent debates on higher education, the tendency has been to ask whether a "great books" curriculum or certain types of core or distribution requirements are good things in general. All too rarely does anyone ask about the circumstances and background of the students for whom requirements are being designed. If we have in mind a general shared goal but, like the Stoics, acknowledge that our students approach the goal from many different starting points, we will naturally conclude that many different curricular approaches are required.

3. *Socratic education should be pluralistic, that is, concerned with a variety of different norms and traditions.* There is no more effective way to wake pupils up than to confront them with difference in an area where they had previously thought their own ways neutral, necessary, and natural. Exploring

the way in which another society has organized matters of human well-being, or gender, or sexuality, or ethnicity and religion will make the pupil see that other people in viable societies have done things very differently. In our complex world, Socratic inquiry mandates pluralism.

There is a widespread fear—reflected, for example, in the argument of Allan Bloom's book *The Closing of the American Mind*—that critical scrutiny of one's own traditions will automatically entail a form of cultural relativism that holds all ways of life to be equally good for human beings and thereby weakens allegiance to one's own. This was the deep fear, too, that led Athenians to charge Socrates with corruption of the young, and led Aristophanes to associate him with father-beating. But of course this is not what Socratic scrutiny implies. Rather, it implies that we should cling to that which we can rationally defend, and be willing to discover that this may or may not be identical with the view we held when we began the inquiry. The Stoics held that a single picture of the flourishing human life could be defended by reason for all human beings in all times and places. Many people today who think about international justice believe, similarly, that certain norms of human well-being and respect for rights will survive critical scrutiny in all places. Confrontation with the different in no way entails that there are no cross-cultural moral standards and that the only norms are those set by each local tradition. If Bloom and others do think that American traditions are so fragile that mere knowledge of other ways will cause young people to depart from them, why are they so keen on endorsing and shoring up these fragile traditions? What is excellent in our own traditions will survive the scrutiny of Socratic argument.

4. *Socratic education requires ensuring that books do not become authorities.* It is an irony of the contemporary "culture wars" that the Greeks are frequently brought onstage as heroes in the "great books" curricula proposed by many conservatives. For there is nothing on which the Greek philosophers were more eloquent, and more unanimous, than the limitations of such curricula. The old Athenian culture described by Aristophanes did favor an idea of education as acculturation to traditional values. This education relied on canonical texts that had moral authority. The young men who marched to school in rows to sing "Athena, dread sacker of cities" learned quickly enough that internalizing these time-honored words and ideas was the goal of their schooling, and that critical questioning brought

swift disapproval. But it was just this conception of uncritical internalization against which the philosophical tradition rebelled, setting its banner in the camp of active reasoning.

Socrates himself wrote nothing at all. If we are to believe the account of his reasons given in Plato's *Phaedrus,* it was because he believed that books could short-circuit the work of active critical understanding, producing a pupil who has a "false conceit of wisdom." Books are not "alive." At best, they are reminders of what excellent thinking is like, but they certainly cannot think. Often, however, so great is their prestige that they actually lull pupils into forgetfulness of the activity of mind that is education's real goal, teaching them to be passively reliant on the written word. Such pupils, having internalized a lot of culturally authoritative material, may come to believe that they are very wise. And this arrogance undercuts still further the motivations for real searching. Such people are even less likely than ignorant people to search themselves, looking for arguments for and against their culture's ways of doing things. So books, when used in education, must be used in such a way as to discourage this sort of reverence and passivity.

Books, furthermore, lack the attentiveness and responsiveness of real philosophical activity (which, as we recall, respects the pupil's particular circumstances and context). They "roll around" all over the place with a kind of inflexible sameness, addressing very different people, always in the same way.[20] The conclusion, once again, is that books, though valuable as reminders of arguing, can be harmful if used as authorities.

The Stoics have some vivid images to make this same point. Epictetus tells the story of a young person who comes to him boasting that he had finally "got" down pat the contents of Chrysippus' treatise on logical problems. Epictetus says to him that he is like an athlete who comes in saying gleefully: "Look, I've got a new set of training weights in my room." This person, he continues, will not get the response, "Great, now you've done it." The response he will get is, "Very well, show me what you can *do* with your weights." So too with the pupil: show that you can use what you read to think well and to take charge of your own reasoning.[21]

Seneca develops the idea further in a letter, warning the pupil against relying on the wisdom contained in "great books" as authoritative:

"This is what Zeno said." But what do you say? "This is Cleanthes' view." What is yours? How long will you march under another person's orders? Take command, and say something memorable of your own

. . . It is one thing to remember, another to know. To remember is to safeguard something entrusted to the memory. But to know is to make each thing one's own, not to depend on the text and always to look back to the teacher. "Zeno said this, Cleanthes said this." Let there be a space between you and the book.[22]

Neither Seneca nor Epictetus repudiates the written text. The analogy of books to weights has a positive side. Books, including some of the great texts from the past of one's own culture, can indeed tone up the slack mind, giving it both the information it needs to think well and examples of excellent argument. Literacy, including cultural literacy, confers both strength and independence,[23] if viewed as a kind of essential training and nourishment, not as itself the goal. Working through the arguments contained in great books can make the mind more subtle, more rigorous, more active. It guarantees that the mind will confront a wide range of options on important questions, and confront them in a challenging presentation, even where popular culture is diffuse and superficial. All this the Stoics knew already; it is even more important for our time.

But the negative side of Epictetus' image is also plain: books are all too likely to become objects of veneration and deference, sitting in the mind without producing strength in the mind itself. This is, of course, especially likely to happen if they are introduced as cultural authorities, as in curricula titled "Western civilization" or "The Great Books." If we were to use a more Senecan title, such as "Some useful and nourishing books that are likely to help you think for yourself," or, following Epictetus' idea, "Some training weights for the mind," then we would be on the right track. Everyone involved would be on notice that there is no substitute for thinking things through, and the hope for a quick fix for complicated problems would no longer be held out. We would see the truth on which Seneca's letter on liberal education ends: that we live in a messy, puzzling, and complicated world, in which there is absolutely no substitute for one's own active searching.

Socratic Reason and Its Enemies

We have not produced truly free citizens in the Socratic sense unless we have produced people who can reason for themselves and argue well, who understand the difference between a logically valid and a logically invalid argument, who can distinguish between the logical form of an argument and the truth of its premises. Logical reasoning, like speaking one's native language, comes naturally to human beings; no doubt it is part of the equipment we evolved in order to survive. Work with young children has shown repeatedly that they can master all the basics of logic readily, through the use of simple examples. But, like mastery of one's native language, it needs help from teachers, at many different levels of education. Most students don't immediately spot fallacious forms of reasoning in a complicated text—or in a political argument they hear on television. Most people carry around inside themselves lots of ill-sorted material, beliefs they have never examined for logical consistency, inferences they have never examined for validity.

This, indeed, was the central way in which Socrates saw himself as making a contribution to democracy. If all we have to work with is what people believe, how will we make progress? By getting people to sort out what they think they know, to test beliefs for consistency, inferences for validity, the way Polemarchus progressed by noticing that the beliefs he shared with his father were not consistent. Students who read the *Republic* should see how Socrates convicts Polemarchus of inconsistency, but at the same time they should ask themselves how well Socrates is arguing, and whether his conclusions really do follow from his premises. This is the primary way in which Plato as a writer overcomes the danger of passivity inherent in the written word: by provoking the reader to logical analysis and criticism.

Logical analysis is at the heart of democratic political culture. When we do wrong to one another politically, bad argument is often one cause. We reason in ways such as the following: "A high proportion of crimes in my community are committed by black people; here is a black person; so he's likely to be a criminal." "All mothers are women. This person here is a woman. So she's going to get pregnant and quit the job, so I'd be better off hiring a man." Of course these are invalid inferences; but we "think" this way all the time. Logical analysis dissipates these confusions. It unmasks prejudice that masquerades as reason. Doing without it would mean forfeiting one of the most powerful tools we have to attack abuses of political power. Although logic will not get us to love one another, it may get us to stop pretending that we have rational arguments for our refusals of sympathy.

Logical analysis, furthermore, shows us healthy ways of interacting as citizens. Instead of claim and counterclaim, we can exchange views critically, examining one another's reasoning. Billy Tucker found it illuminating to learn that one could spend a week thinking about arguments against the death penalty, of which he approved. It showed him a new way of thinking about people on the other side of the issue: they were not just adversaries, they were people thinking as he was thinking, and he came to understand their point of view. At the same time, he came to see how bad the reasoning is in many news accounts. This insight gave him a new wariness, and this wariness again promoted a more fruitful dialogue with people on the other side of the issue.

Socratic reason is not unopposed on today's campuses. It faces two different types of opponents. The first is a conservative opposition, who suspect that Socrates' dedication to argument will subvert traditional values. This opposition is stronger outside the academy than within it, but we can also find it at some institutions. At Belmont, for example, even the separate existence of the Philosophy Department was at one time a matter of controversy. Philosophy majors at Belmont face opposition for their choice. "Secular humanism" was the term chosen by their fellow students to express a basic mistrust of philosophical reason, suggesting that any philosophy major must already have left the Baptist faith behind.

As the students themselves felt, this was a mistaken conclusion. Whatever our personal religious commitments, we are all citizens of a democracy, and we have to deliberate together. Philosophical education plays a valuable role in this sort of deliberation. There is no contradiction between governing one's most personal choices by the faith to which one adheres and learning to argue in a Socratic manner with one's fellow citizens. Indeed, our democracy is unlike many others in the careful protections it accords to private religious choices and to the separation of those choices from the contentious debates of the public realm. It is no sign of disrespect to any religious tradition to ask that its members use in the public realm arguments that can be understood by people from other traditions, or to encourage that sort of argument in class.

More often, however, Socratic goals encounter a different type of resistance, from challenges to truth and reason associated with postmodernist literary theory. Even logic itself is not immune from attack. It is often alleged—not only by bigoted or unsympathetic people but often also by champions of race and sex equality—that logical argument is not for women or not for African-Americans. Some left-wing opponents of Socrates think that logic is all right in its place but impotent as a critical tool, next to the entrenched realities of power. In that sense it is not worth spending one's time on it or investing hope in it. This cynical position, like that of Thrasymachus, can best be refuted by showing what reason can do and has done in the struggle for justice, and by pointing out that if the game is merely power, the powerless will always lose out. Reason has a special dignity that lifts it above the play of forces, and it is only to the extent that reason is respected in a society that minorities will be able to make their just but unpopular claims heard. In Plato's vivid image, reason is a soft golden cord, sometimes pushed around by the iron cord of greed and envy and fear (in operating the imaginary marionette that is the human being), but sometimes prevailing, and always shining with a dignity of its own. It is difficult to imagine how bogus arguments against the equality of women, or of ethnic or religious or racial minorities, could be unmasked without a reliance on the distinction between prejudice and reason; such unmasking will prove futile unless the democratic community as a whole shares that distinction. Cynicism of the Thrasymachean sort is the best recipe for continued oppression of the powerless.

Some left-wing opponents of Socrates, however, make a still stronger attack on logic: they charge that the central forms of logical argumentation don't suit the minds of women, or minorities, or non-Western people. Although these views are sometimes put forward by people who wish to deny full political equality to minorities or to women, their influence in the academy derives from the fact that they are also put forward in a progressive spirit, as if we cannot help disadvantaged groups to make progress unless we recognize the "fact" that logic itself is patriarchal or a tool of colonial oppression. But we do not respect the humanity of any human being unless we assume that person to be capable of understanding the basic issues of consistency and validity and the basic forms of inference. We sell that person short as a human being unless we work to make that person's potentiality for logical thought into an active reality. Such criticisms typically show ignorance of the logical traditions of non-Western peoples and a condescending attitude to the logical abilities of women and racial minorities.[24] There is no sound evidence for such claims, and it is counterproductive for allegedly progressive thinkers to speak as if there were.

But what about the goals of logical argument? Socrates didn't just argue for fun; he had a project: to find an account that was objective in the sense that it was free from bias and prejudice and could withstand critical scrutiny. A further pernicious claim made by postmodernist opponents of Socrates is that the usual goals of Socratic argument, truth and objectivity, are unavailable. A pursuit of these goals, it is alleged, can be nothing other than a mask for the assertion of power or self-interest.

It is important to separate what is plausible in these ideas from what is both naive and dangerous. We should all agree that people who claim to be pursuing truth or to be reasoning objectively (by which we usually mean in a manner free from illegitimate bias) do not always do so. Often, whether consciously or unconsciously, they are using the mantle of truth-seeking to pursue their own interests or to assert the received wisdom of habit—as Socrates so often showed by unmasking pseudoarguments. This defective way of inquiring, however, says very little about the search for truth itself.

We should also agree that modern analyses of truth and knowledge cast grave doubt on one traditional notion: namely, the idea that we can have access to the way things are in the universe entirely independently of the workings of our minds. Technical work in the philosophy of quantum mechanics and the philosophy of language has caused many philosophers to agree with Kant in thinking the world knowable to and truly describable by human beings only as shaped by our concepts and our mental faculties. Even observation would seem to be theory-laden, using salient categories that derive from our own conceptual scheme. (Not all philosophers agree that these points have been established; some would still defend the beleaguered "realist" picture.) At this point, we find intense disagreement: some philosophers hold, with Kant, that we can still defend a single conceptual scheme as the most adequate to reality; some hold that there is a small plurality of adequate schemes governed by stringent criteria of rightness; some adopt a still more elastic pluralism. Philosophers such as Hilary Putnam, Nelson Goodman, Donald Davidson, W. V. O. Quine, and Richard Rorty take up various positions on this spectrum.[25] All, with the possible exception of Rorty, still think we can establish claims as true by arguments that rightly claim objectivity and freedom from bias.

We should agree, further, that one of the factors to be considered in evaluating a claim is the role of social and political power in shaping the concepts it contains. The philosophers named above, focusing on the analysis of scientific knowledge and linguistic reference, have not always thought much about political influences on knowledge-seeking. Consequently, they have not always devoted enough attention to the way in which the desire of a dominant group to retain power can enter into the very articulation of basic ethical and social categories. This insight was grasped already by Plato's characters Thrasymachus and Callicles, when they showed how powerful groups can frequently define moral norms in ways that perpetuate their own superiority—defining "justice," for example, to include obedience to the ruler, so that the ruled would be kept in their place. Michel Foucault developed these ideas further. Although one might take issue with many aspects of Foucault's work, from its historical incompleteness to its lack of conceptual clarity, it contains important insights and remains the only truly important work to have entered philosophy under the banner of "postmodernism."

We should, then, agree with several important claims that postmodernist thinkers have recently stressed. The search for truth is a human activity, carried on with human faculties in a world in which human beings struggle, often greedily, for power. But we should not agree that these facts undermine the very project of pursuing truth and objectivity. The insights of the Kantian tradition—and of its modern heirs such as Putnam, Quine, and Davidson—yield not a radical assault on truth and reason, but a new articulation of those goals. Acknowledging the contributions of language and the human mind invalidates a simpleminded type of empiricism but leaves Socrates on his feet. We need not forgo the aspiration to truth and objectivity; we need only conceive of these goals in a nuanced way, taking account of the shaping role of our categories. Socrates himself made no appeal to truths that transcend human experience, and yet he held that the pursuit of ethical truth is essential to full humanity. Many other pictures of a nontranscendent search for truth have been advanced in ethical philosophy, by figures including Kant and the American pragmatists.

Nor does the recognition of the role of power and interest in shaping concepts give us reason to despair of achieving freedom from bias: it just puts us on notice that we will need to sort out legitimate from illegitimate interests, even as we pursue the other aspects of a conceptual inquiry. This sorting makes Socratic life more complicated, but it doesn't make it in any sense impossible.[26]

What is deeply pernicious in today's academy, then, is the tendency to dismiss the whole idea of pursuing truth and objectivity as if those aims could no longer guide us. Such attacks on truth are not new: we find them, for example, in Thrasymachus and in the ancient Greek skeptics.[27] But they are forms of sophistry whose influence mars the otherwise promising pursuit of Socratic goals on our campuses. Postmodernists do not justify their more extreme conclusions with compelling arguments. Nor do they even grapple with the technical issues about physics and language that any modern account of these matters needs to confront. For this reason, their influence has been relatively slight in philosophy, where far more nuanced accounts of these matters abound. Derrida on truth is simply not worth studying for someone who has been studying Quine and Putnam and Davidson. In other parts of the humanities, however, they exercise a large influence (in part because their work is approachable as the technical work of philosophers frequently is not), causing students to think that those in the know have disdain for Socrates and his goals. This is one further reason why we should insist that philosophy be a large part of the undergraduate curriculum: because this field gives real insight into debates that go on elsewhere, and unmasks in truly Socratic fashion the pretenses of fashionable authorities. It is Socratic to ask critical questions about Socrates' methods and goals; we must continue to do so. But as we do so we should continue to be devoted to the Socratic ideal of sorting things out and finding an account that can endure critical scrutiny.

Socrates in the Modern Curriculum

How can an undergraduate liberal arts education follow Socrates' example? The most important ingredient of a Socratic classroom is obviously the instructor. No curricular formula will take the place of provocative and perceptive teaching that arouses the mind. And a dedicated instructor can enliven the thinking of students in almost any curricular setting. Socratic activity can take place in virtually any humanities or social science course, in connection with readings of many different kinds, as long as the instructor knows a good deal about the particular nature of the student body and strives to develop each individual's capacity to reason.

Although in principle any humanities course might teach Socratic reasoning, many such courses do not focus intensively on critical argument. But such a focus, characteristic of the professional philosopher, is necessary to teach students how to analyze the arguments that they and others make. Given the tremendous importance, for citizenship and for life, of producing students who can think clearly and justify their views, a course or courses in philosophy play a vital role in the undergraduate liberal arts curriculum. If philosophy presents itself as an elite, esoteric discipline preoccupied with formal notation and with questions of little evident human interest, it will not be able to play this role. But professional philosophy has increasingly, over the past twenty years, returned to the focus on basic human interests that it had in the time of John Dewey and William James. Questions about justice and rights, questions about love, fear, and grief, questions of medical and legal and business ethics—all these are now not at the margins of the profession but at its heart. The profession is once again, like Socrates, bringing philosophy from the heavens down to the earth.

Since philosophy is frequently intimidating to students, who (like Billy Tucker) think it is for an elite, students cannot be expected to seek out these courses on their own. In most cases, then—wherever an institution is not confident that students will generally elect such courses on their own with faculty advice—a course or courses in philosophy should be required of all students. This may be done in a variety of ways. One may straightforwardly require a philosophy course, whether one chosen from the established departmental curriculum or from a separate group of introductory courses. One may, as Harvard does, require a course in "moral reasoning" that draws on faculty from several disciplines, with a common mission. One may also aim to infuse philosophical reasoning and analysis into a basic humanities course, for example a course that reads a range of major philosophical texts. The disciplinary base of such courses should not stray too far from philosophy, or the rigor of analysis so important for the Socratic virtues of mind will be diluted.

Institutions that have successful philosophy requirements are those that have studied closely the character of their student body. At Notre Dame the student body is overwhelmingly Catholic and fairly well prepared academically. Like many other Catholic institutions, the university requires two semesters of philosophy in addition to two of theology. This requirement derives from the Catholic tradition's strong emphasis on being able to give reasons for one's religious and moral beliefs. The announced purpose of such courses, for example the course "Science and Human Values" taught by Philip Quinn, is to produce Catholics who don't believe blindly, but can think through their beliefs and reason about them with others, including others who differ in religion. The courses are diverse, but all assign demanding readings and focus a good deal of attention on class discussion and the writing of analytical papers. Class size is rarely more than twenty students. Students express satisfaction with the way in which philosophy classes promote more general goals.

Another very different institution that has profited from a two-semester philosophy requirement is Randolph-Macon College, in Ashland, Virginia. The student body of Randolph-Macon, a midsize liberal arts college, differs from that of Notre Dame in several ways: greater religious diversity, a somewhat lower average of prior academic achievement, a greater tendency to focus on narrow preprofessional semivocational studies. These students would very likely take few demanding courses in traditional humanities and social science subjects without requirements; subjects such as business and computer science would occupy most of their attention. The institution is committed to giving these students an education that does not focus on these narrow instrumental goals, but that gives them something that can impart meaning and discipline to their intellectual lives in a general way, making them both richer as individuals and better informed as citizens. Their experience has been that philosophy, taught in small sections in a highly Socratic manner, plays a crucial role in waking these students up and getting them to take responsibility for their own thinking and choices. In these classes, students participate eagerly. They debate with excitement, for example, about Plato's attack on the poets in the *Republic,* relating Plato's arguments to issues such as violence and sex on television and in the movies. Later a larger group joined in a public discussion of the role of love in the good life, talking about literary examples and relating them to their lives. The greatest enemies of Socratism at Randolph-Macon are vocationalism and indifference. The two-semester philosophy requirement and the dedicated teaching that supports it make at least some headway against these problems.

The University of Pittsburgh is a four-year campus of the state university system, frequently chosen by urban commuting students. Student preparation and skills vary widely. The institution also houses one of the nation's most outstanding philosophy departments, plus an equally outstanding program in the history and philosophy of science. A two-semester philosophy requirement, maintained by a long list of small courses focused on ethics and value, creates a common learning experience for the students and puts them in contact with some of the best young instructors in the nation (since many of the courses are taught by advanced graduate students, who at Pitt are often the stars of the profession's next generation). All involved seem happy with the way this requirement has evolved. Although instructors express some frustration with the amount of remedial work they need to do on writing skills, they feel satisfied that they are getting through to the students well enough to realize their Socratic purpose.

Bentley College, in Waltham, Massachusetts, is a business college that does not claim to give a general liberal arts education. Nonetheless, the administration has decided to require philosophy of all students, for reasons of citizenship and general mental development. Bentley students have little initial motivation to pursue liberal education in the humanities. But they are going to be citizens and voters; therefore the institution judges that they need to develop the ability to reason for themselves about important issues concerning morality, justice, and law. The philosophy requirement is designed to elicit good reasoning on these issues.

Billy Tucker is the sort of student for whom the Bentley requirement is designed. He is highly intelligent but not very confident about his intellectual ability. He still lives with his parents, and his political views are largely derived from his parents, his community, and the popular media. Without such a requirement he would have focused on business courses and left "culture" for others. In Krishna Mallick's course, typical of the courses satisfying the requirement, students begin with several dialogues of Plato, learning to think about arguments by analyzing the examples there. Tucker was drawn into the course by his excitement about these questions, made more vivid for him by seeing a film in class about Socrates' life and death. Why did Socrates refuse to escape from prison, when by doing so he could have saved his life? How does Socrates argue about our obligation to obey the law? Would Socrates have been a draft resister? These things grabbed him— partly on account of the active style of Krishna Mallick's teaching, partly because of the way she had used the film to bring the issues to life. Tucker came to see these questions as about himself and his life, in a way that questions in other required courses were not.

Harvard's Core Curriculum contains a modified philosophy requirement, in the form of a one-semester "moral reasoning" requirement and a one-semester "social analysis" requirement. The moral reasoning courses were designed to get students to think Socratically about central ethical and political issues. Their purpose is very similar to Notre Dame's, though in a secular form: to produce citizens who can give reasons for what they choose, and think reflectively about difficult moral controversies. Harvard students are extremely well prepared and inclined to overconfidence. A strange combination of arrogance that they are at Harvard and fear that they don't really belong there makes them reluctant to expose their real thinking in class. Frequently they cope with fear by adopting a brittle sophistication, which makes it difficult to find out what they really believe. Part of this sophistication may well be a pose of cultural relativism or postmodernism, which the instructor in a moral reasoning course will need to subject to Socratic scrutiny.

Many courses in the area focus on the arguments of historical texts, although to satisfy the requirement historical study must be pursued with a view to developing Socratic reasoning abilities. Others investigate fundamental issues of ethical theory, such as the nature of justice, using both historical and modern readings. A few, finally, focus on contemporary controversies, for example in medical ethics. All are designed to involve the student actively in constructing and analyzing arguments and in criticizing the arguments of others. These courses are taught by a very distinguished group of faculty, including philosopher Thomas Scanlon, political theorist Michael Sandel, aesthetician and political thinker Stanley Cavell, and philosopher/economist Amartya Sen. The drawback of the Harvard system is that the courses are very large: some have close to a thousand students. On the other hand, the instructors usually care a lot about communicating with students, and the program is very well funded, so that discussion sections led by graduate teaching assistants have no more than fifteen to twenty students. As at Pittsburgh, the graduate assistants are themselves a very dedicated group, the leaders of the field in the next generation.

All these courses in diverse institutions combine instruction in Socratic argument with topics of moral urgency, showing students that argument is not just a sterile tool, but makes a difference to their lives. As Amartya Sen describes his goal,

The Sanskrit word for philosophy—*dársana*—also means seeing clearly. Philosophy does have much to do with clarifying matters—not through specialized knowledge but through reasoning. It is possible, of course, to be wonderfully clear and dead wrong. But lucidity does not help the survival of baseless beliefs, silly deductions, groundless prejudice, or the justification of needless misery. Well, that's something for clear reasoning, even though it won't solve all our problems.[28]

His moral reasoning course, which connects the study of different accounts of ethical rationality (in Aristotle, Kant, and the Utilitarians, among others) to pressing issues of social justice, exemplifies these ideas about the practical value of clarity.

Students who take philosophy courses will very likely be exposed elsewhere to postmodernist attacks on truth and argument. One further benefit of requiring a course or courses in philosophy, indeed, is that such courses give students materials they can use to question the attacks on argument they may encounter elsewhere in the humanities curriculum. By getting involved in a philosophy course, students will learn how to think about what they are being asked to do, with a sophistication that is not always present in courses offered in other departments.

Philosophical reflection may also be infused into a broader humanities course or set of courses, but in that case it is very important that philosophers participate in the design and teaching of these courses. Two promising examples of this sort are the revised Western traditions course at the University of Nevada at Reno, where philosopher Deborah Achtenberg has coordinated philosophical discussion (based on Plato and other ancient authors) with literary and historical readings, and the University of New Hampshire's relatively new humanities course, where philosopher Charlotte Witt has worked alongside instructors from literature and the history of science to develop an account of the ancient world that infuses philosophical reflection into the study of history and literature as well as of specifically philosophical works. Both of these courses are well designed for a large group of students with little antecedent preparation in the humanities. Both are well designed and taught but are handicapped to some extent by large size, which inhibits discussion and makes it difficult to assign enough student writing.

At St. Lawrence, a well-funded liberal arts school that attracts an increasingly well-motivated group of students (70 percent receive financial aid), the Cultural Encounters program has managed to infuse philosophy with great success into a variety of undergraduate courses in humanities, social science, and natural science. Indeed, the program was introduced in addition to a non-Western studies requirement for precisely this reason. Because the faculty group running the program received a grant that supported extensive study and group discussion, all have been able to work out a coordinated approach to the teaching of cultural relativism—that is, the view that each local group should be the court of last resort for its own moral practices, and that there are no universal moral standards. All courses dealing with cross-cultural issues are enriched by Socratic examination of the relativist values that students frequently bring to the course. Students confront hard questions about tolerance by thinking about how we should react to others who are themselves intolerant; and they think about differences between tolerance and relativism, between the acceptance of a practice with which one disagrees and the view that there are no criteria of moral evaluation that transcend a local group. Students at St. Lawrence are bright but relatively unmotivated. Socratic inquiry needs to work to overcome student inertia, and this has been done by arousing student interest in cross-cultural comparison and evaluation. Here is a case in which, without a philosophy requirement, Socratic inquiry has been widely and rigorously promoted in many courses. The reasons for this success are the amount of common effort by the faculty group and the dedicated leadership of its two coordinators, Grant Cornwell from Philosophy and Eve Stoddard from English. Not all students, however, get the benefit of this approach.

Some campuses feel that they can infuse Socratic values throughout the curriculum without required courses of any sort. In some cases they recommend the activity of choosing one's own curriculum as itself a setting for Socratic activity as, in dialogue with a faculty adviser, students reflect about their own goals and the courses that might promote them. Three institutions that have successfully practiced this approach to various extents are Grinnell College, in Iowa; Amherst College, in Massachusetts; and Brown University, in Providence, Rhode Island. All are influenced by the Stoic goals of self-command, or taking charge of one's own life through reasoning. (Ralph Waldo Emerson developed his own ideas on "self-reliance" by reflecting on Stoic ideals, and Emerson is a central source for Brown's curriculum.) This approach works best with very well-prepared students and a faculty devoted to teaching. All three are lucky to have that combination. It requires, in addition, an extremely well-supported and well-organized system of advising. Each Brown student is assigned to a faculty adviser who works in partnership with a senior undergraduate; together the team advises about ten entering freshmen, meeting with them regularly throughout the year. Much depends on the faculty member's dedication and knowledge and on the student's willingness to take advice. Furthermore, the procedures, at one level Socratic, don't by any means guarantee a thorough, rigorous exposure to Socratic philosophizing. By giving students so much independence to question and inquire so early, the system sometimes eventually produces upperclassmen who, as a result of naiveté and peer pressure, have fallen prey to intellectual fads and have never really learned habits of rigorous inquiry. It is much harder to get these students to work through the ideas in a Socratic manner than it would be with freshmen. When their arguments are criticized, they tend to react with resentment, as if the activity of criticizing an argument were an illicit and somewhat old-fashioned exercise. One sometimes sees such students in philosophy courses, such as "Feminist Philosophy," that attract students already heavily influenced by attacks on argument. These students are a minority. Most students at Brown take a wide range of courses in humanities and social science, and a large proportion have at least some exposure to philosophy. Most students who do not take philosophy take courses in other areas in which rigorous argument is taught and respected (such as political theory, religious studies, economics, history, and other parts of the humanities). But there is at least some reason for concern that Brown's preference for rational self-government in the choice of curriculum may conduce to an absence of rational self-government at the end of some students' education.

We cannot and should not hope to produce a nation of students who can write excellent papers about Socratic arguments, although this is a sensible goal for some institutions. We can, I think, hope to produce a nation full of students like Billy Tucker at Bentley and the many students like him at Reno and St. Lawrence and Harvard and Notre Dame—students who have examined their beliefs Socratically to some extent and who have mastered some techniques by which they can push that inquiry further, students whose moral and political beliefs are not simply a function of talk-radio or peer pressure, students who have gained the confidence that their own minds can confront the toughest questions of citizenship. To produce this independence we need to rely on philosophy.

We live, as did Socrates, in a violent society that sometimes turns its rage against intellectuals. We may be embarking on a new era of anti-intellectualism in American life, an era in which the anger of Aristophanes' father is all too real a force. In response we should defend the democratic value of Socratic citizenship and of the courses through which our students learn how to reason critically in a Socratic way. We should insist, with Socrates and the Stoics, that our campuses, by doing this, provide a vital democratic service; that in Reno, Nevada, and South Bend, Indiana, and Waltham, Massachusetts, as in ancient Athens, the unexamined life threatens the health of democratic freedoms, and the examined life produces vigor in the nation and freedom in the mind.

CHAPTER TWO

Citizens
of the World

When anyone asked him where he came from, he said, "I am a citizen
of the world."

Diogenes Laertius, Life of Diogenes the Cynic

Anna was a political science major at a large state university in the Midwest.
Upon graduation she went into business, getting a promising job with a
large firm. After twelve years she had risen to a middle-management position. One day, her firm assigned her to the newly opened Beijing office.[1]
What did she need to know, and how well did her education prepare her
for success in her new role? In a middle-management position, Anna is
working with both Chinese and American employees, both male and female.
She needs to know how Chinese people think about work (and not to assume
there is just one way); she needs to know how cooperative networks are
formed, and what misunderstandings might arise in interactions between
Chinese and American workers. Knowledge of recent Chinese history is
important, since the disruptions of the Cultural Revolution still shape workers' attitudes. Anna also needs to consider her response to the recent policy
of urging women to return to the home, and to associated practices of laying
off women first. This means she should know something about Chinese
gender relations, both in the Confucian tradition and more recently. She
should probably know something about academic women's studies in the
United States, which have influenced the women's studies movement in

Chinese universities. She certainly needs a more general view about human rights, and about to what extent it is either legitimate or wise to criticize another nation's ways of life. In the future, Anna may find herself dealing with problems of anti-African racism, and with recent government attempts to exclude immigrants who test positive for the human immunodeficiency virus. Doing this well will require her to know something about the history of Chinese attitudes about race and sexuality. It will also mean being able to keep her moral bearings even when she knows that the society around her will not accept her view.

The real-life Anna had only a small part of this preparation—some courses in world history, but none that dealt with the general issue of cultural variety and how to justify moral judgments in a context of diversity; none that dealt with the variety of understandings of gender roles or family structures; none that dealt with sexual diversity and its relationship to human rights. More important, she had no courses that prepared her for the shock of discovering that other places treated as natural what she found strange, and as strange what she found natural. Her imaginative capacity to enter into the lives of people of other nations had been blunted by lack of practice. The real-life Anna had a rough time getting settled in China, and the firm's dealings with its new context were not always very successful. A persistent and curious person, however, she stayed on and has made herself a good interpreter of cultural difference. She now plans to spend her life in Beijing, and she feels is making a valuable contribution to the firm.

Two years ago, after several years in China, already in her late thirties, Anna decided to adopt a baby. Through her by then extensive knowledge of the Chinese bureaucracy, she bypassed a number of obstacles and quickly found an infant girl in an orphanage in Beijing. She then faced challenges of a very different kind. Even in the most apparently universal activities of daily life, cultural difference colors her day. Her Chinese nurse follows the common Chinese practice of wrapping the baby's limbs in swaddling bands to immobilize it. As is customary, the nurse interacts little with the child, either facially or vocally, and brings the child immediately anything it appears to want, without encouraging its own efforts. Anna's instincts are entirely different: she smiles at the baby, encourages her to wave her hands about, talks to her constantly, wants her to act for herself. The nurse thinks Anna is encouraging nervous tension by this hyperactive American behavior; Anna thinks the nurse is stunting the baby's cognitive development. Anna's mother, visiting, is appalled by the nurse and wants to move in, but Anna, by now a sensitive cross-cultural interpreter, is able to negotiate between mother and nurse and devise some plan for the baby's development that is agreeable to all. To do this she has had to think hard about the nonuniversality and nonnaturalness of such small matters as playing with a baby. But she has also had to think of the common needs and aims that link her with the nurse, and the nurse with her own mother. Her university education gave her no preparation at all for these challenges.

Had Anna been a student at today's St. Lawrence University, or at many other colleges and universities around the United States, she would have had a better basis for her international role, a role U.S. citizens must increasingly play (whether at home or abroad) if our efforts in business are to be successful, if international debates about human rights, medical and agricultural problems, ethnic and gender relations, are to make progress as we enter the new century. As Connie Ellis, a forty-three-year-old waitress at Marion's Restaurant in Sycamore, Illinois, put it on the Fourth of July, 1996, "You can't narrow it down to just our country anymore—it's the whole planet."[2] We must educate people who can operate as world citizens with sensitivity and understanding.

Asked where he came from, the ancient Greek Cynic philosopher Diogenes replied, "I am a citizen of the world." He meant by this that he refused to be defined simply by his local origins and group memberships, associations central to the self-image of a conventional Greek male; he insisted on defining himself in terms of more universal aspirations and concerns.[3] The Stoics who followed his lead developed his image of the *kosmopolitēs*, or world citizen, more fully, arguing that each of us dwells, in effect, in two communities—the local community of our birth, and the community of human argument and aspiration that "is truly great and truly common." It is the latter community that is, most fundamentally, the source of our moral and social obligations. With respect to fundamental moral values such as justice, "we should regard all human beings as our fellow citizens and local residents."[4] This attitude deeply influenced the subsequent philosophical and political tradition, especially as mediated through the writings of Cicero, who reworked it so as to allow a special degree of loyalty to one's own local region or group. Stoic ideas influenced the American republic through the writings of Thomas Paine, and also through Adam Smith and Immanuel

Kant, who themselves influenced the Founders.[5] Later on, Stoic thought was a major formative influence on both Emerson and Thoreau.

This form of cosmopolitanism is not peculiar to Western traditions. It is, for example, the view that animates the work of the influential Indian philosopher, poet, and educational leader Rabindranath Tagore. Tagore drew his own cosmopolitan views from older Bengali traditions, although he self-consciously melded them with Western cosmopolitanism.[6] It is also the view recommended by Ghanaian philosopher Kwame Anthony Appiah, when he writes, concerning African identity: "We will only solve our problems if we see them as human problems arising out of a special situation, and we shall not solve them if we see them as African problems generated by our being somehow unlike others."[7] But for people who have grown up in the Western tradition it is useful to understand the roots of this cosmopolitanism in ancient Greek and Roman thought. These ideas are an essential resource for democratic citizenship. Like Socrates' ideal of critical inquiry, they should be at the core of today's higher education.

The Idea of World Citizenship in Greek and Roman Antiquity

Contemporary debates about the curriculum frequently imply that the idea of a "multicultural" education is a new fad, with no antecedents in long-standing educational traditions. In fact, Socrates grew up in an Athens already influenced by such ideas in the fifth century B.C. Ethnographic writers such as the historian Herodotus examined the customs of distant countries, both in order to understand their ways of life and in order to attain a critical perspective on their own society. Herodotus took seriously the possibility that Egypt and Persia might have something to teach Athens about social values. A cross-cultural inquiry, he realized, may reveal that what we take to be natural and normal is merely parochial and habitual. One cultural group thinks that corpses must be buried; another, that they must be burnt; another, that they must be left in the air to be plucked clean by the birds. Each is shocked by the practices of the other, and each, in the process, starts to realize that its habitual ways may not be the ways designed by nature for all times and persons.

Awareness of cultural difference gave rise to a rich and complex debate about whether our central moral and political values exist in the nature of things (by *phusis*), or merely by convention *(nomos)*.[8] That Greek debate illustrates most of the positions now familiar in debates about cultural relativism and the source of moral norms. It also contains a crucial insight: if we should conclude that our norms are human and historical rather than immutable and eternal, it does not follow that the search for a rational justification of moral norms is futile.

In the conventional culture of fifth-century B.C. Athens, recognition that Athenian customs were not universal became a crucial precondition of Socratic searching. So long as young men were educated in the manner of Aristophanes' Old Education, an education stressing uncritical assimilation of traditional values, so long as they marched to school in rows and sang the old songs without discussion of alternatives, ethical questioning could not get going. Ethical inquiry requires a climate in which the young are encouraged to be critical of their habits and conventions; and such critical inquiry, in turn, requires awareness that life contains other possibilities.

Pursuing these comparisons, fifth-century Athenians were especially fascinated by the example of Sparta, Athens' primary rival, a hierarchical and nondemocratic culture that understood the goal of civic education in a very un-Athenian way. As the historian Thucydides depicts them, Spartan educators carried to an extreme the preference for uniformity and rule-following that characterized the Old Education of Athens in Aristophanes' nostalgic portrait. Conceiving the good citizen as an obedient follower of traditions, they preferred uncritical subservience to Athenian public argument and debate. Denying the importance of free speech and thought, they preferred authoritarian to democratic politics.

Athenians, looking at this example, saw new reasons to praise the freedom of inquiry and debate that by this time flourished in their political life. They saw Spartan citizens as people who did not choose to serve their city, and whose loyalty was therefore in a crucial way unreliable, since they had never really thought about what they were doing. They noted that once Spartans were abroad and free from the narrow constraint of law and rule, they often acted badly, since they had never learned to choose for themselves. The best education, they held, was one that equips a citizen for genuine choice of a way of life; this form of education requires active inquiry and the ability to contrast alternatives. Athenians denied the Spartan charge that their own concern with critical inquiry and free expression would give rise to decadence. "We cultivate the arts without extravagance," they proudly proclaimed, "and we devote ourselves to inquiry without becoming soft." Indeed, they insisted that Sparta's high reputation for courage was ill based: for citizens could not be truly courageous if they never chose from among alternatives. True courage, they held, requires freedom, and freedom is best cultivated by an education that awakens critical thinking. Cross-cultural inquiry thus proved not only illuminating but also self-reinforcing to Athenians: by showing them regimes that did not practice such inquiry and what those regimes lacked in consequence, it gave Athenians reasons why they should continue to criticize and to compare cultures.

Plato, writing in the early to mid-fourth century B.C., alludes frequently to the study of other cultures, especially those of Sparta, Crete, and Egypt. In his *Republic*, which alludes often to Spartan practices, the plan for an ideal city is plainly influenced by reflection about customs elsewhere. One particularly fascinating example of the way in which reflection about history and other cultures awakens critical reflection occurs in the fifth book of that work, where Plato's character Socrates produces the first serious argument known to us in the Western tradition for the equal education of women. Here Socrates begins by acknowledging that the idea of women's receiving both physical and intellectual education equal to that of men will strike most Athenians as very weird and laughable. (Athenians who were interested in cultural comparison would know, however, that such ideas were not peculiar in Sparta, where women, less confined than at Athens, did receive extensive athletic training.)[9] But he then reminds Glaucon that many good things once seemed weird in just this way. For example, the unclothed public exercise that Athenians now prize as a norm of manliness once seemed foreign, and the heavy clothing that they think barbaric once seemed natural. However, he continues, when the practice of stripping for athletic contests had been in effect for some time, its advantages were clearly seen—and then "the appearance of absurdity ebbed away under the influence of reason's judgment about the best." So it is with women's education, Socrates argues. Right now it seems absurd, but once we realize that our conventions don't by themselves supply reasons for what we ought to do, we will be forced to ask ourselves whether we really do have good reasons for denying women the chance to develop their intellectual and physical capacities. Socrates argues that we find no such good reasons, and many good reasons why those capacities should be developed. Therefore, a comparative cultural study, by removing the false air of naturalness and inevitability that surrounds our practices, can make our society a more truly reasonable one.

Cross-cultural inquiry up until this time had been relatively unsystematic, using examples that the philosopher or historian in question happened to know through personal travel or local familiarity. Later in the fourth century, however, the practice was rendered systematic and made a staple of the curriculum, as Aristotle apparently instructed his students to gather information about 153 forms of political organization, encompassing the entire known world, and to write up historical and constitutional descriptions of these regimes. The *Athenian Constitution,* which was written either by Aristotle or by one of his students, is our only surviving example of the project; it shows an intention to record everything relevant to critical reflection about that constitution and its suitability. When Aristotle himself writes political philosophy, his project is extensively cross-cultural. In his *Politics,* before describing his own views about the best form of government, he works through and criticizes many known historical examples, prominently including Crete and Sparta, and also a number of theoretical proposals, including those of Plato. As a result of this inquiry, Aristotle develops a model of good government that is in many respects critical of Athenian traditions, though he follows no single model.

By the beginning of the so-called Hellenistic era in Greek philosophy, then, cross-cultural inquiry was firmly established, both in Athenian public discourse and in the writings of the philosophers, as a necessary part of good deliberation about citizenship and political order.[10]

But it was neither Plato nor Aristotle who coined the term "citizen of the world." It was Diogenes the Cynic. Diogenes (404–323 B.C.) led a life stripped of the usual protections that habit and status supply. Choosing exile from his own native city, he defiantly refused protection from the rich and powerful for fear of losing his freedom, and lived in poverty, famously choosing a tub set up the marketplace as his "home" in order to indicate his disdain for convention and comfort. He connected poverty with independence of mind and speech, calling freedom of speech "the finest thing in human life."[11] Once, they say, Plato saw him washing some lettuce and said, "If you had paid court to Dionysius, you would not be washing lettuce."[12] Diogenes replied, "If you had washed lettuce, you would not have paid court to Dionysius." This freedom from subservience, he held, was essential to a philosophical life. "When someone reproached him for being an exile, he said that it was on that account that he came to be a philosopher."

Diogenes left no written work behind, and it is difficult to know how to classify him. "A Socrates gone mad" was allegedly Plato's description—and a good one, it seems. For Diogenes clearly followed the lead of Socrates in disdaining external markers of status and focusing on the inner life of virtue and thought. His search for a genuinely honest and virtuous person, and his use of philosophical arguments to promote that search, are recognizably Socratic. What was "mad" about him was the public assault on convention that accompanied his quest. Socrates provoked people only by his questions. He lived a conventional life. But Diogenes provoked people by his behavior as well, spitting in a rich man's face, even masturbating in public. What was the meaning of this shocking behavior?

It appears likely that the point of his unseemly behavior was itself Socratic—to get people to question their prejudices by making them consider how difficult it is to give good reasons for many of our deeply held feelings. Feelings about the respect due to status and rank and feelings of shame associated with sexual practices are assailed by this behavior—as Herodotus' feelings about burial were assailed by his contact with Persian and Egyptian customs. The question is whether one can then go on to find a good argument for one's own conventions and against the behavior of the Cynic.

As readers of the *Life* of Diogenes, we ourselves quickly become aware of the cultural relativity of what is thought shocking. For one of the most shocking things about Diogenes, to his Athenian contemporaries, was his habit of eating in the public marketplace. It was this habit that gave him the name "dog," *kuōn*, from which our English label Cynic derives. Only dogs, in this culture, tore away at their food in the full view of all. Athenians evidently found this just about as outrageous as public masturbation; in fact his biographer joins the two offenses together, saying, "He used to do everything in public, both the deeds of Demeter and those of Aphrodite." Crowds, they say, gathered around to taunt him as he munched on his breakfast of beets, behaving in what the American reader feels to be an unremarkable fashion. On the other hand, there is no mention in the *Life* of shock occasioned by public urination or even defecation. The reason for this, it may be conjectured, is that Athenians, like people in many parts of the world today, did not in fact find public excretion shocking. We are amazed by a culture that condemns public snacking while permitting such practices. Diogenes asks us to look hard at the conventional origins of these judgments and to ask which ones can be connected by a sound argument to important moral goals. (So far as we can tell, Cynics supplied no answers to this question.)

Set in this context, the invitation to consider ourselves citizens of the world is the invitation to become, to a certain extent, philosophical exiles from our own ways of life, seeing them from the vantage point of the outsider and asking the questions an outsider is likely to ask about their meaning and function. Only this critical distance, Diogenes argued, makes one a philosopher. In other words, a stance of detachment from uncritical loyalty to one's own ways promotes the kind of evaluation that is truly reason based. When we see in how many different ways people can organize their lives we will recognize, he seems to think, what is deep and what is shallow in our own ways, and will consider that "the only real community is one that embraces the entire world." In other words, the true basis for human association is not the arbitrary or the merely habitual; it is that which we can defend as good for human beings—and Diogenes believes that these evaluations know no national boundaries.

The confrontational tactics Diogenes chose unsettle and awaken. They do not contain good argument, however, and they can even get in the way of thought. Diogenes' disdain for more low-key and academic methods of scrutinizing customs, for example the study of literature and history, seems most unwise. It is hard to know whether to grant Diogenes the title "philosopher" at all, given his apparent preference for a kind of street theater over Socratic questioning. But his example, flawed as it was, had importance for the Greek philosophical tradition. Behind the theater lay an important idea: that the life of reason must take a hard look at local conventions and assumptions, in the light of more general human needs and aspirations.

The Stoic philosophers, over the next few centuries, made Diogenes' insight respectable and culturally fruitful.[13] They developed the idea of cross-cultural study and world citizenship much further in their own morally and philosophically rigorous way, making the concept of the "world citizen," *kosmou politēs,* a centerpiece of their educational program.[14] As Seneca writes, summarizing older Greek Stoic views, education should make us aware that each of us is a member of "two communities: one that is truly great and truly common . . . in which we look neither to this corner nor to that, but measure the boundaries of our nation by the sun; the other, the one to which we have been assigned by birth." The accident of where one is born is just that, an accident; any human being might have been born in any nation. Recognizing this, we should not allow differences of nationality or class or ethnic membership or even gender to erect barriers between us and our fellow human beings. We should recognize humanity—and its fundamental ingredients, reason and moral capacity—wherever it occurs, and give that community of humanity our first allegiance.

This does not mean that the Stoics proposed the abolition of local and national forms of political organization and the creation of a world state. The Greek Stoics did propose an ideal city, and the Roman Stoics did put ideas of world citizenship into practice in some ways in the governance of the empire. But the Stoics' basic point is more radical still: that we should give our first allegiance to *no* mere form of government, no temporal power, but to the moral community made up by the humanity of all human beings. The idea of the world citizen is in this way the ancestor and source of Kant's idea of the "kingdom of ends," and has a similar function in inspiring and regulating a certain mode of political and personal conduct. One should always behave so as to treat with respect the dignity of reason and moral choice in every human being, no matter where that person was born, no matter what that person's rank or gender or status may be. It is less a political idea than a moral idea that constrains and regulates political life.

The meaning of the idea for political life is made especially clear in Cicero's work *On Duties (De Officiis)*, written in 44 B.C. and based in part on the writings of the slightly earlier Greek Stoic thinker Panaetius. Cicero argues that the duty to treat humanity with respect requires us to treat aliens on our soil with honor and hospitality. It requires us never to engage in wars of aggression, and to view wars based on group hatred and wars of extermination as especially pernicious. It requires us to behave honorably in the conduct of war, shunning treachery even toward the enemy. In general, it requires us to place justice above political expediency, and to understand that we form part of a universal community of humanity whose ends are the moral ends of justice and human well-being. Cicero's book has been among the most influential in the entire Western philosophical tradition. In particular, it influenced the just-war doctrine of Grotius and the political thought of Immanuel Kant; their views about world understanding and the containment of global aggression are crucial for the formation of modern international law.

Stoics hold, then, that the good citizen is a "citizen of the world." They hold that thinking about humanity as it is realized in the whole world is valuable for self-knowledge: we see ourselves and our customs more clearly when we see our own ways in relation to those of other reasonable people. They insist, furthermore, that we really will be better able to solve our problems if we face them in this broader context, our imaginations unconstrained by narrow partisanship. No theme is deeper in Stoicism than the damage done by faction and local allegiances to the political life of a group. Stoic texts show repeatedly how easy it is for local or national identities and their associated hatreds to be manipulated by self-seeking individuals for their own gain—whereas reason is hard to fake, and its language is open to the critical scrutiny of all. Roman political life in Seneca's day was dominated by divisions of many kinds, from those of class and rank and ethnic origin to the division between parties at the public games and gladiatorial shows. Part of the self-education of the Stoic Roman emperor Marcus Aurelius, as he tells the reader of his *Meditations,* was "not to be a Green or Blue partisan at the races, or a supporter of the lightly armed or heavily armed gladiators at the Circus."[15] Politics is sabotaged again and again by these partisan loyalties, and by the search for honor and fame that accompanies them. Stoics argue that a style of citizenship that recognizes the moral/rational community as fundamental promises a more reasonable style of political deliberation and problem-solving.

But Stoics do not recommend world citizenship only for reasons of expediency. They insist that the stance of the *kosmou politēs* is intrinsically valuable: for it recognizes in people what is especially fundamental about them, most worthy of reverence and acknowledgment, namely their aspirations to justice and goodness and their capacities for reasoning in this connection. This essential aspect may be less colorful than local tradition and local identity, but it is, the Stoics argue, both lasting and deep.

To be a citizen of the world, one does not, the Stoics stress, need to give up local affiliations, which can frequently be a source of great richness in life. They suggest instead that we think of ourselves as surrounded by a series of concentric circles.[16] The first one is drawn around the self; the next takes in one's immediate family; then follows the extended family; then, in order, one's neighbors or local group, one's fellow city-dwellers, one's fellow countrymen—and we can easily add to this list groups formed on the basis of ethnic, religious, linguistic, historical, professional, and gender identities. Beyond all these circles is the largest one, that of humanity as a whole. Our task as citizens of the world, and as educators who prepare people to be citizens of the world, will be to "draw the circles somehow toward the center," making all human beings like our fellow city-dwellers. In other words, we need not give up our special affections and identifications, whether national or ethnic or religious; but we should work to make all human beings part of our community of dialogue and concern, showing respect for the human wherever it occurs, and allowing that respect to constrain our national or local politics.

This Stoic attitude, then, does not require that we disregard the importance of local loves and loyalties or their salience in education. Adam Smith made a serious error when he objected to Stoicism on those grounds, and modern critics of related Kantian and Enlightenment conceptions make a similar error when they charge them with neglect of group differences. The Stoic, in fact, must be conversant with local differences, since knowledge of these is inextricably linked to our ability to discern and respect the dignity of humanity in each person. Stoics recognize love for what is near as a fundamental human trait, and a highly rational way to comport oneself as a citizen. If each parent has a special love for his or her own children, society will do better than if all parents try to have an equal love for all children. Much the same is true for citizenship of town or city or nation: each of us should take our stand where life has placed us, and devote to our immediate surroundings a special affection and attention. Stoics, then, do not want us to behave as if differences between male and female, or between African and Roman, are morally insignificant. These differences can and do enjoin special obligations that all of us should execute, since we should all do our duties in the life we happen to have, rather than imagining that we are beings without location or memory.

Stoics vary in the degree of concession they make to these special obligations. Cicero, for example, takes a wise course when he urges the Roman citizen to favor the near and dear on many occasions, though always in ways that manifest respect for human dignity. These special local obligations have educational consequences: the world citizen will legitimately spend a disproportionate amount of time learning about the history and problems of her or his own part of the world. But at the same time we recognize that there is something more fundamental about us than the place where we happen to find ourselves, and that this more fundamental basis of citizenship is shared across all divisions.

This general point emerges clearly if we consider the relationship each of us has to a native language. We each have a language (in some cases more than one) in which we are at home, which we have usually known from infancy. We naturally feel a special affection for this language. It defines our possibilities of communication and expression. The works of literature that move us most deeply are those that exploit well the resources of that lan-

61

guage. On the other hand, we should not suppose—and most of us do not suppose—that English is best just because it is our own, that works of literature written in English are superior to those written in other languages, and so forth. We know that it is more or less by chance that we are English speakers rather than speakers of Chinese or German or Bengali. We know that any infant might have learned any language, because there is a fundamental language-learning capacity that is shared by all humans. Nothing in our innate equipment disposes us to speak Hindi rather than Norwegian.

In school, then, it will be proper for us to spend a disproportionate amount of time mastering our native language and its literature. A human being who tried to learn all the world's languages would master none, and it seems reasonable for children to focus on one, or in some cases two, languages when they are small. On the other hand, it is also very important for students to understand what it is like to see the world through the perspective of another language, an experience that quickly shows that human complexity and rationality are not the monopoly of a single linguistic community.

This same point can be made about other aspects of culture that should figure in a higher education. In ethics, in historical knowledge, in knowledge of politics, in literary, artistic, and musical learning, we are all inclined to be parochial, taking our own habits for that which defines humanity. In these areas as in the case of language, it is reasonable to immerse oneself in a single tradition at an early age. But even then it is well to become acquainted with the facts of cultural variety, and this can be done very easily, for example through myths and stories that invite identification with people whose form of life is different from one's own. As education progresses, a more sophisticated grasp of human variety can show students that what is theirs is not better simply because it is familiar.

The education of the *kosmou politēs* is thus closely connected to Socratic inquiry and the goal of an examined life. For attaining membership in the world community entails a willingness to doubt the goodness of one's own way and to enter into the give-and-take of critical argument about ethical and political choices. By an increasingly refined exchange of both experience and argument, participants in such arguments should gradually take on the ability to distinguish, within their own traditions, what is parochial from what may be commended as a norm for others, what is arbitrary and unjustified from that which may be justified by reasoned argument.

Since any living tradition is already a plurality and contains within itself aspects of resistance, criticism, and contestation, the appeal to reason frequently does not require us to take a stand outside the culture from which we begin. The Stoics are correct to find in all human beings the world over a capacity for critical searching and a love of truth. "Any soul is deprived of truth against its will," says Marcus Aurelius, quoting Plato. In this sense, any and every human tradition is a tradition of reason, and the transition from these more ordinary and intracultural exercises to a more global exercise of critical argument need not be an abrupt transition. Indeed, in the world today it is clear that internal critique very frequently takes the form of invoking what is found to be fine and just in other traditions.

People from diverse backgrounds sometimes have difficulty recognizing one another as fellow citizens in the community of reason. This is so, frequently, because actions and motives require, and do not always receive, a patient effort of interpretation. The task of world citizenship requires the would-be world citizen to become a sensitive and empathic interpreter. Education at all ages should cultivate the capacity for such interpreting. This aspect of the Stoic idea is developed most fully by Marcus Aurelius, who dealt with many different cultures in his role as emperor; he presents, in his *Meditations,* a poignantly personal account of his own efforts to be a good world citizen. "Accustom yourself not to be inattentive to what another person says, and as far as possible enter into his mind," he writes (6.53); and again, "When things are being said, one should follow every word, when things are being done, every impulse; in the latter case, to see straightway to what object the impulse is directed, in the former, to watch what meaning is expressed" (7.4). Given that Marcus routinely associated with people from every part of the Roman Empire, this idea imposes a daunting task of learning and understanding, which he confronts by reading a great deal of history and literature, and by studying closely the individual characters of those around him in the manner of a literary narrator. "Generally," he concludes, "one must first learn many things before one can judge another's action with understanding" (11.18).

Above all, Marcus finds that he has to struggle not to allow his privileged station (an obstacle to real thought, as he continually points out) to sever him, in thought, from his fellow human beings. "See to it that you do not become Caesarized," he tells himself, "or dyed with that coloring" (6.30). A favorite exercise toward keeping such accidents of station in their proper place is to imagine that all human beings are limbs of a single body, cooperating for the sake of common purposes. Referring to the fact that it takes only the change of a single letter in Greek to convert the word "limb" *(melos)* into the word "(detached) part" *(meros),* he concludes: "if, changing the word, you call yourself merely a (detached) part instead of a limb, you do not yet love your fellow men from the heart, nor derive complete joy from doing good; you will do it merely as a duty, not as doing good to yourself" (7.13). The organic imagery underscores the Stoic ideal of cooperation.

Can anyone really think like a world citizen in a life so full of factionalism and political conflict? Marcus gives himself the following syllogism: "Wherever it is possible to live, it is also possible to live a virtuous life; it is possible to live in a palace; therefore it is also possible to live a virtuous life in a palace" (5.16). And, recognizing that he himself has sometimes failed in citizenship because of impatience and the desire for solitude: "Let no one, not even yourself, any longer hear you placing the blame on palace life" (8.9). In fact, his account of his own difficulties being a world citizen in the turmoil of Roman politics yields some important advice for anyone who attempts to reconcile this high ideal with the realities of political involvement:

Say to yourself in the morning: I shall meet people who are interfering, ungracious, insolent, full of guile, deceitful and antisocial; they have all become like that because they have no understanding of good and evil. But I who have contemplated the essential beauty of good and the essential ugliness of evil, who know that the nature of the wrongdoer is of one kin with mine—not indeed of the same blood or seed but sharing the same kind, the same portion of the divine—I cannot be harmed by any one of them, and no one can involve me in shame. I cannot feel anger against him who is of my kin, nor hate him. We were born to labor together, like the feet, the hands, the eyes, and the rows of upper and lower teeth. To work against one another is therefore contrary to nature, and to be angry against a man or turn one's back on him is to work against him. (2.1)

One who becomes involved in politics in our time might find this paragraph comforting. It shows a way in which the attitude of world citizenship gets to the root of one of the deepest political problems in all times and places, the problem of anger. Marcus is inclined to intense anger at his political adversaries. Sometimes the anger is personal, and sometimes it is directed against a group. His claim, however, is that such anger can be mitigated, or even removed, by the attitude of empathy that the ideal of the *kosmou politēs* promotes. If one comes to see one's adversaries as not impossibly alien and other, but as sharing certain general human goals and purposes, if one understands that they are not monsters but people who share with us certain general goals and purposes, this understanding will lead toward a diminution of anger and the beginning of rational exchange.

World citizenship does not, and should not, require that we suspend criticism toward other individuals and cultures. Marcus continues to refer to his enemies as "deceitful and antisocial," expressing strong criticism of their conduct. The world citizen may be very critical of unjust actions or policies, and of the character of people who promote them. But at the same time Marcus refuses to think of the opponents as simply alien, as members of a different and inferior species. He refuses to criticize until he respects and understands. He carefully chooses images that reflect his desire to see them as close to him and similarly human. This careful scrutiny of the imagery and speech one uses when speaking about people who are different is one of the Stoic's central recommendations for the undoing of political hatred.

Stoics write extensively on the nature of anger and hatred. It is their well-supported view that these destructive emotions are not innate, but learned by children from their society. In part, they hold, people directly absorb negative evaluations of individuals and groups from their culture, in part they absorb excessively high evaluations of their own honor and status. These high evaluations give rise to hostility when another person or group appears to threaten their honor or status. Anger and hatred are not unreasoning instincts; they have to do with the way we think and imagine, the images we use, the language we find it habitual to employ. They can therefore be opposed by the patient critical scrutiny of the imagery and speech we employ when we confront those our tradition has depicted as unequal.

It is fashionable by now to be very skeptical of "political correctness," by which the critic usually means a careful attention to the speech we use in talking about minorities, or foreigners, or women. Such scrutiny might in some forms pose dangers to free speech, and of course these freedoms should be carefully defended. But the scrutiny of speech and imagery need not be inspired by totalitarian motives, and it need not lead to the creation of an antidemocratic "thought police." The Stoic demand for such scrutiny is based on the plausible view that hatred of individuals and groups is personally and politically pernicious, that it ought to be resisted by educators, and that the inner world of thought and speech is the place where, ultimately, hatred must be resisted. These ideas about the scrutiny of the inner world are familiar to Christians also, and the biblical injunction against sinning in one's heart has close historical links to Stoicism. All parents know that it is possible to shape a child's attitudes toward other races and nationalities by the selection of stories one tells and by the way one speaks about other people in the home. There are few parents who do not seek to influence their children's views in these ways. Stoics propose, however, that the process of coming to recognize the humanity of all people should be a lifelong process, encompassing all levels of education—especially since, in a culture suffused with group hatred, one cannot rely on parents to perform this task.

What this means in higher education is that an attitude of mutual respect should be nourished both in the classroom itself and in its reading material. Although in America we should have no sympathy with the outright censoring of reading material, we also make many selections as educators, both in assigning material and in presenting it for our students. Few of us, for example, would present anti-Semitic propaganda in a university classroom in a way that conveyed sympathy with the point of view expressed. The Stoic proposal is that we should seek out curricula that foster respect and mutual solidarity and correct the ignorance that is often an essential prop of hatred. This effort is perfectly compatible with maintaining freedom of speech and the openness of a genuinely critical and deliberative culture.

In our own time, few countries have been more rigidly divided, more corroded by group hatred, than South Africa. In spelling out its goals for society in its draft for the new Constitution, the African National Congress (ANC) recognized the need to address hatred through education, and specified the goal of education as the overcoming of these differences:

> Education shall be directed towards the development of the human personality and a sense of personal dignity, and shall aim at strengthening respect for human rights and fundamental freedoms and promoting understanding, tolerance and friendship amongst South Africans and between nations.[17]

Some of this language would have been new to Marcus Aurelius—and it would have been a good thing for Roman Stoics to have reflected more about the connections between the human dignity they prized and the political rights they frequently neglected. But the language of dignity, humanity, freedom, understanding, tolerance, and friendship would not have been strange to Marcus. (He speaks of his goal as "the idea of a Commonwealth with the same laws for all, governed on the basis of equality and free speech"; this goal is to be pursued with "beneficence, eager generosity, and optimism".) The ANC draft, like the Stoic norm of world citizenship, insists that understanding of various nations and groups is a goal for every citizen, not only for those who wish to affirm a minority identity. It insists that the goal of education should not be separation of one group from another, but respect, tolerance, and friendship—both within a nation and among nations. It insists that this goal should be fostered in a way that respects the dignity of humanity in each person and citizen.

Above all, education for world citizenship requires transcending the inclination of both students and educators to define themselves primarily in terms of local group loyalties and identities. World citizens will therefore not argue for the inclusion of cross-cultural study in a curriculum primarily on the grounds that it is a way in which members of minority groups can affirm such an identity. This approach, common though it is, is divisive and subversive of the aims of world community. This problem vexes many curricular debates. Frequently, groups who press for the recognition of their group think of their struggle as connected with goals of human respect and social justice. And yet their way of focusing their demands, because it neglects commonalities and portrays people as above all members of identity groups, tends to subvert the demand for equal respect and love, and even the demand for attention to diversity itself. As David Glidden, philosopher at the University of California at Riverside, expressed the point, "the ability to admire and love the diversity of human beings gets lost" when one bases the demand for inclusion on notions of local group identity. Why should one love or attend to a Hispanic fellow citizen, on this view, if one is oneself most fundamentally an Irish-American? Why should one care about India, if one defines oneself as above all an American? Only a human identity that transcends these divisions shows us why we should look at one another with respect across them.

World Citizenship in Contemporary Education

What would an education for world citizenship look like in a modern university curriculum? What should Anna, the future businesswoman in Beijing, learn as an undergraduate if she is to be prepared for her role? What should all students learn—since we all interact as citizens with issues and people from a wide variety of traditions?

This education must be a multicultural education, by which I mean one that acquaints students with some fundamentals about the histories and cultures of many different groups. These should include the major religious and cultural groups of each part of the world, and also ethnic and racial, social and sexual minorities within their own nation. Language learning, history, religious studies, and philosophy all play a role in pursuing these ideas. Awareness of cultural difference is essential in order to promote the respect for another that is the essential underpinning for dialogue. There are no surer sources of disdain than ignorance and the sense of the inevitable naturalness of one's own way. No liberal education can offer students adequate understanding of all they should know about the world; but a detailed understanding of one unfamiliar tradition and some rudiments about others will suffice to engender Socratic knowledge of one's own limitations. It would have helped Anna to have learned a great deal about China; but to have studied the culture of India would have been almost as valuable, since it would have showed her how to inquire and the limitations of her experience.

World citizens will legitimately devote more attention and time to their own region and its history, since it is above all in that sphere that they must operate. This need for local knowledge has important educational consequences. We would be absurdly misguided if we aimed at giving our students an equal knowledge of all histories and cultures, just as we would be if we attempted to provide a bit of knowledge of all languages. Besides the fact that this would produce a ridiculously superficial result, it would also fail in the task of giving students a detailed acquaintance with the local sphere in which most of their actions will be undertaken. Education at all levels, including higher education, should therefore strongly emphasize the history of American constitutional traditions and their background in the tradition of Western political philosophy. In a similar way, literary education should focus disproportionately on the literature of Anglo-American traditions— which, however, are themselves highly complex and include the contributions of many different groups.

On the other hand, it is also extremely important that this material be presented in a way that reminds the student of the broader world of which the Western traditions are a part. This may be done with good educational results in the Western tradition courses themselves, where one can emphasize what is distinctive about this tradition through judicious and illuminating contrasts with developments elsewhere. But it must above all be done by the design of the curriculum as a whole, which should offer students the rudiments of knowledge about the major world traditions of thought and art, and the history that surrounds them, and, even more important, make them aware how much important material they do not know.

Education for world citizenship needs to begin early. As soon as children engage in storytelling, they can tell stories about other lands and other peoples. A curriculum for world citizenship would do well to begin with the first grade, where children can learn in an entertaining and painless way that religions other than Judaism and Christianity exist, that people have many traditions and ways of thinking. (One such curriculum has been developed by E. D. Hirsch Jr. and is being used in a number of elementary-school districts around the country: first-graders tell stories of Buddha under the *boddhi* tree; they think about Hindu myths of the gods, about African folktales, about the life of Confucius.)[18] By the time students reach college or university, they should be well equipped to face demanding courses in areas of human diversity outside the dominant Western traditions.

This exposure to foreign and minority cultures is not only, and not primarily, a source of confirmation for the foreign or minority student's personal sense of dignity—though of course this will be one important function such exposure can often serve. It is an education for all students, so that as judges, as legislators, as citizens in whatever role, they will learn to deal with one another with respect and understanding. And this understanding and respect entail recognizing not only difference but also, at the same time, commonality, not only a unique history but also common rights and aspirations and problems.

The world citizen must develop sympathetic understanding of distant cultures and of ethnic, racial, and religious minorities within her own. She must also develop an understanding of the history and variety of human ideas of gender and sexuality. As a citizen one is called upon frequently to make judgments in controversial matters relating to sex and gender—whether as a judge, deciding a case that affects the civil rights of millions, or simply as a democratic voter, deciding, for example, whether to support a referendum like Colorado's Amendment 2, declared unconstitutional by the U.S. Supreme Court in 1996, which restricted the abilities of local communities to pass laws protecting the civil rights of gays and lesbians. To function well as a citizen today, one needs to be able to assess the arguments put forward on both sides; and to do so one needs an education that studies these issues. There are complex connections between cross-cultural study and the study of gender and sexuality. Cross-cultural study reveals many ways of organizing concepts of gender and sexuality; and thinking about gender and sex is essential to thinking critically about a culture. A good undergraduate education should prepare students to be informed and sensitive interpreters of these questions.

Building a curriculum for world citizenship has multiple aspects: the construction of basic required courses of a "multicultural" nature; the infusion of diverse perspectives throughout the curriculum; support for the development of more specialized elective courses in areas connected with human diversity; and, finally, attention to the teaching of foreign languages, a part of the multicultural story that has received too little emphasis.

Basic "diversity" requirements come in two varieties. There are elective requirements that allow the student to choose one or two courses from among a wide range of offerings. Such, for example, is the requirement at the University of Nevada at Reno, where students, in addition to completing a "World Civilizations" core course, must elect a course focusing on at least one area of human diversity outside the dominant culture of her own society. Areas included are the history and culture of non-Western peoples, the history and culture of minorities in the United States, women's studies, and the study of the varieties of human sexuality. Reno, like many institutions, cannot afford to hire new faculty to create integrative courses or to free existing faculty from many of their other commitments. Making a menu of what is on hand, and then giving students a choice from that menu, is these institutions' only option if they wish to diversify their curricula.

Such requirements can fulfill basic Socratic functions, showing students the possible narrowness and limitedness of their own perspective and inviting them to engage in critical reflection. And they can frequently impart methodological tools that will prove valuable in approaching another area of diversity. But this is not always the case: a student who has taken a course on American women writers of the nineteenth century is still likely to be in a weak position with respect to the sort of cultural diversity she will encounter if she finds herself in dialogue with people from China and the

Middle East. Even a course in non-Western literature may leave the student blankly ignorant of non-Western history and religion. A student who has studied the history and literature of China may remain unaware of the variety and diversity of minorities within her own nation. It is odd and arbitrary to put all these different topics together in an area called "diversity," as if the grasp of any part of any one of them would somehow yield a person the breadth of learning that could be yielded only by some grasp of each area. This problem will be especially grave if, as at Reno, the courses listed as satisfying the "diversity" requirement are unrelated to one another by any common discussion about methodology, beyond the deliberations of the faculty group that put the requirement together in the first place. Such courses may not even produce a student who knows how to inquire about diversity in a new context.

One can make a still stronger criticism of the amorphous elective requirement: that the failure to confront all the areas of diversity undercuts the encounter with each of them. A student of Chinese history who does not have some awareness of the history of women and the family, and of the different ways of understanding gender roles, will be likely to miss a good deal that is of urgent importance to the person who gets involved with China today, whether through politics or through business. If Anna hears the political rhetoric in today's China about the "natural" suitability of a situation in which women leave the workplace to return home, she will need to evaluate these statements and policies. It would be best to evaluate them against the background not only of the Confucian tradition but also of a critical awareness of gender roles and their variety. Successful and fair business dealings with China require such an awareness, which will not be provided by courses on Chinese history alone.

For these many reasons, an amorphous elective diversity requirement does not adequately prepare students for the complex world they will confront. It is better than no diversity program at all, and it may well be the best that many institutions can do. But it does not provide sufficient direction to fulfill completely the goals of world citizenship.

Despite these drawbacks, the particular version of an elective diversity requirement that was designed at Reno has some strong virtues. Particularly admirable is the reasoning that justified the requirement when it was publicly presented to faculty, students, and the community. The argument crafted by the faculty committee focuses on goals of world citizenship rather than on identity politics. Deborah Achtenberg, professor of philosophy, expert on Aristotle's ethics, and chair of the Diversity Committee, reflects that her approach to curricular politics was colored by her own particular history, as "a woman, a Jew, a former sixties activist, a St. John's College alumna, a philosopher." From St. John's, she says, she learned respect for the intrinsic value of great texts; the diversity requirement strongly emphasizes these values. From the civil-rights movement she learned "how exclusion of groups leaves the dominant culture unable to benefit from the perspectives and contributions of those groups"; this experience gave her a strong motivation to work for inclusion of those perspectives in the curriculum. As a woman, she knows how difficult it is to speak when one wonders whether the terms of the debate have been set by someone else; the courses in which she is involved focus on these issues of voice and methodology. As a Jew, she knows how easy it is for excluded groups to internalize demeaning stereotypes of themselves; she therefore urges questioning of all stereotypes, including those fostered by identity politics. Finally, as a philosopher, she is committed to making the continual attempt to "transcend all this particularity towards commonality," communicating what she perceives to others whose perspectives and experiences are different from her own. The curriculum she helped design draws inspiration both from Greek ideas of world citizenship and from biblical demands for equality of attention and love.

For a university that is skeptical of the elective approach and can support a more ambitious undertaking, a more arduous, but potentially more satisfying, approach is to design a single basic "multicultural" course, or a small number of such courses, to acquaint all students with some basic conceptions and methods. A very successful example of such a course, in a nonelite institution with a mixed student body, is "American Pluralism and the Search for Equality," developed at the State University of New York at Buffalo in 1992. This course is required in addition to a two-semester world civilization sequence that provides basic instruction in non-Western religions and cultures. The pluralism course complements the primarily historical world civilization course by enhancing students' awareness of the many groups that make up their own nation, and of the struggle of each for respect and equality. Since these moral issues arise in the international context as well, reflection about them retrospectively enriches the other course.

The outstanding feature of the pluralism course is its careful design. In striking contrast to the catch-as-catch-can approach to diversity that one often finds, the faculty designing this course met for months to work out a coherent set of goals and methodologies. They justified their plan in documents available not only to the university community but also to the general public. The statement of goals and purposes shows the relation of the course to the goals of citizenship:

> A goal of the course is to develop within students a sense of informed, active citizenship as they enter an American society of increasing diversity by focusing on contemporary and historical issues of race, ethnicity, gender, social class, and religious sectarianism in American life. A goal of the course is to provide students with an intellectual awareness of the causes and effects of structured inequalities and prejudicial exclusion in American society. A goal of the course is to provide students with increased self-awareness of what it means in our culture to be a person of their own gender, race, class, ethnicity, and religion as well as an understanding of how these categories affect those who are different from themselves . . . A goal of the course is to expand students' ability to think critically, and with an open mind, about controversial contemporary issues that stem from the gender, race, class, ethnic, and religious differences that pervade American society.

John Meacham, a professor of psychology who is among its architects, enunciates several principles that contributed to the success of the Buffalo course and that should, in his view, guide the development of other such courses.

1. *"Design multicultural courses with broad content."* The Buffalo course is designed to acquaint students with five categories of diversity: race, gender, ethnicity, social class, and religious sectarianism. Each section of the course must cover all five and must focus in depth on three. This approach gives the advantage of breadth and also ensures that students see one category in its relation to the others. Meacham argues persuasively that such a course contributes a deeper understanding of each of its topics than would a narrower course focusing on a single topic.

2. *"Base multicultural courses on faculty disciplinary expertise."* Faculty staffing the course are drawn from ten different disciplines. Meacham comments:

"For example, an intelligent discussion of affirmative action should be grounded at least in history, biology, law, economics, political science, psychology, and sociology." Nothing was included in the course that faculty were not equipped to teach expertly; and different faculty groups in different years approached the basic course plan differently, in accordance with their preparation and training. This allowance for flexibility is very important. Interdisciplinary courses frequently falter if they lack a strong disciplinary base, and faculty cannot do a good job if they are asked to stretch far beyond their training.

The difficulty of finding enough faculty with the relevant expertise is frequently cited as a point against such multicultural courses, as if they were bound to be specially problematic from this point of view. But "great books" courses, for example the countless courses focusing on ancient Greece and Rome, are hardly free of similar problems. The classics department of any university is small, comprising only a few of the faculty who will be teaching such courses. A large proportion of those who routinely teach Euripides and Sophocles and Plato lack disciplinary expertise in classics and never learn either Greek or Latin. They often do a remarkable job within these limits, and sometimes can bring new life to the material in a way that specialists may not. But they do have limits, and need to rely for guidance on secondary literature prepared by specialists. It would therefore be entirely unfair to mention these problems when criticizing new multicultural courses and not to bring the same objections against standard Western civilization courses.

There are, of course, special problems involved in teaching any area in which the relevant scholarly literature is small and still evolving. The nonspecialist teaching Plato can choose from among a wide range of translations and annotated editions of the dialogues, and can prepare by using the many helpful and rigorous books and articles that are easily available. The nonspecialist who wishes to teach the history of women in antiquity, or the history of slavery, would have had a much more difficult time twenty years ago, since the materials for such a study were available only to specialists who knew Greek and Latin—and not easily to these, since many documents had not been edited. But by now this is far less a problem in all the areas of human diversity. In most areas, outstanding volumes responsibly present the results of specialist research to nonspecialist academics. In the areas covered by Meacham's course there is no problem at all, since there is no language barrier, and the topics of the course have by now generated an enormous, excellent, and easily available literature.

3. *"Design programs for faculty development."* Faculty should not be asked to teach material that lies to some extent outside their prior expertise without being given financial support for the time spent in retraining. Retraining involves time taken away from their course preparation in their own original areas, and also from the research that is an integral part of an active scholar's life. First-rate faculty will not choose to get involved in such new courses unless they are compensated for these sacrifices. It is standard practice to pay faculty summer salary for undertaking new course development projects. Where, in addition to retraining, the course will require extensive cooperation among faculty in different fields, such compensation is particularly important. SUNY Buffalo was able to provide funds for four-week faculty development seminars during two consecutive summers. These seminars were absolutely crucial to the program's success, since even faculty who bring a disciplinary expertise to the course are ill prepared for a complex interdisciplinary exchange without concerted preparation, reading, and dialogue. In the seminars the faculty learned about one another's approaches and methods, discussed common readings, and designed readings and methods that were appropriate for the students in their institution.

4. *Spend time reflecting about methodological and pedagogical issues.* Faculty drawn from literature, economics, political science, and philosophy will not intuitively approach a problem such as voting rights or affirmative action with the same set of questions in mind or the same standards of argument and inquiry. This heterogeneity is basically a good thing, since they can complement one another. But careful thought needs to be given to the methods and concerns that will be built into the course. How much, for example, will the course focus on general philosophical questions, such as the nature of rights and the contrast between relativism and universalism? How much empirical information about the history of the relevant issues will students be expected to master? How will quantitative analyses deriving from economics be presented, if at all? If these questions are not settled beforehand, the course will be a grab-bag of issues, with no intellectual cohesion.

Faculty need to devote extra consideration to problems that arise when we approach issues on which people in our society have conflicting and strongly held views. Such issues—and these constitute most of the course—raise particular problems for classroom methodology. Here there is a particular need to be aware of the background and character of one's students and to design classroom methods to elicit the best sort of active critical participation. Buffalo students, Meacham argues, tend to be submissive and deferential. Faculty need to discourage them from simply following authority if the benefits of the course for citizenship are to be gained. In this course more than in others, then, instructors carefully withhold their own personal views, designing strategies for evenhanded classroom debate and not seeking to bring debate to a conclusion prematurely. As one instructor in the course said, it is important "to give students permission to be confused."

The Buffalo course is a success because of the careful thought that went into its design and the availability of funding to support faculty development. One should also commend the determination of faculty to criticize themselves and to monitor carefully the development of the course, insisting on high standards of both expertise and teaching. SUNY Buffalo faculty are under substantial public pressure to justify the development of a multicultural course, since their constituency is aware of many criticisms of such courses. Part of their success is explained by the fact that they have devoted a good deal of thought to public relations both in the university and in the community. They publicize the course and discuss it in a variety of public media, focusing in particular on answering the criticism that such courses are "ideological." They articulate the relation of the course to the goals of democratic citizenship in a convincing way, satisfying the public that the effort contributes to public reasoning, not simply to the affirmation of various groups' identity. This is a legitimate area of public concern, and Buffalo has done more to address it than have many comparable institutions.

A different but equally promising basic core course is the newly designed humanities core course at Scripps College, in Pomona, California. The college enrolls around 700 students, all female; although it shares courses with the other Claremont Colleges, the freshman core course is designed for the entire Scripps entering class, and for them alone. It replaces an earlier Western civilization sequence, which was thought to be too amorphous and unfocused. Called "Culture, Knowledge, and Representation," the course studies the central ideas of the European Enlightenment—in political thought, history, and philosophy, in literature, in religion, to some extent in art and music. Sixteen instructors from all departments in the humanities take turns giving lectures, and each leads a small discussion section. The study of the Enlightenment is followed by a study of critical responses to it—by formerly colonized populations, by feminists, by non-Western philosophy, by Western postmodernist thought. The course ends with an examination of Enlightenment responses to these criticisms. (I was invited to lecture to the group on the ways in which feminists could defend liberalism against the criticisms made by other feminists, and on the responses of the international human rights movement to postcolonial critiques of universal categories.)

This course has produced excitement and lively debate among students. Its clear focus, its emphasis on cross-cultural argument rather than simply on a collection of facts, and its introduction of non-Western materials via a structured focus on a central group of issues all make it a good paradigm of the introductory course. Its ambitious interdisciplinary character has been successful in lecture, less so in sections—where students report that some faculty sections deal far more helpfully with the philosophical texts and issues than do others. This unevenness is to be expected in the first year of such a cooperative venture (the course was instituted in 1995–96) and should not be taken to negate the worth of the experiment. Above all, the course has merit because it plunges students right into the most urgent questions they need to ask today as world citizens, questions about the universal validity of the language of rights, the appropriate ways to respond to the just claims of the oppressed. The college community becomes from the very beginning a community of argument focused on these issues of urgent relevance. (It seemed especially commendable that postmodernism was not given the last word, as though it had eclipsed Enlightenment thinking: students were left with a vigorous debate, as instructors sympathetic to postmodernism welcomed my highly critical challenge to those views.)

Infusing world citizenship into the curriculum is a much larger project than the designing of one or two required courses. Its goals can and should pervade the curriculum as a whole, as multinational, minority, and gender perspectives can illuminate the teaching of many standard parts of the curriculum, from American history to economics to art history to ancient Greek literature. There are countless examples of the successful transformation of familiar courses to incorporate those perspectives. Some involve the redesigning of a basic introductory course. At the University of New Hampshire, a grant from the National Endowment for the Humanities produced a new Western civilization course, team-taught in an interdisciplinary manner by four excellent young faculty hired primarily for this course, from philosophy, the history of science, art history, and comparative literature. The four were given time and support to work together designing a course that integrated all these disciplinary perspectives with a focus on ancient Greece and Rome, at the same time incorporating a comparative dimension that correlated Greek achievements in art, literature, science, and politics with those in China at the same period. (The historian of science specialized in Chinese science; the others were supported in doing research into the comparative dimension of their own discipline.) From the beginning, then, students learned to see familiar landmarks of the Western tradition in a broader world context, understanding what was distinctive about Greek science, for example, in part through the Chinese contrast. As a result of the support and stimulation provided by the program, one of the original four teachers, Charlotte Witt, has gone on to produce not only outstanding scholarship on Aristotle's metaphysics but also admirable discussions of the role of rational argument in feminist criticism.[19]

Some transformations involve the redesigning of a standard departmental course offering. At Brown University, a standard moral problems course has recently taken as its focus the feminist critique of pornography and related issues of free speech. In this way students learn to confront these divisive issues and learn basic facts about them while learning the techniques of philosophical analysis and debate. At Bentley College, Krishna Mallick offers a non-Western philosophy class, focusing on the philosophy of nonviolent resistance. At Harvard University, Amartya Sen offers a course called "Hunger and Famine." Standard topics in development economics are given a new twist, as students learn to think about the relationship of hunger to gender and also to democratic political institutions in areas of the world ranging from Africa to China to India. At the University of Chicago, historian David Cohen has developed a comparative course on war crimes that brings current events in Bosnia and Rwanda together with historical examples from many cultures. Other topics that invite a global perspective, such as environmental studies and climatology, world population, and religious and ethnic violence, are increasingly taking center stage in the social sciences and are an increasing focus of student interest.

Such integrative courses acknowledge that we are citizens of a world that is diverse through and through—whose moral problems do prominently include the problems of women seeking to avoid violence, whose history does include a complex international history of both nonviolence and war, whose thought about hunger and agriculture must take cognizance of the unequal hunger of women and of the special circumstances of developing nations. This way of incorporating diversity has the advantage of relying on the disciplinary expertise of the instructor. Students who study Indian famines with Sen probably learn more that is important about India than will those who take a broad and general introduction to world civilization, although they will profit more from Sen's course if they have already had such an introduction. They will learn about religious and economic diversity in the process of thinking about hunger, but in a way that will be focused and made more vivid by being connected to a specific problem analyzed with rigor and detail. Such focused courses, taught by expert faculty, should be strongly encouraged, whatever else we also encourage.

In many institutions, however, there are few faculty available to teach such international courses, at least beyond the introductory level. If even the introductory level requires combining existing expertise with new interdisciplinary training, as the Buffalo course shows, the generation of more advanced elective courses integrating the perspective of world citizenship requires even more planning and institutional support. One particularly imaginative and successful example of a program for faculty development has recently been designed at St. Lawrence University. Called "Cultural Encounters: An Intercultural General Education," the program exemplifies the values of world citizenship both in its plan and in its execution. Cultural Encounters is a program containing courses at both the introductory and the more advanced levels. But its focus has been on redesigning disciplinary courses toward an emphasis on the student's encounter with a non-Western culture.

St. Lawrence is a small liberal arts college. It is a relatively wealthy institution, able to attract a high-quality young faculty. It is well known for the high quality of its study-abroad programs, and 33 percent of its students do study in a foreign country at some point. Its students are a mixed group. The 70 percent who receive financial aid tend to be stronger academically than the other 30 percent, many of whom are intellectually unaggressive. This circumstance required careful thought by the faculty as they tried to design a program that would awaken critical and independent thinking about cultural diversity, and about the more general question whether values are universal or culturally relative. Since 1987 the college has had a requirement that all students take one course on a non-Western or Third World culture; the Cultural Encounters program is intended to supplement the strong offerings in these areas by promoting rigorous foundational questioning.

The program began when St. Lawrence received faculty and curriculum development grants from the Andrew Mellon Foundation and the Fund for the Improvement of Post-Secondary Education. In its initial phase, grants were given to a group of seventeen humanities faculty from different departments, enabling them to meet in a weekly seminar throughout the year, discussing common readings and eventually generating new courses, each in their separate disciplines. The course was informed from the beginning by three decisions. The first was to put philosophy at the heart of the matter, in the sense that all participants did a lot of serious discussing of issues of cultural relativism, along with whatever cross-cultural readings they also did. Grant Cornwell of Philosophy and Eve Stoddard of English, the two directors of the program, shared an orientation to the material that stressed the universal aspect of human needs and strivings and was critical of cultural relativism. They did not wish, however, to impose this perspective on the program as a whole; they wished to use the issue as a basis for faculty dialogue.

Cornwell and Stoddard's second decision was to focus on just two areas of diversity, by selecting two non-Western cultures, the cultures of India and Kenya. They decided to start from these two concrete areas in raising issues about ethnic and religious diversity, gender, race, and sexuality. They decided that they had a reasonable shot at understanding something of the history and traditions of these two places if they used the grant-supported faculty seminar to spend an entire year doing common research on each, but that they would have no chance at all of achieving responsible coverage if they cast their net more widely. Faculty in the group were drawn from philosophy, art history, anthropology, English, religious studies, biology, government, geology, economics, and Spanish.

The group's third decision was its most surprising. This was that all ten faculty involved should live for a month in the regions they studied, after a year of intensive seminar preparation, so that their teaching would be informed by a firsthand sense of what it was like to live the life of ordinary women and men in these countries. This undertaking was made financially possible because of the grant, and it proved to be the crucial point in the program. During each of the two visits, the group kept a public diary to exchange and refine views. It is clear that this experience permitted a level of insight into controversial issues such as female circumcision and population control that would not easily have been available from reading alone. It also infused the abstract readings with vividness and made the instructors feel that, for a brief time at least, they had been actual participants in the foreign culture.

Returning to St. Lawrence, the group designed courses reflecting their own disciplinary expertise. David Hornung of Biology and Catherine Shrady of Geology teach a seminar called "Cross-Cultural Perspectives of Healing," comparing the Western medical tradition with Islamic, Hindu, and traditional African approaches. Economics professor Robert Blewett teaches "African Economies," comparing several African economic institutions with their North American counterparts, and focusing on the impact of cultural difference on economic structure. "Students," Blewett writes, "will learn not only of the diversity and complexity of economic relationships in African societies but will increase their understanding of economics in their own society." Codirector Eve Stoddard teaches a comparative course on the discipline and management of the female body, studying practices ranging from female circumcision to veiling to plastic surgery, dieting, and exercise. There is no naive assumption that all these practices are on a par—indeed, one of the aims of the course is to get students to make increasingly refined evaluations. Stoddard's teaching was informed by lengthy, complicated discussions with women in the regions she visited; she is therefore able to give an informed account of the societies' internal debates about these practices. Student writing is encouraged to analyze issues of cultural relativism in a rigorous way.

At the same time, the group required that students who chose the Cultural Encounters "track," taking both introductory and advanced courses within the program, should have a foreign language requirement. If at all possible, they must live and study abroad for their junior year. Two-thirds of the students who go abroad go to Europe, the other third to Costa Rica, Kenya, India, and Japan. Not all the programs, then, directly support the intellectual aims of the Cultural Encounters course material. But even the apparently unrelated exposure to a European culture and its language indirectly serves the program's goals, since mastery of a foreign language and the ability to make oneself at home in a foreign culture are essential abilities of the world citizen, and build an understanding that can be used to approach a further and even more remote culture.

The Cultural Encounters program is a model of responsible teaching in several areas of human diversity. By design, it encompasses not only the encounter with a foreign culture but also related issues of gender, ethnic and religious pluralism, and sexuality, presenting issues of American pluralism in relation to those of global cultural diversity. Its interdisciplinary character ensures that these issues will be faced from many interlocking perspectives, including those of literary study and anthropology, long prominent in multicultural teaching, but also those of economics, biology, philosophy, and foreign language teaching. Where faculty are concerned, the program's focus on intensive training and dialogue and its demand for actual immersion in the culture sets it apart from many programs of this sort, as does its focus on foundational philosophical questions of relativism and universality. On the side of the student, the requirement to learn a foreign language and, where possible, to visit a foreign culture makes the "encounter" serious and prolonged, while critical discussion of basic issues about culture and values in the classroom ensures that the encounter will be conducted in the spirit of Socratic searching rather than of mere tourism, and will prompt dialectical reflection on the beliefs and practices of the student's own culture while the student explores a foreign culture.

Cornwell and Stoddard write that they prefer the term *interculturalism* to the terms *multiculturalism* and *diversity,* since the latter are associated with relativism and identity politics, suggesting a pedagogy "limited to an uncritical recognition or celebration of difference, as if all cultural practices were morally neutral or legitimate."[20] *Interculturalism,* by contrast, connotes the sort of comparative searching that they have in mind, which, they argue, should prominently include the recognition of common human needs across cultures and of dissonance and critical dialogue within cultures. The interculturalist, they argue, has reason to reject the claim of identity politics that only members of a particular group have the ability to understand the perspective of that group. In fact, understanding is achieved in many different ways, and being born a member of a certain group is neither sufficient nor necessary. Knowledge is frequently enhanced by an awareness of difference.

The Cultural Encounters program has had an influence beyond St. Lawrence. Its success has spawned imitations in a wide range of colleges and universities, including Northern Arizona University, the University of Tulsa, Towson State University, Colgate University, Mount St. Mary's College, and Bowling Green State University. In 1995 a national conference brought the many participants in this movement together for an institute to discuss experiences and methodology. Much thought needs to be given to how such a program, designed for a small, prosperous college, can be adapted to colleges with larger student populations and fewer resources.

Meanwhile, at St. Lawrence itself, the program received a major grant from the Christian Johnson Endeavor Foundation in 1995 to support further curricular development of "intercultural studies." Over four years, the faculty group will focus on interdisciplinary study of four themes: transmission of culture across boundaries; gender and culture; questioning development: equity and the environment; and health across cultures. Expanding its focus to include Latin America, the faculty group spent the summer of 1996 doing research in the Caribbean. Cheerfully describing the group's members as "pathological workaholics," Stoddard expresses keen excitement about their new task.

The Cultural Encounters program brings us back to the issues raised by the Stoics. Its designers firmly reject an approach to "multiculturalism" that conceives of it as a type of identity politics, in which the student receives the impression of a marketplace of cultures, each asserting its own claim. They insist on the importance of teaching that the imagination can cross cultural boundaries, and that cross-cultural understanding rests on the acknowledgment of certain common human needs and goals amid the many local differences that divide us. Like much of the ancient Greek tradition, beginning with Herodotus, Stoics suggest that the encounter with other cultures is an essential part of an examined life. Like that tradition, they believe that education must promote the ability to doubt the unqualified goodness of one's own ways, as we search for what is good in human life the world over.

Becoming a citizen of the world is often a lonely business. It is, in effect, a kind of exile—from the comfort of assured truths, from the warm nestling feeling of being surrounded by people who share one's convictions and passions. In the writings of Marcus Aurelius (as in those of his American followers Emerson and Thoreau) one sometimes feels a boundless loneliness, as if the removal of the props of habit and convention, the decision to trust no authority but moral reasoning, had left life bereft of a certain sort of warmth and security. If one begins life as a child who loves and trusts its parents, it is tempting to want to reconstruct citizenship along the same lines, finding in an idealized image of nation or leader a surrogate parent who will do our thinking for us. It is up to us, as educators, to show our students the beauty and interest of a life that is open to the whole world, to show them that there is after all more joy in the kind of citizenship that questions than in the kind that simply applauds, more fascination in the study of human beings in all their real variety and complexity than in the zealous pursuit of superficial stereotypes, more genuine love and friendship in the life of questioning and self-government than in submission to authority. We had better show them this, or the future of democracy in this nation and in the world is bleak.

CHAPTER THREE

The Narrative
Imagination

[There] are many forms of thought and expression within the range of human communications from which the voter derives the knowledge, intelligence, sensitivity to human values: the capacity for sane and objective judgement which, so far as possible, a ballot should express. [The] people do need novels and dramas and paintings and poems, "because they will be called upon to vote."

Alexander Meiklejohn, "The First Amendment Is an Absolute"

The world citizen needs knowledge of history and social fact.[1] We have begun to see how those requirements can be met by curricula of different types. But people who know many facts about lives other than their own are still not fully equipped for citizenship. As Heraclitus said 2,500 years ago, "Learning about many things does not produce understanding." Marcus Aurelius insisted that to become world citizens we must not simply amass knowledge; we must also cultivate in ourselves a capacity for sympathetic imagination that will enable us to comprehend the motives and choices of people different from ourselves, seeing them not as forbiddingly alien and other, but as sharing many problems and possibilities with us. Differences of religion, gender, race, class, and national origin make the task of understanding harder, since these differences shape not only the practical choices people face but also their "insides," their desires, thoughts, and ways of looking at the world.

Here the arts play a vital role, cultivating powers of imagination that are essential to citizenship. As Alexander Meiklejohn, the distinguished constitutional scholar and theorist of "deliberative democracy," put it fifty years ago, arguing against an opponent who had denied the political relevance of art, the people of the United States need the arts precisely because they will be called upon to vote. That is not the only reason why the arts are important, but it is one significant reason. The arts cultivate capacities of judgment and sensitivity that can and should be expressed in the choices a citizen makes. To some extent this is true of all the arts. Music, dance, painting and sculpture, architecture—all have a role in shaping our understanding of the people around us. But in a curriculum for world citizenship, literature, with its ability to represent the specific circumstances and problems of people of many different sorts, makes an especially rich contribution. As Aristotle said in chapter 9 of *The Poetics*, literature shows us "not something that has happened, but the kind of thing that might happen." This knowledge of possibilities is an especially valuable resource in the political life.

To begin to understand how literature can develop a citizen's imagination, let us consider two literary works widely separated in place and time. In both cases, the literary work refers to its own distinctive capacity to promote adequate civic perception.

Sophocles' *Philoctetes*, produced in 409 B.C., during a crisis in the Athenian democracy, concerns the proper treatment of a citizen who has become an outcast, crippled by a disfiguring illness. On his way to Troy to fight with the Greeks in the Trojan War, Philoctetes stepped by mistake into a sacred shrine. His foot, bitten by the serpent who guards the shrine, began to ooze with an ulcerous sore, and his cries of pain disrupted the army's religious festivals. So the commanders abandoned him on the deserted island of Lemnos, with no companions and no resources but his bow and arrows. Ten years later, learning that they cannot win the war without his magical bow, they return, determined to ensnare him by a series of lies into participating in the war. The commander Odysseus shows no interest in Philoctetes as a person; he speaks of him only as a tool of public ends. The chorus of common soldiers has a different response (lines 169–176):

> For my part, I have compassion for him. Think how
> with no human company or care,
> no sight of a friendly face,
> wretched, always alone,
> he wastes away with that savage disease,
> with no way of meeting his daily needs.
> How, how in the world, does the poor man survive?

Unlike their leader, the men of the chorus vividly and sympathetically imagine the life of a man whom they have never seen, picturing his loneliness, his pain, his struggle for survival. In the process they stand in for, and allude to, the imaginative work of the audience, who are invited by the play as a whole to imagine the sort of needy, homeless life to which prosperous people rarely direct their attention. The drama as a whole, then, cultivates the type of sympathetic vision of which its characters speak. In the play, this kind of vivid imagining prompts a political decision against using Philoctetes as a means, and the audience is led to believe this to be a politically and morally valuable result. In this way, by showing the public benefits of the very sort of sympathy it is currently awakening in its spectators, the drama commends its own resources as valuable for the formation of decent citizenship and informed public choice. Although the good of the whole should not be neglected, that good will not be well served if human beings are seen simply as instruments of one another's purposes.

Ralph Ellison's *Invisible Man* (1952) develops this tradition of reflection about our failures of perception and recognition. Its hero describes himself as "invisible" because throughout the novel he is seen by those he encounters as a vehicle for various race-inflected stereotypes: the poor, humiliated black boy who snatches like an animal at the coins that lie on an electrified mat; the good student trusted to chauffeur a wealthy patron; the listening ear to whom this same patron unburdens his guilt and anxiety; the rabble-rousing activist who energizes an urban revolutionary movement; the violent rapist who gratifies the sexual imagination of a woman brought up on racially charged sexual images—always he is cast in a drama of someone else's making, "never more loved and appreciated" than when he plays his assigned role. The "others," meanwhile, are all "lost in a dream world"—in which they see only what their own minds have created, never the reality of the person who stands before them. "You go along for years knowing something is wrong, then suddenly you discover that you're as transparent as air." Invisibility is "a matter of the construction of their *inner* eyes, those eyes with which they look through their physical eyes upon reality."[2]

Ellison's grotesque, surreal world is very unlike the classical world of Sophocles' play. Its concerns, however, are closely linked: social stratification and injustice, manipulation and use, and above all invisibility and the condition of being transparent to and for one's fellow citizens. Like Sophocles' drama, it explores and savagely excoriates these refusals to see. Like that drama, it invites its readers to know and see more than the unseeing characters. "Being invisible and without substance, a disembodied voice, as it were, what else could I do? What else but try to tell you what was really happening when your eyes were looking through?"[3] In this way, it works upon the inner eyes of the very readers whose moral failures it castigates, although it refuses the easy notion that mutual visibility can be achieved in one heartfelt leap of brotherhood.

Ellison explicitly linked the novelist's art to the possibility of democracy. By representing both visibility and its evasions, both equality and its refusal, a novel, he wrote in an introduction, "could be fashioned as a raft of hope, perception and entertainment that might help keep us afloat as we tried to negotiate the snags and whirlpools that mark our nation's vacillating course toward and away from the democratic idea." This is not, he continued, the only goal for fiction; but it is one proper and urgent goal. For a democracy requires not only institutions and procedures; it also requires a particular quality of vision, in order "to defeat this national tendency to deny the common humanity shared by my character and those who might happen to read of his experience."[4] The novel's mordantly satirical treatment of stereotypes, its fantastic use of image and symbol (in, for example, the bizarre dreamlike sequence in the white-paint factory), and its poignant moments of disappointed hope, all contribute to this end.

As Ellison says, forming the civic imagination is not the only role for literature, but it is one salient role. Narrative art has the power to make us see the lives of the different with more than a casual tourist's interest—with involvement and sympathetic understanding, with anger at our society's refusals of visibility. We come to see how circumstances shape the lives of those who share with us some general goals and projects; and we see that circumstances shape not only people's possibilities for action, but also their aspirations and desires, hopes and fears. All of this seems highly pertinent to decisions we must make as citizens. Understanding, for example, how a history of racial stereotyping can affect self-esteem, achievement, and love enables us to make more informed judgments on issues relating to affirmative action and education.

Higher education should develop students' awareness of literature in many different ways. But literature does play a vital role in educating citizens of the world. It makes sense, then, to ask how it can perform this function as well as possible—what sorts of literary works, and what sort of teaching of those works, our academic institutions should promote in order to foster an informed and compassionate vision of the different. When we ask this question, we find that the goals of world citizenship are best promoted by a literary education that both adds new works to the well-known "canon" of Western literature and considers standard texts in a deliberative and critical spirit.

It is frequently claimed that it is inappropriate to approach literature with a "political agenda." Yet it is hard to justify such a claim without embracing an extreme kind of aesthetic formalism that is sterile and unappealing. The Western aesthetic tradition has had throughout its history an intense concern with character and community. The defense of that tradition in the contemporary "culture wars" should enlist our support.

Fancy and Wonder

When a child and a parent begin to tell stories together, the child is acquiring essential moral capacities. Even a simple nursery rhyme such as "Twinkle, twinkle little star, how I wonder what you are" leads children to feel wonder—a sense of mystery that mingles curiosity with awe.[5] Children wonder about the little star. In so doing they learn to imagine that a mere shape in the heavens has an inner world, in some ways mysterious, in some ways like their own. They learn to attribute life, emotion, and thought to a form whose insides are hidden. As time goes on, they do this in an increasingly sophisticated way, learning to hear and tell stories about animals and humans. These stories interact with their own attempts to explain the world and their own actions in it. A child deprived of stories is deprived, as well, of certain ways of viewing other people. For the insides of people, like the insides of stars, are not open to view. They must be wondered about. And the conclusion that this set of limbs in front of me has emotions and feelings and thoughts of the sort I attribute to myself will not be reached without the training of the imagination that storytelling promotes.

Narrative play does teach children to view a personlike shape as a house for hope and fear and love and anger, all of which they have known themselves. But the wonder involved in storytelling also makes evident the limits of each person's access to every other. "How I wonder what you are," goes the rhyme. In that simple expression is an acknowledgment of the lack of completeness in one's own grasp of the fear, the love, the sympathy, the anger, of the little star, or of any other creature or person. In fact the child adept at storytelling soon learns that people in stories are frequently easier to know than people in real life, who, as Proust puts it in *The Past Recaptured,* frequently offer "a dead weight that our sensitivity cannot remove," a closed exterior that cannot be penetrated even by a sensitive imagination. The child, wondering about its parents, soon learns about these obstacles, just as it also learns that its parents need not know everything that goes on in its own mind. The habits of wonder promoted by storytelling thus define the other person as spacious and deep, with qualitative differences from oneself and hidden places worthy of respect.

In these various ways, narrative imagination is an essential preparation for moral interaction. Habits of empathy and conjecture conduce to a certain type of citizenship and a certain form of community: one that cultivates a sympathetic responsiveness to another's needs, and understands the way circumstances shape those needs, while respecting separateness and privacy. This is so because of the way in which literary imagining both inspires intense concern with the fate of characters and defines those characters as containing a rich inner life, not all of which is open to view; in the process, the reader learns to have respect for the hidden contents of that inner world, seeing its importance in defining a creature as fully human. It is this respect for the inner life of consciousness that literary theorist Lionel Trilling describes when he calls the imagination of the novel-reader a "liberal imagination"[6]—meaning by this that the novel-reader is led to attribute importance to the material conditions of happiness while respecting human freedom.

As children grow older, the moral and social aspects of these literary scenarios become increasingly complex and full of distinctions, so that they gradually learn how to ascribe to others, and recognize in themselves, not only hope and fear, happiness and distress—attitudes that are ubiquitous, and comprehensible without extensive experience—but also more complex traits such as courage, self-restraint, dignity, perseverance, and fairness. These notions might be defined for the child in an abstract way; but to grasp their full meaning in one's own self-development and in social interactions with others requires learning their dynamics in narrative settings.

As children grasp such complex facts in imagination, they become capable of compassion. Compassion involves the recognition that another person, in some ways similar to oneself, has suffered some significant pain or misfortune in a way for which that person is not, or not fully, to blame. As many moral traditions emphasize the analysis of compassion is remarkably constant in both Western and non-Western philosophy—it requires estimating the significance of the misfortune as accurately as one can—usually in agreement with the sufferer, but sometimes in ways that depart from that person's own judgment. Adam Smith points out that people who lose their mental faculties are the objects of our compassion even though they themselves are not aware of this loss: what is significant is the magnitude of the loss, as the onlooker estimates its role in the life of the loser. This requires, in turn, a highly complex set of moral abilities, including the ability to imagine what it is like to be in that person's place (what we usually call *empathy*), and also the ability to stand back and ask whether the person's own judgment has taken the full measure of what has happened.

Compassion requires one thing more: a sense of one's own vulnerability to misfortune. To respond with compassion, I must be willing to entertain the thought that this suffering person might be me. And this I will be unlikely to do if I am convinced that I am above the ordinary lot and no ill can befall me. There are exceptions to this, in some religious traditions' portrayals of the compassion of God; but philosophers such as Aristotle and Rousseau have plausibly claimed that imperfect human beings need the belief that their own possibilities are similar to those of the suffering person, if they are to respond with compassion to another's plight. This recognition, as they see it, helps explain why compassion so frequently leads to generous support for the needs of others: one thinks, "That might have been me, and that is how I should want to be treated."

Compassion, so understood, promotes an accurate awareness of our common vulnerability. It is true that human beings are needy, incomplete creatures who are in many ways dependent on circumstances beyond their control for the possibility of well-being. As Rousseau argues in *Emile,* people do not fully grasp that fact until they can imagine suffering vividly to themselves, and feel pain at the imagining. In a compassionate response to the suffering of another, one comprehends that being prosperous or powerful does not remove one from the ranks of needy humanity. Such reminders, the tradition argues, are likely to lead to a more beneficent treatment of the weak. Philoctetes, in Sophocles' play, asks for aid by reminding the soldiers that they themselves might suffer what he has suffered. They accept because they are able to imagine his predicament.

It seems, then, to be beneficial for members of a society to see themselves as bound to one another by similar weaknesses and needs, as well as by similar capacities for achievement. As Aristotle argues in chapter 9 of *The Poetics*, literature is "more philosophical than history"—by which he means more conducive to general human understanding—precisely because it acquaints us with "the kind of thing that might happen," general forms of possibility and their impact on human lives.

Compassion requires demarcations: which creatures am I to count as my fellow creatures, sharing possibilities with me? One may be a person of refined feeling and still treat many people in one's world as invisible, their prospects as unrelated to one's own. Rousseau argues that a good education, which acquaints one with all the usual vicissitudes of fortune, will make it difficult to refuse acknowledgment to the poor or the sick, or slaves, or members of lower classes. It is easy to see that any one of those might really have been me, given a change of circumstances. Boundaries of nationality can similarly be transcended in thought, for example by the recognition that one of the frequent hazards of wartime is to lose one's nation. Boundaries of race, of gender, and of sexual orientation prove, historically, more recalcitrant: for there might appear to be little real-life possibility of a man's becoming a woman, a white person's becoming black, or even (*pace* earlier psychiatry) a straight person's becoming gay or lesbian. In these cases, then, it is all the more urgent to cultivate the basis for compassion through the fictional exercise of imagination—for if one cannot in fact change one's race, one can imagine what it is like to inhabit a race different from one's own, and by becoming close to a person of different race or sexual orientation, one can imagine what it would be like for someone one loves to have such a life.

Rousseau thought that people differed only in circumstances: underneath, their desires, aims, and emotions were the same. But in fact one of the things imagining reveals to us is that we are not all brothers under the skin, that circumstances of oppression form desire and emotion and aspiration. Some characters feel like us, and some repel easy identification. But such failures to identify can also be sources of understanding. Both by identification and by its absence, we learn what life has done to people. A society that wants to foster the just treatment of all its members has strong reasons to foster an exercise of the compassionate imagination that crosses social boundaries, or tries to. And this means caring about literature.

Literature and the Compassionate Imagination

The basis for civic imagining must be laid in early life. As children explore stories, rhymes, and songs—especially in the company of the adults they love—they are led to notice the sufferings of other living creatures with a new keenness. At this point, stories can then begin to confront children more plainly with the uneven fortunes of life, convincing them emotionally of their urgency and importance. "Let him see, let him feel the human calamities," Rousseau writes of his imaginary pupil. "Unsettle and frighten his imagination with the perils by which every human being is constantly surrounded. Let him see around him all these abysses, and, hearing you describe them, hold on to you for fear of falling into them."[7]

For older children and young adults, more complex literary works now should be added. It was in connection with the moral education of young adults that ancient Athenian culture ascribed enormous importance to tragic drama. Going to a tragedy was not understood to be an "aesthetic experience," if that means an experience detached from civic and political concerns. The tragic festivals of the fifth century B.C. were civic festivals during which every other civic function stopped, and all citizens gathered together. Dramas were routinely assessed as much for their moral and political content as for their other characteristics. Indeed, as the literary criticism preserved in Aristophanes' *Frogs* makes plain, it was well understood that formal devices of meter, vocabulary, and verse form conveyed, themselves, a moral content. What, then, was the civic education that tragedies were intended to promote?

Tragedies acquaint the young citizen with the bad things that may happen in a human life, long before life itself does so. In the process they make the significance of suffering, and the losses that inspire it, unmistakably plain to the spectator; this is one way in which the poetic and visual resources of the drama have moral weight. By inviting the spectators to identify with the tragic hero, at the same time portraying the hero as a relatively good person, whose distress does not stem from deliberate wickedness, the drama makes compassion for suffering seize the imagination. This emotion is built into the dramatic form.

The sympathies of the spectator are broadened in the process, through the notion of risks that are common to all human beings. Tragedies are obsessed with the possibilities and weaknesses of human life as such, and with the contrast between human life and other, less limited lives, belonging to gods and demigods. In the process they move their spectator, in imagination, from the male world of war to the female world of the household. They ask the future male citizen of ancient Athens to identify himself not only with those he might in actual fact become—beggars, exiles, generals, slaves—but also with many who in some sense he can never be, such as Trojans and Persians and Africans, such as wives and daughters and mothers.

Through such devices the drama explores both similarity and difference. Identifying with a woman in a drama, a young male spectator would find that he can in some sense remain himself, that is to say, a reasoning human being with moral virtues and commitments. On the other hand, he discovers through this identification much that is not his own lot: the possibility, for example, of being raped and being forced to bear the enemy's child; the possibility of witnessing the deaths of children whom one has nursed oneself; the possibility of being abandoned by one's husband and in consequence totally without social support. He is brought up against the fact that people as articulate and able as he face disaster and shame in some ways that males do not; and he is asked to think about that as something relevant to himself. So far from being "great books" without a political agenda, these dramas were directly pertinent to democratic debates about the treatment of captured peoples in wartime. With their efforts to overcome socially shaped invisibilities, they participated actively in those debates.

Literature does not transform society single-handed; we know that these powerful and in some sense radical dramatic experiences took place in a society that was highly repressive of women, even by the standards of its own era. Certain ideas about others may be grasped for a time and yet not be acted upon, so powerful are the forces of habit and the entrenched structures of privilege and convention. Nonetheless, the artistic form makes its spectator perceive, for a time, the invisible people of their world—at least a beginning of social justice.

The tragic form asks its spectators to cross cultural and national boundaries. On the other hand, in its universality and abstractness it omits much of the fabric of daily civic life, with its concrete distinctions of rank and power and wealth and the associated ways of thinking and speaking. For such reasons, later democratic thinkers interested in literature as a vehicle of citizenship came to take a particular interest in the novel—a genre whose rise coincided with, and supported, the rise of modern democracy.[8] In read-

ing a realist novel with active participation, readers do all that tragic spectators do—and something more. They embrace the ordinary. They care not
only about kings and children of kings, but about David Copperfield, painfully working in a factory, or walking the twenty-six miles from London to
Canterbury without food. Such concrete realities of a life of poverty are
brought home to them with a textured vividness unavailable in tragic poetry.

Again, the reader's learning involves both sameness and difference. Reading a novel of class difference (for example, a novel of Dickens), one is aware,
on the one hand, of many links to the lives of the characters and their
aspirations, hopes, and sufferings. There are many ways, however, in which
circumstances have made the lives of the poorer characters very different
from those of middle-class readers. Such readers assess those differences,
thinking of their consequence for aspirations to a rich and fulfilling life.
They also notice differences in the inner world, seeing the delicate interplay
between common human goals and the foreignness that can be created by
circumstances. Differences of class, race, ethnicity, gender, and national origin all shape people's possibilities, and their psychology with them. Ellison's
"invisible man," for example, repels the easy and facile sympathy that says
"we are all brothers" because his inner world strikes the reader as dark and
frightening, as the secure child of a loving home gradually takes on more
savage and pessimistic sentiments. In this way we start to see how deeply
racism penetrates the mind and emotions. Consider, for example, the scene
in which the narrator buys a yam from a Harlem street vendor. His emotions
of homesickness, delight, and recognition are in one sense familiar; but the
struggle with shame, as he decides not to hide his pleasure in something he
has been taught to see as a sign of negritude, will be unfamiliar to the white
middle-class reader, who probably will not be able to identify with such an
experience. Such a failure of sympathy, however, prompts a deeper and more
pertinent kind of sympathy, as one sees that a human being who initially
might have grown up free from the deforming experience of racism has been
irrevocably shaped by that experience; and one does come to see that experience of being formed by oppression as a thing "such as might happen"
to oneself or someone one loves.

This complex interpretive art is what the Stoics required when they asked
the world citizen to gain empathic understanding of people who are different.[9] This idea, however, needs to be developed in a specifically democratic
way, as an essential part of thinking and judging well in a pluralistic dem-

ocratic society that is part of an even more complex world. One literary figure from our own tradition who gives us particular help in this task is Walt Whitman, who saw the literary artist as an irreplaceably valuable educator of democratic citizens. "Their Presidents," he wrote, "shall not be their common referee so much as their poets shall."[10] He went on to argue that literary art develops capacities for perception and judgment that are at the very heart of democracy, prominently including the ability to "see eternity in men and women," understanding their aspirations and the complexity of their inner world, rather than to "see men and women as dreams or dots," as mere statistics or numbers. Whitman makes it clear that his idea of a democratic poetry is his own translation of the ancient Athenian idea to the situation of modern America: in "Song of the Exposition" he imagines the Muse of ancient Greek poetry migrating to the New World and inspiring his poetry, "undeterr'd" by America's mixture of peoples and its surprising love of machinery.

The poet's ability to "see eternity," Whitman holds, is especially important when we are dealing with groups whose humanity has not always been respected in our society: women and racial minorities, homosexuals, the poor and the powerless. A major part of the social role of the literary artist, as he saw it, was to promote our sympathetic understanding of all outcast or oppressed people, by giving their strivings voice. "I am he attesting sympathy," the poet announces (*Song of Myself* 22.461–24.5) :

> Through me many long dumb voices,
> Voices of the interminable generations of prisoners and slaves,
> Voices of the diseas'd and despairing and of thieves and dwarfs,
> . . .
>
> Through me forbidden voices,
> Voices of sexes and lusts, voices veil'd and I remove the veil,
> Voices indecent by me clarified and transfigur'd . . .
>
> Dazzling and tremendous how quick the sun-rise would kill me,
> If I could not now and always send sun-rise out of me.

The poet in effect becomes the voice of silenced people, sending their speech out of himself as a kind of light for the democracy. Like Ellison much later, Whitman focuses on our failures to see the flesh and blood of those with whom we live; his poems, like Ellison's novel, portray themselves as devices of recognition and inclusion. The imagining he demands promotes a respect for the voices and the rights of others, reminding us that the other has both agency and complexity, is neither a mere object nor a passive recipient of benefits and satisfactions. At the same time, it promotes a vivid awareness of need and disadvantage, and in that sense gives substance to the abstract desire for justice.

As in Athens, so in America: the fact that sympathy inspired by literary imagining does not immediately effect political change should not make us deny its moral worth. If we follow Whitman's idea, we will conclude that it is essential to put the study of literature at the heart of a curriculum for citizenship, because it develops arts of interpretation that are essential for civic participation and awareness.

Marcus Aurelius made a further claim on behalf of the narrative imagination: he argued that it contributes to undoing retributive anger. He means that when we are able to imagine why someone has come to act in a way that might generally provoke an angry response, we will be less inclined to demonize the person, to think of him or her as purely evil and alien. Even if we never fully understand the action, the very activity of asking the question and trying to depict the person's psychology to ourselves in the manner of a good novelist is an antidote to self-centered rage. It is easy to see how this psychological mechanism operates in our personal lives, where the ability to tell ourselves the story of a parent or a lover or a child who has angered us can often help us avoid selfish vindictiveness. In our political lives, this ability has an equally prominent role—especially when we are dealing with people different from ourselves, whom it would be all too easy to treat as alien objects without the sort of psychological and historical complexity we habitually impute to ourselves.

This point is itself repeatedly dramatized in literary works dealing with characters against whom society has directed its anger. The reader of Richard Wright's *Native Son* contrasts the demonized version of criminal defendant Bigger Thomas, in the novel's account of the press coverage of his trial, with the complicated person she has come to know. The reader of E. M. Forster's posthumously published *Maurice* in a similar way contrasts the demonizing stereotypes of the homosexual purveyed by most characters in the novel with the inner world of Maurice himself, as the reader has come to know it, his dreams of companionship and his intense longing for love. As Whitman insists, literary understanding is a form of imaginative and emotional receptivity that can seem profoundly threatening to the sort of person who would demonize a group. To allow inside one's mind people who seem alien and frightening is to show a capacity for openness and responsiveness that goes against the grain of many cultural stereotypes of self-sufficiency.

Whitman's insistence on receiving the voices of the excluded suggests a further point: that for literature to play its civic function it must be permitted, and indeed invited, to disturb us. If we can easily sympathize with a character, the invitation to do so has relatively little moral value; the experience can too easily deteriorate into a self-congratulatory wallowing in our own compassionate tendencies. The challenge of Sophocles' *Philoctetes* to its audience was to see without flinching what the characters found disgusting and vile: pus, blasphemous cries, Philoctetes' body covered with sores. The challenge of Wright's *Native Son* was and is to look into the life of a violent criminal who kills his lover Bessie more casually than he kills a rat. Similarly, the challenge of *Invisible Man* is to see what it is like to be seen through, or seen in terms of various demeaning fantasies—again, a difficult experience for the novel's likely audience.

These works are all written in a conventional literary language, a fact that explains their relatively easy acceptance into the realm of "literature" despite the radical character of their subject matter. It can also be argued, however, that literary art most fully fulfills its Whitmanesque mission of acknowledging the excluded when it allows the excluded to talk as they really talk, to use a daily language that is nonliterary and that may shock our sensibilities. The 1994 Booker Prize for Fiction, Britain's most distinguished literary award, was given to James Kelman's *How Late It Was How Late*, a novel of working-class life in Glasgow, Scotland. The novel, which is set in the mind of its protagonist, uses throughout the working-class Scots dialect that such a character would actually speak, and includes all the words that such a character would be likely to use in thought and speech. The award created a minor furor, since many cultural critics objected strenuously to giving such a prestigious artistic prize to a work that, by one count, uses the word *fuck* over four thousand times. In interviews given during the controversy, Kelman defended his project in Whitmanesque terms. The voices of working-class people, he claimed, have generally been excluded from "English literature" in his still highly class-conscious society. For generations, at least since Dickens, there have been gestures of inclusion, in which working-class characters figure in a literary novel; but their voices first had to be assimilated to a middle-class norm of literary discourse. This was a way of rendering real working people invisible.

A central role of art is to challenge conventional wisdom and values. One way works engage in this Socratic enterprise is by asking us to confront— and for a time to be—those whom we do not usually like to meet. Offensiveness is not all by itself a sign of literary merit; but the offensiveness of a work may be part of its civic value. The inclusion of new and disturbing works in the curriculum should be assessed with these ideas in mind. When we do consider such works we should bear in mind that it is difficult to know in advance, or quickly, which unconventional works, or parts of works, will have a lasting power to illuminate the situation of a group and which are merely shocking. Most of us have fears and blind spots that militate against the acknowledgment of some of our fellow citizens, and we should recognize that our reactions of disturbance may therefore be highly unreliable, leading us to regard as merely shocking what will eventually be seen to have genuine merit. (To give just one example, contemporary sensibilities required the excision of a crucial scene from Wright's *Native Son*, in which Bigger and his friend masturbate in the movie theater while looking at the image of a white woman. This scene, too shocking for publication in 1940 and not included in editions of the novel until 1993, can now be seen as crucial to the narrative development of the work, and to its exploration of the social formation of Bigger's imagination and desires.) We do not need to deny that there are defensible criteria of literary merit in order to recognize that we ourselves are unreliable judges of merit when works touch on our own lives and the controversies of our own time. For this reason we ought to protect the opportunity of the arts to explore new territory with broad latitude, and we should also protect the right of university teachers to explore controversial works in the classroom, whether or not we ourselves have been convinced of their lasting merit.

Compassion in the Curriculum: A Political Agenda?

If the literary imagination develops compassion, and if compassion is essential for civic responsibility, then we have good reason to teach works that promote the types of compassionate understanding we want and need. This means including works that give voice to the experiences of groups in our society that we urgently need to understand, such as members of other cultures, ethnic and racial minorities, women, and lesbians and gay men.

Recall Reno student Eric Chalmers, who, in connection with the readings assigned in his English class, was asked to think about the experience of a gay person and to write a letter to his parents in that persona—to let that person's voice emerge from his mouth. "I probably didn't say anything," he quickly explained; "I just rambled." This otherwise aggressive and crusty young man, extremely confident and even dogmatic, showed a moment of confusion and uncertainty. He acknowledged that the "off-the-wall" assignment had had a point—because "we met, you know, all sorts of people," and fulfilling the assignment is "like an understanding of their belief system." Such Whitmanesque experiences of receptivity and voice should be cultivated. They are closely connected to the Socratic activity of questioning one's own values and to the Stoic norm of becoming a citizen of the whole world, but they cannot be engendered without works that stimulate the imagination in a highly concrete way, including works that unsettle and disturb.

To produce students who are truly Socratic we must encourage them to read critically; not only to empathize and experience, but also to ask critical questions about that experience. And this means cultivating an attitude to familiar texts that is not the detached one that we sometimes associate with the contemplation of fine art. This more critical attitude has its roots, in the West, in the ancient Greek tradition of the tragic festivals, where watching a work of art was closely connected to argument and deliberation about fundamental civic values. It has been revived and vividly depicted in quite a few critical works of the present day—among them, Wayne Booth's fine work, *The Company We Keep: An Ethics of Fiction.*[11] Drawing on his own reading of ancient Greek texts, Booth proposes a valuable metaphor for the interaction of reader with a literary work. A literary work, he writes, is, during the time one reads it, a friend with whom one has chosen to spend one's time. The question now is, what does this friendship do to my mind? What does this new friend ask me to notice, to desire, to care about? How does he or she invite me to view my fellow human beings? Some novels, he argues, promote a cheap cynicism about human beings and lead us to see our fellow citizens with disdain. Some lead us to cultivate cheap sensationalistic forms of pleasure and excitement that debase human dignity. Others, by contrast, show what might be called respect before a soul[12]—in the way the text itself depicts the variety of human goals and motives, and also, it may be, in the interactions among the characters it displays.

Booth makes it clear that this critical attitude is perfectly compatible with immersion in the work; his idea is that immersion and experience precede, and ground, a critical assessment that we should ideally carry on in conversation with others whose perceptions will complement and challenge our own. He calls the process "co-duction" to stress its communal and comparative character. Through this process we attain insight into what we have become while we were enjoying the work. This insight will illuminate the nature of the literary experience and its role in our lives. Booth considers the classroom a paradigmatic scene of such critical activity.

Booth is famous for a distinction that we need to bear in mind: between the narrator or characters and the "implied author," that is, the sense of life embodied in the text taken as a whole. A work that contains few or no sympathetic, admirable characters may still promote sympathy and respect in the reader through the sort of interaction the work as a whole constructs. (Both of these figures are distinct, in turn, from the real-life author, who may have all sorts of properties that are not realized in the text.)

Thinking about Booth's metaphor of the literary work as friend shows us a further dimension of the experience of sympathy. When we read a novel with close attention, we frequently will be led by the text to have sympathy with characters of many different kinds; but frequently, too, the text will cultivate sympathy unevenly, directing our attention to some types of human beings and not to others. Literary works are not free of the prejudices and blind spots that are endemic to most of the political life. A novel that sees the experience of middle-class women with great sympathy may (like the novels of Virginia Woolf) render working-class people invisible. A novel that recognizes the struggles of working-class people—as, up to a point, the novels of Dickens do—may have little sensitivity to the lives and experiences of many types of women. If we are reading and teaching such novels with democratic ideals of equal concern and respect in mind, we will probably come to feel that there is something incomplete or even defective in these works. In this sense sympathetic reading and critical reading should go hand in hand, as we ask how our sympathy is being distributed and focused. One learns something about the text when one asks these critical questions: one sees its internal structure with a new sharpness, and one makes one's own relation to it more precise.

This civic and evaluative approach to reading is both moral and political. It asks how the interaction between reader and text constructs a friendship and/or community, and it invites us to discuss texts by making moral and social assessments of the kinds of communities texts create. Wayne Booth's version of this approach, like the one defended here—and like that of Lionel Trilling in the previous generation—is liberal and democratic, informed by a conviction that all citizens are worthy of respect and that certain fundamental freedoms deserve our deepest allegiance.

But conservative critics have recently charged that the whole idea of reading in this way is an illicit and antiliterary activity, alien to the high tradition of the humanities.[13] To take a fairly typical example, in a column titled "Literary Politics," George Will recently wrote of the "supplanting of esthetic by political responses to literature," arguing that this approach "aims at delegitimizing Western civilization by discrediting the books and ideas that gave birth to it."[14]

It is not clear what notion of the aesthetic George Will has in mind when he contrasts the aesthetic with the political. The questions raised here about compassion and community are hardly new, faddish questions. Indeed, they are as old as literary interpretation itself. In ancient Greece alone, one can find them in Aristophanes and Aristotle, Plato and Plutarch. How, all these works ask us, does literature shape the character of the young citizen? What moral weight do its forms and structures have? This, we might say without distortion, is *the* dominant question asked about literature in the Western aesthetic tradition. And it is asked, when it is asked well, in a manner that does not neglect the literary form of the text. In fact, one of the greatest contributions of both Plato and Aristotle to aesthetics was their subtle account of the ways in which literary forms themselves convey a content, a view of what is worth taking seriously, and what the world is like.

What could someone mean by saying that these questions are not aesthetic? Such a claim can be seriously supported only by defending a picture of the aesthetic that has had a relatively narrow and recent history in the Western tradition, namely the Kantian and post-Kantian formalist tradition, according to which the proper aesthetic attitude is one that abstracts from all practical interests. Kant's own thought on this topic is complex and susceptible of multiple interpretations. But his claim that beauty gives pleasure without interest has certainly led many people to suppose that he was urging us to look at art without thinking of any practical questions at all, including very general questions, such as what is worth caring for, what is just and good. More recently, formalist aestheticians such as Bloomsbury writers Clive Bell and Roger Fry advocated that sort of detachment as characteristic of a truly aesthetic response.[15] In a famous example supplied by their ally, aesthetician Edward Bullough, people caught in the fog will usually prove unable to look at the fog aesthetically, because they are preoccupied with their safety.[16] They will succeed in doing so only if they can suspend their practical interests in safety and well-being, and attend to the pure color and shape that surround them. George Will needs to defend such a view to make sense of his claims. On other more common views of the aesthetic, political criticism is a central part of aesthetic attention.

Is the formalist view an adequate view of the aesthetic? It has a certain intuitive appeal. It seems true that if I am preoccupied with how to get out of the fog, there are many features of its shape, color, and form to which I am probably not attending. Similarly, if I am reading Ellison's novel as a set of instructions on how to bring about racial harmony, or Dickens' *Hard Times* as a blueprint for labor reform, much will elude me. Ellison described his novel as "a raft of hope, perception, and entertainment"; the person who ignores the entertainment loses a crucial dimension of the perception and hope. But this does not mean that the texture of Dickens' or Ellison's language is not profoundly moral and political, aimed at creating a community of a certain sort and at acknowledging certain parts of the human world as worthy of our attention and love.

Most great aesthetic theorists in the Western tradition have ultimately rejected the extreme formalist view. The long list includes Plato, Aristotle, the Stoics, Hegel, Nietzsche, Tolstoy, and fine present-day theorists such as Arthur Danto, Nelson Goodman, and Richard Wollheim. Ironically, it includes, as well, the Renaissance humanists who shaped the canon of literary classics that conservative theorists defend: for these thinkers saw their focus on the Greeks and Romans as part of the "political agenda" of reacting against medieval scholasticism and promoting a more human-centered view of the world.

One can at least comprehend how one might look at a Monet canvas in the way Bell and Bullough recommend—although I doubt that it is the most richly rewarding way to look, if it neglects ways in which Monet's forms express joy, and serenity, and even a certain ideal of community. One can at least comprehend what it might mean to listen to a Mahler symphony that way—though, once again, it seems that one would lose much by refusing the music's invitation to feel compassion, disgust, despair, and triumphant joy, and one would certainly be doing violence to Mahler's own self-conception, which seems a remarkably fruitful one. (He repeatedly speaks in letters of the ways in which his works address questions about the meaning of life and seek to create a compassionate, nonhierarchical community.) It is at least possible to look at dances of some modern choreographers in this way—though, once again, one would, I think, be missing a great deal that is both ethical and political, for example Martha Graham's narrative investigations of myth, sexuality, and ethical conflict.

But it is next to impossible to see what it could mean to read a drama of Sophocles, or a novel of Dickens or George Eliot, in the detached way. It is impossible to care about the characters and their well-being in the way the text invites, without having some very definite political and moral interests awakened in oneself—interests, for example, in the just treatment of workers and in the reform of education. Both Dickens and Eliot frequently address the reader, alluding to such common interests. This commitment to the making of a social world, and of a deliberative community to think critically about it, is what makes the adventure of reading so fascinating, and so urgent.

There was a brief moment in the recent history of literary criticism when it did seem possible and desirable to hold such concerns in abeyance. This was the moment of the flourishing of the so-called New Criticism, which held (to simplify) that when one read a poem one should bring nothing external to that reading—no historical and social context, no questions of one's own about life and how to live it.[17] Not surprisingly, this movement produced its best work in the area of lyric poetry, and even there only by a degree of inconsistency—for critics did allow themselves to ask what a word could have meant in 1786, say, and did permit themselves the extraneous knowledge that a certain other meaning came into being only in 1925. If they had not done so they would have produced gibberish. Other elements of context crept back in, as did normal human concerns about love and death, meaning and emptiness. Indeed, claims were ultimately made about the political meaning of literary irony and complexity. But even in its more elastic version, this movement had a difficult time doing justice to complex narrative works with a social dimension. For this reason it was resisted all along by some of the finest minds in the field, among them British moral critic F. R. Leavis and American social thinker Lionel Trilling. Both of these men had a political agenda. Trilling's *The Liberal Imagination* made explicit his own commitment to liberalism and democracy, and argued brilliantly that the novel as genre is committed to liberalism in its very form, in the way in which it shows respect for the individuality and the privacy of each human mind. He connected his criticism of the fiction of Henry James very closely with his general social criticism. *The Liberal Imagination* juxtaposes essays on James with essays on contemporary social issues.

What Wayne Booth and many other contemporary critics are doing today, feminist critics prominently among them, is to continue such approaches and to render them more sophisticated by asking more subtle questions about the ways in which works construct desire and thought, inviting the imagination to be active in these or those ways. Such a critical stance sometimes leads the critic to be harsh toward famous works of literature. Thus Wayne Booth argues that Rabelais's works display a contemptuous and cruel attitude to women, and that such an attitude is intrinsic not only to certain characters, but also to the works as a whole and their humor. Booth finds Rabelais distasteful because of this lack of empathy, and reports that he can no longer really enjoy the work's humor now that he has come to see it in this critical light, as tinged with cruelty. He is therefore probably somewhat less likely to teach and recommend the works, though in his book he does continue to "teach" them in this critical spirit.

On the other hand, considerations of empathy more frequently lead to an expansion of the traditional list of works read, as critics, searching for accounts of the experience of silenced people, discover powerful accounts of that experience that have previously been overlooked. A representative example of this type of criticism is the article "In the Waiting Room," by the young feminist critic Judith Frank. In the first portion of her article, Frank, a scholar of eighteenth-century English literature who teaches at Amherst College, describes her own teaching of unfamiliar works by women. She notes that these works focused on the vicissitudes of the female body in a way unparalleled, not surprisingly, in male works of that period. Three of them, in fact, dealt with breast cancer—one being Fanny Burney's journal account of her mastectomy, "an operation performed during the eighteenth century with only a wine cordial as anesthesia." Frank's brilliant idea of setting her account of curricular controversies in the context of a vivid, unsentimental, and powerful account of her own radiation treatment for breast cancer—diagnosed the semester after she taught the three nonstandard works alluding to breast cancer—reminds her reader vividly of the fact that this historically and ethically situated kind of criticism responds to an age-old conception of what gives literature its importance in human life. ". . . isn't that, after all," she asks, "what many people think good literature should do: sustain us when we're weak, deepen our understanding of history, expand our sense of what it's possible to think and feel?" She makes us ask why we might suspect a teacher who assigns the three nonstandard works of having a "political agenda": is it political to acknowledge the bodies of women and the illnesses to which women are subject, and apolitical to deny such recognition? Is criticism political only when it asks us to look and see, acknowledging what we might not have acknowledged before, and apolitical when it does not invite such acknowledgment?

The move to include noncanonical works and to scrutinize the ways in which such works construct desire and recognition does not necessarily lead to "delegitimizing Western civilization," as George Will fears. Says Frank,

> Despite the picture Will paints of contemporary academic life, I did not whine to my colleagues that Shakespeare and Milton don't talk about breast cancer; nor did I, deciding that the lack of a poetic treatment of breast cancer in their works makes them bad writers, demand that my department replace our courses in Shakespeare and Milton with courses on Maria Edgeworth and Audre Lorde. Rather, like many of my colleagues, I taught the noncanonical alongside the canonical: Edgeworth and Burney, for example, alongside Defoe, Richardson, Fielding, Smollett, and Sterne. Will is anxious about the wholesale destruction of Western civilization, I think, because canon revision reveals the canon to be a social institution rather than a self-evidently sublime entity unsoiled by the grime of human interest.

If literature is a representation of human possibilities, the works of literature we choose will inevitably respond to, and further develop, our sense of who we are and might be.

Once we start to think of literature this way, we notice something else: that the New Critics' decision *not* to concern themselves with the social and historical dimensions of literary works was itself a political act, an act of a quietistic type. Turning to the ethical interpretation of a standard text, Frank defends an interpretation of Defoe's *Robinson Crusoe* that links it closely to its own historical context, one in which moral issues involved in colonialism and slavery were hotly debated. As Frank puts it, "You need to do a lot of work to ignore the historical context of *Robinson Crusoe,* no matter how mythically it presents itself." The willful choice to remain ignorant of such issues, and to treat the work as distant myth, betrays a certain stance, a stance of detachment from concrete human problems. The detachment of the Bloomsbury formalists was less innocent of politics than it might at first seem. Indeed, it seems evident, when one studies the writings of Bell, Fry, and other members of the Bloomsbury group, that their stance was closely connected with Bloomsbury's own complicated political stance, radical in matters of sex and aristocratic in matters of taste and education. The idea was that the cultivation and defense of fine-tuned, detached aesthetic responses allowed them to rise above everyday moral judgments (and thus to protect unconventional forms of sexual life), but also to neglect reformist proposals of the day that focused on the education of the masses, concentrating instead on the cultivation of small elite communities of friends. (The Bloomsbury ideal was closely linked not only to disdain for the working classes but also, frequently, to anti-Semitism and other forms of ethnic and racial prejudice. These prejudices also infect much of the New Criticism.) There is of course no reason why the political attitudes of Bloomsbury or the related ideas of the New Criticism should not be found in the literary classroom. We all learn most from a curriculum that contains dissent and difference, an interaction of opposing views. Even in the process of coming to grips with one work in a single class we should seek out a plurality of contrasting judgments. And different classrooms will properly differ greatly, as they foster approaches with political dimensions of many different types. The important thing to recognize is that we don't avoid the political dimension by pretending it isn't there; and insofar as we do, we drain the works, especially narrative works, of much of their meaning and urgency. This sort of frank debate about the moral content of art has been a staple of the Western tradition, in both philosophy nd literature. There is no reason why it should not continue to make our teaching of literature more truly Socratic. The addition of new works will enhance our understanding both of history and of human beings. A critical examination of more standard works will yield new insights—frequently (as in the case of *Robinson Crusoe*) by revealing a dimension of unease or criticism in the text that a more morally detached style of criticism might have missed.

World Citizenship, Relativism, and Identity Politics

What, if anything, should worry us in the current political criticism? It is not a cause for concern that some political critics are more radical than

Wayne Booth and Lionel Trilling, just as some are more conservative. It would be dull if all academics were liberals; criticism, like moral and political philosophy, profits from vigorous debate. It is far more healthy for students to hear debates between opposing views than for them to hear only refined talk about a poem's irony, divorced from any historical or ethical considerations.

Nor is it a cause for grave concern, ultimately, that many contemporary critics espouse forms of moral relativism deriving from French postmodernist philosophy, denying the objectivity of value judgments. One may certainly take issue with the conclusions of these critics, and find fault with their arguments. On the whole, philosophers thinking about truth and objectivity have not been very impressed by the arguments of the postmodernist critics, even when they defend versions of relativism on other grounds. The full assessment of these issues requires an arduous engagement with arguments, frequently technical in nature, drawn from the philosophy of physics, the philosophy of mathematics, and the philosophy of language. Any scholar who moves between philosophical debates on these issues and the related debates in literary theory cannot help noticing a difference in sophistication and in complexity of argument. (Literature is not the only field guilty of lapses in conceptual clarity: when economists talk about values, they are equally likely to espouse a naive form of relativism that would not withstand philosophical scrutiny.) We should demand more philosophical rigor in literary discussions of relativism, which otherwise risk superficiality and triviality.

But to ask for more rigor is not to say that relativist positions should be ignored or dismissed. The humanities classroom ought to contain vigorous debate between relativists and antirelativists of many kinds, just as between conservatives and liberals. When carried on at a high level, such a debate about the objectivity of value judgments enriches our understanding of alternatives in a useful way.

Such reflections about the philosophical shortcomings of literary teaching suggest that the teaching of literature can prepare world citizens better if it becomes more truly Socratic, more concerned with self-critical argument and with the contribution of philosophy. Interdisciplinary teaching, such as the work done at St. Lawrence by Grant Cornwell of the Philosophy Department and Eve Stoddard of the English Department, is an especially good way of promoting this rigor, both in the work of faculty and in their un-

dergraduate teaching. Any literature classroom in which views of decon-
structionist critics are discussed or exemplified should also contain some
basic analysis of the arguments for and against various forms of cultural
relativism. This can most easily be done in a climate of interdisciplinary
dialogue and debate, in which literature teachers can observe the way these
issues are handled by philosophers in courses on issues ranging from ethics
to the philosophy of science, and in which the philosophers become aware
of the subtle issues involved in discussions of literary interpretation. There
is indeed a risk that our newly theory-conscious departments of literature
will produce an outpouring of bad philosophy on these issues, both in research and in teaching. Interdisciplinary dialogue is the best way to prevent
this from happening more than it already has.

Interdisciplinary dialogue about literature takes a variety of forms on
today's campuses. Many introductory courses in "world civilization" or
"Western civilization" bring philosophers together with literary scholars for
the discussion of central literary texts. Such courses are most successful if
they give the faculty support for course-development time, during which
they can talk together and bring the resources of their disciplines to their
common readings. Faculty also frequently team-teach courses at a higher
level, integrating the perspectives of different disciplines. And finally, faculty
may join in interdisciplinary dialogue outside the classroom, in ways that
shape their classroom teaching. At St. Lawrence, the interdisciplinary faculty
seminar, which focused extensively on theoretical issues of relativism, influenced the design and the methods of each individual faculty member's departmental courses. Such approaches need strong support, since without
them the facile relativism that many undergraduates bring to the classroom
is likely to remain unexamined and the goals of world citizenship to that
extent unfulfilled.

The really grave cause for concern in the current teaching of literature,
however, is not the presence of defective arguments, which can easily be
criticized. It is, instead, the prevalence of an approach to literature that
questions the very possibility of a sympathy that takes one outside one's
group, and of common human needs and interests as a basis for that sympathy. The goal of producing world citizens is profoundly opposed to the
spirit of identity politics, which holds that one's primary affiliation is with
one's local group, whether religious or ethnic or based on sexuality or gen-

der. Much teaching of literature in the current academy is inspired by the spirit of identity politics. Under the label "multiculturalism"—which can refer to the appropriate recognition of human diversity and cultural complexity—a new antihumanist view has sometimes emerged, one that celebrates difference in an uncritical way and denies the very possibility of common interests and understandings, even of dialogue and debate, that take one outside one's own group. In the world-citizen version of multiculturalism, the ethical argument for adding a work such as *Invisible Man* to the curriculum will be Ellison's own argument: that our nation has a history of racial obtuseness and that this work helps all citizens to perceive racial issues with greater clarity. In the identity-politics version of multiculturalism, by contrast, the argument in favor of *Invisible Man* will be that it affirms the experience of African-American students. This view denies the possibility of the task Ellison set himself: "of revealing the human universals hidden within the plight of one who was both black and American."

These different defenses of literature are connected with different conceptions of democracy. The world-citizen view insists on the need for all citizens to understand differences with which they need to live; it sees citizens as striving to deliberate and to understand across these divisions. It is connected with a conception of democratic debate as deliberation about the common good. The identity-politics view, by contrast, depicts the citizen body as a marketplace of identity-based interest groups jockeying for power, and views difference as something to be affirmed rather than understood. Indeed, it seems a bit hard to blame literature professionals for the current prevalence of identity politics in the academy, when these scholars simply reflect a cultural view that has other, more powerful sources. Dominant economic views of rationality within the political culture have long powerfully promoted the idea that democracy is merely a marketplace of competing interest groups, without any common goals and ends that can be rationally deliberated. Economics has a far more pervasive and formative influence on our lives than does French literary theory, and it is striking that conservative critics who attack the Modern Language Association are slow to criticize the far more powerful sources of such anticosmopolitan ideas when they are presented by market economists. It was no postmodernist, but Milton Friedman, who said that about matters of value, "men can ultimately only fight."[18] This statement is false and pernicious. World citizens should vigorously criticize these ideas wherever they occur, insisting that they lead to an impoverished view of democracy.

An especially damaging consequence of identity politics in the literary academy is the belief, which one encounters in both students and scholars, that only a member of a particular oppressed group can write well or, perhaps, even read well about that group's experience. Only female writers understand the experience of women; only African-American writers understand black experience. This claim has a superficial air of plausibility, since it is hard to deny that members of oppressed groups frequently do know things about their lives that other people do not know. Neither individuals or groups are perfect in self-knowledge, and a perceptive outsider may sometimes see what a person immersed in an experience fails to see. But in general, if we want to understand the situation of a group, we do well to begin with the best that has been written by members of that group. We must, however, insist that when we do so it may be possible for us to expand our own understanding—the strongest reason for including such works in the curriculum. We could learn nothing from such works if it were impossible to cross group boundaries in imagination.

Literary interpretation is indeed superficial if it preaches the simplistic message that we are all alike under the skin. Experience and culture shape many aspects of what is "under the skin," as we can easily see if we reflect and read. It is for this reason that literature is so urgently important for the citizen, as an expansion of sympathies that real life cannot cultivate sufficiently. It is the political promise of literature that it can transport us, while remaining ourselves, into the life of another, revealing similarities but also profound differences between the life and thought of that other and myself and making them comprehensible, or at least more nearly comprehensible. Any stance toward criticism that denies that possibility seems to deny the very possibility of literary experience as a human social good. We should energetically oppose these views wherever they are found, insisting on the world-citizen, rather than the identity-politics, form of multiculturalism as the basis for our curricular efforts.

Literature makes many contributions to human life, and the undergraduate curriculum should certainly reflect this plurality. But the great contribution literature has to make to the life of the citizen is its ability to wrest from our frequently obtuse and blunted imaginations an acknowledgment of those who are other than ourselves, both in concrete circumstances and even in thought and emotion. As Ellison put it, a work of fiction may contribute "to defeat this national tendency to deny the common humanity shared by my character and those who might happen to read of his experience."[19] This contribution makes it a key element in higher education.

We are now trying to build an academy that will overcome defects of vision and receptivity that marred the humanities departments of earlier eras, an academy in which no group will be invisible in Ellison's sense. That is in its way a radical political agenda; it is always radical, in any society, to insist on the equal worth of all human beings, and people find all sorts of ways to avoid the claim of that ideal, much though they may pay it lip service. The current agenda is radical in the way that Stoic world citizenship was radical in a Rome built on hierarchy and rank, in the way that the Christian idea of love of one's neighbor was and is radical, in a world anxious to deny our common membership in the kingdom of ends or the kingdom of heaven. We should defend that radical agenda as the only one worthy of our conception of democracy and worthy of guiding its future.

CHAPTER FOUR

The Study of
Non-Western Cultures

Oh, East is East, and West is West, and never the twain shall meet . . .
But there is neither East nor West, nor Border, nor Breed, nor Birth,
When two strong men stand face to face, though they come from the
ends of earth!

Rudyard Kipling, "The Ballad of East and West"

At Belmont University in Nashville, students in Ronnie Littlejohn's course "Advanced Moral Theory" find that the focus of the course is Japanese moral theory and practice. After learning to analyze Japanese concepts related to Western ideas of justice, love, and care, students are asked to write essays assessing the validity of the following claim: "Whereas Japanese moral practice considers maintenance of relationships to be the primary guide for moral practice, Western civilization privileges adherence to abstract rules and duties for this purpose."[1]

At Bryn Mawr College, Aristotle scholar Steven Salkever and historian of Chinese thought Michael Nylan teach "Comparative Political Philosophy" by studying Socrates and Confucius. They look at the different ways in which both thinkers challenged traditional cultures with new questions about virtue, stirring up doubts about the adequacy of time-honored ideas. They ask students to notice strategies by which each educator masks the innovative character of his philosophical program—Socrates' profession of ignorance, Confucius' claim to follow tradition. "The intention to innovate yet conserve, to tell all yet not to say too much," they conclude, "are goals fundamental to each educator." The class debates the merits of the two thinkers' criticisms of traditional ideas of honor and manliness.

At the University of Chicago, students in the course "Compassion and Mercy in the Western Philosophical Tradition" talk with a visitor, Paul Griffiths of the Divinity School, who has just lectured to them on Indian Buddhist views of compassion. After discussing the different terms standardly translated as "compassion," Griffiths explains that the Buddhist view is not easy to compare with views of compassion or sympathy in thinkers such as Rousseau and Adam Smith, who have been the focus of the course. Unlike its Western counterparts, the Buddhist view rests on a radical attack on the concept of the individual self, asking us to respond to suffering in a way that denies the distinctness of each person's individual life course. Students ask Griffiths to what extent this moral view could support (as Rousseau's would appear to) the demand for political equality.

Students in U.S. colleges and universities are learning more about non-Western cultures. Curricula that once focused exclusively on "the Western tradition" have recently made efforts to incorporate comparative courses and courses focusing exclusively on the cultures of "the East" in a wide range of disciplines, including history, philosophy, political theory, economics, religion, musicology, and literature. Even when courses retain a "Western" focus, they frequently incorporate a comparative perspective. Many people today are asking whether there are good reasons for these changes. They fear that by diluting our focus we will produce students who no longer grasp their own tradition. This is a legitimate worry, and we should be sure that new knowledge does not lead to ignorance. A new and broader focus for knowledge, however, is necessary to adequate citizenship in a world now characterized by complicated interdependencies. We cannot afford to be ignorant of the traditions of one half of the world, if we are to grapple well with the economic, political, and human problems that beset us.

Rudyard Kipling declared that there is a total gulf between "East" and "West," and that there can be no understanding across this gulf—except, he thought, in the limiting case of military and quasi-military confrontation, where he believed (somewhat naïvely) that some elements of common (male) humanity become unavoidably clear, and a man is a man no matter what his origins. Unlike Kipling, we live in a world in which "East" and

"West" do, and must, meet constantly, and must strive to understand one another without resort to conflict. Whether we are discussing the multinational corporation, global agricultural development, the protection of endangered species, religious toleration, the well-being of women, or simply how to run a firm efficiently, we increasingly find that we need comparative knowledge of many cultures to answer the questions we ask. Moreover, Americans are now increasingly working with and alongside people from other cultures, in business and in political and social projects of many kinds. We need to find ways of crossing the gulf that Kipling thought unbridgeable. Our task is made more difficult by the fact that we can no longer assume, as Kipling apparently did, that there is a universal language of strong manliness that makes "breeding" and "birth" irrelevant: we are aware that ideas of peace and war, of proper norms of manliness and aggression, vary greatly across cultures and are shaped in many different ways by different cultural and religious traditions.

Indeed, many of these foreign cultures are now among us in America. Once-distant religious practices and beliefs shape our business activities, our laws, our understanding of what religion is. To be ignorant of Islam, of Buddhism and Hinduism, of the traditions and religious practices of China and Japan, is not only to lack an essential prerequisite of international enterprise and political debate. It is also, frequently, to lack the equipment necessary to talk to one's neighbors, to vote with understanding on measures connected with immigration and diversity, to think about the legal issues involved in a Buddhist prisoner's request for sacred books and chapel services,[2] to deliberate well about bringing up an adopted child of Chinese origin, or to understand why author Salman Rushdie faces an edict of death.

We need to learn more about non-Western cultures—above all for these reasons of good citizenship and deliberation in an interlocking world. But this learning is valuable for other reasons as well. It will enhance our self-knowledge as Americans. We will get a better picture of our own diverse nation by becoming aware of the many traditions, both Western and non-Western, that intermingle within it. And we will also understand the specifically Western aspect of our American origins, more precisely, "the Western tradition," by comparison with other ways and practices. As John Searle has argued, "one of the most liberating effects of liberal education is in coming to see one's own culture as one possible form of life and sensibility among others."[3]

We will also come to understand how our own history has erred in its understanding of other human beings. Our relationship to non-Western societies has frequently been mediated by projects of colonial domination, usually accompanied by complacent attitudes of religious superiority. Both our romantic longing for a mysterious Eastern "other" and our closely related denigration of "the East" as nonrational, superstitious, and amoral stem from an attitude that assumes Western values to be normative for morality and culture. Whether a thinker is rebelliously praising "the East" for its spiritual richness and sexual opulence or, more conventionally, denigrating it for its mysticism and immorality, the tendency to take some vaguely articulated version of Western middle-class Christianity as the benchmark obscures real thought about both self and other. These oversimplifications are certainly not unconnected with the fact that Western colonial authorities ruled politically over India and other parts of the non-Western world and were eager to justify their presence. We need to gain a more adequate understanding of non-Western cultures partly because in so doing we come to understand intellectual and moral wrongs in which our predecessors have been implicated. To gain this sort of self-critical vantage point on history does not entail suspending criticism about practices and beliefs of non-Western cultures or portraying them as free from domination or misrepresentation. It does mean perceiving our own projects of simplification, avoidance, and self-avoidance in our relations with other cultures.

So far, America has not done very well in producing the sort of citizen who can interact well with distant cultures. Our nation's great size and its distance from most others make it easy to forget that it is part of a complex world. Its economic and political strength make it easy to feel that one does not need to know about any other nation. The preeminence of English as the first language of economics, science, and world business makes it easy to believe that little would be gained from knowledge of another language. In consequence, Americans are insular and ignorant to a degree unparalleled in Europe, where a plurality of Western cultures, at least, is a fact of everyday life. Both Americans and Europeans, however, are alike in knowing little about religions such as Islam, Hinduism, and Buddhism, which govern the daily lives of millions of the world's people. We know far too little about other nations' ideas of work, of business dealings, of family, of morality. This ignorance has led to moral and political error, to failures in human sensitivity and in sheer common sense. In business it has led to blunders that might have been avoided had our educational system done a better job.

(Recall Anna, the businesswoman who found herself ill prepared to run an office in Beijing.) To correct this situation, which jeopardizes our future, we need to rely on our colleges and universities. They must press forward with curricular broadening; but they must do so in a way that adequately meets the needs of today's citizens.

The study of non-Western cultures is extremely challenging. Cultures are not monolithic or static. They contain many strands; they contain conflict and rebellion; they evolve over time and incorporate new ideas, sometimes from other cultures. It is not surprising, then, that many difficult questions should arise when we add the study of other cultures to the curriculum. When we decide to teach "Chinese values" in a course on comparative philosophy, what should we be studying? The Confucian tradition? The Marxist critique of that tradition? The values of contemporary Chinese feminists, who criticize both Confucianism and Marxism (often by appeal to John Stuart Mill, whose *The Subjection of Women* was translated into Chinese early in the century)? Much depends on our purposes, in the course in question. But we should not fail to ask these questions. To make things still more complex, we must remember that even "the Confucian tradition" was itself not monolithic. Salkever and Nylan remind their class that much that we now think of as the "traditions" of ancient China (and ancient Athens) was really the work of subversive antitraditional intellectuals, engaged in argument with their surrounding societies. Similarly, Griffiths warned students to be aware of the radical challenge posed by Buddhism to people's everyday ways of thinking and speaking about the self. If they fail to do this, thinking of Buddhism as a straightforward picture of daily thoughts and ways in India, they will greatly exaggerate the differences between Indian ways and our own.[4] Non-Western cultures are complex mixtures, often incorporating elements originally foreign. This is true of our own traditions as well, and one aspect of studying these cultures will be to understand how much we have derived from them.[5] Cultural influence does not flow only, or even primarily, in a single direction.

Given these complexities, and given our urgent need for better understanding of cultures with which we are in constant interaction, we need academic instruction to steer us. We cannot rely on personal experience alone to convey all that we need to know in order to be informed and sensitive citizens. But this instruction will be helpful only if it does grapple well with the difficulties of cross-cultural description. Once we set out these difficulties in more detail, getting a clearer understanding of the defects we have when we approach foreign cultures without adequate instruction, we will be able to identify the methods of instruction that are likely to yield good results, promoting enlightened citizenship where enlightenment is urgently needed.[6] We will understand why it is important for our colleges and universities to build further on the good beginning they have made, and why their efforts deserve our support.

The Descriptive Vices: Chauvinism and Romanticism

When we study another culture or another era, we often encounter customs that strike us as strange. (This may also happen when we go next door to visit our neighbors or when we try to understand the thoughts of a person whom we love.) If we care enough to pursue matters further, we try to interpret what we see before us. At this point, two contrasting vices often make their appearance, vices that any good education for global understanding will need to combat.[7] The first we may call *descriptive chauvinism:* it consists in recreating the other in the image of oneself, reading the strange as exactly like what is familiar. This vice is very common in teaching in the history of philosophy. Historians of ancient Greek thought, especially those drawn to the ancient Greeks by an interest in the philosophical problems of the historian's own era, very often leave to one side what they regard as alien, representing the Greeks as very like nineteenth-century Englishmen or, today, twentieth-century Americans. Such assimilations are not always bad. One of the joys of doing the history of philosophy is to discover in an ancient text a subtle analysis of a problem that still vexes us today. But all too frequently the historian motivated by contemporary concerns will miss something important in the Greek sources. Thus nineteenth-century descriptions of ancient Greek religion tended to make it look much more like Christianity than it really was. The role of Zeus as king of the gods was subtly distorted to produce the picture of a kind of monotheism, and notions of faith and grace were liberally imported into the reading of ritual and prayer, in ways that misrepresented their meaning.

Similarly, when the ethical thought of Aristotle was taught, concepts that seemed foreign to the dominant ethical traditions of nineteenth- and twentieth-century British thought were subtly distorted until they looked like what was familiar. The Aristotelian concept of *eudaimonia*, which means a complete and flourishing human life that lacks no activity that would make it better or more complete, was standardly understood (and even translated) as "happiness," a term that in modern English usage suggests a state of being pleased or satisfied. This made Aristotle's ethical theory look more like a form of utilitarianism, concealing for a long time the fact that Aristotle's theory cannot accurately be assimilated to either of the two categories of ethical theory (the "teleological" and the "deontological"), which were taken to be exhaustive.

What was wrong with these enterprises? The fact that Aristotle was highly regarded in his own time should make us seek an interpretation that makes his ideas powerful in their own historical context, insofar as we know it. And, more important, our belief that human life does not change altogether from one century to another—that many of the basic problems tackled by Aristotle's work (the fear of death, moderation in appetite, distributive justice, the balance between friendship and self-sufficiency) are still, in some form, problems for us—should make us seek an interpretation that makes them make sense for us, at least in a general way. In general, human interpretation across a gulf, whether of place or of time, generally, and rightly, involves some background assumptions about the rationality of the other: we rightly prefer interpretations that make the person say something coherent and meaningful to interpretations that make the person speak nonsense. In some areas, such as physics, we should be prepared to find the theories of another time no longer relevant to us, even though we should try to see how they made sense in their context. But in ethics, where life's problems don't altogether go away, we should be prepared to find both contextual good sense and at least some present-day plausibility.

The problem with many interpreters of Aristotle in the nineteenth and early twentieth centuries was that they refused to consider that there might be plausible views other than those their philosophical culture was currently discussing. They assumed that theirs was the best philosophical culture, and that everything meaningful about ethical matters was already being articulated in it. When that chauvinistic assumption was questioned, other plausible views could be discovered in authors of the past. Thus, it was recognized that Aristotle saw people not as striving to maximize a state of satisfaction, and also not as striving to perform a list of duties. He saw them, instead, as striving to achieve a life that included all the activities to which, on reflection, they decided to attach intrinsic value. He thought of the problem of life-planning as one that fundamentally involved deliberation about a rich plurality of rather general ends, in which the deliberator asked what concrete form of "moderation" or "courage" made most sense for his own life. Put in these terms, Aristotle's ethical enterprise is not unreachably "other" or impossibly foreign. Indeed, it might well be argued that it fits what real people do when they think about their lives—even in present-day America—better than do the abstractions of utilitarian moral theory.[8] So a description of Aristotle's ethics that was chauvinistic in philosophical terms, assimilating Aristotle's theory too closely to reigning ethical theories, caused readers to lose a distinctive philosophical option that might actually have made better sense of their lives.

If descriptive chauvinism is a problem even when we think about a relatively familiar culture, such as the culture of ancient Greece, we can expect it to be far more problematic when we approach an unfamiliar culture. If one knows little about the society one is encountering, it will be tempting to suppose that at least some very important things are the same. Thus, many who know that Indian music sounds very different from Western music are likely to be unaware that the whole concept of a "musical work of art" is one that does not exist in the same form in Indian traditions, with their emphasis on the creative role of the interpreter. The concept of the musical artwork that organizes our practices of concertgoing is in fact of relatively recent origin, even in the West; and yet this fact is far from widely recognized.[9] A listener who brings that concept to a performance by Ravi Shankar is likely to miss many aspects of his creative contribution, which is that of improvisation within the limits of a classical form with long traditions of performance. Such a listener would also fail to consider some more pertinent cross-cultural similarities—for example, between Shankar's activity and that of a modern jazz musician. Only when certain differences are recognized can more interesting similarities come into view.

Again, although most Americans are aware of the fact of religious difference, they may be unaware that difference encompasses what counts as worship itself and what a ritual of worship is. We see this problem even in our daily lives in America. Many Christians visiting an Orthodox or Conservative Jewish worship service will find that the relationship between worship services and ritual practice is differently organized in the two religions, and that proper norms of behavior during a worship service vary greatly. Walking in and out of the service at odd hours, talking and even laughing during the service—all this the Christian is likely to think exceedingly bad behavior; it is, however, acceptable behavior, indeed the norm, in Conservative Jewish services.

These puzzles, again, are even more likely to arise in the encounter with a completely unfamiliar religion. Many who are aware that Confucianism is in many ways very different from Christianity may still expect it to have concepts of divinity, of faith, and of prayer that are roughly comparable to their Christian counterparts. Only a further inquiry would show the extent to which ideas of ritual practice, rather than beliefs about deity, are central in Confucian religion. Again, a Christian approaching Hinduism with expectations formed by an upbringing in a strongly monotheistic religion is likely to find it easy to think of Rama as the central divinity and to feel that the Hindu tradition centers upon that god and his sacred places. Such assumptions would cause this person to distort the polytheistic and extremely diverse Hindu traditions of the past and thus, for example, to miss the extent to which the recent emphasis on Rama and his birthplace by the BJP (Bharatiya Janata Party, the leading Hindu fundamentalist party) involves a distortion of tradition. Good academic instruction could have prevented this political error.

If errors of descriptive chauvinism are common in areas where we generally acknowledge diversity, they are far more common, and troubling, in areas of life that we take to be culturally invariant. An American who arrives India, no matter how well prepared for difference, is likely to be overwhelmed by the sheer absence of physical space, the sheer lack of concern for solitude and privacy. The concept of the privacy of the person or the household, so dear to most Americans, does not exist in India in anything like the same form. Visitors may call unannounced, and the general level of bustle and interruption is, by American standards, painfully high. Street life in an Indian city or even town allows none of the contemplative solitude that one may have walking along the lakeshore in Chicago, however crowded it is—because one's physical space is not regarded as sacrosanct in the same way, because one may find oneself offered a guided tour, or assistance with luggage, and in many other ways find one's space invaded (a very Western description of the phenomenon).

An example of the bad political judgment that can result from descriptive chauvinism is in Paul Ehrlich's book *The Population Bomb*. Ehrlich reports that the idea that there is a world population emergency occurred to him while he was riding in a taxi "one stinking hot night in Delhi" and got stuck in traffic; he looked around him at the seas of people: "people eating, people washing, people sleeping. People visiting, arguing, and screaming... People, people, people, people ... the dust, noise, heat, and cooking fires gave the scene a hellish aspect." Ehrlich then felt a sudden panic, expressed in the remarkably Western thought, "Would we ever get to our hotel?"[10] Whether Ehrlich's analysis of the global population emergency is accurate is, of course, another story. (There are many reasons to think it inaccurate.)[11] What was descriptively chauvinistic was his assumption that daily life in Delhi should be expected to be rather like that in a major American city, where one proceeds to one's hotel smoothly without incident. If it wasn't like that, then some worldwide emergency must be in the making. Of course another diagnosis is possible: Delhi is, on a perfectly normal day, rather different from Chicago, with different traffic patterns, different norms of horn-blowing, and, indeed, different expectations about the time it might take to get to one's hotel.

We all have biological parents, and many of us grew up with one or two parents, whether biological or adoptive. We all have assumptions about what a parent is and what a child is. We rarely recognize the extent to which these assumptions are shaped by a specifically Western tradition, in which the idea of the two-parent nuclear family living in its own house has a prominence probably unequaled elsewhere in the world.[12] When one sees the extended families of an Indian town, in which relatives of many sorts are all close to the children and in which regular visits by a number of aunts and uncles and friends form a large part of the child's world, one may well feel a sense of strange impropriety: where are the child's own parents, and why are they leaving so much to others? Why are these nosy relatives showing up at the door again, unannounced? Our own norms lead to a confusion that could have been dispelled by earlier recognition that the culture has a different understanding of who is ultimately responsible for the child's well-being. Education could have prevented these confusions.

Or consider Anna, the American businesswoman working in Beijing who adopted a Chinese baby. She was prepared to find many things different in China, but she had assumed that people all over the world hug and talk to babies in the same way—that the aggressive style of parenting common in America, with its interest in early interaction and its emphasis on cognitive and motor stimulation, reflected a universal human norm. Her surprise at the fact that her Chinese nurse wrapped the baby's limbs tightly, discouraging movement, and refused to interact with the child led her, at first, to blame the nurse, thinking her a bad caregiver; only later did she recognize that she was dealing with a cultural difference.

Anna wished that her undergraduate education had prepared her to confront Chinese culture in a more sensitive manner. And indeed, good classroom teaching can prepare students to confront such problems well. Paul Griffiths told the students at the University of Chicago that even aspects of ourselves that we may easily think of as universal and invariant—such as our emotional responses of sympathy and pain at the suffering of others—are actually shaped in complicated ways by the culture's or religion's view of personal identity and of continuity in space and time. We cannot intelligently compare Buddhist compassion with Western compassion until we become aware of larger descriptive differences. Ronnie Littlejohn urged the students at Belmont not to assume that Japanese culture shares our ideas of what an ethical norm is, or what the sense of duty is. He urged them to think hard about the importance of community and relationship in Japanese moral practice—a thought that would have importance for any student doing business with that country or trying to understand the reasons for its success. We urgently need such teaching to equip students for our multinational world.

Do our campuses themselves avoid the error of descriptive chauvinism? This error is relatively common in teaching about all foreign cultures (including those of ancient Greece and Rome)—especially at the more subtle level at which we assume we know what a "religion" is, what an "artwork" is, what a philosophical problem is, and so forth. It is, however, a vice that teachers at most schools I visited are making earnest efforts to avoid in their teaching of non-Western cultures. Long-term immersion in another culture, as in the St. Lawrence program, and cooperative teaching, such as the Salkever/Nylan course at Bryn Mawr, are two very good ways to avoid this vice. And indeed, I saw less of descriptive chauvinism in the teaching of non-Western cultures than I observe in teaching about ancient Greece, where it is all too easy to assume that this is "our" culture, with "our" great books and "our" ways of thinking.

Descriptive chauvinism has its opposite in what we might call *descriptive romanticism,* the expression of a romantic longing for exotic experiences that our own familiar lives seem to deny us. This vice consists in viewing another culture as excessively alien and virtually incomparable with one's own, ignoring elements of similarity and highlighting elements that seem mysterious and odd. This form of distortion is at least as common in our daily lives as descriptive chauvinism, since people are often drawn to foreign cultures by a desire for mystery and strangeness or for alternatives to familiar ways of thinking.

Thus young people who were drawn to Indian culture in the 1960s and 1970s frequently ignored the side of India that seemed familiar—the long traditions in mathematics and economics, the traditions of atheism and hedonism, the zeal for rational classification, the elaborately rhetorical intellectualism of the Bengali intelligentsia. They sought out mystical versions of Hindu religion because they felt that these supplied what America seemed to lack—spirituality divorced from economic necessity and military aggressiveness. In so doing they, like many people before them, portrayed India as the mystical other, a portrait that distorts the real variety of Indian traditions. People brought up in one set of habits frequently notice in the foreign only what seems different; they take the similar things to be evidences of international Westernization (as, of course, in some cases they are) and refuse to acknowledge the authenticity of anything that looks like what they associate with the West. Similar distortions are frequently put forward by Indian scholars themselves, who are eager to distance their own traditions from those of the colonial oppressor. Indian feminist Veena Das, for example, argues that Indian women are not capable of thinking about their own well-being as distinct from the well-being of the rest of their family—despite ample empirical evidence that women who are hungry while others in their family have food do take note of this fact, that women who are forbidden to work outside the home do view this as a constraint on their ability to feed themselves and their children.[13]

Descriptive romanticism can lead to disastrous errors in our encounters with others. Consider the plot of Puccini's *Madame Butterfly*. Pinkerton's view of Japanese culture as exotic and totally unlike his own leads him to believe that a Japanese woman does not need to be treated with the moral regard he shows his Western wife. She is a delicious plaything, to whom loyalty and promise-keeping are entirely unnecessary. Of course no culture, Eastern or Western, is really a realm of free sensuality, lacking all moral prescriptions surrounding sexual expression and the treatment of a sexual partner. Pinkerton was ignorant of the Japanese moral order. Moreover, there are unlikely to be in any culture women who don't care how they are treated, who exist simply as morsels to be consumed by men. The tragedy of the opera is a tragedy of descriptive romanticism: for Pinkerton just doesn't notice that the woman he desires is a human being with feelings of love and demands for moral respect that are very similar to those of his own wife. Americans abroad still make such mistakes.

Descriptive romanticism, moreover, distorts "the West" just as surely as it distorts "the East." The student (or scholar) who turns to India as a source of non-Western spirituality and poetry is likely to downplay, in the process, the existence of poetic and spiritual traditions in the West. The person who thinks of India as enjoying a monopoly of spirituality is likely to be selling Western religions short, and Western music and poetry and art. She may also be ignoring many cultures within the West: the cultures of Russia and Finland, for example. It is all too easy to misunderstand ourselves in the light of a simplistic contrast with the other.

Clearly, it is of urgent importance to produce citizens who can avoid chauvinism when they think about and deal with non-Western cultures. Equally clearly, we are unlikely to avoid it without good academic instruction.

Some academic instruction about non-Western cultures is not helpful because it is itself excessively romantic and simplistic. In a book closely related to courses they teach at Smith College and at Harvard University, anthropologist Frédérique Marglin (Smith) and economist Stephen Marglin (Harvard) have argued that Indian culture lacks "binary oppositions," for example the polar opposition between life and death. They also claim that, while the West makes a strong distinction between the values that prevail in the workplace and those that prevail in the home, Indian culture makes no such distinctions, cultivating (largely through mystical spirituality) what they call "the embedded way of life."[14] Such simplistic claims about a complex culture like India's can easily be shown to be inadequate to the many-faceted reality.[15] Similar problems infect widely used textbooks. A student who reads that "the chief mark of Indian philosophy in general is its concentration upon the spiritual" will be likely to be thrown onto the wrong track.[16] She will be encouraged by such a statement to neglect the rich logical traditions of India, the complex debates about perception and knowledge (which closely parallel Western debates about the foundations of knowledge),[17] and also the presence of atheist and materialist traditions (above all, the "Carvaka" school) that assailed religiosity and spirituality. Bimal Matilal, until his premature death several years ago professor of Indian thought at Oxford University and a leading authority on the history of Indian philosophy, concludes: "Too often the term Indian philosophy is identified with a subject that is presented as mystical and non-argumentative, that is at best poetic and at worst dogmatic. A corrective to this view is long overdue."[18]

By now, however, it is not difficult to find books and instructors that present balanced and accurate portrayals. The textbook *Beyond the Western Tradition: Readings in Moral and Political Philosophy,* edited by philosophers Daniel Bonevac, William Boon, and Stephen Phillips, is a good basic undergraduate introduction.[19] Original texts are now available in a variety of well-translated editions, and some of the best courses on Indian thought do not use a textbook at all. One outstanding example is the course "Philosophy East and West," taught by James van Cleve at Brown University. Van Cleve, who is an expert in the history of Western philosophy but who has lived and taught in India, has a detailed grasp of India's primary logical and epistemological traditions and is well equipped to present them alongside the more familiar religious traditions of India. There is something seductive in the idea that hard logical thinking is unnecessary, that a great and noble culture did without it by cultivating the inner world of spirituality. Such stereotypes are false, and good courses resist them from the start.

Descriptive romanticism is common, as well, in academic accounts of other non-Western cultures. Zhang Longxi, professor of comparative literature at the University of California at Riverside, described these errors in a lecture to the faculty titled "Knowledge, Skepticism, and Cross-Cultural Understanding."[20] Longxi, whose academic career was delayed by years of labor on rural farms during China's Cultural Revolution, speaks of the pernicious influence of Jacques Derrida's view that Western culture is "logo-centric," focused on verbally articulated argument, and that nonphonetic Chinese written characters, by contrast, preserve "the testimony of a powerful movement of civilization developing outside all logocentrism." Longxi argues that Derrida's discussion of Chinese culture gives no evidence of serious study. Such a study would have revealed not utter difference, but a complex tradition of thought about language, thinking, and writing that is in many respects closely comparable to Western traditions. Similarly oversimple are claims that Chinese culture lacks the notion of the individual or distinctions between subject and world, between fact and value.

Both descriptive vices frequently rely on simplifications—of both self and other. Perhaps the greatest obstacle to descriptive adequacy, whether in teaching or in life, is the desire to summarize the essence of a culture in a pithy way—for this almost always leads to a neglect of complexity and internal debate, and to a corresponding oversimplification of the person's own culture for purposes of contrast. As Salkever and Nylan note, many contrasts of Chinese with "Western" philosophy involve "pronouncements like this: 'We might sum up the Chinese attitude to reason in these terms: reason is for questions of means; for your ends in life, listen to aphorism, example, parable, and poetry.'" This oversimplification is then put to work in analyzing alleged shortcomings (or virtues) of "Western philosophy"—before an adequate account of the complexities of either one has been put before the student.

Good teaching of non-Western cultures is becoming more and more common. Like Salkever and Nylan, good instructors in many colleges and universities are increasingly stressing the following points about the idea of "culture":

1. *Real cultures are plural, not single.* Any real-life culture contains diverse regions, classes, ethnic and religious groups, and distinctive men and women within each group. We would easily see the defects in a monolithic portrayal of "American values"; we should be equally critical of such descriptions of China or India.

2. *Real cultures contain argument, resistance, and contestation of norms.* Any description of what "Indian values" are should include not only the dominant norm but also the voices of resistance to that norm. Divisions between urban and rural, female and male, rich and poor are ubiquitous in cultures, and one should recognize that the most influential texts do not always reveal these debates. To discover them we must frequently move beyond the texts of high culture into the study of history.

3. *In real cultures, what most people think is likely to be different from what the most famous artists and intellectuals think.* It would be bizarre to treat Plato (an aristocrat disdainful of the democratic culture around him) as representative of "ancient Greek values," just as it would be bizarre to treat Karl Marx as representative of "German values," or James Joyce as repre-

sentative of "Irish values." Such errors are commonly made, however, in studying distant cultures. They can be avoided only by reading broadly and doing one's best to discover a wide spectrum of popular thinking.

4. *Real cultures have varied domains of thought and activity.* Descriptions of "non-Western culture" too often focus on philosophy, religion, and literature, since those are relatively easy to teach, ignoring music, sculpture, architecture, science, agriculture. They also tend to focus on an urban elite, ignoring daily life and the lives of rural people.

5. *Real cultures have a present as well as a past.* One of the oddest features of contemporary descriptions of India and China is that interpreters frequently identify the culture with its oldest or most traditional segment. We would not accept a description of American values that identified them with the values of Plato, with those of the seventeenth-century Puritans, or even with those of Madison and Jefferson; so why should we accept a description of Indian traditions that focuses on the laws of Manu, or of Chinese traditions that focuses on Confucius? Just as America has evolved, in part by borrowing good ideas from elsewhere, so too India and China have evolved. Confucius is a part of Chinese values; by now, however, so too are the ideas of contemporary Chinese critics of Confucianism; so too are the borrowed ideas of Mill, Spencer, Marx, and modern economics. Indian values are shaped by traditional Hindu ideas; they are shaped, as well, by the internationalist cosmopolitanism of Rabindranath Tagore, by the humanist religious eclecticism of Rammohun Roy, by the philosophical/economic thought of Amartya Sen, by filmmaker Satyajit Ray's love of Hollywood movies and Indian cultural traditions, by secularism and Islam and Christianity. It is arrogant and mistaken of the Westerner to judge that Hindu fundamentalists are "really Indian" and that secularists are "Western," that Confucian authoritarianism is really Chinese and that the human rights movement is not. The fact that people die for an idea is usually a good indication that the idea is theirs.[21]

Instructors who include material about non-Western cultures in their courses should be alert to all these warnings. This is difficult enough for expert scholars, but nonexperts have additional difficulties, since they often do not know the languages or which specialists they can trust. Obviously, we should not encourage sloppy and impressionistic teaching. These are real obstacles. Some people feel that they give us a reason not to include the study of non-Western cultures in the undergraduate curriculum. But if we judge, as we should, that we badly need to encourage better understanding in this area, we must try to answer this objection.

We should begin by asking the objector to reflect on the way in which "Western culture" is currently being taught. Ancient Greece is a foreign culture; all the problems just enumerated arise in attempts to teach it well. If one really held to the maxim that someone who does not know the language of the culture and cannot expertly judge about research materials and translations should not be teaching that culture to undergraduates, approximately 90 percent of the courses in classical civilization or Western civilization that currently exist in American colleges and universities would have to be scrapped. Most faculty who teach Sophocles and Plato do not know Greek; many teachers of medieval history, philosophy, or literature do not know Latin. Among those who do, few are expert enough to criticize different translations.

We encounter these problems because we are determined to bring a liberal education in these books to undergraduates of widely varying backgrounds. In Europe, by contrast, the Greek and Latin classics are studied only by a narrow group of specialists. Europeans tend to be shocked by our way of teaching Sophocles and Plato in general undergraduate courses. Our way ensures less expertise in teaching; but it is in keeping with our democratic ideal, which holds that all students, regardless of preparation, should have the opportunity to receive a liberal arts education that will open to them the works judged most likely to help them think and live well. Because we are determined to make these works available, scholars have worked to produce acceptable translations for students. The system is not perfect; but it is infinitely better than the old aristocratic system of reserving the study of Sophocles for a narrow elite that knew Greek.

In teaching non-Western cultures, our situation is different in degree, not in kind. Many teachers of non-Western topics will not know the relevant languages; but it is likely that in any large university or college some will, and can give guidance to their colleagues about the choice of reference materials and translations. (We should remember, too, that it is a rare citizen of India who knows all ten of the official languages of India, and a small minority who know Sanskrit, the ancient language; given this situation, English has for a long time been the main intellectual and political language of the nation.) The professional organizations make many research tools and bibliographies available, and in this day of rapid communication via the

Internet, scholars can seek advice from their peers at other institutions. The range and quality of available translations is rapidly expanding, and the market created by new courses can be expected to produce further expansion. As Ronnie Littlejohn points out, study in translation often motivates students to pursue language study, since they "discover that other language worlds . . . may capture moral realities" unfamiliar to them, and this shows them an urgent reason to get involved in this learning.

A key strategy in overcoming the two descriptive vices is cooperative teaching. At the University of New Hampshire, the comparison of ancient Greek and ancient Chinese science was made fruitful by the presence, on the four-person teaching team of the introductory humanities course, of an expert in ancient Greek philosophy and an expert in the history of Chinese science. At Bryn Mawr College, Salkever teams up with Nylan to teach comparative political philosophy. At the University of Chicago, Indologist Wendy Doniger has teamed up with classicist David Grene to teach drama and myth; in my own course "Compassion and Mercy in the Western Philosophical Tradition," Indologist Griffiths visited to lecture on Buddhist views. Choice of comparative materials should be guided by the availability of colleagues willing to advise and/or coteach.

Salkever and Nylan suggest, on the basis of their experience, that it is always easier to avoid the descriptive vices if one chooses a plurality of contrasting texts from each culture. Then it is difficult to talk about "Chinese values" or "Indian values" in a simplifying manner. They also stress the importance of situating each text carefully in its historical and social context, so that it can be understood not as the voice of "the culture," but as an active and individual voice within a complex plurality of voices. When they teach a course on Socrates and Confucius they devote a good deal of time to this sort of stage-setting, which does require collaboration, in order to ensure the right degree of expertise. Texts should be seen as elements in a cultural conversation—although this emphatically does not mean treating them as mere products of cultural forces.

The Normative Vices:
Chauvinism, Arcadianism, Skepticism

Description is rarely altogether separate from evaluation. When we describe what we see, we try to make sense of it, and our descriptions are therefore likely to be limited by our experience, by our habitual ideas of the sensible. We are also influenced by what we find interesting or arresting, and in that way description is likely to be biased in favor of what has caught our eye. These two evaluative tendencies in description often pull in opposite directions, though not necessarily with a tendency to balance description nicely in the middle. Descriptions of India frequently show at one and the same time the ill effects of habit, as the describer underestimates the difference of attitude to worship or the family, and an overemphasis on the strange and colorful.

But once we have described a culture we are to some extent free to evaluate it in different ways. A person who believes that India is the land of mystical spirituality, indifferent to logic and "Western" rationality, may despise India on that account, or, if she abhors all "logocentrism," she may think India the best of nations. Any reasonably accurate description of a culture is likely to portray a plurality of views and perspectives, so simple praise or condemnation will be rendered difficult by the very fact of precision. Nonetheless, when we turn from description to evaluation, we need to guard against a new set of vices. Again, these are very difficult to avoid in daily life unless we are prepared by academic instruction. And they pose a sharp challenge to academic instruction itself.

The first and most obvious is *normative chauvinism*. The evaluator judges that her own culture is best, and that insofar as the other culture is unlike it, it is inferior. Normative chauvinism has a complex relationship to descriptive chauvinism. Both may, of course, be present: the describer may make the foreign culture look more homelike than it really is, and then proceed to criticize it for the differences that remain. But very often, normative chauvinism is grounded in descriptive romanticism: having made the foreign culture look foreign and strange, the evaluator condemns it for that very strangeness.

This combined error is very common in cross-cultural encounters, and has been so for centuries. In ancient Greece and Rome, description of distant nations frequently takes the form of imagining an impossibly, weirdly different "other," and than of criticizing that other for lacking the civilized characteristics of Greece or Rome. Tacitus' *Germania*, for example, first describes German customs in a way that inaccurately overstresses their distance from Roman values, and then criticizes the Germans for barbarity on the basis of that description. Much later, John Locke made a similar normative error when he characterized Indian philosophy as holding the mythical view that the earth rests on an elephant who in turn is supported on the back of a tortoise—and then, having offered a quite ludicrously inaccurate description of "the poor Indian Philosopher," proceeded to "show" how much better Western philosophy can do.[22] As Bimal Matilal notes, the image is taken from an old religious myth, but "it would be impossible to find a text in classical Indian philosophy where the elephant-tortoise device is put forward as a philosophical explanation of the support of the earth."[23] Modern analytic philosophers sometimes continue the same error, first characterizing Indian philosophy inaccurately as altogether mystical and antilogical, then condemning it for that alleged fact.

Many contemporary attacks on "multicultural" education go wrong through a similar combination of descriptive and normative error. Allan Bloom, for example, asserts that "only in the Western nations, i.e. those influenced by Greek philosophy, is there some willingness to doubt the identification of the good with one's own way."[24] This inaccurate description neglects rich critical traditions in many non-Western philosophical cultures and, of course, the everyday critical rationality of most human beings in all places and times. On this shaky basis Bloom then judges the West to be superior and the non-West to be not worth studying.

But normative chauvinism does not require inaccurate description as a basis. Even if a student has been given a rich, descriptively accurate portrayal of a culture, she may still err at the evaluative stage if she has been encouraged to think that nothing can ever be learned from the foreigner, and that one's own culture has the best answers to all human questions. To return to my earlier example, a music-lover who is enamored of the recent Western classical tradition of the "musical artwork" may get a very accurate idea of Indian classical music and still condemn that music for lacking a concept she finds habitual and central. Probably such a blanket condemnation would be an error. Again, Saul Bellow's rhetorical question—where would we find "the Tolstoy of the Zulus, the Proust of the Papuans"—has been widely repeated as a normative statement critical of the cultural achievements of these societies.[25] The person who repeats it in this spirit is to a degree observing accurately; many non-Western cultures do lack a form comparable to the novel. (Japan, of course, is a salient example of a non-Western novel-writing culture, and by now we certainly find first-rate novels in more or less every world culture. Even though writers such as Naguib Mahfouz and

Chinua Achebe and Vikram Seth are influenced by Western traditions, their novels still seem deeply rooted in their own cultures.) Descriptive difficulties to one side, however, users of the remark appear to be making the astonishing move of requiring novel-writing as evidence of cultural value. Even if we grant the odd assumption that aesthetic excellence is the only reason for taking a curricular interest in a culture—political, historical, and economic factors being presumed irrelevant—such a conception of aesthetic worth is remarkably narrow. It neglects the existence, in India and Africa and China, of epic and lyric poetry, of drama, and of complex traditions in music, dance, sculpture, and architecture. This is surely normative chauvinism in its most straightforward sense, the novelist's admirers seeing his own craft as at the center of the world of ideas.

Normative chauvinism in our relation to "the East" has frequently been linked with the aims of religious missionaries. Because of their sincere conviction that Christianity was the one true religion and that the heathen would lack salvation without conversion, many people did make earnest efforts, often successful, to convert the inhabitants of foreign cultures. Their convictions about the superior worth of Christianity usually included not only metaphysical but also moral notions: they tended to believe not only that the "heathen" lacked the right beliefs about divinity but also that they were immoral, simply because they did not share all Christian ethical views. Sometimes the moral critique made sense, and sometimes it did not. What was chauvinistic was to assume that every difference from one's own way was in itself evidence of immorality. We see very much the same set of assumptions at work today at Brigham Young University, where the study of non-Western cultures tends to be organized around the aims of missionary work. One need not think those projects illegitimate in order to feel that they are incomplete as education, prematurely foreclosing inquiry into the value of distant practices and ideas.

Normative chauvinism can easily poison a citizen's encounter with a foreign culture, whether in business or in politics or simply in reading and thinking. It is difficult for people avoid this error unless, as undergraduates, they have been exposed to instruction that shows them how to think about a very different way of life. Students cannot have courses on every culture with which they may possibly come in contact. But a good course about one culture will show them how to inquire about others.

The best antidote to normative chauvinism is curiosity. This is a trait most people have, but it needs to be stimulated and steered by good teaching. Good comparative instruction should, above all, encourage students to keep their minds open and alive, prepared to find something interesting and valuable in the new civilizations they may encounter. The ancient Greco-Roman world did contain Tacitus' hostile and simplistic portrayal of the Germans; it also contained the *History* of Herodotus, who went to Egypt and Persia with an inquiring mind, prepared to find that foreign customs would contribute significant scientific and moral and political ideas, ideas that might even be better than those of his own city. We need to produce citizens who are more like Herodotus than like Tacitus. On the whole, I think, our colleges and universities do produce such students in courses on non-Western cultures. Such courses frequently contain the excitement of new discovery and adventure; professors teaching them rarely seem to suffer from boredom or burnout. Salkever, Nylan, Griffiths, and many others convey to their students their own excitement about what a cross-cultural encounter has shown them.

The vice opposed to normative chauvinism consists in imagining the other as untouched by the vices of one's own culture. Since this frequently takes the form of imagining the non-West as paradisiacal, peaceful, and innocent, by contrast to a West that is imagined as materialistic, corrupt, and aggressive, we may call this vice *normative Arcadianism.* The non-West as seen by the Arcadian frequently has many of the features associated with images of Arcadia in pastoral poetry. It is a green, noncompetitive place of spiritual, environmental, and erotic values, rich in poetry and music, and lacking the rushed, frenetic character of Western life. Like the classical image of Arcadia, the normative image of "the East" is often a reverse image of whatever is found impoverished or constraining in one's own culture. Thus many young enthusiasts about Indian religion think of India as a country of spiritual harmony, without the competition that they dislike in the West. Thus Frédérique Marglin, who characterizes Western medicine as dehumanizing and bureaucratic, imagines with Arcadian nostalgia a country where smallpox avoidance was mediated by a colorful and poetic ritual.[26] She does not succeed quite so well in imagining the pain of smallpox; nor does she ask what proportion of the contemporary Indian population would prefer to return to the days of smallpox and its presiding goddess Sittala Devi. In the same volume, Stephen Marglin describes an Arcadian way of life in rural India, in which religious values permeate both home and workplace. He portrays in a highly favorable light religious prohibitions that keep menstruating women out of the workplace: for (he argues) here we have an example of the same values existing both in the workplace and in the home (where menstruating women may not enter the kitchen).[27] This, then, is the "embedded way of life," by contrast to Western alienation. In a similar fashion, Jacques Derrida imagines China as a realm free from the vices of hierarchy and subordination that he has traced to Western culture's fascination with language and reason. (Often such critiques of the West are inspired by a specific philosophical critique of the Enlightenment—for example, Nietzsche's or Heidegger's—and have rather more to do with controversy within the history of Western thought than with anything real about the East.)[28]

Normative Arcadianism, once again, is a difficult error to avoid for people who have no solid preparation for cross-cultural encounters in their undergraduate education. Young people in America are inclined to be reluctant to criticize that which is different; they often feel that it is unfair or tyrannical to criticize someone else's values and beliefs. They also often feel rebellious toward the culture in which they were raised, and eager to find an alternative. They badly a solid grounding in cross-cultural evaluation if they are to develop the combination of sensitivity and firmness that good citizenship requires.

It is, of course, no easy matter to distinguish normative Arcadianism from positive evaluations that are plausible and interesting. I have chosen some rather extreme examples, in which it is easy to see that the blanket dismissal of "the West" and exaltation of "the East" are unlikely to be entirely right. These examples are easy to spot in part because they rest on crude and inadequate description, description that already betrays romantic oversimplification. (One afternoon in Orissa was enough to convince Stephen Marglin that everyone loved the religious taboos and that women were better off than in the West; Derrida did not investigate the complex hermeneutic traditions of China.) But when we turn to cases in which we have an adequate description, it becomes far more difficult to identify errors of normative Arcadianism. We have to have answers to the evaluative questions themselves before we can do that; and we should not be too confident that we do have all the answers. A good classroom will be full of debates on these questions. Eve Stoddard's class at St. Lawrence contained many different views about the practices of veiling. Along with Stoddard, I find some of them excessively Arcadian and uncritical; what was good about her class was that it made the appropriateness of criticism a central theme, opening up a vigorous debate on the issue. Paul Griffiths finds Buddhist ethical views attractive in a way that many of the University of Chicago students did not; that is why the dialogue between them was illuminating. Amartya Sen's students may initially find Indian religious traditions attractive in a way that he does not. Vigorous debate is the best way to make progress toward sensitive evaluation. It is possible, though difficult, to find such debate outside the classroom. But we should not leave these important matters to chance. We should make sure that our students learn how to think and debate well, by giving them well-taught courses like the ones I have described. Fortunately, most courses I have encountered do strive for this sort of debate even when the instructor has a definite view. Frédérique Marglin's students at Smith, for example, report that her teaching is extremely open to different positions and much less dogmatic than I found her scholarship to be.

Because it is so difficult to get the balance right, a third vice often makes its appearance: *normative skepticism.* The inquirer simply narrates the way things are, suspending all normative judgment about its goodness and badness. This position is very different from toleration. The tolerant person may have, and usually does have, definite views about what is proper and improper, right and wrong. On the other hand, in certain spheres of life—religion being paramount among these in the Western tradition—such a person decides not to inhibit or perhaps even to criticize, but to allow others to go their own way. Tolerant people usually do not tolerate everything: where real harm to others is present, their interest in the protection of liberty will require them to draw a line. Our ideas of religious toleration themselves demand that we not tolerate bigoted or violent acts that interfere with others' free exercise of their religion—even when these acts are themselves motivated by religious belief. In many contexts, however, tolerant people will indeed refrain from interfering with, and possibly also from criticizing, the practices and beliefs of others. This, however, does not mean that they suspend normative judgment. Their interest in liberty does not require them to regard all choices as equally good. For example, people who are tolerant in the area of sexual conduct may have definite moral views of their own about what conduct is good and bad; they will probably teach those views to their children. But so long as there is no harm to others, they are prepared not to be nosy about the private conduct of their neighbors.

Our nation has a long and distinguished tradition of tolerance in religious matters, and to some degree in related moral matters. It is easy for tolerant Americans, confronted with the confusingly different practices of another culture, and aware of the dangers of normative chauvinism, to react by suspending all evaluation. We may be confused about the distinction between tolerance and the refusal of evaluation, thinking that tolerance of others requires us not to evaluate what they do. Many undergraduates make this mistake, thinking that the only way to treat their friends with toleration is to take a hands-off attitude to all criticism. Or we may just find the whole business of evaluating another culture so difficult that we throw up our hands and stop trying.

Skepticism is the initial position of many students on moral differences. If they do not encounter good teaching about other cultures, it is likely to remain their position. If it remains their position, they are likely to be weak-spirited citizens when they encounter evil elsewhere in the world. When they encounter violence against women, or assaults on democracy, or discrimination against members of a religious or ethnic minority, they are likely to say, "Well, that is their culture, and who are we to speak?" In this way, Americans all too frequently lack conviction about evil elsewhere. Good teaching does not force the student to abandon skepticism, where this is a seriously held and well-thought-out position. But it does push the student hard, raising tough questions about how skepticism can coexist with the determination to protect liberty. Students writing on female genital mutilation in Eve Stoddard's class at St. Lawrence showed strong initial inclinations to normative skepticism. One outstanding student argued that our culture has made so many mistakes that the only way to treat another culture with respect is simply to accept whatever they do, without criticism. The hands-off attitude to criticism runs so deep in today's students that they will sometimes try to take this position even toward actions that strike them intuitively as paradigms of evil. Stoddard repeatedly shows her classes that this is not the only acceptable way for a tolerant person to think, and that, indeed, there are some serious problems that arise for the tolerant person who begins to defend practices that involve limitations on liberty.

Students tend to think that skepticism is a way of being respectful to others. But good teaching will show that to refuse all application of moral standards to a foreign person or culture is not really a way of treating that person with respect. When we refuse to make judgments that we make freely in life with our own fellow citizens, we seem to be saying that this form of life is so alien and bizarre that it cannot be expected to be measured by the same set of standards. This is another way of being patronizing. As anthropologist Dan Sperber says, "In pre-relativist anthropology, Westerners thought of themselves as superior to all other people. Relativism replaced this despicable hierarchical gap by a kind of cognitive apartheid. If we cannot be superior in the same world, let each people live in its own world."[29] This refusal of acknowledgment and communication is not an ideal way of showing human respect. As Salkever and Nylan put it, "By assigning cultural differences to some sacrosanct spot safe from our critical faculties, cultural relativism, which begins by urging us to respect the other, ends by denying other cultures and other human beings the serious consideration they deserve."[30] Much of the cross-cultural teaching I encountered makes students aware of this difficulty.

The best way to begin avoiding these pitfalls in teaching is to think in terms of common human *problems,* spheres of life in which human beings, wherever they live, have to make choices. All human beings have to confront their own mortality and cope with the fear of death; all human beings have to regulate their bodily appetites, making judgments in the areas of food, drink, and sex; all have to take some stand about property and the distribution of scarce resources; all need to have some attitude to the planning of their own lives. Beginning a cross-cultural comparison from these common problems will put us in a position to recognize a shared humanity and at the same time to notice the very considerable differences in the ways in which different cultures and individuals have faced these problems. Of course we should not assume that the problems themselves are always understood in a shared way. What death is thought to be will vary greatly among traditions; emotions and even bodily appetites exhibit considerable cross-cultural variation. But there is enough similarity and overlap in the area of these basic problems that we can organize our teaching around them, and in that way portray the different traditions as intelligent attempts to make a viable existence for human beings in the midst of the very considerable limitations that are endemic to human life.[31] Steven Salkever and Michael Nylan write that in teaching comparative political thought they have attempted

to have each course focus on one such permanent human problem as confronted in two very different places: the originating moment of philosophy, broadly understood, in China and Greece, when the issue is how to think one's way outside the limits of prescribed social roles; the problem of how to imagine and respond to death; and the problem of how to combine innovation and continuity in societies in which traditional authority has been shaken, with our texts here coming from Western Europe and China in the 16th to the 19th centuries.[32]

This sort of teaching—also represented in Eve Stoddard's class on the female body—has the greatest hope of overcoming the dangers inherent in cross-cultural study, producing both understanding and the potential for further fruitful inquiry.

Freedom and Individuality

Two stereotypes dominate current thinking about the West and the non-West. These are the idea that "the East" values order whereas "the West" values freedom; and the idea that "the East" values community whereas "the West" values the individual. These claims have recently been made from a variety of normative directions. Arthur Schlesinger, claiming that the noble idea of human rights is purely Western in origin, uses this claim to cast doubt on the value of non-Western cultures, and on their place in the college curriculum.[33] Lee Kuan Yew, former prime minister of Singapore, has used similar claims to repel criticism, arguing that Eastern peoples must be permitted to follow their own traditions of authoritarianism and must not be taken to task by international human rights movements.[34] Western Arcadians point to the alleged absence of "individualism" in India as a good thing; Indian and Chinese feminists criticize Gary Becker for assuming too little individualism in his portrayal of the family.[35] Sorting through this confusion of claims and counterclaims will be an important task for many courses in non-Western values.

Such courses need, more than most, to bear in mind the fact that cultures have a present. When we are talking about India or China we should not identify their values with the oldest strand of tradition. Nobody could doubt that ideas of human rights are a very deep part of the Chinese tradition at this point, as of pretty well every non-Western tradition. As Amartya Sen writes, "To the extent that there has been any testing of the proposition that the poor Asians do not care about civil and political rights, the evidence is entirely against that claim."[36] (He points to struggles for these rights in India,

South Korea, Thailand, Bangladesh, Pakistan, China, Myanmar, and elsewhere.)

But Schlesinger insists, it would seem, that we measure the worth of a culture by its ancient history, and blame it if it derives crucial components of its ethical view from another culture. It is not clear why it is supposed to be a mark of inferiority in a culture that it appropriates good ideas from elsewhere—but let us follow Schlesinger's proposal consistently. By the standard he seems to propose, America will not have a lot of culture left, and what is left will be that of the Native Americans. Even "Western culture" as a whole will have to get rid of a great deal, including most of its mathematical achievements, to which Indian and Arabic discoveries were crucial, and its dominant religion, Christianity, which derives, as we remember too rarely, from Semitic cultures of the Near East. If we really want to reject everything given from "outside," we may have to go back to the dead end of Greek mathematics, with its geometrical interpretation of number, which made many mathematical problems insoluble and others intractably cumbersome. In religion, we may need to embrace the polytheism that worshipped the not-very-ideal Olympian gods. This, in turn, may mean that the Enlightenment's notion of human rights will not fare so well, since both mathematics and Christianity had some role in producing it. Neither Greek nor Roman society contained any developed notion of basic human rights or of religious toleration.

Perhaps we should be even stricter, and get rid of all the languages of Europe, since we know that Indo-European languages originated in Asia, as did Hungarian and Finnish, the two most common non-Indo-European languages. If we relentlessly purify our tradition of all Asian elements, we will be left with some exiguous scraps of information about the indigenous peoples of Europe and their cultures before the advent of the Indo-Europeans. This would not yield us a very robust notion of human rights.

However, let us put the question of "our" culture to one side for a moment and ask how we should pose Schlesinger's question about the non-West. How should we ascertain to what extent the older traditions of a non-Western culture contain an idea of human rights?

The first thing any such discussion must do is make the concepts involved more precise. The notion of human rights is far from a clear notion (as is shown clearly, for example, in the intense debates over whether Aristotle had elements of such a notion),[37] nor is there a single agreed-on version of rights theory and its basis. Some theorists have grounded rights-claims in theology, others in a view of human nature and its capacities. Some, like John Locke, have done both, in a way that is difficult to sort out. Many of these elements can be compared to some element in non-Western culture. The notion of a right is the notion of a claim that a being has in virtue of some trait that it has: usually the idea is that this claim has a special force or is indefeasible by other claims. There are many accounts of who the right-bearers are, what the right-conferring facts about them are, and how powerful the claims are. Once we spell the ideas out, asking what it means to say human beings have a right and on what basis they are taken to have these rights, we will find that many cultures have at least some of the elements that are involved in the various different views of rights that we inherit from the Enlightenment—and also that Western thinkers do not agree at all about which features are the ones to be prized. The Greek Stoics, who were of great importance to the human rights tradition on account of their notion of the equal worth of all human beings, tolerated slavery because they did not think external conditions mattered much. They therefore did not think equal worth gave one a right not to be held as a slave. Such, for less philosophical reasons, has been the view of many modern rights-thinkers. Seeing all this will put us in a position to begin to investigate the relationship between our various rights traditions and the views about human worth held, for example, by Mencius in the Chinese tradition, or by Indian thinkers such as Kautilya and Ashoka.

If we turn to the well-worn notion of "Western individualism," we will find a similar situation. If individualism is defined as the view that each person has but one life to live and that one person's death does not logically entail the death of any other person, most human beings in all times and places have been individualists, and individualism is an obvious truth of human circumstances. If individualism is defined as the view that one ought to maximize the satisfaction of one's own personal interests, some Western people and some Eastern people have had this view. The Carvaka school in India defended the pursuit of personal pleasure and satisfaction in a way closely comparable to the classical Utilitarianism of the West. But it is equally true to say that many Western people and many Eastern people have not held that view. Most dominant moral and religious traditions in both East and West give a prominent place to altruism and duties to others. If individualism is defined as the view that one should not subordinate one's own well-being too much to the needs and demands of others, that one also has duties to promote one's own happiness, then most great moral traditions of both West and East have, once again, been individualist. Different norms of appropriate self-sacrifice obtain in different parts of each tradition; no tradition lacks norms of courageous self-sacrifice, but none teaches that human life should always be a matter of putting the needs of others first. When we ask more precisely what we are talking about, we will at least get to a position where we can begin a fruitful comparison—for example, between norms of appropriate female self-sacrifice in Christianity and in Hinduism.

The question of human freedom is similarly complex. When it is claimed that "the East" values order and "the West" values freedom, several different ideas are at issue: (1) the value of personal reflection and choice of a way of life; (2) the value of certain specific institutionally guaranteed freedoms, such as religious freedom, freedom of speech, and freedom of the press; and (3) the value of the equal distribution of these freedoms—the idea that they are not just important, but important for all. Once again, taking these ideas apart will permit us to start a fruitful comparison. If we focus on the value of personal reflection and choice, we will observe that this value was stressed by Aristotle in the Western tradition, but also by Kautilya (a contemporary of Aristotle) and Ashoka (two generations later) in the Indian tradition. Kautilya and Aristotle did not believe that personal choice was important for women, or slaves, or the lower classes; they thought it important for well-positioned males.[38] Ashoka insisted on the importance of personal freedom for all male inhabitants of his kingdom, including the pre-agricultural "forest people"—meaning that they should not be indentured or taken in captivity. He described his goal in government as "non-injury, restraint, impartiality, and mild behaviour" applied "to all creatures."[39]

If we ask about religious freedom and toleration, we discover that India has a strong and ancient tradition on this issue. The enlightened emperor Ashoka, in the third century B.C., converted to Buddhism. He not only helped to make Buddhism a world religion by sending missionaries to both east and west; he also erected a large number of public stone inscriptions describing the essentials of good public life. These inscriptions give essential emphasis to the value of religious plurality and toleration, both in public policy and in the private conduct of citizens. His Edict XII puts the issue thus:

. . . the growth of essentials (of Dharma [conduct including religious behaviour] is possible) in many ways. But its root (lies) in restraint in regard to speech, (which means) that there should be no extolment of one's own sect or disparagement of other sects on inappropriate occasions, and it should be moderate even in appropriate occasions. On the contrary, other sects should be duly honoured in every way (on all occasions). If (a person) acts in this way, (he) not only promotes his own sect, but also benefits other sects. But, if (a person) acts otherwise, (he) not only injures his own sect but also harms other sects. Truly, if (a person) extols his own sect and disparages other sects with a view to glorifying his own sect owing merely to his attachment (to it, he) injures his own sect very severely by acting in that way.[40]

Thus what we take to be a crucial aspect of the Enlightenment turns up in India, well before any Western thinker dreamed of it, as a humane response to the fact of religious pluralism.

If we now leap ahead to a time contemporaneous with Grotius and other humanist precursors of the Western Enlightenment, we encounter the great Moghul emperor Akbar, who reigned from 1556 to 1605. Akbar was no democrat; but he did put various human rights, including freedom of worship and religious practice, at the heart of his program in a way that could not have been found in the Europe of that time. Akbar, a Muslim, took a deep interest not only in Hindu philosophy and culture but also in Christianity, Jainism, and the Parsi religion. Unlike Ashoka, who proselytized for Buddhism, Akbar refrained from giving his own religion any privileged position in the state, and indeed attempted to create a synthetic state religion for India, called the Din Ilahi, drawing on the different religions in the country. He sought out ministers, advisers, and court artists and intellectuals from every faith. Later, a highly intolerant Moghul emperor, Aurangzeb, who violated basic rights of Hindus, encountered severe criticism and even armed rebellion from members of his own family, who defended freedom of action and worship for Hindus.

Moreover, conscious theorizing about tolerance and xenophobia is found throughout this tradition. To give just one example, the eleventh-century Iranian writer Alberuni, who came to India with the invading Muslim army, studied Indian society, culture, and mathematics. (His translations of Indian mathematical treatises influenced the Arab world and thus, in turn, the development of Western mathematics.) Intolerance of the unfamiliar was one of his central topics. Pointing out that Hindus are receiving the new Islamic arrivals with hostility and suspicion, describing examples of normative chauvinism in Hindu dealings with him and his fellows, he concludes: "By the bye, we must confess, in order to be just, that a similar depreciation of foreigners not only prevails among us and the Hindus, but is common to all nations towards each other."[41]

The standard polar contrasts, in short, are descriptively crude and therefore inevitably out of focus in their normative evaluations. Once we dissect the values we prize (or in some cases despise) into their several components, we find that world history contains many useful parallels. Even if a number of these component parts came together in the European Enlightenment in a unique and highly influential way, it does not follow from this that the Enlightenment had no non-Western sources, nor that its parts had no non-Western parallels.

Thus the history of human rights suggests that a dismissive attitude to non-Western cultures is based to at least some degree on uninformed normative chauvinism. Even if non-Western cultures did lack some essential moral notions, this would not give us good reasons not to learn all we can about them: for I have argued that good teaching should not be uncritical, and we need to know about the world in which we live. In fact, however, the assumption of Western superiority needs critical examination, and the need for that examination gives us further reasons to study cultures other than "our own."

Aims and Limits of Cross-Cultural Teaching

The primary goal of the teaching of non-Western cultures should be to awaken curiosity and begin a conversation. No set of courses, however well designed, can tell students everything they should know about the primary cultures of the non-Western world. Nor should we think of education as a smorgasbord, in which students dabble in a variety of cultures without getting a solid grounding in any one. Since our colleges and universities are in America, it makes sense that our students should begin from and focus on their own sphere of life, the sphere in which they will need to act. This means giving a primary place to American history and to a study of major sources of the complex culture we have inherited. Of course not all these sources are Western, and a good education in Western culture will make such connections evident. It will also frequently illuminate a Western idea by the judicious use of comparison and contrast with a highly different culture. A real grasp of Western liberal individualism requires a sense of what its alternatives might be; we can gain this through, for example, a judicious study of Buddhist ethics. Most general courses in Western civilization would be more illuminating if they contained a comparative component, its scope and nature to be determined by the training of the faculty. The same is true of many courses at a more advanced level, where a single comparative session can frequently illuminate a range of issues. But the question remains, how far and in what ways the curriculum should foster courses explicitly devoted to non-Western cultures.

This question cannot be answered in a monolithic way. The high school preparation of our students is in a state of extreme flux; college instructors need to keep reviewing their students' preparation and adjusting their curricular demands in this light. In 1996, in a group of University of Chicago undergraduates, about half reported that their high school education had lacked training in non-Western cultures; the other half, however, reported that their high schools had prepared them better on non-Western cultures than on the West. No rigid set of curricular requirements would have served this diverse group; at present we should prefer flexible systems that give students lots of advice but allow them to judge, to some extent, what they need to learn. The Chicago system accomplishes this by offering a large variety of core civilization courses, some of them Western in focus, some comparative, and some focused primarily on the non-West. The overall plan, however, should establish some definite goals for students to meet, whether through course requirements or through advising.

All students should gain some understanding of the major world religions. This is an area of such fundamental importance to all political and economic interactions with the world's varied cultures that we simply cannot afford to have citizens who are ignorant of Islam, or Hinduism, or Buddhist and Confucian traditions. This may be achieved through a world civilization course or in some other way; but in some form it should be a nonnegotiable part of the undergraduate curriculum.

All students should also master a foreign language, to a level of proficiency that makes possible the reading of newspapers and simple literary texts, and the understanding of radio and television broadcasts. It should be difficult to place out of this requirement through achievement tests taken in high school; high school instruction seldom has the cultural richness of college instruction. Even if the language involved is Spanish or French, and not the language of a non-Western culture, language study puts the problem of cross-cultural understanding before the student in a way nothing else does. Expressing your own ideas in a foreign tongue is as good a way as any of seeing the relationship between sameness and difference; it should shape all cross-cultural study.

Beyond this, it seems sensible for students to be required to study in some depth one non-Western culture, through a requirement in most cases, and from a group of courses designed to awaken conversation and reflection across cultural boundaries. Each such course should have a historical and a cultural component. To be prescriptive beyond this point would be unwise, since faculty have been discovering so many excellent ways of doing this sort of comparative teaching. Often these ways involve focusing on a single set of issues in a comparative perspective. Ronnie Littlejohn's moral philosophy students, setting their Japanese course side by side with their other philosophy courses, arrived at a rich and complicated account of one central area of Japanese culture. (Littlejohn concludes that a course like this, though confined to a single area of a single culture, "motivates [students] to study the language and culture further and seek to understand other ways of being human.") Salkever and Nylan's students, focusing on political philosophy, got insight into two cultures' ways of pursuing questions about "the examined life." Eve Stoddard's students learned to think about American views of the female body together with African and Middle Eastern views. At Notre Dame, an "Anthropology of Work" course discusses conceptions and practices of productive activity in both pre- and postindustrial societies in both the West and the non-West. At Brown in the Comparative Literature Department, Chinese literature expert Dore Levy offers a course called "Tales and Talemakers," which compares practices of narration in works from several non-Western cultures, including Babylon, China, and classical Arabic culture. Meanwhile her colleague Meera Visvanathan offers an extremely popular course in the history of Japanese literature. At Harvard, as we have seen in Chapter 2, Amartya Sen's students learn to think about hunger and famine in the modern world by considering a variety of nations, both Western and non-Western. Many other types of interdisciplinary cross-cultural teaching focus on an artistic or musical genre, or a set of economic issues.

The best way to make sure that students get involved with non-Western cultures is to infuse these studies throughout the curriculum, drawing on the diverse areas of faculty expertise. Where there is a non-Western requirement, it should not be satisfied by extremely narrow courses that give no insight into the larger issues under debate in a culture; but a well-chosen set of central figures or issues can frequently focus inquiry better than a vast survey. Faculty do best teaching issues they know about, even if some of the texts are new to them. At Brown, despite the fact that faculty advising has been substituted for core requirements, a large proportion of students elect a course in some non-Western culture, responding to the wide availability and excellence of such courses, in departments ranging from Music to Religious Studies to Comparative Literature to Anthropology to History and Political Science.

Our primary goal should be to produce students who have a Socratic knowledge of their own ignorance—both of other world cultures and, to a great extent, of our own. These students, when they hear simplistic platitudes about cultural difference, will not be inclined to take them at face value; they will question, probe, and inquire. Because they have a basic awareness of cultural and methodological issues, they will have a way of pursuing their questions further. They will approach the different with an appropriate humility, but with good intellectual equipment for the further pursuit of understanding. These traits, so important in a citizen of today's interdependent world, are very unlikely to be developed by personal experience alone. At present we are not doing well enough at the task of understanding, and these failures are damaging our nation—in business, in politics, in urgent deliberations about the environment and agriculture and human rights. We must, and we can, cultivate understanding through a liberal education; and an education will not be truly "liberal" (producing truly free and self-governing citizens) unless it undertakes this challenge.

☆☆☆

CHAPTER FIVE

African-American
Studies

Herein the longing of black men must have respect: the rich and bitter depth of their experience, the unknown treasures of their inner life, the strange rendings of nature they have seen, may give the world new points of view and make their loving, living, and doing precious to all human hearts.

> W. E. B. Du Bois, "Of the Training of Black Men," in *The Souls of Black Folk*

At Morehouse College, in Atlanta, Algernon Campbell, a senior English major, talks fast, with exuberance and energy. He has come from a predominantly white high school where there was never any discussion of the topic of race. Nobody understood that topic, he says, certainly not Campbell himself, who was simply trying to fit in. Coming to Morehouse, he has found an open forum, where he can explore these issues all the time, without anxiety about racism and trying to fit in. He can seek a scholarly historical understanding of the role of racial identities in America, and this will help him to know himself. Campbell is extremely proud of Morehouse, and happy with his current life.

At Brown University in the spring of 1992, Alvin Jameson discusses the sudden decline in his work in philosophy. An upper-middle-class African-American student—when I first met him he was wearing an Andover sweatshirt—Alvin did so well in my undergraduate course on philosophy and the novel, writing a stunning paper on time in Samuel Beckett, that I gave him permission to attend my graduate seminar on the same topic. But he has not been in class most of the semester, and when he does show up he seems half asleep. He tells me now that he is increasingly anxious about his black identity. He has joined an all-black fraternity. The brothers have been putting pressure on him not to care about philosophy and literature—besides giving him initiation assignments that keep him up all night. He no longer has a plan to go to graduate school in philosophy.

At the University of Alabama at Birmingham in March 1994, former Atlanta mayor Andrew Young visits just when the African-American Studies program is campaigning to become a full-fledged department. Addressing an African-American Studies class, Young opposes the change. "One of my daughters majored in black studies, and I tried my best to talk her out of it. If you are paying for an education, you ought to get people to teach you things [you] can't learn on [your] own. Spend your time in math, finance, accounting, and sciences."

In December 1994 I talk to Angela Kaufmann, one of my freshman advisees. One of her reasons for choosing Brown was the diversity of its curriculum; in her first semester she elected a course in the Afro-American Studies Department. She loves the reading, but as the only white person in the class she feels increasingly uncomfortable in class discussion. Last week the instructor, a young African-American woman, sympathetically discussed theories of racial memory, implying that people without a blood connection to a particular racial group cannot understand its sufferings. Angela asked whether having relatives who died in the Holocaust might not be one way of understanding sufferings inflicted by racism. Her question, she says, was met with a stony silence.

At Harvard University, Kwame Anthony Appiah, professor of philosophy and African-American studies, discusses the relationship between group identity and world citizenship. The son of an Englishwoman and a London-trained lawyer who became one of the founding fathers of the Republic of Ghana, Appiah, educated at Bryanston and Cambridge, an expert in modal logic and a leading scholar in African-American studies, speaks eloquently of his biracial and binational identity, arguing that one may be intensely loyal to a particular nation or group without forgetting that one's primary moral loyalty is to "the human future." On his death, Appiah's father left his children a letter reminding them to remember that above all they are "citizens of the world." Wherever they are, he urged, they should ask how the world has become better through their efforts.

At the University of California at Riverside, the black students group has invited Khalid Muhammed, associate of Louis Farrakhan, to give a public address. Muhammed is known for his view that the Jews were responsible for the slave trade; it is expected that his speech will contain anti-Semitic material. The administration has agreed to Muhammed's request for unusual security measures—each person in attendance will be searched at the door. Some faculty believe that the administration should have prevented Muhammed from speaking on campus, or should at least have refused the unusual security request. Others believe that he should be allowed to speak on his own terms but that his speech should be greeted with public protest. As students and members of the community file past the security guards to enter the auditorium, a group of faculty led by philosopher Bernd Magnus, director of the University's Center for Ideas and Society and a survivor of Bergen-Belsen, stand outside in grim silence with placards protesting Muhammed's anti-Semitism.[1]

No topic divides American universities more painfully than the topic of race. In no area do we need more urgently to learn about one another, and in no other area are there so many barriers to that understanding. The African-American community is itself divided. Should the goal be an inclusive, humanistic vision of culture such as that envisaged by W. E. B. Du Bois, in which black culture is embraced by all Americans even as black Americans embrace all of culture? Or should it instead be the creation of an identity apart from others, and linked at times with the disparagement of other people and groups? Should young black students focus on African-American culture in their undergraduate education, or should they be doing something more economically useful, such as engineering or math? The white community responds to these divisions with confusion and distress. Already riven by conflicts between racism and antiracism, aware of the continued presence of racism in the mostly white academy, and unsure what will count as effective antiracism, sympathetic white educators frequently find themselves paralyzed, even when, as at Riverside, public protest of vicious lies seems morally appropriate.

It seems more important than ever to defend the vision of culture mapped out by Du Bois, in which all U.S. citizens would study the art and history of African-American people, even as black men—and black women—would embrace the study of the whole world. This new, inclusive academy would continue to teach engineering or accounting, preparing students for careers. But it would also provide its students, both black and white, with an education of the spirit, building the basis for a richer sort of citizenship.

Can we build this inclusive and spiritually rich academy, despite the fact that we must build on a foundation that includes the suffering and fear that have divided us? If we are to have any hope of doing so, we need to get beyond the current tendency to see any demand for the study of a minority group as mere identity politics, or as mere whining or "victimology." Equally unhelpful is the anxious shrinking that is a natural expression of white people's discomfort and guilt about our nation's legacy of vicious racism. Instead, people from all backgrounds must engage one another honestly. (This is true in other areas of racial tension as well, but the history of white-black racism will stand here for other, related exclusions.) We must all seek to understand the history of the demand for Afro-American studies and the academic exclusions that gave rise to it. We must understand how even those African-Americans who were grudgingly included were until recently required, as the price of admittance, to repudiate their origins and to avow the superior value of European civilization. We can then try to grasp the complex reactions of shame, pride, longing, and hatred that this academic history must surely have engendered in any rational black person who was made to live through it. And we should acknowledge that such reactions were and are rational, that even what most troubles and frightens us is worthy of our respect, inasmuch as it has grown out of a genuine and valid concern. Only at this point will we be in any position to sort through the controversies about race and Afrocentrism that vex today's curricula.

Any writer who pronounces on such divisive issues should locate her own history among them. In Bryn Mawr, Pennsylvania, in the early 1960s, I encountered black people only as domestic servants. There was a black girl my age named Hattie, daughter of the live-in help of an especially wealthy neighbor. One day, when I was about ten, we had been playing in the street and I asked her to come in for some lemonade. My father, who grew up in Georgia, exploded, telling me that I must never invite a black person into the house again. Nor was school very different: my private school included black people only as kitchen help, and we were encouraged to efface them from our minds when we studied. My history courses said little about slavery. Never, in high school or afterward at Wellesley and New York University, did I read any work of literature by a black writer. W. E. B. Du Bois, Frederick Douglass, Booker T. Washington, Richard Wright, Ralph Ellison, Zora Neale Hurston—all these names were unknown to me. It was not possible to study them anywhere; they simply were not taught. Martin Luther King Jr. could not be avoided, because he was in the news, but my father called him a communist agitator, and my teachers said nothing. No music teacher among the many with whom I studied piano and voice mentioned jazz, and I hardly heard it until I was in my twenties, although it was a major source of more or less all the modern classical music (by Copland, Ravel, Bernstein, Poulenc) that I did play and sing.

My career in philosophy has continued my segregated academic life. In twenty years of teaching in departments of philosophy and classics I have taught only two black graduate students and have had no black colleagues. Now that I am in a law school, I have had two black colleagues—one of whom, a visiting professor, was one of my two black philosophy graduate students. Very few black students take nonrequired courses in philosophy, and even in my current law teaching I see few black faces. I find things out mostly by reading and imagining.

Race, Culture, and Shame: The Case of Harvard

To understand today's conflicts over African-American studies, it is essential to go back to the beginning of the history of African-Americans in the American university. Fortunately, a comprehensive documentary history of African-American life at Harvard gives us a case study we can scrutinize.[2] Harvard was among the more liberal of the American universities on this issue from the eighteenth century onward,[3] so it provides a case of relatively progressive white response to the presence of racial difference, showing us how limited even the progressive vision was in these times; but it shows, as well, tensions between humane aspiration and lack of imagination.

In the early years, blacks could enter the academy (if at all) only by accepting the superiority of Christian European culture and the primitive status of African culture. American universities were for the most part religious in origin, and often highly sectarian. (Brown, founded in 1745, was the first in America that did not have a religious test for entrance.) In the view of the dominant Protestant tradition, the culture of Africa was not a culture, but a primitive, quasi bestial form of life that left real doubts about the inhabitants' human status. There was little or no knowledge of African cultures; only late in the nineteenth century did African music and art begin to make an impact in the West, and serious description of African political institutions was later still. Africa was imagined to be a land of undisciplined aggression and sexuality. As is common in the history of mythology, a culture expresses its own sense of value by imagining a distant land that contains the opposite of everything that is prized. Ancient Greeks imagined hypothetical barbarian lands where women ruled, or wantonness ran riot; Roman authors described a Germany that was the mythic inversion of Roman values. Likewise, the Africa imagined by Americans was an inversion of Puritan values, and Puritan America defined its worth by contrasting itself with the hypothetical bestial other. African-Americans could prove their human status only by accepting Christ as savior and confessing the benighted character of their origins. Often blackness of skin was taken—by both blacks and whites—to be a symbol of the moral and intellectual degradation of African ways of life.

Such views were advanced not only by opponents of education for black Americans, but by many African-Americans themselves and by their most progressive white supporters. Indeed, one of the most prominent arguments made for educating blacks was the need to raise them above their brutish origins. The first published African-American poet, slave girl Phillis Wheatley—examined by Cotton Mather and a team of Puritan divines, who ascertained that she knew Latin and therefore might be considered capable of writing the poems she had written—speaks passionately, in a 1767 poem addressed to the students of Harvard, of the moral force of the Christian teaching that has rescued her from brute sensuality and darkness.

> While an intrinsic ardor prompts to write,
> The muses promise to assist my pen;
> 'Twas not long since I left my native shore
> The land of errors, and *Egyptian* gloom:
> Father of mercy, 'twas thy gracious hand
> Brought me in safety from those dark abodes.[4]

Wheatley depicts her poetic impulse as "intrinsic." But, she suggests, it cannot find expression in verse unless and until the "muses" of classical learning give her assistance. This is all the more important because she has only recently left "the land of errors," whose moral and spiritual "darkness" is correlated with, and, presumably, thought to be represented by, the blackness of Wheatley's skin. (The next stanza identifies those "errors," as Wheatley associates Africa with "sin" and its "transient sweetness.") The favor shown Wheatley by the divines who published her work is not unrelated to her poetic admission of shame.

White progressive arguments similarly assume the baseness of African culture, defending the humanity of the Negro by insisting that their failure to be Christian results from ignorance rather than from natural vice. Thus, in a debate about the morality of slavery at Harvard in 1773, Eliphalet Pearson, who makes many excellent moral arguments against the institution, takes it as an undisputed starting point that African culture is totally benighted, without either art or thought: "It is acknowledged that they are extremely unacquainted with the politer arts, and almost wholly ignorant of every thing belonging to science, and consequently strangers to all the pleasures of a scholar and a philosopher." But God has organized things this way, Pearson continues, because if they did have knowledge of "science and the politer arts" and the benefits of ordered political society, they would be even more unhappy as slaves than they now are: "A keen excruciating sense of liberty forever lost must still predominate, till, the spirit broken by the fatigue of incessant distress, they sink into a state of lifeless insensibility." Besides, he continues, our own treatment of them has blunted their intellects:

> And then forsooth we are presently disposed to tax them with natural stupidity; and make the very thing that our unnatural treatment has occasioned the ground of our justification. It is well known, that stupidity is by no means the natural characteristic of these people; and when we consider the nature of their condition in this country, how miserably dejected, depressed and despised, instead of marking their want of apprehension, we ought rather to admire that there are any the least appearances of sensibility remaining in them.[5]

Pearson's argument seems internally confused: for how can absence of cultivation be a beneficent gift from God to prevent further misery, if it is also a pernicious result of human ill treatment? (And why did the beneficent God not prevent slavery from existing, rather than depriving people of culture in order that they should bear it?) What is even more striking, however, in his basically humane account, is the presumption throughout that the culture the slaves brought with them from Africa is no culture or art at all.

What idea of culture did these early supporters of black education employ in making such determinations? It was a model of Christianized classical learning, in which knowledge of Latin and Greek was firmly allied to Christian commitment and practice and, indeed, to a knowledge of the Bible and of Christian theology. (Until the reforms introduced by Benjamin Jowett at Oxford in the late nineteenth century, the Greek and Latin classics were always taught in conjunction with Christian theology. The two subjects were understood to be interdependent elements of a single culture—in a way that grossly distorted the nature of ancient Greek and Roman life and thought.) So strong was the identification between culture and classical learning that in 1833 two Boston lawyers told the following story, in the presence of an alert errand boy:

> While at the Capitol they happened to dine in the company of the great John C. Calhoun, then senator from South Carolina. It was a period of great ferment upon the question of Slavery, States' Rights, and Nullification; and consequently the Negro was the topic of conversation at the table. One of the utterances of Mr. Calhoun was to this effect—"That if he could find a Negro who knew the Greek syntax, he would then believe that the Negro was a human being and should be treated as a man."[6]

Here, as in Wheatley's poetry, human worth is defined in terms of willingness and ability to take on the dominant culture. The selection of the somewhat arbitrary example of Greek syntax was probably motivated by memory of the difficult struggle most students have with it in school, and the humiliation that used to be heaped upon those who did poorly. Greek was thought to be an especially taxing mental exercise—too taxing, it was often said, for the frail physiques of women.[7] The young American culture, always on the defensive about its relationship to Europe, insisted on this exercise with uncommon zeal, as a prerequisite of full humanity.

The errand boy who preserved the story was Alexander Crummell, then employed by the New York Antislavery Society office, later among the most distinguished African-American intellectuals of his generation. Crummell devoted much of his career to the defense of African culture. We can begin to see why this project would have seemed not only attractive, but even imperative, in the service of full citizenship and self-respect.

There is a common human tendency to think of one's own habits and ways as best for all persons in all times. Today we don't think that all good people know Greek, so we can laugh at the old assumption that such knowledge was a necessary mark of humanity. We know that every language has a complicated syntactic structure and that no one language is "higher" than another. The human infant will learn the language it hears, whatever it is; the ability to learn a specific language does not require a specific genetic heritage. But when Greek was the mark of the gentleman, and when gentlemen were all of white European stock, it was hard to see the arbitrariness of the choice of Greek as the mark of the human. Greek served as a self-congratulatory validation of the culture of the gentleman who happened to have learned Greek—while a constructed image of Africa, the land without Greek culture (rather like ancient Greek contrasts between "the Greek" and "the barbarian"), reinforced Americans' sense of cultural superiority and warded off their anxieties about shortcomings vis-à-vis Europe.

At times, such distortions were described as such—by educated African-Americans who had the opportunity both to participate in and to observe them. The first black man to graduate from Harvard College was Richard T. Greener, class of 1870, son of a failed gold miner and a mother keen on education, former shoe salesman, wood engraver, and Oberlin student. Greener eventually became professor of mental and moral philosophy at the University of South Carolina, where he also taught Latin, Greek, mathematics, and constitutional history—until the university closed its doors to blacks in 1877. At the same time he had studied law and been admitted to the bar, and he soon became dean of the Law school at Howard University, later moving into private practice and politics. He also served as consul in Bombay, India, and as commercial agent of the United States in Siberia. In 1892 the Chinese government conferred on him the Order of the Double Dragon, for aid to famine victims in Shansi Province. After his retirement from the foreign service in 1905, he lived in Chicago, where he was active in the Harvard Club. In 1894 Greener wrote a remarkable address titled "The White Problem." The rhetorical device of the lecture, and its deep insight, is to turn around and study as pathology what white culture has taken for its own normalcy and superiority. Greener pillories the tendency to see white behavior as unproblematic and what deviates from those customs as "a problem." He exposes the related pathology of subservience that made talented black people obsequious to those conventional norms, and consequently ashamed of themselves.

> A phase of the white problem is seen in the determination . . . to treat the Negro as a member of a child-like race . . . All the traditions seemed against the Negro, all the arguments surely were. He was rarely given a real chance . . . to talk freely for himself, and when such opportunity was afforded, he generally took his cue from his audience, and talked to the jury, and usually with bated breath. When he spoke humbly, apologetically, deprecatingly, he was an intelligent, sensible fellow, a milder form of "good nigger" before the war.[8]

Citing achievements of notable blacks in public service and the arts, citing Antonín Dvořák's praise of black musical traditions as the origin of all that is worth taking seriously in American music, Greener concludes: "These facts taken at random would tend to show that the American Negro has traditions—far more, and more honorable than many of his traducers." As for Christianity, which is often held out as the mark of white culture's superior morality and the African's degradation, Greener points to white bigotry as evidence of that religion's incompleteness, at least as generally practiced: "How far from solution seems the white problem, when the Negro reflects how powerless is Christianity to repress race prejudice; how often indifferent to real brotherhood, while affecting deep denominational interest."[9]

Greener notes with deadly accuracy the tendency of whites, and of many blacks, to agree that blackness and black traditions are basically something to apologize for. He notes that Lawrence Lowell, president of Harvard, famously remarked, "I am glad I was not born a Jew; but if I had been a Jew, I should be prouder of that fact than any other." What white leader, Greener asks, would say the same today of blackness? (That it was in present circumstances a misfortune, yet nonetheless a mark of pride?) And yet the fact of black merit and accomplishment and decency and justice is abundantly evident, giving ample reason for pride. If, despite those reasons, shame, rather than pride, is the norm, and if even blacks have been taught to internalize this shame despite the rich resources of their own traditions, "then is it not demonstrated that it is not the Black but the White Problem, which needs most serious attention in this country?"[10]

One thing an education at Harvard might teach black men, Greener concludes, is the complexity of the question as to which traditions truly promote morality: "From their reading, observation, and reflection, they are not sure but that the very fact of their origin may have been the means, under God's guidance of the Universe, of saving them from illiberal prejudices, from over-weening race-pride, from utter disregard of other races' rights, feelings and privileges, and from intellectual narrowness and bigotry."[11] The solution to the problem of black cultural shame lies in redirecting this shame to its source, at the same time reclaiming with pride the right to investigate the African-American past.

Let us now, following Greener's lead, imagine the talented and aspiring young African-American of the late nineteenth century—and from now on we shall focus on males, since similar educational opportunities became available to females only much later. This young man is raised as a Christian, and he is taught that the place from which he originated was a Godless, sinful place. He is taught that his dark skin and the darkness of that place are somehow connected. Both brand him with shame in the eyes of the white community. He learns that blackness is his problem, but in certain circumstances it can be redeemed—if he makes a sincere effort to excel in the lessons of the dominant culture, putting his past as far as possible behind him. He can sing "Fair Harvard," and, like W. E. B. Du Bois, he can talk about Kant with George Santayana and about epistemology with William James and Josiah Royce. He may even, again like Du Bois, stage a production of an ancient Greek drama in a Boston colored church.[12] (Du Bois' significant choice was Aristophanes' *Birds,* a mordant political satire about two men who leave a city that mistreats them to found an ideal realm in the clouds, eventually establishing dominance not only over Athens but over the Olympian gods themselves.) Still, he lives, as Du Bois famously expressed the idea, in two worlds, and has the "double consciousness" of belonging to two worlds. If, like Du Bois, he is possessed of unusual determination and self-esteem, he may harbor an ironic disdain for the mores that exclude him from full membership. ("I was in Harvard but not of it," writes Du Bois, "and I realized all the irony of my singing 'Fair Harvard.' I sang it because I liked the music, and not from any pride in the Pilgrims.")[13]

But if he is more like Phillis Wheatley than like Du Bois—and many young people of Du Bois' own time remained in these respects like Phillis

Wheatley—he will internalize the white community's cultural self-congrat-ulation and feel a secret shame about his own cultural origins, which he will see as the source of an unspecified taint. He must perpetually atone for Africa by singing "Fair Harvard" all the louder. This doesn't mean that he does not also partake in the life of the African-American community: in-deed, he cannot help doing so, when social relations between the two groups are exceedingly strained. But as a scholar and a Harvard man, he is a classicist and a Christian—only he knows that he isn't, not fully or authentically.

In short, for a black student being asked to study the great books was not like being asked to do so for a white student. For the latter, it was an initiation into the elite stratum of one's own world. For the former, it was like going to a debutante party in whiteface and knowing that one wasn't on the invitation list.

Harvard, however, offered its young black students more than hypocrisy and reminders of shame. These young men were there, having overcome great obstacles, because they loved learning. What Harvard offered them was, above all, the "Veritas" expressed in its motto. They therefore found in the university a double and somewhat contradictory character. They saw that Harvard was an elite men's club that excluded them; but it was also, at the same time, a noble institution dedicated to understanding, through whose invitation to pursue truth they might approach any truth at all, not least the truth of their own dignity and the badness of racism. The value of truth seemed to these men, rightly, to be a universal good, something that empowered them rather than oppressing them. Racism, as they saw it, re-sulted from a failure of intelligence and imagination, qualities that Harvard fostered, even while it also fostered racism.

A remarkable example of this use of the academy's core commitment to expose and invalidate its racism is a letter written to Harvard's President Lawrence Lowell in 1922 by Roscoe Conkling Bruce Sr. Bruce, son of the first black to serve a full term as U.S. senator, was a graduate of Exeter and Harvard (class of 1902), where he was president of the debating team, a member of Phi Beta Kappa, Class Day orator, and a *magna cum laude* grad-uate. At the time of the incident he had recently completed a thirteen-year stint as superintendent of colored schools in Washington, D.C. His son, an Exeter student, had been admitted to Harvard for the following fall, and Bruce wrote to the registrar to reserve a room for his son in one of the freshman dorms (in which all freshmen were required to reside, and where at least two black undergraduates had lived already). He received the following letter from Lowell, who had recently decided to close these dorms to blacks, simultaneously instituting a quota for Jewish undergraduates:

> Dear Mr. Bruce: Your letter to the Registrar about your son has been given to me. I am sorry to have to tell you that in the Freshman Halls, where residence is compulsory, we have felt from the beginning the necessity of not including colored men. To the other dormitories and dining rooms they are admitted freely, but in the Freshman Halls I am sure you will understand why, from the beginning, we have not thought it possible to compel men of different races to reside together.[14]

Bruce's remarkable reply argues that Harvard has a grave responsibility for leadership in education—and, if in education, then also in American public life, since the American democracy rests on education. Lowell's deference to prejudice seems to Bruce to traduce the very mission and spirit of the institution. He concludes:

> To me whose personal indebtedness to Harvard is immeasurable, the University is neither a mere mechanism of instruction nor a social club, but a centre of enlightenment and idealism and service rendered holy by aspiring centuries.
> Few words in the English language, I submit, are susceptible of more poignant abuse than two you have seen fit to employ. The first is "race"; the second, "necessity." As the one is often nothing more than a term of social convenience, so the other is quite often a means of buttress[ing] prejudice. But, "veritas" is less elusive.

Although Lowell (under heavy pressure from southern alumni) did not retreat, replying to Bruce that "we" do not owe "the colored man" such required integration, Bruce's letter was instrumental in causing the Harvard Board of Overseers to consider the matter. In 1923 they voted to overturn Lowell's decision. As Du Bois noted in an editorial, the fact that Bruce outclassed Lowell in their exchange was itself a victory in the cause of winning public respect for African-American culture: "In its logic and its English, its flavor and restraint [Bruce's letter] is as far above Lawrence Lowell's labored and obscure defense as can be imagined . . . Imagine, my masters, six decades after emancipation, a slave's grandson teaching the ABC of democracy to the Puritan head of Harvard!"[15]

Shame, Self-Respect, and the Study of Africa

Progress was being made in integrating some academic institutions—though at a snail's pace, and at only some of the leading institutions. African-Americans were increasingly permitted to excel in aspects of the dominant culture—although many racist prohibitions remained. This progressive movement did not, however, address curricular matters, or draw connections between racism and the curricular neglect and denigration of African and African-American cultures. More was needed, then, in order to embody the ideal of Veritas: a systematic scrutiny of paradigms for concealed bias, and a better understanding of history.

Some of the best black scholars concluded that they would need to write their own history, attempting to create a complete and unbiased record. Their commitment to this quest was reinforced by the indignities of discrimination—in library use, in housing, in collegial life. John Hope Franklin, one of the most eminent and influential American historians of the century, had to contend with the segregation of southern archives and libraries in order to write southern history, and with segregated housing markets in order to live near his campus wherever he was. He concluded that the black scholar's quest needed to combine the interest in truth with a concern for political justice: "It was necessary, as a black historian, to have a personal agenda, as well as one dealing with more general matters, that involved a type of activism."[16] Similar historical work was undertaken by other distinguished black authors, such as Benjamin Quarles, Merze Tate, and Frank Snowden—whose pioneering *Blacks in Antiquity* took a careful scholarly look at the presence of dark-skinned people in the ancient Greco-Roman world.[17] Other black authors produced excellent works in the arts and their history and criticism. At the same time, the "Harlem Renaissance" had brought the excellence of African-American artistic achievement to the attention of the nation as a whole.[18]

As the debate about blacks in higher education developed, the topic of African origins kept returning. Both white and black academics, confronting the history and current culture of African-Americans, felt a need to situate it with reference to those origins, so long a source of shame for one, of loathing for the other. Critics of African-American art did not hesitate to reinvent the old stereotypes of the dark, sexual, primitive African and the Olympian, intellectual white man. Soon these same stereotypes were taken up by the defenders of African-American culture and appropriated for its defense more or less unchanged, with only the value judgments inverted. Thus praise of African-American sculpture from the white community spoke of its superior "harmony of rhythmic movement," its closeness to "elemental need," its "tremendous emotional endowment," and "the ideal of man's harmony with nature." These phrases, all used by the great art collector Albert C. Barnes, among the first prominent collectors of African sculpture, were typical of the tendency to romanticize African origins and to criticize white culture as excessively intellectual. Barnes writes, "The white man in the mass cannot compete with the Negro in spiritual endowment. Many centuries of civilization have attenuated his original gifts and have made his mind dominate his spirit." The black American, by contrast, has "in superlative measure that fire and light which, coming from within, bathes his whole world, colors his images and impels him to expression."[19]

This striking tribute makes contact with reality—but not without incorporating a good deal of fantasy. While it does acknowledge high cultural achievement, it does so at the cost of perpetuating a stereotype of black naturalness and white intellectuality that since the eighteenth century has served, more or less without real inquiry, to marginalize or exclude African-Americans from American academic life. Such contrasts between the passionate African and the cold white person are likely to prove unhelpful in approaching the complexities of individual lives and artworks. Once entrenched, they can also inhibit the development of individuals: for any African-American student who likes math or science, for example, or any black artist whose work is formal and intellectual, will in some quarters be disparaged, and may disparage himself, as excessively "white," a sellout to the dominant culture. Such stereotypes are difficult to eradicate, in part on account of their self-confirming quality. The African-American who doesn't conform tends to be seen not as a counterexample to the generalization, but as an imitator of whiteness. The African-American who does appear to conform is taken as evidence of its eternal validity.

Similar cultural insularity and stereotyping exist in the field of music. It is difficult today to find a major twentieth-century composer who does not owe a considerable debt to jazz. Gershwin, Copland, Bernstein, Dvořák,

Ravel, Poulenc, Stravinsky, and many others were exhilarated by the rhythmic sophistication and vitality of African and African-American work. In the minds of these creative musicians, and many conductors and musicians as well, there was nothing "primitive" or "natural" about African-American music: it was work of tremendous sophistication, which challenged the resources of traditional notation and of the traditional ways of playing instruments. This sophistication was less apparent to early scholars and musicologists, who continued, without serious inquiry, to speak of the "primitive" character of jazz, and of the African music that appeared to lie behind it. In 1959, the publication of A. M. Jones's authoritative *African Music* showed the inaccuracy of such descriptions; his work was followed by Gunther Schuller's analytical history *Early Jazz,* which discusses extensively the relationship between the rhythmic, harmonic, and melodic properties of jazz and those of the African music that might plausibly be connected with it.[20]

Schuller describes the difficulty Western musicologists had in even notating African music, when they first began to do fieldwork in Africa. Before the fieldwork of Jones (an Englishman who had lived most of his life in Africa), the expectation of visiting scholars was that they would encounter "primitive" musical forms. But European-trained musical ears, accustomed to hearing all voices strike together on a downbeat, proved unable to notate correctly the complicated polyphonies of African ensemble music, in which often each of twelve or more voices will go its separate way, weaving and interweaving. Reconstructions based on the flawed notation seemed to Africans laughably crude, in the way in which a child's copy of a complex artwork would seem crude. Nor could European ears catch the small rhythmic differences that were crucial to the correct notation of African song, as intervals of a twelfth of a second or less were routinely deployed by the African performer. European music simply did not operate with such small rhythmic intervals, so European-trained notators made errors.

This humbling experience showed European musicologists that the label "primitive" was a misnomer, and that they were dealing with great sophistication, though not the type of sophistication to which they were accustomed. (Schuller suggests, plausibly, that the downbeat structure of ragtime was black musicians' effort to simplify African rhythmic traditions for Western ears, and that it was only in the 1950s, for audiences by then more sophisticated in jazz listening, that the free-voice movements characteristic of African traditions could be successfully reintroduced into jazz.)[21] Nonetheless, in the popular mind, the image of the Negro as a pulsating musical animal, in touch with the earth and with "primitive energies" deriving from nature, persisted and flourished, as it persists to this very day, untouched by musical reality.

How, then, could the African-American scholar or artist conceive his identity, in a world that appeared to offer only two images of human achievement—that of the Christian, classically trained European, and that of the African primitive? The answer mapped out by Albert Barnes was chosen, as well, by a number of leading black artists, who vindicated their claim to culture by presenting a romanticized image of African passion and spiritual power. One especially striking example in this period is a poem titled "The Shroud of Color," published in 1925 by much-honored black poet Countée Cullen.

The speaker, addressing God, begins by expressing a despair caused by racism and its internalized psychological correlate, shame:

> "Lord, being dark," I said, ""I cannot bear
> The further touch of earth, the scented air
> . . .
> I strangle in this yoke drawn tighter than
> The worth of bearing it, just to be a man.

The speaker now seeks solace in nature, but comfort eludes him. His passionate embrace of the earth only makes him long the more for death. God then shows him the structure of the earth, its tremendous variety of plants and animals, of angels and devils, its sometimes fierce and bloody struggle for survival—but in all this wondrous variety he finds that he is the only creature that hates itself and wants to die. Next, however, God shows him Africa, with its "strange wild music," its rhythmic tom-toms, its "primitive" jungles. After experiencing Africa's freedom, and also the anguish of the slave ships and the suffering of his fellow Africans, the speaker decides for life, exclaiming, "Lord, I will live, persuaded by mine own." He dedicates his life to the cause of telling "truth" about his people and their history.[22]

This poem expresses a terrible pain. A great part of the pain is the sense of being an outcast, homeless and without identity. The speaker travels all round the earth and still feels himself an exile from every way of life. But the solution the poem proffers rings false, as do the lines in which "primitive" Africa is described, the weakest lines in the work. Cullen is a sophisticated, worldly, somewhat decadent poet, whose art has links to Coleridge, Tennyson, and Swinburne, to Baudelaire and to Rimbaud. (He was a professor of both French and English literature.) Like Baudelaire's fantasies of an innocent voluptuous paradise, Cullen's nostalgic depiction of Africa is a poetic fiction that has little connection with any real place. But Baudelaire's poet-speaker has a culture and dwells, however uncomfortably, in its midst, singled out for abuse only by the fact of being a poet. Thus his poetic fiction of the primitive can confess itself to be imaginary without rendering the poet-speaker homeless. Cullen's speaker, by contrast, has no culture and no home—not simply because of being a poet but, above all, because of race. His urgent need to invent a home, both for himself and for others of his race, leads him inexorably back to the crude cultural fiction of the primitive jungle rhythms of Africa, a fictive place that can hardly be a home for a poet such as Cullen, and can hardly confer on him the identity he seeks. But if Cullen's speaker cannot find his home in (the stereotype of) Africa, then, the logic of the poem goes, since the white world has repudiated him already, he is nothing and nobody.

This potentially tragic dilemma underlies many of our current debates. We need to ponder it, before we condemn the search for African origins of culture, judging the demand for the study of Africa to be mere "identity politics" or "victimology." The culture that put people in such a position of shame and homelessness, the culture that refused to recognize the sophistication of their art until more or less forced to do so by foreign scholars such as Schuller and Jones, cannot afford to treat lightly the cultural dissonance that is the legacy of that conduct.

Cullen's poem, however, suggests a solution to its own problem, as the speaker dedicates himself to the "loyal dream" of uncovering the history of his people. For a fictional image of Africa that mirrors white stereotypes, it might, then, be possible to substitute a subtle and true image, both of Africa and of the history that led black people from Africa to America. Both Bruce and Cullen suggest, in their different ways, that a fuller pursuit of Veritas, one that includes black Americans as inquirers and their history and traditions as part of the curriculum, is the only honorable solution to the social and intellectual legacy of racism.

The "Loyal Dream": African-American Studies in the Modern American University

Already in 1913, Arthur A. Schomburg, the black bibliophile (born in Puerto Rico) whose collection became the origin of the Schomburg Collection for Research in Black Culture at the New York Public Library, stated, "The American Negro must remake his past in order to make his future . . . History must restore what slavery took away, for it is the social damage of slavery that the present generations must repair and offset." Schomburg's essay *Racial Integrity: A Plea for the Establishment of a Chair of Negro History in Our Schools and Colleges* concludes with a plea for the serious study not only of the history of African people in America, but also of the culture and art of Africa:

> The bigotry of civilization which is the taproot of intellectual prejudice begins far back and must be corrected at its source . . . The Negro has been a man without a history because he has been considered a man without a worthy culture. But a new notion of the cultural attainment and potentialities of the African stocks has recently come about, partly through the corrective influence of the more scientific study of African institutions and early cultural history. Already the Negro sees himself against a reclaimed background, in a perspective that will give pride and self-respect ample scope, and make history yield for him the same values that the treasured past of any people affords.[23]

And yet Schomburg's sensible proposal that American universities should support serious scholarship in the study of Africa and the African-American past bore little fruit for decades. The assumption that there was no African or even African-American culture or history continued to dominate in the university, even though increasingly controverted by the internationally recognized art and scholarship that continued to be produced by black Americans.

Only with the political traumas of the 1960s and 1970s did the idea of African-American studies finally win recognition in a substantial number of major U.S. colleges and universities—and then frequently only as the result of fear-ridden negotiations with student pressure groups. At Harvard, for example, the Rosovsky report, which recommended the creation of a program rather than a department, was eventually rejected by the faculty in favor of departmental status, in conjunction with demands of the black students' group. As Nathan Huggins, historian of the Harlem Renaissance and longtime chair of the Harvard Afro-American Studies Department, describes the events:

> It was a bitter decision, many of those voting in favor doing so under a sense of intimidation. In that mood of crisis and perceived threat, the department was born. It would suffer, during its first ten years, from the lingering doubts and resentments harbored by faculty never fully convinced of Afro-America as a legitimate field of study, doubtful of it as a "discipline," and suspicious of what often appeared to be separatist tendencies on the part of its advocates.[24]

Such origins for a time crippled the development of departments of African-American studies—for their intellectual legitimacy was never acknowledged by leaders of the academic community. At Harvard, after having voted to create the new department, the academic community did little to support its efforts. Residual doubts caused established Harvard departments such as English and History to be reluctant to appoint scholars to joint appointments with Afro-American Studies. The failure to extend these joint appointments frequently caused nationally recognized black scholars to decline Harvard's offer altogether. Only very recently has the leadership of Henry Louis Gates Jr. brought to Harvard a nationally recognized group of scholars, including philosophers Kwame Anthony Appiah and Cornel West and sociologist William Julius Wilson. Many universities have not had this success, since academic careers have not proved as attractive as other options to talented black students, and the pool is consequently very small.

Since many of the difficulties faced by African-American studies result from a lack of consensus about their rationale and curricular legitimacy, an assessment of the current situation should begin by looking at these issues. Three distinct justifications for such programs have emerged.[25] One is the interest of African-Americans in redressing the imbalance in the academy by having a "turf" of their own. Having been forced for so long to enter an academy organized around the traditions of the dominant culture, African-Americans seek at least one department organized around their own traditions and culture. The academy that has asked them to repudiate their culture and "confess" its inadequacy should now acknowledge the dignity of both people and culture by giving research about them serious academic standing. This is a legitimate demand, indeed an important one—so long as it is not taken to imply that African-Americans should not study other aspects of history and culture, or that white students should not learn about African-Americans.

A second rationale, while legitimated by the unique history of Africans in America, is more problematic: an interest in discovering, and to some extent forging, a cultural identity. The dilemma posed by Cullen's poem persists. African-Americans often feel that they do not fully belong to a dominant culture that still expresses disdain for them; they cannot fully identify with its history or derive pleasure from its memories and ritual observances. (Like Du Bois, they feel that they would be right to sing "Fair Harvard" without any pride in the Pilgrims.) A turning to Africa is now, as it was for Cullen, an understandable response to this feeling of nonbelonging. And yet African-American culture is by now irretrievably different from any known African culture or cultures, past or present. The nostalgia for an African past, though seductive, is fraught with dangers of historical error and cultural oversimplification. Even more important, the idea that one's identity must be sought first and foremost in a racially based group identity, rather than in a larger world identity, is itself full of dangers for citizenship and understanding.

As Du Bois argued long ago, questions of identity and history cannot and should not be neglected when colleges think of how to teach their students, since they must begin with the students as they are and address their predicaments and concerns as they are:

> A university in Spain is not simply a university. It is a Spanish university. It is a university located in Spain . . . It starts with Spanish history and makes conditions in Spain the starting point of its teaching . . . In the same way, a Negro university in the United States of America begins with Negroes . . . it is founded on or it should be founded on a knowledge of the history of their people in Africa and in the United States, and their present condition. Without whitewashing or translating wish into fact, it begins with that; and then it asks how shall these young men and women be trained to earn a living and live a life under the circumstances in which they find themselves or with such changing of those circumstances as time and work and determination will permit.[26]

This sensible statement, as applicable to integrated as to black colleges, implies that the racial identity of students will legitimately enter into instruction as a starting point, a life situation from which instruction must begin and whose understanding should be central in the process of instruction. But this idea of beginning from one's own experience should not be taken to imply—and Du Bois insisted that it did not imply—that the goal of education should be to pit group against group, identity against identity. From different starting points, he saw students embarking, through education, on a voyage into the human, "beginning with the particular, and going out to universal comprehension and unhampered expression."[27] One had to understand the particular identity in order to approach the universal; and yet an identity that remains focused on the particular will properly be seen as incomplete.

By far the most compelling rationale for African-American studies, then, is that of truth and understanding for all students, as from their different starting points they approach the inclusive goal of world citizenship. Given the history of our nation, it is imperative for all citizens to understand the achievements and sufferings of its African-American people. Given the way in which misrepresentations about African history and culture figured in the injustice done, it seems all the more urgent for scholarship to redress these wrongs, replacing manufactured images of Africa and black America with true stories of cultural variety and human particularity. The goal of such instruction should, however, be not the formation of separate identity groups, but the creation of a truly inclusive academy and a public culture that acknowledges the contributions of all its constituent groups. As Henry Louis Gates expresses this idea, our universities should "prepare our students for their roles in the twenty-first century as citizens of a world culture, educated through a truly human notion of the humanities."[28] Walter Massey, now president of Morehouse College, has adopted a similar policy, arguing that a Morehouse education must connect African-American studies with the goal of "emphasizing the global scope of our commitment to a culture of excellence."[29] The most productive way to conceive of African-American studies is as a crucial contributor to such a program.

The understanding that results from research in African-American studies should be spread throughout the curriculum, in courses on American and world history, in literature, music, and art. It cannot properly be cordoned off in departments of African-American studies. But such departments are urgently needed as centers for new research in areas of American and African culture that have not been documented, and as places where students interested in a more specialized pursuit of these interests can learn the techniques necessary to go further.

African-American studies has frequently been said to lack disciplinary integrity and to exist as a unity only on account of political pressures. But like other interdisciplinary departments, such as classics, Near Eastern Studies, and American Studies, the African-American Studies department has the potential to generate valuable new research that crosses traditional disciplinary boundaries. It can bring the history of music together with the history of literature and sculpture, political and social history together with a study of the arts. It will fulfill this potential best if many of its faculty are jointly appointed in established departments, but these interdisciplinary ties give no reason to deny the new field its own disciplinary legitimacy.

Can the field, however, have such legitimacy, given that it oddly chooses to blend the study of Africa with that of the history of African peoples in America? We can see by now that this choice is not so odd, given the role played by misunderstanding of Africa in the oppression of black people in America. Indeed it would be difficult to write the history of African-American people without understanding their African heritage. Given, too, the great importance of African traditions in the development of African-American music and art, the linkage makes as much sense as do many other studies of tradition that cross geographic and temporal boundaries. A similar disciplinary choice was made by the field that is usually thought to be a paragon of legitimacy: classics, which brought Greece and Rome together precisely in order to study the role of the parent culture (that of Greece) in the forging of a derivative and yet to some extent independent culture (that of Rome). Just as one cannot see what a Roman writer is doing unless one understands both the Greek traditions in which he is working and the independent contribution of his own local milieu, so too one has a fuller understanding of the art of Duke Ellington, Charlie Parker, or Wynton Marsalis if one can situate them in a tradition that both derives from Africa and is distinctively American.

Doing justice to the history and cultures of Africa, and of African-American people, will require some transformations not only in the content of traditional courses but also in their methodology. It is easy and relatively inexpensive to organize a course around a list of "great books." Even faculty who are not experts in a given field, such as the Greek and Latin classics, can read the books (usually in translation) and make at least a show of teaching them, little though they may know about the rest of the culture. This is an inadequate way to teach ancient Greece, modern Europe, or any culture. It obscures the contribution of the nontextual arts, such as music, sculpture, architecture, and dance, and also important parts of verbal culture—oral poetry, myths and narratives, religious rituals—that did not get written down in transmitted texts of high culture but can still be reconstructed and studied. It studies history only by reading historians. But this inadequate approach is particularly defective for the cultures of Africa, where oral traditions are such a central part of the literary heritage, and where major contributions in sculpture, music, and dance require a highly sophisticated and specialized understanding. The research on African music that was supplanted by the sophisticated musicology of Jones and Schuller exemplifies the bad work that can be produced and taught by scholars who are insufficiently specialized—and yet, how many American academics can recognize an interval of one-twelfth of a second?

Can such gaps be filled? Of course the long-term answer is that primary and secondary curricula need reform to become more culturally sophisticated, especially in areas such as music, in which instruction in general tends to be seriously deficient. But where college liberal arts education is concerned, the filling of these gaps requires support of specialized research in departments of Afro-American studies, whose results can then be disseminated in the curriculum at large. (One of the first chairs of Afro-American Studies at Harvard was Eileen Southern, a distinguished ethnomusicologist.)[30] No amount of specialized research can educate all ears. But at least it can create good verbal descriptions of musical works that can be used in courses, as guides to listening and as historical context for what is to be heard.

Much the same is true in other areas of history and culture: expert research in departments of African-American studies can produce work that nonexpert faculty can use to teach African-American history, the African-American novel, African literatures, African sculpture, African and African-American religious life, and many other areas of human culture. These departments must undergird and complement efforts to integrate the truth about Africa and African-Americans into basic courses of many kinds.

Such a fruitful integration of specialized and general teaching exists in the SUNY–Buffalo course "American Pluralism and the Search for Identity." Faculty with special expertise in African-American studies collaborated with faculty from other departments in the design of this required course, integrating material about slavery and racial divisions into a larger study of America's struggle to extend equal rights and privileges to previously oppressed groups. Readings include slave narratives, theoretical writings by Du Bois, Richard Wright, and other prominent black writers, Supreme Court cases pertaining to race, reports from the U.S. Civil Rights Commission— all combined with related readings from the history of debates about the equality of women and various ethnic and religious minorities. The course offers all students a serious academic understanding of racial equality, and the African-American student a historical grasp of his or her own tradition in relation to those of other groups.

Andrew Young assailed African-American studies for minority students, on the grounds that they do not advance economic well-being. Far better, he said, to focus on science, engineering, economics, accounting. Young is of course correct that students must consider their future and that no group can advance in America without thinking about jobs. But the narrow vision of education suggested by his statement, increasingly prominent in a world anxious about job security, threatens to do away with some of education's most important benefits for all students, white as well as black. We have to think not only about how we will earn enough to live, but also about why we live, and what makes life worth the living. The humanities are essential to address these questions. If we become a population who can relate, as citizens, only on the narrow parched terrain of financial interest, we will have lost much that makes us fully human.

Race and the Academy: Tensions and Conflicts

The pursuit of truth about African-American history and culture has given rise to many tensions. The academy, like most of America, contains racial emotions that are irrational because they are based on, and serve to perpetuate, dangerous racial stereotypes.

In such an atmosphere, it is not too surprising that deliberation does not always go well. Even the question who should study and learn in this area is a matter of painful debate, as some defend racial qualifications for both teaching and learning in African-American studies, while others insist strongly on inclusiveness in the classroom and in hiring.

All citizens, not only African-Americans, need an education in African-American history and culture. This principle must be the starting point for any discussion of the issue of inclusiveness and separatism. African-Americans may have especially urgent reasons to seek this education and to promote the research that lies behind it. An interest in truth is not at all incompatible with a special interest in self-respect and in the undoing of insult and prejudice. Schomburg said this well in 1913:

> Of course, a racial motive remains—legitimately compatible with scientific method and aim. The work our race students now regard as important, they undertake very naturally to overcome in part certain handicaps of disparagement and omission too well-known to particularize. But they do so not merely that we may not wrongfully be deprived of the spiritual nourishment of our cultural past, but also that the full story of human collaboration and interdependence may be told and realized.[31]

In the contemporary academy, Schomburg's observation still holds: black students may have a special interest in or even need for such a historical understanding of their culture. But it is vital to insist that this learning is there for all students, as is the whole of liberal arts education. It must be made fully available to all, in an atmosphere of mutual respect and collaboration.

Some classrooms in African-American studies, like the one encountered by my freshman advisee, make white students feel uncomfortable. Many white students avoid taking such courses in the first place, assuming that they will be made to feel out of place. We should criticize this situation whenever it arises. The need to learn about African-American history and culture is a need all Americans share. A classroom is a place of inquiry that should be open to all who will do the work in a spirit of inquiry and mutual respect. If we ask white students to agree that their black classmates can read Arthur Miller and John Updike, it is preposterous, and morally bad, to bar them from inquiry when they seek to understand the art of Toni Morrison or Ishmael Reed. The racialist view of "blood memory" has no place in the academy—except as an object of study, a pathology that has at times afflicted many communities who want to ward off the outsider. (We could say the same of the concept of race as well, which has little biological validity.) Such modes of teaching and learning have rightly been vigorously criticized by most of the leading intellectuals in the African-American community, including Henry Louis Gates, Anthony Appiah, and Cornel West. Such internal criticism is becoming ever more effective.

If "blood memory" is unacceptable as a theory about the suitability of students, it is equally unacceptable as a theory about their professors. It was always laughable to suppose that we were genetically close to the ancient Greeks. It was not even true that twentieth-century Americans have a culture that is in any meaningful sense continuous with that of ancient Greece, so many differences have been wrought by intervening centuries, above all by the history of Christianity. But the really baneful fiction was the idea that either a genetic or a cultural heritage gives any person a special claim to teach and do research in a subject. They do not: interest, insight, imagination, hard work, and dedication are what give someone a claim to teach in a subject.

We sometimes see this rather easily. We do not insist that the teacher of German be a person of German stock. Even if we sometimes have a preference for the native over the acquired speaker, we are well aware that the native speaker may have been born from parents who were not themselves native speakers. We do not insist that the teacher of Indo-European linguistics be a person of Indo-European stock, whatever that is. Indeed, despite the prejudices of some older German Indo-Europeanists, for whom Indo-European studies had a racist agenda, Jewish linguists have made major contributions to Indo-European studies. So too with all subjects. Although there are reasons why more African-Americans and fewer whites may gravitate to this field, when once they are there their academic work should be judged like anyone else's—for its range, insight, and excellence. If we say anything else, we hold up to our students a false and pernicious image of the limits of the imagination and open the door to the very racism we hope to combat. For if we do say that only blacks can teach African-American studies, what is to prevent the white racist from saying that only whites can teach white studies, or that only people of Greek descent can teach ancient Greek?[32]

Not all academics agree in repudiating separatist hiring. In 1982 black students at Harvard Law School, with some faculty support, protested the appointment of the courageous civil-rights lawyer Jack Greenberg to coteach a course in civil rights law with a black colleague. The incident was complex, since the students were protesting the fact that a short course taught by a visitor was replacing a regular course, and that the law school had failed to make plans for regular teaching in the area.[33] Nonetheless, to the extent that Greenberg's race became the focus of complaint, the episode displayed a regrettable racialist character. Today, however, most leaders of the black intellectual community are in agreement that racial affiliation should not be a necessary condition of teaching African-American studies. Nathan Huggins some time ago insisted that the Harvard department was "interested in making the best possible appointments, regardless of race."[34] Henry Louis Gates more recently wrote: "our subject is open to all—whether to study or to teach. After all, the fundamental premise of the academy is that all things ultimately are knowable; all are therefore teachable. What would we say to a person who said that we couldn't teach Milton because we are not Anglo-Saxon, or male, or heterosexual—or blind!"[35]

There is an element of truth in the separatist claim about teaching. The experience of being black in America is an unusual experience; some things about that condition will be more difficult to understand if one has not had the experience. A white person who walks down the street or goes grocery shopping is not perceived as a threat, and may not be aware of the extent to which a black man, however well dressed or well behaved, will be likely to see people cross to the other side of the street or clutch their purses in fear. These experiences can be understood by the empathic and imaginative, but people more commonly universalize their own experiences and filter out what is different. At the very least, one would not want to attempt to teach in this area without having spent a lot of time talking with black Americans and hearing their experiences, any more than one would want to teach in women's studies without having spent a great deal of time talking to women—or in ancient Greek studies without immersing oneself for a very long time in the culture and language of ancient Greece. But it is not impossible for a white to develop a rich understanding of black history or culture, nor for blacks to lack self-understanding. People often fail to know themselves, and sometimes an outsider can see what escapes an insider. The element of truth, however, tells us simply that understanding is difficult without experience, and that all instructors in this area need understanding. It provides no reason to insist on a racial standard for appointments.

Black students, furthermore, should be encouraged to pursue whatever academic interest exhilarates them, without feeling undue pressure to define their academic identity in racial terms. Many black students become intensely race-focused when they leave home and enter college, deciding—

often in rebellion against successful assimilationist parents—to define their goals in terms of the identity politics of race. One can sympathize with the struggle for identity any young African-American in America faces, without conceding that a major determinant of the academic life of every such student should be a search for a specifically black identity. Arthur Jameson will have to figure out what sort of manhood he wants to claim for himself. But that undertaking need not prevent him from studying philosophy and literature, even choosing a career in those areas. One of the most influential African-American faculty members at Brown is a young historian who specializes in the history of seventeenth-century China. He gives students of his race (and others) a valuable signal: do whatever you care about, and do not fear that in so doing you will forfeit your individual identity.

Many blacks believe that traditional academic subjects are spoiled by the taint of racism. They might even perceive as a traitor the young black who likes such studies. And yet this belief is false. Neither philosophy nor the study of literature nor even the study of ancient Greece and Rome is per se a white racist undertaking. They are ways of seeing the world that are open to all people. Sometimes we may indeed find racist ideas deeply lodged in the standard ways of approaching a subject. Many approaches to the Greek and Roman world were once distorted by ideas of racial superiority. The very project of studying ancient Greece and Rome was not so tainted, but one might have had a struggle in some places to approach it in a nontainted way. Some influential approaches to the teaching of music embody racial views of musical culture and of innate musical ability grounded in a specific ethnic and cultural heritage that are closely linked with the history of racism: Carl Orff's system for teaching music to children was closely related to his Nazi affiliations. If one found an entire musical establishment organized around the Orff system, one might plausibly attack that establishment as racist. Music and musicology would, however, remain. The study of Indo-European linguistics in Germany and Austria was at one time intimately bound up with Nazi views about the Aryan people and their racial heritage; it might have seemed that to study Indo-European was to be absorbed into a racially tainted profession. By now, good scholarly work has rigorously dissociated the history of language from such myths, establishing Indo-European as an area of study open to all. In general, whenever a domain of learning has been deformed by bias or prejudice, this circumstance should be regarded as a challenge to pursue the truth more rigorously and to get rid of all that stifles it.

One of the most pernicious developments in debates about race and the curriculum, as in debates about women's studies, has been the suggestion that standard structures of argument, and logic itself, are racially tainted and not for African-American students. This suggestion has been heard even within the Committee on Blacks in the American Philosophical Association. It was urged, for example, that summer recruitment programs for talented black undergraduates should avoid formal logic because black students do not feel comfortable with it; it was suggested that a study of African philosophy should replace logic. This suggestion was greeted by a storm of protest from other black philosophers, who saw the statement, rightly, as reminiscent of racist disparagement of the intelligence of African-Americans that they had long fought to overturn.

Of course no program intended to make philosophy attractive to potential graduate students should focus on formal logic, since it is not philosophically exciting and few students enjoy it. It is a necessary tool, and should be presented as such, in the context of more exhilarating material. Among those exciting materials might well be—for all students—a cross-cultural study of what philosophy has meant in different traditions. There are some excellent anthologies that such a cross-cultural course segment could use,[36] and of course it may be of special interest to the African-American student to find the philosophical traditions of Africa presented in a scholarly way. But it is crucial to avoid the suggestion that philosophical argument itself is a matter of racial inheritance or that black students cannot think logically.

In general, we should remember the vision of W. E. B. Du Bois, when he imagined a world in which no human being would be cut off by the color line from access to any profound work of culture:

> I sit with Shakespeare, and he winces not. Across the color line I move arm in arm with Balzac and Dumas, where smiling men and welcoming women glide in gilded halls. From out the caves of evening that swing between the strong-limbed earth and the tracery of the stars, I summon Aristotle and Aurelius and what soul I will, and they come all graciously with no scorn nor condescension. So, wed with Truth, I dwell above the Veil. Is this the life you grudge us, O knightly America?[37]

For Du Bois, the world of the mind is common to all. To judge that truth, logic, and literature written by whites are all inappropriate objects of study for the African-American is to yield to the feudal society of "knightly America," which made Truth and Beauty off-limits to all but an elite.

Many curricular problems have arisen as institutions try to include African-Americans and their heritage. Among these, none is more difficult than the demand for an "Afrocentric" curriculum. While the liberal cosmopolitan demands inclusive learning for all citizens, a more radical and more retributive approach to the legacy of racism is to demand a curriculum that is unbalanced in a direction opposite to that of earlier imbalances, Afrocentric where the old curriculum was Eurocentric. Gates puts the current situation well: "We Liberal Reformists say: Do unto others as you would have them do unto you; and—hope for the best. The Left says: Let's do unto you what you *did* unto Others; and then see how you like that."[38] Such a retributive approach has a limited place in the academy, when it prompts us to uncover prejudice that has been parading as objectivity. But it cannot be productive when it departs from the pursuit of truth and substitutes a new distortion for the old one.

Many "Afrocentric" courses pursue truth and apply rigorous standards of evidence. These are courses that direct the student to the study of African and African-American history as a central part of their curriculum, while gathering the material with a scrupulous regard for evidence and argument. A good example is the required course at Spelman College called "The African Diaspora and the World," a two-semester sequence that studies the histories of African peoples as they have been scattered by the slave trade into different regions of the world. Spelman connects the purpose of the course to the college's internationalist mission of preparing students for leadership in an increasingly interdependent world culture:

> Cultural exchange as a dynamic force is emphasized. An appreciation of the interaction of political, social, and economic factors within and across continental boundaries and throughout history is stressed. To put it another way, this course seeks to provide students with a formal introduction to their own background and culture (a very legitimate need); the connection of that background and culture to those of other communities of African descent; the relationship between this comprehensive experience and developments in the larger world; and the fostering of a process whereby students learn to reflect critically upon

methods and strategies of addressing contemporary political, economic, and social maladies. In short, the course seeks to develop a
more capable leadership.[39]

The course follows Du Bois' idea that students must begin from their own
situation, understand that situation historically, then move outward toward
a more inclusive understanding. The course traces the history of African-
American people from African origins through the time of the civil rights
movement. At each stage, however, this history is connected to other, related
histories—of the slave trade and colonialism in other parts of the world, of
antislavery and anticolonial movements in different countries, of other
groups in America who have striven for full equality. An interdisciplinary
course, its organizing perspective is that of history and political science; but
economics, literature, music, dance, and visual art all play a role. There is
emphasis throughout on rigorous critical argument and on the goal of citizenship. Here we see a way in which a curriculum can contain an Afrocentric focus and yet not lose sight of Du Bois' more embracing goal. Integrated
colleges could also profit from a course of this quality, and indeed the
SUNY–Buffalo course has many common features with the Spelman course.

Morehouse College, Spelman's brother institution, has recently initiated
curricular changes that follow this same promising pattern. New President
Walter Massey, a well-known scientist and scientific administrator, has taken
as the motto of his administration "creating a world house at Morehouse."
This goal, he argues, requires strengthening the offerings in African-American studies by insisting on a rigorous structure for the departmental major
and in general by infusing new depth and excellence into the curriculum.
But it also requires an emphasis on the interdependence of all the world's
peoples and their need for mutual understanding. The "world house" theme,
Massey continues, takes its inspiration from Morehouse alumnus Dr. Martin
Luther King Jr., who wrote in his book *Where Do We Go from Here: Chaos
or Community:*

> We have inherited a large house, a great world house, in which we
> have to live together, black and white, Gentile and Jew, Catholic and
> Protestant, Moslem and Hindu, a family unduly separated in ideas,
> culture, and interest, who, because we can never again live apart, must
> learn somehow to live with each other in peace . . . we cannot ignore
> the larger world house in which we are also dwellers.

Massey also cites the words of John Dewey, insisting that a liberal education ought to produce "hospitality of mind, generous imagination, trained capacity of discrimination, freedom from class, sectarian or partisan prejudice and passion, faith without fanaticism."[40]

It is noteworthy that these humane values infuse the description of the Morehouse African-American Studies major itself: among the goals of the major is said to be to "encourage students to appreciate the ideals of brotherhood, equality, spirituality, humane values, and democracy."[41] Massey has, courageously and commendably, taken an aggressively inclusivist approach to the mission of the African-American college, setting its efforts within the context of a program of preparing all students for effective world citizenship.

At other institutions we find many courses and curricula that incorporate African-American studies in ways that make valuable contributions to citizenship. Often a topic-oriented approach produces good results. At St. Lawrence, a comparative fine arts course studies the process by which the art of different cultures became recognized as "fine art" in Western museums; a comparative literature course studies the tradition of orally transmitted and written epic poetry in the Greek, Indian, and African traditions; a religion course compares fundamentalisms in the African-American and white Protestant communities with other varieties of fundamentalism worldwide. All of these are valuable ways in which material about Africans and African-Americans are being integrated into curricula.

But not all Afrocentric instruction is as responsible as the Spelman courses and the new Morehouse curriculum, and not all courses about Africa are as rigorous as those at St. Lawrence. In some cases the retributive approach described by Gates leads to distortion of the historical record. Even in the time of Arthur Schomburg, such compensatory distortions were well known, and Schomburg attacked them:

> history cannot be written with either bias or counter-bias. The blatant Caucasian racialist with his theories and assumptions of race superiority and dominance has in turn bred his Ethiopian counterpart—the rash and rabid amateur who has glibly tried to prove half of the world's geniuses to have been Negroes and to trace the pedigree of nineteenth century Americans from the Queen of Sheba. But fortunately today there is on both sides of a really common cause less of the sand of controversy and more of the dust of digging.[42]

Schomburg spoke, it seems, too quickly. Today, more than eighty years later, we still find "rash and rabid amateur[s]" who assert a number of demonstrably false claims about Africa: that Beethoven is of African descent, that Aristotle stole his ideas from Egyptian libraries, that Greek language and Greek culture derive largely from the language and culture of black-skinned Egyptian people. Such hypotheses are defended by abuse of linguistic and textual evidence and have no scholarly legitimacy. The linguistic evidence for the priority of Egypt over Greece is a central part of the argument in Martin Bernal's *Black Athena,* the most scholarly work to publish such assertions. But Bernal's understanding of the principles of historical linguistic reconstruction is completely unscientific and has been decisively refuted by the analyses of expert Indo-European linguists.[43]

There is no reason to suppose that Bernal (who is white and Jewish) has been motivated by a racialist agenda. Many equally unreliable stories about the alleged borrowing of Greek culture (whether from Egypt or India or Babylonia) have been produced, independently of issues of race. In the 1960s Cyrus Gordon, a well-known professor at Brandeis University, held that Greek culture derived from biblical culture, and that the Greek and Hebrew languages were related. This claim involved gross linguistic error. Recently Martin West, an extremely conservative British classicist and in general a very fine scholar, argued that early Greek philosophy derives from Iran and India.[44] West's claim is even less historically plausible than Bernal's, since some Greeks did go to Egypt, whereas there is no evidence that any went to India before Alexander's campaigns in the fourth century B.C. Where evidence is scarce, speculative scholarship abounds. We should not suppose that Afrocentric writers are doing anything unusually sinister when they advance their own unreliable speculations, nor should we cry out that there is a political conspiracy to subvert scholarship.[45] Nonetheless, unreliable scholarship should be rejected. Other accounts of an allegedly "stolen legacy" of Africa to Europe are even less credible and more amateurish.[46]

Other retributive fantasies of culture begin with biology; an example is the notorious "melanin theory" of culture, articulated by black authors such as Richard King, Carol Barnes, and Frances Cress-Welsing and made famous by Leonard Jeffries, controversial chair of Black Studies at the City University of New York.[47] Combined with a typology of "sun people" and "ice people" first articulated by white Canadian author Michael Bradley,[48] the "melanin theory" holds that the pigment melanin is the natural inheritance of the human species, and that white skin is produced by a genetic abnormality. Because of color inferiority, whites respond with vindictiveness and aggression to people who do have melanin, and thus racism is born. These theories are not novel; they recreate in new terms the very stereotypes of African sensuality and white intellectuality that have been current since Phillis Wheatley's time.

It is important to understand the genesis of such mistaken and unscientific theories. A scare image of Africa shaped more by bigotry than by inquiry has dominated in the academy for centuries. It seems perfectly understandable that many black students and scholars today, like Cullen and others earlier, would be drawn to a correspondingly positive fantasy of African cultural power. Such fictions, however, do a tremendous disservice to the legitimate study of African-American history and cultures. They create the impression that black scholars are interested in propaganda rather than truth, something that is not accurate about the vast majority. They promote theories of the racial origins of culture that have been used for years to keep black students out of academic pursuits for which they are eminently well qualified. They do violence to human variety and particularity, to the sophistication and intricacy of black music and art, to the literary achievements of writers from Du Bois to Baldwin and Morrison. They provide a handy supply of scare stories that white critics of African-American studies can use to give a distorted picture of these studies. It is urgent to criticize such accounts of Africa. Most leading African-American intellectuals have already done so. Leonard Jeffries' conception of Afrocentrism has been repudiated by Gates, by Appiah, by Cornel West, by Michael Eric Dyson, and in general by leading black thinkers in many academic fields.[49]

It is particularly urgent for all interested in truth to speak out when these fictions are associated with anti-Semitism, as they have been by Jeffries, Khalid Muhammed, and historian Tony Martin of Wellesley College. Once a reputable historical scholar who did sound work on Marcus Garvey, Martin has recently become an anti-Semitic polemicist. His privately published pamphlet, *The Jewish Onslaught,* contains vicious statements about the role of the Jews in the oppression of black Americans, related to the scurrilous pseudohistory *The Secret Relationship between the Blacks and the Jews,* a volume endorsed by Khalid Muhammed and taught by Martin in his courses at Wellesley. Such associations between the Jews and the slave trade were also endorsed by Jeffries in remarks for which he was suspended from his chairmanship of the Black Studies Department at the City University of New York. (He was reinstated as the outcome of a protracted lawsuit, but a higher court overruled the decision, and the U.S. Supreme Court has recently refused to hear the case.)

These are extreme and highly atypical cases of ugly and unacceptable racism. The presence of such racist teachers on American campuses raises serious moral issues. When a black student group at the University of California at Riverside invited Muhammed to speak, the gesture raised issues of free speech and the proper role of the university administration in suppressing student speech. Many who deplored both the invitation and Muhammed's message nevertheless believed that the administration behaved rightly in refusing to prevent him from speaking once he had been duly invited. On the other hand, the presence of hate propaganda on a campus must always be met by public protest and official dissociation of the institution from the message of hatred. That American campuses have sheltered racist and anti-Semitic propaganda in the past is no excuse for them to do so now.

When tenured faculty speak in a racialist manner, we should remember that any attempt to terminate their employment is fraught with danger for academic freedom. Faculty and administrators rightly shrink from taking up tenure-removal procedures on the basis of the content of a colleague's teaching (as opposed to criminal activity, mental incompetence, academic fraud, or the sexual harassment of students). Not very long ago left-wing faculty members were dismissed because of some link, real or alleged, with the Communist party. Untenured faculty are still vulnerable to dismissal for their political views. Even though an African-American professor who teaches that the Jews caused the slave trade may seem different from a philosopher who was once a Communist—since the former is actively teaching falsehood and thus subverting the academic process—we cannot have confidence in the ability of administrators to make such distinctions. Many politically unpopular views look to some administrators like dangerous falsehoods. We should therefore permit such a tenured faculty member to remain, in order to draw a line protecting other legitimate work from politically motivated persecution. This protection would not be defensible, however, if he or she threatened or coerced students or faculty. Meanwhile, the institution should publicly disclaim any complicity in the anti-Semitic views such a scholar expresses, and colleagues should condemn them, as most have. In this context, it seems especially significant and commendable that Walter Massey, new president of Morehouse, has made Martin Luther King Jr.'s idea of a "world house," in which all people, including "Gentiles and Jews," will live in peace and friendship, the central goal of his administration.

If Tony Martin and Leonard Jeffries are highly atypical of the black academy, why do they attract so much publicity? Why are their ideas so frequently discussed in the press, while the principled cosmopolitanism of Kwame Anthony Appiah and Walter Massey, the liberal pluralism of Gates, the progressive integrationism of Cornel West, and the brilliant Henry James scholarship of Ken Warren (chair of Afro-American Studies at the University of Chicago) are rather less discussed, although they teach in more prestigious positions, have more academic publications, and far surpass the others in all traditional measures of academic influence and respect? One part of the answer is that these extremists do have a substantial student following on some campuses. Another answer is that American popular culture is sensationalistic, and extreme positions always get more discussion than moderate positions. None of this suffices, however, to explain the disproportionate emphasis on extreme anti-Semitic Afrocentrism in recent works that purport to depict American campus life. Extreme behavior by a white male in the academy is rarely taken as exemplary of the nature of white men. When Martin Heidegger is revealed as a Nazi, John Rawls and Hilary Putnam are under no public pressure to write editorials disclaiming anti-Semitism on the part of white male philosophers. And yet Heidegger was a leader in the field; this is hardly true of Martin or Jeffries. Nonetheless, Martin and Jeffries are brought to the door of figures like Gates and Appiah in a way that Heidegger is not brought to the door of Rawls. Shouldn't we ask why?

The reason appears to be that Martin and Jeffries confirm a stereotype. It is easy to see them as paradigmatic rather than eccentric or pathetic because—both in doctrine and in violence of language—they confirm fictions that have been perpetuated by members of both races for centuries, with what African novelist Chinua Achebe calls a "wilful tenacity."[50] Such stereotypes of black aggression and irrationality, like other myths of Africa, can be combatted only by truth—by describing the work of black scholars and artists, and emphasizing repeatedly the fact that the extreme positions have been repudiated by acknowledged leaders of the black intellectual community.

The engagement with truth that lies at the heart of African-American studies has a goal, well expressed by Achebe. It is to show the West and its citizens, black and white alike, what both Africa and the history of America may look like "once [we] rid [our] mind[s] of old prejudices and beg[i]n to look at Africa not through a haze of distortions and cheap mystifications but quite simply as a continent of people—not angels, but not rudimentary souls either—just people, often highly gifted people and often strikingly successful in their enterprise with life and society."[51] That goal demands that we renounce stereotypes (except to study them) and pay attention to the individual. This undertaking may be less dramatic and romantic than focusing on stirring images. But it is the only way to pursue real enlightenment. And when we do pursue enlightenment, we may discover that the study of people in their individuality and idiosyncrasy is really not so pedestrian after all, but full of delight.

When we consider the tortuous and sometimes tragic history of these issues in our colleges and universities, it is easy to feel pessimism. We see, over two hundred years, so much distortion and malice, so little *veritas*. W. E. B. Du Bois, writing in 1933, expressed a challenge that still lies before us all. Discussing the pain of racism in the academy, Du Bois quotes a line from Jamaican poet Claude McKay: "If we must die, let it not be like hogs." Du Bois comments:

> But the alternative of not dying like hogs is not that of dying or killing like snarling dogs. It is rather conquering the world by thought and brain and plan; by expression and organized cultural ideals . . . We hold the possible future in our hands but . . . only by thought, plan, knowledge, and organization. If the college can pour into the coming age an American Negro who knows himself and his plight and how to protect himself and fight race prejudice, then the world of our dream will come and not otherwise.[52]

Du Bois addressed this challenge to the black community, in an essay focused on the mission of the Negro college in a largely segregated America. For us, living in an America nominally integrated but still consumed by bigotry, this challenge must be heard as a challenge for black and white educators alike, to build colleges and universities that conquer racism by thought and brain and plan, by the dissemination of truth and the demolition of pernicious myths and stereotypes. More like human beings than like snarling dogs, we must commit ourselves to producing citizens, white and black, who know themselves and their historical plight and how to fight race prejudice. Then the world of our dream will come, and not otherwise.

CHAPTER SIX

Women's Studies

[W]e may safely assert that the knowledge which men can acquire of women, even as they have been and are, without reference to what they might be, is wretchedly imperfect and superficial, and always will be so, until women themselves have told all that they have to tell.

John Stuart Mill, *The Subjection of Women* (1869)

At the University of Nevada at Reno, there is a change in the syllabus of the general education course on great books of ancient Greece. Deborah Achtenberg of Philosophy has persuaded the faculty committee to add the poetry of Sappho, together with background readings on the situation of women in the ancient Greek world. These readings present absorbing new research about daily life and the household, data that would not have been available from the great books themselves or from focusing on the events of political history. The faculty learn how scholars have reconstructed women's lives by combining data from visual art, archaeology, tax records, "documentary papyri" such as laundry lists, and little-known medical treatises.

At Stanford University, students of political theorist Susan Moller Okin, chair of the university's Ethics Program, learn to examine texts and issues in Western political thought through what Okin calls "the prism of gender." Okin argues that the most influential contemporary American theories of political justice have neglected women's situation in society and the distribution of resources and opportunities within the family. They have done so, for the most part, because they have simply assumed that the family is an institution characterized by bonds of love and affection, and that it would injure those bonds even to raise questions of justice about its internal operations. Students learn that John Stuart Mill presented powerful arguments against this failure to consider family justice, arguments that have, says Okin, been wrongly neglected. How can we expect to produce a nation of just citizens, Okin asks with Mill, if they have not learned justice in the place that is the source of their most powerful moral instruction?[1]

At Harvard University, students in an economics course on hunger and famine taught by economist Amartya Sen learn how to look at the distribution of food through "the prism of gender." With Sen, they estimate the number of females in the world who are likely to have died because of their sex—whether through sex-selective infanticide or through receiving nutrition and health care unequal to that given to males. In the world as a whole, the number of these "missing women," Sen argues, is approximately 100 million.[2] Sen shows that the family, which can be a source of love, care, and even justice, can also be a place in which women are slowly or quickly killed. He notes how frequently estimates of a nation's general prosperity fail to ask how women are doing, remarking that dominant economic models of the family discourage the investigator from posing that question.

At Brown University, students who sign up for the popular course "Biology of Gender" learn from Professor Anne Fausto-Sterling that many of the experiments purporting to discover innate differences between men and women have scientific defects that call their conclusions into question. They study the results of experiments showing how early cultural norms of gender shape the lives of infants. Infants labeled male are bounced and tossed in the air; the same infants, when believed to be female, are cuddled and held tightly. Even an infant's crying is described differently—as anger when the observer thinks the baby is male, as fear when the observer believes it is a female. Fausto-Sterling (like John Stuart Mill) argues that the pervasive influence of these cultural patterns makes it impossible for us, so far, to know what, if any, natural differences exist between women and men.[3]

Caroline Bynum, professor of religious studies at Columbia University, speaks at a memorial service for David Herlihy. Herlihy was professor of history at Bryn Mawr, Harvard, and finally Brown; at his death in 1991, he was president of the American Historical Association. Describing barriers to the study of women's history created by dominant models of research, Bynum shows how Herlihy broke down those barriers through his fundamental work on medieval property rights. Forging new demographic and statistical techniques, he made it possible to learn about the lives of people who did not play a big role on the political stage. Herlihy, she says, took those steps when it was unfashionable to do so, a religious Catholic inspired by a medieval ideal of spiritual friendship between men and women.

New scholarship about women's lives is changing the academy. Highly diverse, filled with debate and contention, scholarship about and by women pervades curricula, transforming not only the content but often also the methodology of established courses. These changes are controversial. Critics of women's studies often look back to an earlier era when there seemed to be a general consensus about what the traditional academic disciplines were doing and what their methods were. If women entered these disciplines at all, they did so without questioning the traditional methodology and subject matter of the disciplines. They did not demand that they be allowed to do research on the lives of women, and thus these lives remained largely unstudied, in disciplines ranging from art history to classics to psychology and history.

But there were large gaps in the disciplines, gaps created by a failure to study women with the seriousness with which men's lives had long been studied. What Mill observed in 1869 was still true a hundred years later: we knew very little about the history of women, about their psychology, their bodies, their religious attitudes, their philosophical ideas. The very generalizations about women's "nature" that Mill mocked as inadequate and lacking a basis in true research still dominated many discussions—when women were discussed at all.

Mill predicted that this situation would not change until women themselves did research and told their own story. He might have been proved wrong. The imagination can cross boundaries of gender and class and race, and David Herlihy's idea of "spiritual friendship" between women and men can be realized. But the absence of women in the academy was in fact accompanied by a culpable failure to study the lives of those who had been excluded from academic citizenship. Gaps in knowledge and understanding undermined both teaching and research concerning one-half of the human race. These gaps hindered students in their civil, political, and familial lives.

Nor could these gaps be addressed by simply plugging some new information about women into the existing research paradigms and the curricula stemming from them. In many cases the defects were methodological as well, and the remedy required rethinking how to gather reliable information about the lives of those who were marginalized in a nation's culture, economy, or religious history. For example, as Caroline Bynum argued, historical research focusing on large-scale political events, and using the techniques appropriate to study such events, proved unable to provide a rich account of the lives of women. In order to discover what work women did, how much property they controlled, how children were raised, what they thought about politics or religion, new techniques, both narrative and demographic, needed to be forged.

Again, when the gross national product of a modern nation is reported in fields such as public policy and economics, domestic labor is not counted as productive labor.[4] And yet domestic labor is essential to understanding a nation's overall economy and the quality of life of its members. Without new methods of inquiry, it was difficult to take account of this labor or to estimate its importance. There were similar failures in biology and medicine, in psychology, in philosophy, in art history, in many other fields. Families, and the work women do in them, were often assumed, but at the same time ignored. Mill's criticism was still valid.

As Okin argued, the family is one of the most important topics studied by political science and economics, since its influence on human development is pervasive and deep. The most influential economic model of the family has been that proposed by Nobel Prize–winning economist Gary Becker.[5] This model is widely used to make predictions, to chart the direction of public policy, and even to gather information. A prominent assumption of this model is that the male head of household is a beneficent altruist who adequately represents the interests of all his family members and can be relied on to distribute resources fairly. Relying on this assumption, users of the model do not ask how each particular member of the family is doing. When gathering information, they ask only about households. A recent attempt to study the situation of widows in India, for example, found that there were no data on widows' nutritional or health status because the data did not disaggregate households into their members.[6]

The assumption, however, is false. Conflicts of interest over occupational choice, division of labor, basic nutrition, and health are pervasive parts of family life the world over.[7] A closer look at the family reveals that in many parts of the world girls are fed less well than boys, less frequently taken to the doctor when ill, less well educated, less well protected from violence—all this if they are permitted to survive infancy in the first place. To reveal these facts, new methods needed to be devised.

The silence about women in the academy was not a benign or neutral silence. It supported, as it was supported by, the exclusion of women from the dignities of the scholarly community. Treating women as of such little account that they were not worth studying was a way of denying respect to women's lives; this denial of respect went hand in hand with the denial of academic employment. Worse still, the silence concealed evils in the larger world, ranging from unequal opportunity to domestic abuse and malnutrition.

Women had many urgent and justified grievances, in short, against traditional male research and teaching. These failures were failures in scholarship for all, since all need to know the truth. Men should have been asking these questions and doing this research, and in some cases they did. But on the whole, correction of these deficiencies in scholarship awaited the arrival of women in the disciplines in sufficient numbers to influence the direction and character of research, seeing traditional topics through "the prism of gender."

Already in the fourth century B.C., Plato recognized that an unbiased look at the reality of women's lives was an uphill struggle, in a culture long accustomed to restrict women to a domestic role. Socrates says to Glaucon in the *Republic* that most Athenians will find it ridiculous to think of women doing exercise out of doors, or studying philosophy—and therefore they will avoid asking sincerely and objectively whether women have the capacity to do these things. Any question that challenges deeply rooted habits seems threatening, especially when the challenge is to entrenched structures of power. Socrates reminds Glaucon, however, that many things we now know to be fruitful seemed absurd when they were first introduced—for example, the custom of public exercising that is now at the heart of Greek culture. When we reflected well about that change, however, "the appearance of absurdity ebbed away under the influence of reason's judgment about the best." He later reminds Glaucon that rational reflection can be crippled by habit even at the level of language: if they do not use both the masculine and the feminine forms of the participle when they talk about rulers (equivalent to our practice of saying "he or she"), they will be likely to forget what they have agreed, that women should have the opportunity to attain the highest functions in the city. Reason can falter through a failure of imagination.[8]

Women's studies, at its best, makes just such an appeal to reason. It asks the scholarly community not to surrender to the tyranny of habit and to habitual ideas of what is "natural," but to look for the truth in all its forms, using arguments that have been carefully sifted for bias. In this way, it has opened up many fruitful lines of research.

Women's Studies and the Exclusion of Women

Mill suggested, correctly, that ignorance about women's lives was supported by the exclusion of women from the academy. In 1969, one hundred years after the publication of Mill's call for women's studies, there were two tenured women on the faculty at Harvard University, one in a chair endowed through Radcliffe for a woman. This was typical in the elite universities that trained young scholars. Women were allowed to dine at the Faculty Club only in a small side room. Until 1967 they had been forbidden to use Lamont Library, where reserve books for undergraduate courses were kept; their own separate facility (with separate though not entirely equal resources) was almost a mile from most classrooms. A female teaching assistant, assigned to teach a section of a large course in a seminar room inside Lamont, asked what she should do about the fact that women were forbidden to enter the building. She was told, "Go around to the side entrance, and do not use the elevator." Harvard, which had taken a strong stand on racial integration in university facilities since 1923, had no hesitation in denying the equal use of its facilities to women.

Nor were women equal in graduate student financing. They could not hold prestigious traveling fellowships that helped graduate students with their research. Until 1971 they could not hold the three-year Junior Fellowship, which freed a small group of young scholars for interdisciplinary study. Married women had to declare their husband's income when filling out their expense account for a fellowship, but married men did not have to declare their wife's income.

Lives of young female scholars were difficult in other ways. The university, like most at that time, had no grievance procedure for sexual harassment, and few women escaped some form of unwelcome pressure by their male supervisors and instructors. If a woman wore fashionable clothing and looked attractive, she was blamed for the aggressive behavior her appearance elicited. If a man looked good, however, it was assumed that women would behave like professionals and avoid aggressive behavior. (This asymmetry still exists.) Job placement was governed by male networks and word of mouth rather than by public advertisement and procedures embodying a notion of fair search. As a result, women were usually not recommended for jobs at the all-male Ivy League schools, and in many cases were low on the list of students to be placed, regardless of merit, often with the argument that they did not need to support a family whereas male students did. The first faculty committee formed at Harvard to consider the interests and grievances of women—headed by Caroline Bynum, then a powerless, untenured faculty member—led to charges that its members were unscholarly "agitators."

During this period Harvard began to consider fully integrating women into its undergraduate student body. For some time Radcliffe students had attended Harvard classes. Radcliffe had never had a separate faculty, so the separate identity of Radcliffe in the early 1970s served above all as a quota system for admissions. Radcliffe had a separate admissions office and a limit on its numbers, which ensured a roughly four-to-one male-to-female ratio. It was well known that the academic credentials of students admitted to Radcliffe were on average stronger than those of Harvard students. Thus full coeducation basically meant fewer places for men and more for women. While this discussion was in progress, a master of one of the Harvard residence halls received a letter from an alumnus asking for his view about equal admissions. His reply, published widely (presumably because the recipient found it somewhat shocking, a sign of better times to come), stated that Harvard should not be producing housewives and mothers the way Wellesley did, it should be producing male leaders. This statement, once published, was much criticized; and yet there was widespread awareness that it expressed a view that was commonly held though rarely uttered in public.

In such a climate, it is not surprising that there were few courses at Harvard that touched on women's lives, as there were few in any institution of that time. Female students and scholars, in general, and indeed all scholars and students, received the message that women's lives were not the stuff that serious scholarship was made of. This situation was typical in the academy.

By 1980, when Harvard created a committee on women's studies, many things had changed. Several Ivy League institutions had begun to study the problem of sexual harassment. Once sex blind admissions were adopted in most Ivy League institutions, the numbers of men and women in the student bodies rapidly became roughly equal. The number of women in graduate school and in at least the lower levels of many university and college faculties was increasing. Most of the fellowships that had previously been closed to women were opened.

Since the late 1960s, women had already been developing courses on women's issues in many disciplines; in some cases men had joined in this effort. Many of these courses were linked to the consciousness-raising efforts of the women's movement, just as the far-from-neutral status quo ante reflected a male political consciousness skeptical of women's full intellectual and civil equality. Yet there was no single political line that was espoused by these early teachers of women's studies—though all were committed to full equality for women in citizenship and opportunity. Then as now, the women's movement was full of debate, containing liberals and Marxists, communitarian defenders of caring and family along with advocates of gender separateness and self-sufficiency.[9] Even core values such as equality of opportunity were understood in different ways, as was the relation between feminism and sexuality.

At this time the increased number of women on college and university faculties, and of men concerned with women's issues, made it possible to develop new areas of research about women and to transform departmental curricula accordingly. Women's studies developed more rapidly in some departments than in others: history, for example, was one of the earliest. Many colleges and universities began interdisciplinary programs in women's studies, some offering undergraduate majors. Then as now, women's studies is carried on chiefly within traditional departments. Special programs tend to be poorly funded, and make few appointments on their own. An accurate account of what is going on in women's studies should therefore look both at departments and at the specialized programs, whose primary function is to stimulate interdisciplinary research and dialogue. Most courses that make up most undergraduate majors in women's studies are departmental courses, although they may be cross-listed in a special program.

Early proponents of women's studies had to confront a number of objections. The most common, then as now, was that these studies were motivated by a political agenda. Yet opponents could not truthfully assert that the old organization of study was apolitical; in countless ways, the traditional focus of scholarship reflected the highly political judgment that it was more important and more interesting to study the activities, bodies, and experiences of men. If opponents, recognizing this fact, continued to oppose women's studies on account of its political character, they would have to do so by making a substantive argument to show that the goals allegedly promoted by women's studies were bad goals, something that on the whole male scholars did not publicly do. Even if an objector were willing to argue that women should be confined to their traditional domestic roles and should not be allowed to take on an expanded role in the professions, it was hard to see how that conservative position could justify scholarly omissions and distortions of the type that new women's scholarship revealed. The best way to answer the charge of a suspect political motivation was, therefore, to keep producing good, truth-revealing work. That remains the best answer today, and it is because women's studies has proved its credentials in many areas that it has had a major influence not only on the academy but also on the law and on many other areas of our lives.

The second common objection, a more substantial one, was that women's studies does not form a single discipline with a single methodology. This was of course not a valid objection to pursuing women's studies within each department. Nor could it plausibly be thought a valid objection to the collaborative pursuit of research and scholarship at the faculty or graduate level, since it is well known that one discipline frequently learns from another. Psychologists cooperate with sociologists and biologists, philosophers with economists and political scientists, historians with specialists in music and art. Fields such as comparative literature, public policy, environmental studies, and classics are interdisciplinary in their very nature. On the other hand, such possibilities of fruitful collaboration do not suggest that each interdisciplinary focus should generate its own doctoral program. Women's studies in particular is such a vast field that it seemed then, and usually seems now, imprudent to offer a Ph.D. in it, both because the student in such a program might not have mastery of any single discipline and because he or she would not find a job. Interdisciplinary doctoral programs such as the University of Chicago's conservative Committee on Social Thought have sometimes generated exciting work; and yet their students almost always enter the academic job market at a disadvantage, encountering skepticism about whether they have really mastered any single set of techniques. Women's studies is in a comparable position.

Skepticism about disciplinary unity was less acute when the topic under discussion was an undergraduate major or concentration, but it still had some validity. The student who pursued a major in this "field" might not be mastering any recognized body of knowledge or preparing for any future career or job. Undergraduate programs in general, however, do not necessarily prepare students for a job; the whole point of a liberal arts education is to enrich the life of a citizen in far-reaching ways. Nonetheless, a student completing a major in women's studies should exhibit mastery of some structured body of knowledge. This problem also plagues many established disciplines. Classics, as currently practiced in the academy, is not a structured body of knowledge. The undergraduate classics major frequently emerges with a smattering of language, history, archaeology, philosophy, literature, and history of science, ranging over two cultures and twelve centuries. The new discipline of women's studies focused attention on this issue of disciplinary unity from the start. The most fruitful approach has been to base the interdisciplinary field firmly between the disciplines rather than apart from them. This type of interdisciplinarity required most faculty to be jointly appointed in an established discipline and, frequently, students to have a dual major, one of which is in a more established field. This practice had and has the additional advantage of integrating the new studies into the traditional disciplines and thereby transforming them.

Women's Studies and the Disciplines

By now, new scholarship about women's lives has transformed virtually every major discipline in the undergraduate curriculum in the social sciences and the humanities.[10] Transformations in the *content* of the disciplines are ubiquitous and easy to understand. Students now read more literary works by female writers, more religious texts by female thinkers, more about women's lives in various periods of history. Classes in biology are more likely to use a female body as an example of the human body alongside a male body, classes in psychology to use women as subjects alongside men. But the more profound contribution of women's studies, and the one that has proved more controversial, is its challenge to traditional methods of inquiry. Women's studies has asked new questions of the old data, sought new data in ways that require new methods, in some cases rejected the old methods as inadequate. These are the issues on which critics of women's studies focus, holding that a radical fringe has assailed standards in ways that damage scholarly inquiry. Any defense of women's studies should begin, then, by arguing that many of these transformations have been highly beneficial to the search for truth.

Philosophical theories of justice, like economic theories of distribution, have rarely considered the family as an institution to which basic insights about distributive justice and injustice must apply. Philosophers in women's studies have forced the field to confront this issue, challenging the reasons usually given for this neglect. Far from being a realm of love "beyond justice," the family, these scholars show, is a place where gross violations of justice frequently occur, as well as defects in moral development that mar children's capacity for just citizenship. Far from being a realm that exists "by nature," unaffected by legal and institutional factors, the family is shaped in countless ways by laws regulating marriage, divorce, and childrearing, and by general economic policies that govern people's opportunities and living standards.

Contemporary theorists of the family such as Jean Hampton, Virginia Held, Susan Moller Okin, and John Rawls—working, by and large, in close connection to the tradition of Kantian liberalism—have asked how legal changes could promote respect for women's worth and autonomy, and ensure norms of fair equality of opportunity; others have addressed issues of child welfare and the legal definition of parental responsibility.[11]

The new focus on women's lives has also opened other fruitful areas of inquiry neglected by conventional male philosophy. New attention has been given to important human phenomena such as love and imagination, and to the role they play in a truly rational judgment. Emotions such as love of a child, fear for that child's welfare, grief at the death of a parent are held to be not mindless unreasoning forces, but intelligent ways of recognizing the importance of what is occurring. A person who does not respond emotionally could properly be criticized, not only as callous, but also as not fully rational. These ideas about emotion and judgment are not altogether new in the history of Western philosophy. Some of them, for example, were adumbrated by Aristotle, who, despite his misogynistic attitude toward real-life women, said many things that contemporary feminists find appealing.[12] Philosophers such as Rousseau and John Dewey also played a part in their development. Nor do all feminist philosophers hold a single position on these issues; they disagree strongly not only about the proper analysis of emotions but also about how reliable emotions are. But before women's studies began to influence philosophy there was little support for this whole line of inquiry; it would have been scorned as soft and slightly embarrassing. Feminist scholars deserve most of the credit for restoring these topics to the agenda of the profession.[13] In a related domain, the explanation of scientific rationality, feminists have again broken new ground, insisting on the role of affiliation and cooperation in the process of knowledge acquisition. Again, these claims are not altogether new in the history of thought: many of them, for example, can be found in the work of David Hume.[14] But feminist thought has played a major role in their contemporary articulation.

Not all challenges to traditional professional philosophy have been equally successful. Some challenges to notions of objectivity and rationality have been unconvincing—especially when they have suggested that the very norm of objectivity, of a judgment free from bias and distortion, is a mythical male ideal that we should jettison. Feminist argument, from Plato onward, has depended on the ability to distinguish between a judgment that is truly objective and truly rational, and one that is tainted by bias and prejudice. That distinction is not always easy to discern; philosophers will rightly differ not only about where to draw the line but also about what concepts are useful in articulating a norm of objectivity (whether, for example, an emotion-based judgment is by definition nonobjective). They will also differ about whether an objective judgment should be said to require truths that are altogether independent of human experience and history (most thinkers today would deny this). But our best accounts of the limits of human understanding do not imply that we should abandon our norms of rationality and objective truth. The Society for Analytical Feminism, a satellite organization of the American Philosophical Association, has actively promoted rigorous debate about these questions; two of its leading members have recently published an excellent anthology showing the importance for feminism of ideas of truth, objectivity, and rationality.[15] The profession now has a lively exchange about these matters in which no starting point, methodological or empirical, remains unchallenged.

In classics, until 1975, there was no reliable history of the lives of women in the ancient world. Many of the most important sources for these lives were neglected and unedited texts and documents. History was written primarily as political history, including the history of personal connections among influential males. The techniques most often used by ancient historians, which focused on textual and inscriptional evidence, were insufficient to write the lives of women. The reading of documentary papyri is a highly specialized skill possessed by only a handful of experts, none of whom had been interested enough in women to use it extensively to that end. Yet two decades later we know a great deal about the lives of women in ancient Greece and Rome. Sarah Pomeroy's pioneering work on women's lives in ancient Greece derived, in the first instance, from her expert training in the reading of papyri.[16] But she and her followers have also had to correlate these findings with the reconstruction of data about propertyholding and inheritance, with evidence about religious cult practices, and with the evidence of visual art and archaeology. Each piece of evidence representing women had to be carefully sifted for its origins, since little of it will have been written by women. Such work, like work on ancient homosexuality, requires scholars who can go back to the beginning, assuming that nothing is really known, and forge techniques by which real knowledge can be gained. Since this work has produced new questions in a field that for a long time lacked new challenges, it has become a focal point for young scholars. The new edition of the *Oxford Classical Dictionary*, a standard (and very mainstream) reference work, now has an editor for women's subjects in order to ensure that this new scholarship is integrated into articles on many different topics.

"The prism of gender" in classics has revised many established ideas about the ancient world, including standard characterizations of the ancient economy. Before scholars in women's studies came on the scene, the dominant methodological approaches to the study of the ancient economy, whether Marxist or neoclassical, failed to take into account the central role of the household and its "domestic economy." As Sarah Pomeroy characterizes the situation, the economy of the household was standardly treated "as part of a primitive world predating the formation of the polis."[17] This approach was anachronistic, distorting the reality of ancient Greece to make it fit modern categories. And yet it took the dogged effort of scholars in women's studies, insisting on a focus on women's experience, to gain recognition for questions that are now acknowledged to be central to the proper study of the ancient world.

The new focus on women's lives requires new paradigms of instruction in the undergraduate curriculum. A course focused on "great books" of the ancient world will rightly be seen as unable to convey an accurate and complete sense of what the ancient Greek and Roman world was like. To give a full picture, teachers will need to go beyond the most famous literary and philosophical texts, consulting sourcebooks and other presentations of data in order to discover the lives of ancient women. Even specialized courses in the literature or art or philosophy of the ancient world should set the texts in their historical context, which contained women as well as men.

In anthropology, women's lives have been a focus of research since the days of Margaret Mead, and the field was among the earliest to understand the importance of taking women's points of view into account when describing a society. Recent research in social anthropology has emphasized the importance of the concepts of emotion used by a society, asking how fear and anger and love function in transactions between people and in their dealings with the natural world.[18] This new methodological emphasis has involved correction of some common male paradigms of rationality. These tended to contrast emotion with reason in an excessively simple way, denying that emotions could ever be sources of information. Anthropologists—led by those with a feminist orientation, such as Catherine Lutz and the late Michelle Rosaldo—were quick to see the extent to which a culture's norms of appropriate anger, shame, grief, and love expressed evaluations, not simply unintelligent biological reactions.[19] They proposed a new research project for observers of society: the precise description of the society's emotion taxonomy and its relation to behavior and to social norms. This new research focus has led to corresponding transformations in the understanding of social dynamics.

In physical anthropology, feminist scholars have again produced new methods and questions. When researchers describe the behavior of a primate species, they often use human concepts. Behavior becomes intelligible to them on the basis of their own experience; thus they project onto the primate's behavior perceptions conditioned by the habitual norms of their world. This approach does not always lead to good data-gathering. Male primatologists depicted primate gender roles in a manner strongly influenced by their assumptions about human female roles: the female primate, they repeatedly said, was "coy" in her courting behavior, reserving her sexual favors for the male who won the courting competition. This projection led to distortion. It had long been known that females in other animal species— birds, cats, certain fish—accept multiple sexual partners, though this phenomenon had been ignored in most studies—largely, concludes primatologist Sarah Blaffer Hrdy, "because theoretically the phenomenon should not have existed and therefore there was little theoretical infrastructure for studying it." Only when a substantial number of female researchers got involved in primate research was it noticed that similar promiscuous behavior is present in quite a few primate species. Female sexual initiative, female promiscuity, and other forms of female control are ubiquitous features of primate life. Indeed, Hrdy concludes, it seems likely "that a polyandrous component is at the core of the breeding systems of most troop-dwelling primates: females mate with many males, each of whom may contribute a little bit toward the survival of the offspring." It took the perspective of female researchers to notice aspects of primate behavior that had been there all the time. These findings have thrown sexual selection theory into a state of upheaval, previous male bias has been generally acknowledged, and new research has focused intensively on female reproductive strategies.[20]

What explains the fact that it took "the prism of gender" to introduce these observations? Some studies, Hrdy notes, indicate that female researchers are simply better field observers—on average, they perform better on tests measuring recognition and tracking of particular species members over time, an ability crucial to the detection of polyandry. But Hrdy concludes that the most important factor is that females were more capable of imaginative empathy with the female primates being studied, more capable of supplying an imaginative narrative that put together pieces of observed behavior in a coherent way. (She stresses that this could lead to error, and suggests that the best strategy for avoiding error is to establish a diverse and mutually critical research community.) We may add, as well, that male researchers may have had a strong desire to imagine the "natural order" in a certain way, with females firmly relegated to a position of chaste domesticity, and this narrative bias may simply have marred their vision. As Hrdy says: "When generalizations persist for decades after evidence invalidating them is also known, can there be much doubt that some bias was involved?"[21]

Dutch researcher Frans de Waal has recently added to these criticisms evidence that the very selection of species to describe displayed a bias in favor of familiar human gender roles. Chimps, whose society is to at least some extent patriarchal, with male sexual initiative, have been extensively researched and form a primary basis for accounts of our own alleged sociobiological evolutionary heritage. But the bonobos of Zaire, who are just as close to us genetically as chimps, show an altogether different pattern: female initiative in sexual matters, a society kept at peace by constant sexual activity and surprisingly deficient in aggression. Bonobos were not discovered until 1929, but soon after that a great deal was known about them, including their remarkable closeness to humans—they share about 98 percent of our genetic makeup. Sociobiologists in the 1970s, however, made chimps their species of choice. As a result of this deliberate decision, writes de Waal, "male superiority remained the natural state of affairs," since chimp males "reign supremely and often brutally." Not so the bonobo, whose whole physical style, graceful and nonaggressive, differs sharply from that of the chimp—in the way, says de Waal, that a Concorde differs from a Boeing 747. As intelligent as chimpanzees, bonobos appear to have a more sensitive temperament, and are unusually imaginative in play and joking. Most striking are the ubiquity of sexual contact and its diversity—including frequent male-male, female-female, and male-female contact, and, in terms of acts, oral sex and prolonged kissing in addition to the more usual primate repertoire of vaginal and anal acts. De Waal writes that our view of our evolutionary heritage would have been utterly different had bonobos, rather than chimps, been the species of choice for researchers: we would have believed "that early hominids lived in female-centered societies, in which sex served important social functions and in which warfare was rare or absent."[22] Once again, scientific methods that claimed to be objective really were not objective and did not attain the whole truth—or even amass the entirety of the data.

These are only three fields out of the dozens in the humanities and social sciences. Similar stories could be told about every other field. In religious studies, women's studies has produced new accounts of women's religious lives in ancient societies, new proposals in religious ethics emphasizing the roles of compassion and care, new theological accounts of divinity. In psychology, "the prism of gender" has opened up new avenues of research into the social learning of gender roles, the psychology of the emotions, and the attitudes of the two sexes to intimacy. In history, the new attention to women's lives has prompted a shift in paradigms of research and teaching: at this point social history focused on daily life is at least as creative and lively a field as political history. Like Socrates' gadfly, women's studies has challenged every discipline to wake up, to confront new arguments. Usually this has led to profound transformations, both in the content of knowledge and in methodology.

The Women's Studies Classroom: Indoctrination?

In her recent book *Who Stole Feminism?* philosopher Christina Hoff Sommers grants that here and there we find "some solid scholarly courses offered by women's studies programs, where the goal is simply to teach subjects like women's poetry or women's history in a nonrevisionist way." Such courses, however, are not the norm, she contends: most women's studies courses are heavily "ideological," committed to a process of political conversion that disdains reasoned argument and traditional scholarly standards in favor of a process of "consciousness raising" that resembles "indoctrination."[23]

Sommers' contrast assumes what it purports to argue, namely that new "revisionist" approaches cannot be "solid" or "scholarly," supplying genuine illumination. Yet even the few examples presented above demonstrate that solid scholarship in many cases required revision of traditional methods. There would have been no way to teach women's history had women-oriented scholars like Herlihy and Pomeroy not pioneered the techniques to do such work. There would have been no way to teach about sexual initiative in female primates had "revisionist" female primatologists not come on the scene. There would have been no way to talk about the contribution of family love to human rationality had the paradigms of social rationality currently in use not been broadened to include the roles of emotion.

Is the feminist classroom a place of indoctrination instead of a place of reasoned debate? Hoff Sommers' claim has been echoed by former women's studies professors Daphne Patai and Noretta Kortge, in their book *Professing Feminism.*[24] Their claim is weakened by certain aspects of their study. Like Hoff Sommers, they base their conclusions on a small number of anecdotes, and professors interviewed for the volume make their comments anonymously. It is easy to find disgruntled individuals in any profession, and it is difficult to weigh such anonymous claims. Moreover, both researchers examine only courses offered in programs labeled "Women's Studies," rather than looking at the much larger number of courses offered by scholars of women's studies in traditional departments, frequently in direct response to the research and cross-fertilization generated by interdisciplinary programs.

The full impact of women's studies can be assessed only by examining the treatment of women's lives across the whole breadth of the curriculum. Nor do these authors ask whether the amount of conformity in women's studies is any greater that what we would find in economics, or classics, or musicology.

What is indoctrination, and how is it different from regular instruction? Indoctrination, suggests Hoff Sommers, is characterized by three features: the major conclusions are assumed beforehand, rather than being open to question in the classroom; the conclusions are presented as part of a "unified set of beliefs" that form a comprehensive worldview; and the system is "closed," committed to interpreting all new data in the light of the theory being affirmed.[25]

Whether this account gives us sufficient conditions for indoctrination, and whether, so defined, all indoctrination is bad college pedagogy, may certainly be debated. According to these criteria, for example, all but the most philosophical and adventurous courses in neoclassical economics will count as indoctrination, since undergraduate students certainly are taught the major conclusions of that field as established truths which they are not to criticize from the perspective of any other theory or worldview; they are taught that these truths form a unitary way of seeing the world; and, especially where microeconomics is concerned, the data of human behavior are presented as seen through the lens of that theory. It is probably good that these conditions obtain at the undergraduate level, where one cannot simultaneously learn the ropes and criticize them—although one might hope that the undergraduate will pick up in other courses, for example courses in moral philosophy, the theoretical apparatus needed to raise critical questions about these foundations.

Nor will a first-year American medical student be permitted to debate the merits of Western medicine from the viewpoint of alternative medical paradigms, such as acupuncture or Ayurvedic medicine. Again, there is some merit in this situation, since intellectual apprenticeship needs intense focusing within a single paradigm. Mathematics and physics, as taught at the undergraduate level, have all three of Hoff Sommers' features, and this is almost certainly a good thing. One probably should try to learn college mathematics and to engage in foundational theoretical questioning about the nature of number at the same time.

Hoff Sommers' scare term *indoctrination* has not yet succeeded in isolating a phenomenon that is really bad; more argumentation is surely needed. In particular, it would be important to spell out how much ought to go unquestioned in a class on issues in social thought generally. Does Hoff Sommers object, for example, to taking it as given that slavery is bad, or that cruelty is to be avoided? Surely most courses in moral and political philosophy make such assumptions—unless their purpose is to focus on debates about precisely that foundational issue. If they did not rely on some core of moral judgments—which, of course, can always be questioned in the context of some other inquiry—they would lack a moral bedrock on which to test the explanatory adequacy of the competing ethical theories. And yet we would have a hard time concluding that rational debate could not go on within that framework.

But should we even grant that women's studies courses and the scholarship associated with them are typically characterized by the three features Hoff Sommers finds problematic? It is admittedly difficult to teach issues that lie deep in people's personal lives. A judicious instructor will exercise unusual sensitivity when discussing rape, or child sexual abuse, or attitudes to pornography. Many basic courses in criminal law do not address the topic of rape for precisely this reason, and those that do so exercise special care to promote a sensitive atmosphere in the classroom. For example, at the University of Chicago, Stephen Schulhofer, author of the first basic criminal law casebook to have a full chapter on rape, spends a lot of time preparing students for the topic and discussing the likelihood that the class contains victims of the crime.[26] While the tension in the class remains palpable, a wide-ranging discussion is promoted, and many different views are expressed.

Not all classrooms address such tensions this well. On several campuses I studied, students complain that some of their courses seem more like therapy sessions lacking in rigor—although typically these courses are singled out as exceptions that one can learn to avoid. Another common complaint is that men are made to feel uncomfortable in some courses—and even, on occasion, discouraged from attending. Here as in the case of African-American studies, we should strongly object to any such practice, and we should applaud the fact that it is becoming rare. At Brown, the course "Feminist Philosophy" in 1994–95 was about 50 percent male; this is an excellent result, since the issues studied by the course—the situation of women in developing countries, theories of justice in the family, pornography, domestic violence—are topics that it is at least as important for men to think about as for women.

Finally, a number of courses I visited seemed to err in the direction of withholding criticism. Feminists often feel that they are such an embattled minority that they should seek solidarity, viewing any public criticism of another woman as bad form or even betrayal. This shrinking from criticism is, however, profoundly subversive of the central aim of women's studies, which is to establish scholarly inquiry about women as a central part of a university education. Ultimately this goal can be attained only by establishing an outspoken and truly Socratic critical culture.

But charges of indoctrination and politicization cannot be adjudicated in the abstract. We can best proceed by selecting a single area and looking in depth at representative examples of teaching. Since philosophy has always been an area of special importance to women's studies, providing it with much of its theoretical basis, let us return to that field. Do philosophical courses about women's issues exhibit a single party line and an atmosphere closed to critical debate?

Philosophical courses on women's issues cover a wide range of topics, and topics relating to women may also be raised within many standard philosophy courses in moral and political philosophy, theory of knowledge, and philosophy of mind. At Princeton University, political theorist Amy Gutmann has examined arguments for and against abortion in a basic moral problems course. At Brown, philosopher David Estlund teaches freedom of expression, focusing for a substantial portion of the course on feminist arguments about pornography. At Syracuse University, philosopher Linda Alcoff focuses on women's attitudes to knowledge, examining the claim that women have a distinctive contribution to make to the process of knowledge acquisition in science. At the University of Houston, philosopher Cynthia Freeland examines the contribution that Aristotle, despite his misogyny, can make to the development of feminist ethics. At the University of New Hampshire, Aristotle scholar Charlotte Witt examines the claims made by several recent feminist writers that we should not speak of women as sharing any common "essence." My own course in feminist philosophy at Brown focused on problems faced by women in developing countries, using these issues to pose the problem of what standards we should use when assessing the practices of another culture. Other courses focus on justice within the family, on the nature of the emotions, and on the relationship between autonomy and community. There is no one way to teach feminist philosophy, no standard list of problems; but the standard philosophical problems in all these areas frequently reveal a new complexity when examined from the point of view of women's experience.

This heterogeneity of topics already creates difficulties for the hypothesis that there is a single feminist "party line." But how are the diverse topics themselves considered? On every campus I visited, I found vigorous debate about the merits of different philosophical positions, both within a given classroom and across classrooms. At Brown, to take just one example, teachers and students in philosophy courses differ strongly about violent pornography. Some argue that violent pornographic materials are liberating to women's sexuality, some that they are morally objectionable and supportive of women's social subordination. A campus forum, set up when a recruiter from *Playboy* came to campus, staged these differences vividly, as my colleague David Estlund and I debated each other, and students in turn argued the merits of our respective cases. There are also sharp differences about the value of universal categories such as "human rights" and "human flourishing" in addressing the concerns of women in other parts of the world. Some students argue that standards of evaluation should derive from the local culture; others defend universal norms. This is typical of the situation on most campuses.

Philosophers in the Western tradition are followers of Socrates. Choice of that profession reveals a commitment to the human value of reason. Even if a philosopher has strong views about a topic, she does not want her students to take those views on trust; she wants to impart tools with which the student can herself reach a justified conclusion. Thus even instructors who have arrived at strong views of their own about the morality and legality of pornography typically seek a vigorous classroom debate on the issue. Indeed, the likely presence of diverse opinions is what makes the topic so interesting to teach: in pursuing this diversity to its source, we arrive at complex underlying issues about the value of art, the connection between fantasy and action, the moral worth of privacy. A large proportion of philosophers who teach women's issues probably would favor a duly qualified right of choice on abortion, whatever their own personal moral and religious views; and yet when the topic is taught in the philosophy classroom, it is taught precisely in order to uncover the arguments for and against this right. The students' conclusions are always less important, in this academic field, than the quality of their arguments. Philosophy teachers are not cheerleaders. Whether or not they reveal their own personal conclusions on an issue—a matter on which instructors differ—they typically view unanimity in the classroom as a sign that they have failed in their task. Since recent feminist inquiries have raised challenges to received philosophical positions about knowledge, scientific inquiry, and the nature of reason itself, the feminist philosophy classroom is actually less given to "indoctrination" than are many other philosophy classrooms, which often take received views for granted. And even when it is the traditional norm of reason that is being challenged, feminist philosophers typically challenge with arguments that are highly rational and logical.

Feminist philosophy teachers, in short, have no "party line" to impart to their students, any more than they agree on a single view in their scholarship. They include Rawlsian liberals, Utilitarians, followers of the "discourse ethics" of Jürgen Habermas, postmodernists, analytic philosophers of science, theorists of "care ethics," Wittgensteinian communitarians, and many others, including religious ethicists both conservative and liberal. Mary Ann Glendon, who led the Vatican delegation to the United Nations Conference on Women, is a feminist political thinker; so too are lesbian separatist feminists, who would disagree with many of Glendon's concrete ethical conclusions—although the two types could agree about the importance of combatting violence against women, women's hunger, and women's unequal education. On no major theoretical proposition in feminism would we get general agreement from all current groups, except perhaps the proposition that women should be treated as ends rather than as means to the ends of others, and also that this situation does not yet obtain universally in the world in which we live.

Feminist philosophy, like women's studies generally, has developed in close connection with the political aims of feminism. Reflecting about issues of sex inequality is hard to separate from an interest in reform. Much feminist teaching about women has made these connections. This does not seem to be a bad thing. To see what one takes to be an urgent human need and not to care whether that need ever gets addressed would appear to be a defect of character, a false kind of detachment that is not a virtue in the academic life. That is why most faculty teaching women's issues in philosophy would call themselves "feminists"—meaning, broadly, that they have a practical political interest in social justice for women.

Such a connection between theory and practice, however, is not something new in the Western philosophical tradition. In Plato's *Republic,* Socrates reminds his conversation partners that "it is no chance matter we are discussing, but how one should live" (352D). Reaching conclusions about life should be closely connected to attempts to put those conclusions into practice. Aristotle argues that the goal of moral and political philosophy ought to be "not theory but practice."[27] The Hellenistic philosophers who followed him strongly concurred, holding that the philosopher or political thinker was like a doctor, who did not fulfill his task if he just talked about the state of the patient and made no recommendations for cure. This paradigm of a committed and worldly philosophy profoundly influenced distinguished modern political thinkers, such as Locke, Kant, and Mill, all of whom closely connected their theoretical analyses to practical political concerns. And yet the same critics who charge feminists with a political agenda are slow to make such criticisms of Mill's *On Liberty* or Kant's *Perpetual Peace.*

To illustrate these general claims let us now examine three sample classrooms—focusing, again, on philosophy, broadly construed. Eve Stoddard's Cultural Encounters course on the female body at St. Lawrence begins from a rigorously developed theoretical basis. Students (most of whom have no previous philosophy background) learn to define precisely concepts such as "cultural relativism" and "ethnocentrism" and to differentiate them. The committed relativist makes claims to universality for his moral position, saying that all cultures should be evaluated only on their own terms, and no culture should interfere with the values and practices of another. An ethnocentrist simply speaks from within a single culture, claiming that his or her culture is founded on the principles and practices that are appropriate for all. Much of the course is spent on examining paradoxes in the relativist position: how can a relativist make this universal claim, when so many cultures are themselves nonrelativist and use nonrelative criteria of evaluation? How can the relativist consistently defend a no-interference policy toward other cultures, when it is obvious that many cultures believe in interfering with the practices of others? Then not to interfere will be to countenance interference. Such general discussions are woven through the course.

Stoddard's teaching is guided by her own scholarship on Kant's moral philosophy and its influence on Wordsworth.[28] She writes eloquently about the development of the idea of personal autonomy in the eighteenth century, and these concepts clearly influence her own approach to women's issues. Her manuscript on Kant and Wordsworth includes extensive criticism of some contemporary feminists (psychologist Carol Gilligan and others influenced by her) who have been understood to denigrate the concept of autonomy. Stoddard (along with feminist philosophers Barbara Herman and Onora O'Neill) stresses that Kant's idea of autonomy does not deny the importance of bodily need, friendship, and community.[29] Kant offers, in fact, a valuable paradigm for contemporary feminists who seek relationships in which each party is truly self-governing.

Student writing in a course is one index of what a professor has communicated and of the atmosphere prevailing in a classroom. Papers from Stoddard's Cultural Encounters course show that some first-year St. Lawrence students do not write very well—and Stoddard is plainly distressed by this fact, spending a good deal of time correcting grammar and style. But in this course they are learning to think for themselves about these very controversial issues. Stoddard has evidently fostered a climate of vigorous disagreement and mutual respect. She does not conceal her own nonrelativist moral view, but she makes it clear to students that the aim of the course is to produce good arguments, not to agree with the instructor. The paper receiving the highest grade is one with which she vigorously disagrees—a defense of a "hands off" relativist position toward female circumcision. "Because it is impossible to judge a practice so foreign to our own conception of establishing social identity," writes Student Q (a male), "it is better to take a neutral position on the issue, and to accept . . . choices made by a culture with graciousness." Stoddard writes in the margin, "Where do you draw the line? If a country were slaughtering all male children, should we intervene?" As the argument unfolds, Stoddard commends parts of Q's strategy—his insistence, for example, that internal critique and opposition are likely to be more knowledgeable and precise than Western judgment at a distance; she commends his careful exegesis of material about two African cultures from books read in the course. She asks some hard questions about his claim that outsider Alice Walker should not have criticized African practices. Why not? she asks. And is this always so? Q concludes that the West has its own domestic problems of hunger, homelessness, violence, and inequality to attend to, and should get those fixed before casting aspersions on Africa. Stoddard expresses her disagreement with Q in her comment, and commends his argument and his class participation generally.

Student R (a female) addresses the issue of circumcision by focusing on Jomo Kenyatta's claim that female circumcision is a practice that symbolically cements cultural identity, rather like Jewish male circumcision. R is not convinced by this argument. It may be true, she says, as Kenyatta argues, that female circumcision helps males of a tribe bond together and gives women the right to be married by men with status and power. But Kenyatta, she argues, has not sufficiently considered the point of view of the women themselves, and their interest in self-respect and control over their lives. "The conflict between the traditional and dehumanizing aspects of circumcision needs to be examined further . . . Doctors and operators need to discuss the harmful effects of circumcision through community talks and religious teachings." R writes awkwardly and diffusely, and Stoddard comments repeatedly on this, letting her know that she has a strong argument, but one whose effectiveness is undermined by poor writing skills. She receives a lower grade than Q.

The St. Lawrence class shows feminist discussion going on in the context of rigorous theoretical argument and extensive empirical reading. Students have been enabled to confront some very hard, distressing moral issues about women's lives in an atmosphere of vigorous Socratic disagreement. If Stoddard has not entirely succeeded in making up for the uneven preparation of her students in reading and writing, she has certainly produced a group of more thoughtful world citizens, prepared to exchange ideas reflectively in a world that is increasingly committed to supporting women's rights to bodily autonomy.

At Washington University in St. Louis, philosopher Marilyn Friedman holds a seminar in "Topics in Feminist Philosophy." The enrollment is half undergraduate and half graduate; there are eight women and two men. The course works through four recent books in feminist political thought, one being Friedman's own *What Are Friends For? Feminist Perspectives on Personal Relationships and Moral Theory.*[30] Friedman argues in the book that some criticisms made by feminists against traditional moral philosophy are correct: philosophy has spent far too little time thinking about friendship, family, and other close personal relationships. She holds that a good description of ethical reasoning must include not only abstract concerns of justice but also an empathic consideration of the interests of particular others. But Friedman is critical of some of the "care theorists" for their lack of concern with questions of fairness. She insists that love and friendship can flourish best in an atmosphere in which justice is guaranteed to all; and she warns that displacing justice in favor of community may leave feminists with no way to criticize traditions that denigrate or oppress them. A witty, determined woman in her forties, Friedman (whose husband, Larry May, is also in the Washington University Philosophy Department) adopts a Socratic style of teaching, in which students form their views by dialogue and debate, with little imposition of authority from Friedman herself.

When I visited Friedman's class, the book under discussion was Iris Young's *Justice and the Politics of Difference,* a defense of strong participatory democracy against more traditional liberal norms of impartiality.[31] The seminar was conducted as a dialogue among the students. Karen Hoffman, a graduate student visiting from St. Louis University, presented a clear summary of the argument of Young's chapter attacking impartiality. Hoffman then raised some pointed questions for Young's account: how can the democratic process protect its own values of openness and tolerance without appeal to some universal norms of a traditional liberal kind? What does Young's open and inclusive dialogue do with people who use the openness to preach intolerance or hate? Should the fact that someone stands up and says "I feel this way" count in discourse and public policy, especially if that person can't give any reasons for what has been said? And finally, if Young rejects consensus as a democratic goal, what does she offer to take its place? The students debated these points for ninety minutes, with only brief interventions from Friedman. Their opinions and backgrounds seemed highly diverse, ranging from the conservative-libertarian to the radically egalitarian. If there was a party line in the classroom, it was that some communitarian criticisms of liberalism had been successful; even this conclusion did not go unargued. Friedman's class seemed to me full of lively debate, balanced and judicious in its treatment of Young's book, and noteworthy for the fact that almost every student participated strongly, and with good humor. The plurality of opinions was so obvious that one student, discussing Young's critique of consensus as a political goal, said as a joke, "Maybe this room will have a consensus!"

Stanford University has an undeserved reputation as the home of fanatical multiculturalism, of radical approaches to cultural diversity that scorn the great works of the Western tradition.[32] To judge from those caricatures, a women's studies class at Stanford could be expected to be a place of strident polemic against the West and ill-argued proposals for change. This is not the case in Susan Moller Okin's course "Gender and Political Theory," Political Science 266 or Feminist Studies 270. Okin describes the course as follows:

> We shall read and analyze major works and parts of works from the Western tradition of political thought, viewing them through the prism of gender. In order to understand better the ideological roots of inequalities between the sexes, we'll examine the ways in which assumptions about sexual difference have shaped some of the central concepts of the tradition, including reason, nature, politics, justice, and the separation of public from private life. Different and sometimes contrasting interpretations of the primary sources will also be read and discussed.

Okin is a serene, soft-spoken woman in her late forties, whose gentle style of lecturing does not conceal a powerful theoretical mind and a wide command of fact. Her own personal commitments to her husband and children are evident in almost any exchange with her, and yet she also maintains a position of sympathy and fairness toward women who have different views of the best way to live. Interacting with women from seven different countries at an international meeting on women's rights, for example, she was among the most effective Americans in establishing a rapport with the other women present, whatever their attitudes to the traditional family. I have observed the same responsiveness and care in her interactions with students.

Okin's course follows closely the outline of her own much-praised book *Women in Western Political Thought*.[33] In that work she analyzes arguments for and against women's equality in a variety of writers, including, most prominently, Plato, Aristotle, Rousseau, and Mill. (Okin has also edited Mill's *The Subjection of Women*, and her own *Justice, Gender, and the Family* owes a large debt both to Mill and to Kant.)[34] In general, Okin's concern is to show that from the very beginning of the Western political tradition there have been two strands of thought about women: one, exemplified by Plato and Mill, that raises skeptical doubts about claims of "natural" difference and demands a full equality of opportunity for women, together with social circumstances designed to minimize the impact of traditional hierarchy on women's development. A second strand, exemplified in different ways by

Aristotle and Rousseau, begins from the assertion of innate immutable difference and derives moral imperatives from those starting points, defending
asymmetrical roles for men and women. Okin is severely critical of the
second group of thinkers for ignoring the arguments of the first group. She
finds no solid argument backing the claims of innate difference—this is what
she means by the claim that the roots of these ideas are "ideological." They
express, in her view, a vested interest in the status quo of sex asymmetry
rather than a disinterested search for truth. At the same time, however, she
shows how a complex and distinguished thinker such as Rousseau actually
argues on more than one side of the issue, and one of the outstanding parts
of the book is Okin's treatment of internal tensions in Rousseau's thought.

The stance from which Okin herself approaches the material, as her
Justice, Gender, and the Family shows, is that of a liberal in the Kantian
tradition, profoundly committed to both political and economic equality for
women. At the same time, that work offers a strong defense of the family,
as an institution essential to the well-being and moral education of children.
Okin's project is to show that this institution, which has sheltered great
harms and inequalities, can in fact be just, and to argue that justice would
not subvert, but would very much improve, the ability of its members to
share love and impart virtue.

Okin's course readings are drawn largely from the major works of the
Western political tradition: Plato, Aristotle, Aquinas, Hobbes, Locke, Rousseau, and Mill, along with relevant articles from the secondary literature. As
the course description announces, the course focuses on these writers
through "the prism of gender," asking what each has had to say about gender
relations and the inner workings of the family. The assumption of the course
is that the family and the distribution of rights and resources within it are
important topics of political theory—so it is fair to ask how any major
theorist has handled them.

Following the lead of Mill, Okin dissects the concept of "nature," showing
how many different things it has meant in philosophical argument, and how
easily thinkers have slipped from one sense of the term to another, in ways
that render their arguments invalid. People frequently infer from the fact
that something is customary the conclusion that it is fitting and proper, the
way things should be. Even a fact that is not just customary but also innate
would not be for that reason alone "fitting and proper": for, Okin emphasizes repeatedly, many things with which people come into the world are

not so good, and we try to change them. We must ask, as Mill reminds us, whether we know anything at all about innate differences between men and women. Mill believes that we do not, since we have seen men and women only under conditions of inequality. But even if we did have a good argument for saying that there are innate differences, we would still need to make a further argument to show that these differences should have some political weight.

Students in Okin's course will not emerge skeptical about all rational argument in politics—for they will have seen, studying Plato and Mill through Okin's eyes, a strong defense of the value of reason in securing justice. But they will emerge more skeptical about the *pose* or *claim* of rationality, and better able to dissect arguments, asking whether they are sound or are based on mere habit or prejudice.

Courses such as Okin's, Friedman's, and Stoddard's produce better citizens, citizens better able to sort through complex issues about women that they will almost certainly need to handle in their lives, public and private. These discussions are valuable for all students, not only for women. Each campus should think how to incorporate these questions and perspectives into basic, core courses, so that all undergraduates will have at least a brief experience of looking at history through "the prism of gender."

The philosophical part of women's studies is doing its job well. Such high standards are also the norm in classics and in history, and in empirical courses in anthropology, political science, sociology, and economics. Such courses may indeed leave some basic notions unchallenged. For example, courses on women's hunger and nutrition, such as those taught by Valerie Hudson at Brigham Young and Amartya Sen at Harvard, typically leave unchallenged the assumptions that it is bad for any human being to die prematurely from malnutrition, and morally unacceptable that a human being should suffer these bad things on account of sex. This seems a good place to begin an academic discussion of hunger. If this is indoctrination, then most good teaching in social science involves indoctrination.

In literature, we find imaginative and innovative teaching—like that of Judith Frank at Amherst, focused on the detailed investigation of a period and the role of works by and about women in the literary history of the period. Literary theory inspired by deconstruction does produce empty jargon and argument lacking in the rigor that one should demand of human-istic argument. Scholars influenced by it teach some bad classes—empty, windy, and contemptuous of argument. But this is a problem for the pro-fession as a whole, and certainly not a particular problem for feminism. Feminist criticism has retained an ethical foundation in a way that much literary work has not, since feminist critics have on the whole remained focused on issues of justice and equality. Nor have feminist critics been quick to take the view that all criticism is play, since they have thought, rightly, that serious issues are at stake in the evaluation of a literary work. They are the heirs, on the whole, of ethical critics such as F. R. Leavis and Lionel Trilling far more than of deconstruction, even and especially when they raise uncomfortable questions that Leavis and Trilling did not raise and look at familiar texts from a new moral viewpoint.

Feminist Thought, Deformed Preferences, and Democracy

If all this is so, and if the scare term *indoctrination* does not capture anything of real importance that marks off women's studies from other academic fields, what is the real source of anxiety among the critics of the new field? It would seem to be, ultimately, a concern about the content of some views commonly taught by feminist thinkers, especially thinkers in political theory and philosophy. Hoff Sommers, for example, says that contemporary femi-nists are committed to a view that is radical and highly dangerous to de-mocracy. "Respect for people's preferences is generally thought to be fun-damental for democracy," Hoff Sommers observes in a chapter titled "The Gender Wardens"; any feminist who holds that on occasion women may be wrong about their true interests, as many feminists do, is "prepared to dis-miss popular preferences in an illiberal way."[35]

If this critique is correct, despite all that has been said so far, it seems plausible that women's studies is indeed based on a dangerously radical political agenda. What, more precisely, are the views that Hoff Sommers is worried about? She cites feminist philosopher Marilyn Friedman:

Liberal feminists can easily join with other feminists in recognizing that political democracy by itself is insufficient to ensure that prefer-ences are formed without coercion, constraint, undue restriction of options, and so forth. Social, cultural, and economic conditions are as important as political conditions, if not more so, in ensuring that preferences are, in some important sense, authentic.[36]

Friedman is "quite wrong", says Hoff Sommers: "anyone, liberal or conservative, who believes in democracy will sense danger in" her ideas. "Who," she asks, "will 'ensure' that preferences are 'authentic'? What additions to political democracy does Friedman have in mind? A constitutional amendment to provide reeducation camps for men and women of false consciousness?"[37]

Such ideas about preferences, she continues, might have had some truth in the days when Mill uttered them—for in those days women were not only taught that their own subjugation was "fitting and natural"; they were also prevented from changing things by voting. But now that women have the vote, "their preferences are being taken into account." So we must reject the idea that any criticism of their preferences is appropriate or even admissible. "Since women today can no longer be regarded as the victims of an undemocratic indoctrination, we must regard their preferences as 'authentic.' Any other attitude to American women is unacceptably patronizing and profoundly illiberal."[38]

Hoff Sommers grants, significantly, that the ideas she criticizes are to be found in Mill, perhaps the greatest of the liberal political philosophers, and are not the private property of a radical feminist cabal. And of course Mill did not believe that women's preferences were deformed merely by the fact that they did not have the vote, or that the suffrage would correct the situation. The denial of suffrage explained why their preferences were not duly *recorded*. But Mill's account of why these preferences were in any case *distorted* is a different matter altogether. Here he speaks of a multitude of factors: the absence of equal education; the absence of accurate information about women's potentialities and abilities; the hierarchical behavior of men, who treat women with condescension and cast aspersions on their achievements; the pervasive social teaching that women are fit only or primarily for domestic and nonintellectual functions; women's own justified fear of questioning authority, which leads them to shy away from new functions and pursuits; their equally justified fear of moving from a position of comfortable inequality to a position that would be both unprotected and still unequal. Men's preferences, too, were corrupt, he argued: for to be taught that without any personal distinction, just in virtue of being male, one is superior to the most talented woman engenders a diseased view of oneself and one's conduct, and leads men to endorse irrational and self-protective social choices. In short, Mill thought that a liberal democracy—even one with women's suffrage—could contain preferences deformed by a legacy of social hierarchy and inequality. Because of the priority he attached to liberty, he did not argue that people with diseased preferences should suffer political disabilities, except in the case of marital rape and domestic violence. But he did believe that moral education should urgently address the problem.

Mill's idea is at the heart of respectable Utilitarian thought of the present day, both in philosophy and in economics. Utilitarians, unlike some other democratic political thinkers, do hold that ultimately social policy should be based upon the preferences and desires of individuals. But most Utilitarian thinkers recognize that preferences may be distorted by a variety of factors, in such a way that they will fail to be the individual's own "true" or "authentic" preferences. And most hold that democratic deliberation must try very hard to separate the "authentic" from the "inauthentic" preferences, basing social choice on the former rather than the latter where this can be done. Nobel Prize–winning economist John Harsanyi, for example, holds that the "social utility function" must steer clear of all preferences that are "inauthentic" in the sense that they are distorted by absence of information, by logical errors, or by the failure of the person in question to be in a state of mind "conducive to rational choice." We must also omit all preferences that are deformed by "sadism, envy, resentment, and malice."[39]

Harsanyi's analysis is typical of claims made by academic feminists in political theory, many of whom contend that women's preferences are frequently confused by lack of correct information, or by strong emotions deriving from their upbringing in a gendered society. And it is precisely the contention of Catharine MacKinnon, the feminist thinker most strongly criticized by Hoff Sommers, that men's preferences are frequently deformed by "sadism, envy, resentment, and malice," women's preferences by adaptation to (even eroticization of) a state of affairs in which men's desire for control governs the course of life.[40] One can of course argue about whether the case for seeing various preferences of women and men as distorted in this way has been made; and there is danger in leaping prematurely to such a conclusion. But insofar as they can be shown to be so deformed, it is a standard conclusion of utilitarian liberalism that such preferences should not be the basis of social policy. Once again, Utilitarian thinkers do not suggest that we should deny such people the vote; they do suggest that a reflective and deliberative democracy should criticize such people, should instil suspicion of such preferences in the young, and should view the signs of preference deformation in the proponents as a strong reason for skepticism about the merits of a proposed law or a policy. In some especially grave cases of distortion by malice, for example racist preferences for segregation, or some males' preference for sexual harassment, our society has judged that legal restrictions on personal liberty are required.

Economists have reached similar conclusions about another type of preference distortion, which is standardly called "adaptation," a phenomenon in which an individual shapes her preferences to accord with the (frequently narrow) set of opportunities she actually has. Some have argued that women in many parts of the world exhibit preferences that are deformed in this way, even where very basic matters such as physical health, nutrition, and security are concerned.[41] If one does not know what it is like to feel well nourished, it is especially easy to be content with the undernourished state in which one lives; if one has never learned to read, and is told that education is not for women, it is very easy to internalize one's own second-class status and learn not to strive for, or even to desire, what tradition has put out of reach.[42] The existence of such "adaptive preferences" gives us strong reasons to be highly mistrustful of existing preferences in choosing social policies. We have good reasons, for example, to support public investment in female literacy, even in the absence of female demand. Such a suggestion is fully compatible with democracy.[43] Democratic choice need not be understood as the aggregation of uncriticized preferences, and most theorists of democracy, even those in the Utilitarian tradition, by now do not so construe it. They construe it, instead, as a more reflective exercise, in which we attempt to ascertain which among our preferences are conducive to the general welfare. Feminists are asking, in effect, for this more reflective type of democratic choice-making.

Nor is the recognition of diseased preferences a new discovery. It is a pervasive feature of the most prominent accounts of emotion and desire in the Western philosophical tradition. Cultural forces, including ideas of self and other imparted through moral teaching, are widely held to produce emotions and desires that are inimical to self-development, self-expression, and rational autonomy. These views are prominently found in Mill, a liberal democrat. They are also found, in one or another form, in thinkers as diverse as Plato, Aristotle, Aquinas, Epicurus, the Greek and Roman Stoics, Spinoza, Kant, and many others. Kant is especially important in this history for the way in which he criticizes sexual desire itself for leading people to treat one another as objects, in an argument that is the direct antecedent of the arguments of Catharine MacKinnon.[44]

Some of these thinkers, above all Plato, did indeed hold that this problem made democracy unworkable. (In an earlier phase of her argument Hoff Sommers actually labeled her feminist opponents "Platonists.")[45] But of course one need not reach this conclusion, and one will not reach it if one is convinced, as are, in different ways, Aristotle, Kant, and Mill, of the overwhelming importance of individual choice and self-determination. Instead, while supporting coercive legislation in some especially urgent cases of preference deformation—supporting a system of taxation, for example, or a series of laws against racial discrimination—one will tend to focus on the role of public persuasion and moral education, hoping that inappropriate preferences, whether competitive or acquisitive or sexist or racist, can be eradicated through a voluntary program of reform within a democratic society.

Feminist argument continues this long tradition of analyzing the social formation of preferences. Once the social origin of a pattern of desire is recognized, moral evaluation of that desire is invited. When the desire is associated with harm, legal restriction on its expression may at least be considered. Thus feminist arguments about preference and desire have supported nondiscrimination legislation, which does not allow employers with sexist preferences to act in accordance with their desire. They have focused new attention on the role of law in hindering marital rape and domestic violence; they are the basis of the Beijing Meeting's recent declaration that a woman, married or not, has the right to refuse sexual intercourse. They have focused attention on the problem of sexual harassment—until by now the asymmetry of power in many workplace situations has been recognized as a fact that no judge may responsibly overlook. In 1994, for example, Reagan appointee Richard Posner made just such a judgment in the case of the first woman to work in the tinsmith shop at General Motors. Mary Carr's co-workers hounded her over a five-year period, defacing her toolbox and overalls, urinating at her, exposing themselves to her, using obscene language. Posner, citing feminist authors, held that the asymmetry of power in that situation was an essential part of the facts of the case, wrongly overlooked by the lower court judge.

Is this recognition of asymmetrical power subversive of democracy? It seems plausible to think that it would have been far more dangerous to democracy to permit workers to be intimidated and hounded on account of their sex. If feminist teaching has promoted a new attention to such issues, as it clearly has, then it has served democracy well.

Moral judgments do not and should not lead directly to political policies. Whether we accept any particular policy recommendation made by any particular group of feminists, however, we should acknowledge the power of the idea at the heart of much recent feminist writing: the idea that we can and should *morally* criticize desires that have been deformed by a legacy of hierarchy and oppression, and seek to make our children, and ourselves, free of such hatreds and resentments. The fact that this idea is central in feminist classrooms, as indeed it often is, should not alarm us. For good reasons, this idea has become central in democratic theory and social science generally, and feminist thinkers have been instrumental in turning the attention of social science to an issue of crucial importance. In this sense, by now most classrooms that discuss rationality, including the libertarian rational choice workshop at the University of Chicago, are feminist classrooms, debating the topic of preference deformation in ways that reflect and use feminist insights. It is good for students to be goaded into thinking about these issues when they are undergraduates, so that as citizens they may approach their choices with a grasp of fact and of argument.

Feminist ideas about preference and desire are radical—in much the way in which the civil rights movement was radical. It is always radical to ask citizens to look searchingly into their own hearts with the suspicion that some of their most deeply rooted motivations may be deformed by a legacy of injustice. But these core ideas are also, in the best sense, liberal and democratic—because they embody the deepest insights of the liberal tradition about personhood and freedom. If we do not teach our students these ideas, we are failing in an obligation to present them with the best that is being thought on central matters of human choice.

Women's studies is not a single topic. It is a wide, interconnected network of topics. In striving to incorporate adequate instruction in these many areas, the academy is striving to arrive at a more adequate account of reality. The effort to see women more clearly and to give a more adequate account of their lives has transformed the disciplines; it has also transformed the law and public policy of our nation. Critics of feminism are wrong to think that it is dangerous for democracy to consider these ideas, and dangerous for college classrooms to debate them. Instead, it is dangerous not to consider them, as we strive to build a society that is both rational and just.

CHAPTER SEVEN

The Study of
Human Sexuality

Ideally we should love everyone. Yet it is often difficult to love someone
unknown, or different from oneself.

Scott Braithwaite, a gay Mormon graduate of Brigham Young University,
at a Sacrament Meeting Talk in Cambridge, Massachusetts

In 1990 an American judge, a Reagan appointee to the U.S. Court of Appeals
for the Seventh Circuit, read the *Symposium* for the first time, in order to
"plug one of the many embarrassing gaps in my education." In his 1992
book *Sex and Reason*, Richard Posner describes the impact of this experience:

> I knew it was about love, but that was all I knew. I was surprised to
> discover that it was a defense, and as one can imagine a highly inter-
> esting and articulate one, of homosexual love. It had never occurred
> to me that the greatest figure in the history of philosophy, or for that
> matter any other respectable figure in the history of thought, had at-
> tempted such a thing. It dawned on me that the discussion of the topic
> in the opinions in *Bowers v. Hardwick* . . . was superficial . . .[1]

Discussing those opinions later in his book, Posner argues that they betray
both a lack of historical knowledge and a lack of "empathy" for the situation
of the homosexual, the two being closely connected: "The less that lawyers
know about a subject, the less that judges will know, and the less that judges
know, the more likely they are to vote their prejudices." Thus he suggests
that the "irrational fear and loathing" expressed in the Georgia statute under

which Michael Hardwick was prosecuted, and endorsed in the opinions, might have been dispelled by a study of history—beginning, it would appear, with a study of Plato, but including, as well, a study of relevant scholarship in history, social science, and science. *Sex and Reason* was his own attempt to advance this educational process, and "to shame my colleagues in the profession" for failing to educate themselves.[2]

In at least one subsequent judicial opinion Posner has shown the effects of his own belated education; for in a recent blackmail case he speaks eloquently and with empathy of the special vulnerability of the closeted homosexual in contemporary American society, describing in some detail the nonnecessary and nonuniversal character of the prejudices that make this class of persons so painfully susceptible to the blackmailer's schemes.[3]

Human sexuality is an important topic of scholarly inquiry, as it is an important aspect of life. In many fields—including medicine, anthropology, sociology, psychology, history, religious studies, classics, and literature—the relaxing of legal restraints on discussion of sexual activity has led to a flowering of research. Indeed, this is one of the most lively research areas in the current academy, in part because it is so unusual to find a central area that has not been thoroughly studied. The fruits of this research are now becoming available in the curriculum. But their introduction has been controversial, because they involve aspects of life about which citizens have intense feelings, and often deep differences. Such research is sometimes said to have a radical "political agenda" that will corrupt the young.

It is not clear why learning about a subject should be associated with the erosion of moral judgment on that subject. In many other areas of our lives we do not think this way. We do not think that studying the history of slavery or of religious intolerance would be likely to make students lose their grip on moral judgments about the badness of slavery or of religious persecution. On the contrary, we tend to think that historical understanding is an indispensable aid to moral judgment, since it confronts us plainly with what we do and have done. This is why the denial of the Holocaust is understood, correctly, to be subversive of moral judgment, and why the study of the truth of the era of the Holocaust is so urgently important. What, then, is the source of the resistance to historical, anthropological, and scientific teaching about sexuality?

It is, it would seem, the thought that in such a setting of dispassionate scholarly inquiry, moral judgment will not be dominant enough or unitary enough. Perhaps more precisely, it is the worry that historical and cross-cultural study of sexuality will make apparent the actual variety of moral norms and judgments in this area throughout history, and that this will encourage relativism. Once again, however, we should note that this does not happen in cases in which we feel that we have a compelling moral argument that we can recommend to all our fellow citizens. Learning that many of the Founding Fathers thought slavery all right does not shake our conviction that it is evil; learning about German anti-Semitism does not produce anti-Semites. So far, then, it appears unclear why learning how different people think about sex should erode any moral judgments that are well founded.

And yet the hostility to research and teaching about sex in the academy endures and increases. Even the most cautious and respectable work on this topic encounters difficulty. In 1987 a group of respected social scientists led by Edward O. Laumann of the University of Chicago set out to do an ambitious study of sexual behavior in America, whose results have now been published in the two books *Sex in America* and *The Social Organization of Sexuality*.[4] The study was conceived as a response to the AIDS crisis. From the beginning the researchers were aware that they needed a large sample in order to answer the questions they wanted to ask about sexual behavior. They were highly critical of the data gathered by early sex surveys, both because of the numbers involved and, more important, because of the methods by which subjects were selected. They contended, convincingly, that we currently had no reliable information about sex in America; they set out, rigorously, to provide such information. Their project won support from the National Institute of Child Health and Human Development, the Centers for Disease Control and Prevention, the National Institute on Aging, and the National Institute of Mental Health. Scientists in these agencies "wanted more general studies of sexuality to examine such issues as teen pregnancy, sexual dysfunction, and child abuse."[5] The team of Edward O. Laumann, John H. Gagnon, Robert T. Michael, and Stuart Michaels was awarded the contract to do the study after a public competition. Already, however, "our national squeamishness about sex" was emerging, the authors note; for the competition was announced under the rubric "Social and Behavioral Aspects of Fertility Related Behavior," with no hint of the original conception that this was to be a comprehensive sex survey.[6]

Political obstacles proliferated. Many government officials were reluctant to include questions that went beyond a narrow repertoire of disease-related inquiries. For example, they did not want the researchers to include questions about masturbation, whereas the researchers reasoned that this was a little-known topic of potentially considerable importance to public thought about topics ranging from pornography to sexual dysfunction. Eventually the whole idea of the sex survey came under attack, when Senator Jesse Helms introduced an amendment to a funding bill that specifically prohibited the government from paying for such a study. The amendment passed, sixty-six to thirty-four. As a result the research team, operating with private money, could study a sample of only 3,500 adults instead of the originally projected 20,000; data about subgroups, for example gays and lesbians, are therefore for the most part unavailable.[7] Suspiciousness of sex research had triumphed, impeding the progress of inquiry. The resulting volumes are still valuable, but the original plan could not be fulfilled.

Opposition to inquiry is a fairly typical response in curricular debates as well; proponents of these studies are greeted with suspicion, as if they were proposing a subversive activity. The situation recalls Aristophanes' portrayal of the Old and the New Education. The Old Education, its proponent suggests, is the one that produced real he-men. The New Education softens the manly body, producing a citizen who is soft and receptive, whose large genitals symbolize his obsession with pleasure, whose large tongue indicates both his elite intellectual pursuits and his readiness for sexual "deviance."

We should agree with Aristophanes to this extent: an education that frankly studies the history and variety of human sexuality is linked with Socrates and his goal, the "examined life." And this goal does require us to depart from Aristophanes' anti-Socratic ideal of the manly citizen who asserts himself unreflectively, in sex as in every other area of life. But it is that idea of the unreflectively assertive citizen that is the real danger to democratic citizenship, because it asks us not to think about things that urgently require informed debate. And it is the Socratic ideal of a citizen who reflects and compares, in the area of sex as in every other, that promises to create a richer, because more truly deliberative, democratic community.

Sex is a topic of concern to us all as citizens, in many roles. As jurors, we may be asked to reach fair and impartial verdicts in cases dealing with child molestation, spousal abuse, recovered memory, rape and sexual violence, sexual harassment. We may be asked to evaluate testimony on gay parenting, on the "homosexual panic" defense for manslaughter, on the battered-woman syndrome, on marital rape, on the relative claims of adoptive and biological parents. As voters we may be asked to cast ballots in referenda such as Colorado's Amendment 2, which restricted the right of local communities to pass ordinances protecting lesbian, gay, and bisexual people from discrimination. As members of professional groups, firms, universities, businesses of many types, we may be asked to form opinions about what policies our group should adopt on sexual harassment, or whether spousal privileges in health care and benefits should be extended to same-sex couples. As members of religious groups, we may be asked to take part in the debates about the family, women's rights, and same-sex relationships that are intense in all major U.S. religious denominations. As world citizens, we are called upon to talk about these issues with people from other nations, whose traditions and norms in these areas are likely to be different from our own.

The position of the world citizen in the university should be a very simple one: that these choices should be made with knowledge rather than in ignorance. We should therefore produce students who have knowledge of relevant aspects of history, anthropology, social science, biology, and the history of literature, of relevant arguments in moral and political philosophy and in the history and current practice of religions.

Sexuality and "Social Construction"

A central contention about sex in the academy today, and a central source of public controversy about current academic work, is the claim that sexuality is a "social construct." This idea, because of its association with the work of philosopher Michel Foucault, is widely understood to be connected to a radical agenda that subverts customary moral values. But the idea itself is usually not clearly analyzed, or its connection to normative moral argument well understood. It is therefore important to formulate it precisely, in order to give a sense of what is and is not claimed.

We can best accomplish this if we begin by illustrating the claim of "social construction" by turning to a different but related area, the area of the emotions—fear, grief, anger, envy, jealousy, love, and other relatives. Emotions are a good starting point because they are somewhat easier to analyze into their social and nonsocial dimensions than are sexual desires and actions.

What, then, would someone mean by saying that emotions such as anger, fear, grief, and love are at least in part "socially constructed"? The social constructionist's claim is that such emotions are not simply given in our biological makeup (although they may have a biological basis); they embody a good deal of learning. A further claim is that this learning takes place in society and is crucially shaped by society. Fear, for example, is not just a tingling at the back of the neck. It involves thoughts about significant danger impending. Anger is not just a boiling of the blood. It, too, requires thoughts about an offense and an offender. Both fear and anger are therefore highly responsive to changes in belief. If I discover that I am not really threatened, or that the threat is trivial, I can expect my fear to abate. If I discover that not A but B has offended me, I will be angry at B instead of A. If I discover that the offense did not occur at all, my anger will go away. If I discover that it is not a serious offense but a trivial one, I can expect anger to become irritation.

Societies shape people's beliefs and expectations in many ways that are relevant to these emotions. They teach people what events are offenses, what offenses are important, and how a reasonable person would behave in response. It is important to distinguish at least five different areas of social construction.

1. *Behavior.* Society teaches people how to manifest or not manifest their anger, their fear, their grief, and what expressions of these emotions are appropriate or inappropriate. There is great social variation in these teachings. Forms of lamentation that are mandatory in Greece would be considered vulgar and shameful in England. Outbursts that once were regarded as reasonable expressions of anger in our own country—for example, murdering a wife's lover (which was not a criminal offense in Texas until 1967)—are no longer so regarded.[8]

2a. *Norms about the whole emotion category.* Societies give people different views about how they should view their fear, their anger, their grief. Some societies, for example that of ancient Rome, teach that anger is a good and pleasant thing, a valuable assertion of manly dignity and control. Other societies teach that anger is socially divisive and to be avoided when possible. The society of the Utku Eskimos, described by anthropologist Jean Briggs, teaches that anger is only for small children; adults should never get angry.[9]

We can expect these variations in normative teaching to affect not only the judgments people make about emotions, but also the experience of the emotion itself. An ancient Roman is likely to enjoy getting angry, feeling the experience to be linked with pride and manly self-assertion. For an Utku, getting angry would be linked with feelings of shame, and would feel like a regression to childishness.

2b. *Norms about evaluations within the category.*   Society teaches people what is worth getting angry about and what not, what is worth fearing and what not. These evaluations are likely to contain much similarity and overlap: all known societies teach the fear of one's own death. But there are also many variations that are socially shaped. An ancient Roman will get angry at his host if he is seated one seat too low at table, seeing this as an affront to his dignity. A contemporary American is not likely to pay much attention to table seating. Anglo-American common-law definitions of "reasonable provocation" hold that some offenses are such that a "reasonable man" will be provoked to violence by them. Once again, what these norms are varies over time. In the last century, a paradigm of such "reasonable" anger was the situation in which a husband discovers his wife in bed with a lover. In our century, other examples are displacing this—anger, for example, at sexual abuse of one's child. On the other hand, our society thinks that the anger caused by racial prejudice is especially baneful and unreasonable, and that crimes caused by such anger are especially odious. Because anger would not exist without some beliefs about what is worth getting upset about, and because the relevant beliefs appear to be socially formed, we can say without paradox that anger is a social construct. Similar arguments can be made for the other major emotions.

These social norms enter into the experience of the emotion itself. A feeling of "righteous indignation" is different, for most people, from the experience of a forbidden and stigmatized anger. A modern American who did get furious at his hostess for seating him one seat away from the top might well experience that anger differently from the ancient Roman in a similar situation, who would have been taught that it was manly and good to feel that way.

3. *Categories.*   Sometimes social shaping enters into the way in which the whole emotion category is conceived. We can see this phenomenon very

clearly, for example, if we focus on the history of erotic love in the Western tradition. If we look at the passion of Phaedra for Hippolytus in Euripides' play, at the love of Paolo and Francesca in Dante's *Inferno,* at the love of Cathy and Heathcliffe in Emily Brontë's *Wuthering Heights,* and at a pair of lovers in a contemporary novel by John Updike, we will see some features that all the relationships have in common, which make it reasonable to call them all "love." On the other hand, there are big differences in the understanding of what love *is,* which we should not ignore or efface in thinking about it. These differences shape not only what people say about love but also, it seems, the way in which they enact and experience it. An ancient Greek seems to think of *erōs* as an intense desire for possession of an object, linked with distraction and something akin to madness. The medieval paradigm of courtly love is very different: it makes respectful distance and worship essential, and cultivates a norm of tender receptivity, the *cor gentil.* Heathcliffe and Cathy's love involves Romantic ideas of the opposition between social convention and nature; they experience their love as deriving from deep sources of authenticity that link them to nature rather than to civilization, and thus they repudiate many elements of the courtly tradition. The love described by Updike contains complex combinations of all these traditions, with some distinctively modern elements. In each case, society shapes not only the tradition, but also the experience of people who grow up in it.

4. *Placement of individuals within the categories.* The role that fear, anger, and jealousy play in the life of a given person is likely to have a complicated etiology. Differences of early experience in the family are likely to play a large role. But here, too, it is plausible to think that social factors are important. Experiments show, for example, that when infants cry their emotions are frequently labeled in accordance with the viewer's beliefs about the infant's sex. The very same crying baby will be called "frightened" when the observer believes it to be a girl, but "angry" when the observer believes it to be a boy.[10] Further evidence shows that these differences in labeling (linked, as they clearly are, to common social stereotypes of the masculine and the feminine) have behavioral consequences: girl and boy babies are held differently, tossed in the air differently, and so forth. Such differences are likely to shape the emotional repertoire of the developing child.

    Cross-cultural variety is neither necessary nor sufficient for the claim of social construction. Variety is a likely sign that social shaping has been at work. But we can have social shaping with considerable overlap and concordance, since societies face many similar problems. The fact that the fear of death is ubiquitous does not mean that it is not socially shaped. Nor is variety inevitably a sign of social forces at work, since the observable variety might conceivably have been produced by other factors, such as psychological or even biological causes. (The social constructionist need not deny that biology also plays an important role in shaping emotions.)

Social construction, moreover, is fully compatible with normative moral evaluation. Noting that the ancient Romans and the modern Utku have different experiences and ideas of anger does not prevent us from asking which conception seems the more socially fruitful. Noting the variety in conceptions of love across the centuries does not prevent us from evaluating the different conceptions in the light of human well-being. The social constructionist will be cautious in assigning moral blame to individuals for what their society has engendered. It seems unfair to blame the average Roman for not being just like a cooperative, peaceable Utku. On the other hand, we can also expect individuals to exercise a degree of critical reflection about their society and its norms, and every known society contains disagreement and debate on such matters. Deciding that one society's conception is preferable to another's does not make change easy. We cannot easily adopt the emotional values of the Utku, even if we decide they would be best for us. But the power of habit does not mean that moral evaluation is powerless. As the ancient Greek and Roman Stoics knew, when they diagnosed the ills of their society and recommended the removal of anger and hatred, small, piecemeal changes are always within our power, even when a utopian revolution is not.

The person who holds that sexuality is "socially constructed" typically holds that at least some of these types of social shaping exist in the domain of sexual behavior and desire.

1. *Behavior.* Societies shape norms of proper sexual behavior in varying ways, fostering norms of what sexual behavior is appropriate for parties at different ages and in different social relationships and settings, what sexual acts are appropriate or inappropriate for parties engaged in a sexual relationship.

2a. *Norms about sexuality itself, as a whole,* vary greatly as well, in ways that affect experience. Some societies teach that sex is a basically good thing in need of control, rather like the appetite for food and drink; others, that it is a basically evil thing to be tolerated for the sake of procreation. Most societies today contain complex mixtures of these views. These differences color experience. The person brought up on the view that sexuality is essentially sinful is likely to experience shame and guilt in connection with sexual desire in a way that a person differently brought up will not.

2b. *Norms about other evaluations within the category.* We are familiar with many other norms in the area of sexuality: norms, for example, of what is desirable in a sexual partner. Age, breast size, weight, musculature, coloring, dress, gender—all these characteristics are marked in varying ways as desirable and undesirable. There is much evidence that these norms, too, are socially shaped and vary greatly from culture to culture, and from time to time in the same culture.

3. *Categories.* More controversially, the social constructionist claims that the basic sexual categories themselves undergo social shaping. Sexual actors may be categorized in a number of ways, for example by whether they are active or passive and by whether they choose partners of the same or opposite gender. How these categories are interwoven and which of them is primary involve much variation. The social constructionist claims that this variation can most plausibly be explained as deriving from social norms, rather than purely from biology or from individual familial variation. A prominent social constructionist claim is that our society's division of people into the heterosexual and the homosexual lacks precise parallels in many times and places, and is to that extent a social artifact. Of course both same-sex and opposite-sex partner choices are ubiquitous, and people in other cultures have not failed to notice these choices. But the social constructionist claims that these choices are not always taken as very salient, certainly not as determining an "identity" that charts the whole course of one's sexual life. Elsewhere, for example, the salient division may be, instead, between preference for the active and for the passive role, and it may be this that gives a person his or her sexual "identity."

Such claims may be disputed: sociobiological explanations for basic categories have been advanced, as well as genetic explanations of other types. If the story of a single gene controlling same-sex preference is established as true, this will certainly cast doubt on the claims of social construction, since it will indicate that over a long period of human history and in all places within that time, a single, unvarying biological marker has divided agents into two categories. On the other hand, such biological markers assume importance only when societies decide to notice them and to accord them importance; so invariance does not inevitably create two marked categories of social actor. It is difficult, furthermore, to know exactly what gene theorists hold to be the culturally invariant trait associated with the gene. Is it a preference for same-sex partners? A preference for the passive role? Without distinguishing these two concepts and still others, it is difficult to establish a plausible cross-cultural thesis. For these and other reasons, biological explanations of sexual categories, while they may eventually illuminate some aspects of our lives, are still too uncertain to be truly explanatory.

4. *Placement of individuals within the categories.* The social constructionist can plausibly argue that fulfilling society's norms of proper male or female behavior is something to which individuals are strongly pushed by social pressures and sanctions. Identified as male or female by the appearance of genitalia at birth, children are socially shaped from a very early age in accordance with those roles and the social expectations associated with them. It is much more difficult to make this case for heterosexual or homosexual orientation. No external mark separates infants into two groups, to receive differential social conditioning. How does a young man growing up in a pious Christian family in the Midwest, a young man who loves sports and who wants nothing more than to serve his country as a naval officer, become a homosexual?[11] What in his parents' and community's treatment of him could possibly explain a difference that sets him apart so painfully from those he emulates? Like E. M. Forster's character Maurice, many gay and lesbian people seem undistinguishable from nongay people—or, rather, distinguishable only by the experience of discovering that they want what is socially unacceptable. Social construction may explain how the norms and categories got there, but it seems difficult for them to explain such cases. It seems that some more individualized explanation, whether biological or psychoanalytic, must also be invoked.

Sexuality: Ancient Greece and Modern America

The case for the social construction of sexuality can best be understood if we consider a complex historical example whose relevant features have been thoroughly described. Ancient Athenian culture of the fifth century B.C. is such an example. Athens is a good starting point for historical inquiry on these issues, since some of the best historical work on sexuality has been done using this material. Most important is the magisterial work of scholarship *Greek Homosexuality*, by Sir Kenneth Dover,[12] but other, more recent works have developed the inquiry further.[13]

It has been difficult to study Greek views of sexuality, because for some time scholarly puritanism and evasiveness have exerted a pernicious influence, eclipsing or distorting straightforward matters of scholarship. Whether prompted by shame or by the desire to make the revered Greeks look more like proper Victorians, such evasiveness has influenced the editing and translation of ancient texts, the formation of lexica and other technical tools of scholarship, and thence our understanding of the ancient world.[14] Until very recently there were no reliable translations of Greek and Latin texts involving sexuality, and no reliable scholarly discussions of the meanings of crucial words, metaphors, and phrases. As Kenneth Dover writes: "On sexual behaviour, and homosexual behaviour in particular, translations and authoritative-sounding statements until quite recent times are not to be relied on, because turbulent irrationality impaired the judgement of translators and scholars."[15] In short, the type of open-ended inquiry into sexual norms and conduct that the world citizen should favor was virtually absent in the academy of previous generations.

A single illustration will show the extent to which prudery produced distortion. In 1961 the prestigious Clarendon Press in Oxford published a new scholarly edition of the Roman poet Catullus prepared by C. J. Fordyce. Although this is an ambitious and in many ways exhaustive edition, it does not contain all the poems of Catullus: as the preface states, "a few poems which do not lend themselves to comment in English have been omitted."[16] The jacket blurb, which may be presumed to have Fordyce's approval, calls these "a few poems which for good reason are rarely read." The editor's principle of selection is of interest, for he has included some offensive poems of a scatological nature, as well as all poems dealing with heterosexual sex-

233

uality. It is same-sex acts, and allusions to them, that he finds inappropriate for English commentary.

Nor, in those days, did the dictionary help the curious reader of those poems. If, for example, readers of Catullus 16 wanted to know the meaning of *pedico* (which means "to play the insertive role in anal intercourse"), they would find it defined in a dictionary only as "to practise unnatural vice." If, again, they wanted to know the meaning of *irrumator* (which means "one who plays the insertive role in oral intercourse"), they would find only "one who practises beastly obscenity."[17] They had to guess which "beastly obscenity" was meant. This was the situation across the board.

In the English translations in which most of the public approached these authors, the situation was even more acute. Until very recently almost no sexually explicit passage was available in anything like a faithful translation. Thus the humor of Aristophanes disappeared, in great part, from public view, and was not even well understood by expert scholars. Only after a 1957 decision in which the U.S. Supreme Court took what seemed to be a more liberal stance on obscene materials, holding that obscene material had to be without redeeming social value, did U.S. publishers dare to issue literal versions of these plays.[18] This was pretty much the situation with all authors. Nor did one see reproductions of the vase paintings that are among our most important sources for ancient sexual norms and practices.

This suppression of texts and visual art gave the public a distorted image of ancient Greco-Roman culture. When accurate translations were finally made available, the public experienced shock and disbelief, seeing that the revered Greeks made jokes that seem daring even by relatively liberal American sensibilities. In 1966 in Ypsilanti, Michigan, a town near Detroit with a large Greek-American population, a new professional repertory company staged a production of Aristophanes' comedy *Birds,* starring the great comic actor Bert Lahr, the Cowardly Lion of *The Wizard of Oz.* The production used the accurate translation of William Arrowsmith. A local newspaper expressed strong disapproval: the ancient Greeks may have enjoyed such humor, but need we inflict it on the families of Ypsilanti?

The crucial turning point in scholarly inquiry on Greek sexuality was the decision of a great scholar, Sir Kenneth Dover, to embark on a comprehensive study of Greek attitudes to homosexual desire and conduct. He did so because he judged that "practically everything said during the last few centuries about the psychology, ethics and sociology of Greek homosexuality was confused and misleading. The root of the confusion was the failure to understand how quite different attitudes to the 'active' and the 'passive' role coexist, and extreme reluctance to admit that the Greeks regarded homosexual arousal as natural or normal."[19] Carefully sifting the different types of evidence (vase paintings, law court speeches, literary and philosophical texts), Dover came to a number of striking conclusions about behavior and norms in fifth-century Athens.

Athenian culture, Dover argues convincingly, did not consider sexual arousal or desire per se problematic or shameful. Sex is an area of our appetitive life that needs careful monitoring and control, but it is not in that respect different from hunger and thirst. In short, we do not find the special problematizing of sexual desire that is frequently linked to the Christian notion of original sin. This problematizing could be expected to affect the experience of sexual satisfaction as well as judgments about it.[20]

Moreover, same-sex desire and arousal were considered natural and normal. As Dover shows, the vocabulary of "nature," even "compulsions of nature," was standardly used of a male's desire for a (usually younger) male—and used not by social deviants, but by people represented or seen as respectable. Even in works of conservative writers, such views are ascribed to moral exemplars. (For example, the conservative thinker Xenophon imagines the morally admirable Hieron speaking of "the compulsions of nature" in connection with his erotic passion for a young man.) The gods are depicted as enjoying, and consummating, such desires. Such sexual experiences were widely thought to be unusually intense and powerful. It was thought, moreover, that only in a male-male sexual relationship would one be likely to have a deep spiritual and emotional bond with one's lover: women were sequestered and relatively uneducated.

The primary distinction around which norms revolved was that between the active and the passive. Being an active penetrator was thought to be manly and good, and it was usually a matter of moral indifference whether one penetrated a woman or a man. It was understood that a person of strong sexual appetite would seek out both sources of satisfaction; the concept of a person with an exclusive orientation toward women or toward men was rare, if it existed at all. On the other hand, to be passive, for a male, was thought to be shamefully "womanish," especially if one preferred that role.

For these reasons, elaborate protocols of courtship developed to regulate erotic relationships between older and younger citizen males. (Frequently these two groups were not very far apart in age: the older might be in the early twenties, the younger in the late teens.) The intercourse of an active citizen male with a male prostitute was unproblematic, and no social sanctions attached to visiting a prostitute of either sex, so long as it was understood that one played the active role. Where a young male citizen was concerned, however, care had to be taken to protect his future standing in the community. Such a young man must make sure that people did not think he had been bribed for sexual favors. This would be taken as an indication that he was up for sale to the highest bidder. Nor would a future adult citizen want to be thought of as someone who desired the passive sexual role or who was habituated to it. Therefore, as at least a public norm, intercrural intercourse (intercourse between the thighs) was preferred, since it did not require any bodily penetration.

It is difficult to know how far these social norms correspond to real practices. There is some reason to suppose that penetrative intercourse was more common than popular norms suggest, and may have been indulged so long as it was not publicly discussed. Much in the area of private, undiscussed behavior must remain conjectural. Clearly, however, if we go by the evidence of vases and of texts representing widespread popular norms (such as the speech of Pausanias in Plato's *Symposium*), it was thought all right for sexual relations to occur between older and younger citizen males, provided these protocols were observed. Such relationships frequently involved intense mutual devotion and high social and personal aspiration.[21] It was widely believed that males who wanted something more than bodily pleasure in a sexual relationship would seek these relationships.

Why should this information be important for a modern undergraduate, beyond the sheer interest of accurate knowledge itself? We do not have the option of becoming ancient Greeks. Nor, if we did, would we want to borrow that culture's misogynistic ideas. Probably we would also reject its extreme devaluing of sexual passivity. Given that young people mature more slowly in our world than they did in the ancient world, we would probably set the age of consent higher than the ancient Greeks informally did. What is significant in this encounter is the experience of seeing difference where we expect to see timeless natural divisions, the discovery that a group of people, whom we in general respect, organized this intimate side of life very differently. It is no exaggeration to say that in the ancient world our modern conception of the homosexual really did not exist, since people did not classify themselves, and others, on the basis of a binary division focused on the gender of object choice. Bisexual desire was assumed to be ubiquitous, and gender of object was simply far less significant than the choice of the active or the passive role. Male-male relationships, furthermore, were seen to be, and often clearly were, vehicles of intense romantic devotion, frequently combined with refined intellectual and political aspirations. Thus we have learned something about human possibilities that we might not have seen without studying history, especially living in a culture that frequently portrays male-male relationships as promiscuous and unconcerned with spirituality.

When we notice things of this sort, we begin to see our own norms and practices as ours rather than as universal and necessary. In that way we learn something about ourselves and the choices our history and culture have made. We also begin to ask questions that we didn't ask before, such as whether we have good reasons for the judgments and the distinctions we make. If we have no good reasons for our sexual norms, that is not necessarily a bad thing; much of human life is based on habit rather than on reason. But it does mean that we should hesitate before we disadvantage fellow citizens who experience life differently and who have different habits.

Cross-cultural study can show us that appeals to "nature" and "the natural" are ubiquitous in the sexual realm. By displaying the sheer variety of customs that have been so defended, it can show us how slippery these appeals actually are, and how thoroughly bound up with culturally shaped images of proper behavior.

Even if something were "natural" in the sense of being an innate part of our biological equipment, it would not follow that we cannot and should not change it; many aspects of our innate endowment need, and get, improvement. To call something "unnatural" in that sense is not to make a moral criticism: many good things, such as art, virtue, and political justice, are unnatural in the sense that they require us to depart from some of our innate tendencies and to develop new ones. Cross-cultural history, by showing us the variety of norms that have been endorsed by a species sharing a common biological heritage, prepares us to inquire further into the morality of our sexual choices.

By now there is a great deal of high-quality material that studies sexual norms and classifications cross-culturally. Ancient Greece is a good place to begin, because the relevant texts have been well translated and provided with good historical commentaries, and because Dover's book is one of the best in the area on any culture. It is also useful to begin with a culture about which, in general, quite a lot is known, rather than with the fascinating but elusive material available from Native American traditions or from New Guinea. But increasingly it is possible for solid scholarship to be made available from a variety of different times and places. This material can be integrated into the curriculum in a variety of areas, where appropriate, such as classics, history, philosophy, anthropology, and sociology.

When we study sexuality in any place or time, we are in some sense gaining knowledge of ourselves. But we should also study ourselves more directly, trying to get an accurate sense of what the norms and practices of sexual conduct and desire are in our own nation at this time. There is now a rich body of material, historical and sociological, that does study our own norms and practices. To take only a single example, Laumann's study of sexual behavior in America is, by the authors' own account, incomplete, since the size of the sample had to be reduced. Its conclusions have also been disputed in other ways—particularly by those who doubt that any survey, however carefully designed, will elicit true reports. But it is more complete and methodologically careful than any other survey of American sexual attitudes and practices, especially because it uses a randomly selected population. Therefore, with whatever defects it may have, it should be one starting point for the curricular investigation of sexuality in our own society.

Laumann's data, like much recent research on American sexual mores, strongly support the claim that sexual behavior and classifications are socially constructed. "We find in fact," the authors conclude, "that sexual behavior is very much like other sorts of social behavior. Without consciously thinking about it, we play by the rules." With respect both to behavior and to the subjective experience of sexuality, sex "should not be seen as operating solely, or even primarily, at the level of the individual . . . [but as] mediated by ongoing social and sexual interaction."[22]

The frank study of these behavioral patterns, norms, and experiences and their complex interweavings in our own culture is, as Laumann and his fellow authors plausibly hold, a valuable contribution to our development as a society: "With efforts to know and interpret the facts about our sexual lives, we as a nation can become more effective in respecting diversity in our sexuality and in formulating coherent and effective policies that enhance the sexual aspects of our private and public lives."[23]

The Study of Sexuality in the
Undergraduate Curriculum

Curricula face these issues in many ways. When they begin to do so they encounter some tricky problems, both political and intellectual. One illustrative case is that of Brown University, which in 1985 had virtually no curricular coverage of these issues, but which now is among the few to offer an undergraduate concentration in the study of sexuality. Brown, often identified with "political correctness" in public discussions of higher education, is widely believed to be a campus on which "multiculturalism" flourishes. In some areas pertinent to world citizenship Brown has in fact played a pioneering role. For example, it had one of the earliest and still has one of the best departments of Judaic studies in the country. It has a distinguished Center for Women's Studies and a strong associated undergraduate program. It has a fine World Hunger Program and associated programs in international relations and development studies. Though not a leader in African-American studies, it has a respectable small department in this area, with strong links to History and to American Civilization, and to a recently developed Center for the Study of Race and Ethnicity. On issues of sexuality, however, Brown did not take the lead, either in curriculum development or in basic matters of tolerance and antidiscrimination. By the mid 1980s it was the only Ivy League school that did not include sexual orientation in its statement of nondiscrimination with respect to admissions, hiring, and promotion.

In 1985–86 Brown's Educational Policy Committee created a new subcommittee called "Minority Perspectives in the Curriculum." The charge of this committee was to study the extent to which the curriculum as currently constituted incorporated studies pertaining to the history and the experiences of American minority groups. Although the groups that were to be the committee's concern were not named in its formal charge, it was understood that they would include major ethnic and racial minorities. It was also understood that the committee would not deal with Judaic Studies or Women's Studies (not a minority study in any case), since those programs were viewed as healthy and well integrated into the curriculum. What was left totally unclear was whether the committee was to include in its fact-finding inquiry the curricular treatment of homosexuality. At a preliminary meeting, leaders of the gay and lesbian student group asked that this issue be included, since they were eager for more information about the way it was being addressed in the curriculum; it would be relatively easy to add one further group to the list about whom questions would be asked. There was some support for this proposal, since faculty were aware that issues of sexuality were frequently not discussed where discussion would have been intellectually appropriate.

This issue arose at the first meeting of the committee. The dean stated categorically that the "legitimate concerns" of the ethnic and racial groups would not be mingled with a treatment of homosexuality. Asked for her reasons for omitting an area that would have been easy to include in a fact-finding mandate, she argued that our community had reached a consensus about the importance of the concerns of ethnic and racial minorities, but not about those of sexual minorities. It was unclear why this lack of moral consensus was an argument against including these topics in the curriculum, and still less clear why it was an argument against studying how and whether they were currently being addressed.

The faculty arrived at a compromise, creating a small separate fact-finding group to discover whether further study of this issue was needed. Interviews with both faculty and students in relevant departments revealed something interesting. For example, the course "Abnormal Psychology" did not study homosexuality, on the grounds that it was no longer considered an abnormality by the psychiatric and psychological professions. Nor did the course "Sociology of Deviance" study the topic, although in principle it might have, since "deviance," the instructors told me, was used in that department as purely a statistical and not a normative category (as implying only relative rareness, not moral depravity). In fact what emerged was how few courses treated the topic at all. "Biology of Gender," taught by renowned feminist biologist Anne Fausto-Sterling, was the only regularly offered course that devoted any time at all to the topic, and this was approximately a week in a semester-long course.

Moreover, when the ongoing minorities committee interviewed the chair of the African-American Studies Department, he took the position that although it would be a good thing to increase university offerings in African-American Studies, the most pressing issue of minority knowledge and understanding at Brown was that of homosexuality. Students, he argued, were exceedingly ill informed about this topic and brought their prejudices into class in a way that impeded learning. He found the atmosphere in his own courses to be so hostile, and so uninformed, as to undermine the dignity of the university.

Support for a fuller study of the issue was growing. By the spring of 1986 the dean agreed, with some reluctance, to appoint a committee to study the curricular treatment of homosexuality. She asked me to chair the committee. I agreed, and the committee began to meet. Its members included a behavioral psychologist, a professor emeritus of medicine, and several others, none with much apparent interest in the topic. Indeed, it appeared that the dean had deliberately created a reluctant committee. But we drew up a fact-finding questionnaire for all departments and programs, and waited for the results. Then an odd thing happened.

An old friend of the dean's invited me out to lunch. After much general discussion, it emerged that what he wanted was to discover my *real motivation* for this keen interest in sexual minorities. In this connection, he began asking numerous questions about my personal life. In the moment, I reacted by answering his questions. They were irrelevant to the curricular issue, and I immediately regretted having been put on the defensive in this way. I then told him that there were three reasons for my interest. First, I believed it to be an important issue of justice. Second, I read Plato's *Phaedrus* when I was an adolescent and found that account of male-male love the most appealing paradigm of love I had seen. It combined aspiration, passion, friendly concern, and shared intellectual goals in a way that I had never seen in fictional accounts of male-female love, which usually contained either asymmetry of power or a lack of real erotic passion. Since it described what I myself wanted from love (albeit with a man), it seemed to me very odd to suppose that same-sex lovers who emulate Plato's paradigm today should be stigmatized. Third, since my adolescence, partly as a result of having been a professional actress, I have had numerous gay male friends, and have had reason to be very grateful to them for friendship, especially in a male-dominated academic setting in which collegial friendships with non-gay men are full of complexity.

How odd this personal scrutiny was—and yet a very common fact of life for faculty who show an interest in the study of homosexuality. One might have thought there were two issues on the table: the curriculum, and social justice. Neither of these seemed to involve the personal life of the faculty member, and in other areas of study personal questions would not have been raised. Did this professor really believe that any person who defends the study of a group as legitimate is (whether openly or secretly) a member of that group? And did he really hold that if someone defends a claim of justice involving a group, he or she, again, is (openly or secretly) a member of that group? It may be a dogma of American life that all actions are motivated by self-interest. And yet this dogma seems false; there are claims of justice, and there are people who pursue them for their own sake. Why can't that be allowed to be so in this area? Why must there be a personal story, bringing forward a personal motive?

The fact was, however, that on this one issue of sexual orientation, straight scholars' fear of contagion was so deep that it was rare indeed to find support for those claims of justice, or for the closely related claims of scholarly legitimacy. The world citizen's desire for understanding was virtually absent, and the governing assumption was that the only reason to pursue the issue was one of personal identity politics. This belief proved self-confirming, since its prevalence discouraged people not personally involved from taking a stand on the issue, lest they fall under embarrassing suspicion. A straight man who took a public stand either on gay civil rights or on the importance of curricular study of homosexuality would immediately be the subject of rumors, as if only a tainted person would get involved. No conversation about the topic could begin until it was possible to define "who you really are," one's sexual orientation being taken to be fundamental to one's stance in what was supposed to be a reasoned argument about knowledge and justice.

Michel Foucault's analysis of modern sexual categories is not always convincing. But events like those at Brown show the truth of his claim that our society makes questions of sexual orientation fundamental to all its dealings with a person, more fundamental, often, than kindness, or excellence, or fairness. At Brown—and in many comparable institutions around the country—asking about the "identity" of the person frequently took the place of examining the quality of the person's argument. This is not the life of reason, the life that our campuses should promote.

Once duly constituted, the Brown committee examined the curriculum to find out what resources it offered for any person who wished to understand the phenomenon of homosexuality. Our questionnaire posed three questions: (1) Did the department have any courses that dealt with homosexuality? (2) Did it have any plans for course development in that area? (3) Did it have any faculty member who could advise students who wished to do reading and research in that area? The following departments, among many others, answered all three questions in the negative: Psychology, Sociology, History, Japanese Literature, German, French. In all those areas, the response betrayed a scholarly gap. Only Religious Studies and Biology had any formal curricular offerings (in each case a subsection of a single course, and the Religious Studies offering was a temporary, one-time course taught by a graduate student), although English pointed out that in effect the whole department did lesbian and gay studies, since a large number of the greatest authors were lesbians or gays, and Psychology took the time to write a lengthy and helpful answer, explaining that they did not teach the topic because their approach was not oriented to the study of human beings in any case: they focused almost exclusively on animal experimentation.

Our students' knowledge of psychology and literature and history was not being well served. This refusal of knowledge was linked with prejudice and injustice, as both cause and effect. Lesbian and gay students interviewed by the committee reported the feelings that seized them when, as so often happened, an instructor arrived at a portion of a historical event or a literary text in which the issue of homosexuality arose—and passed over it with embarrassment, saying something like, "Well, we all know what *that* is." The point is, we didn't, and on the whole didn't want to.

Discussion with lesbian and gay students proved to be a turning point in the work of the committee. Some committee members reported later that they had expected to see a group of radicals conforming to various imagined stereotypes, pushing a strident and simplistic "political agenda" connected with identity politics. What they saw was a group of diverse young men and women, students any of us might have taught. We heard them reflecting seriously and poignantly about the gaps in their education occasioned by embarrassment and ignorance about homosexuality. We heard them describe, as well, the ways in which those deliberately crafted silences were linked with an experience of second-class citizenship: they felt that they were being told, on each such occasion, that a feature of themselves was so embarrassing that it could not even be a topic of reasoned discussion in the academic community. And we understood, as well, the likely effect of these silences on other students in attendance, as their own imaginations were refused the material requisite for understanding the lives of some of their fellow citizens. The initially reluctant committee became united in the view that our curriculum had gaps that were damaging to the pursuit of knowledge.

An interdisciplinary group of faculty decided that the best way to address the situation was to bring high-level scholarship on sexuality to the campus.

A conference on Homosexuality in History and Culture, sponsored by departments including History, Religious Studies, Classics, and Philosophy, brought to Brown a group of distinguished scholars to present new research on aspects of homosexuality in history and society. Held in early 1987, it was the first major academic conference devoted to this topic, at least in that part of the country. Speakers, including classicists David Halperin and the late John J. Winkler, historians Henry Abelove and the late John Boswell, literary scholars Catherine Stimpson and Biddy Martin, gave a large, diverse audience a sense of the variety and high quality of the new scholarship currently being done on the history of sexuality. Care was taken to send the community the message that this was material of interest to all students and scholars, not only to those who were personally involved. Distinguished social historian David Herlihy, a pioneering scholar in women's and family history and a religious Catholic known for his strong family commitments, chaired the opening session. The provost of the university, engineer Maurice Glicksman, sat with his wife in the front row.

Two years after this, Brown adopted a nondiscrimination statement that included sexual orientation among the categories. Beginning in 1988, under the new presidency of Vartan Gregorian, the social situation of gay and lesbian students on campus improved considerably, as it was made clear by the administration that insults and abuse directed at a person on account of his or her sexual orientation did not belong in an academic community any more than did racist taunts. It became increasingly apparent that it was possible to have reasoned discussion on this issue.

By 1994, many departments offered courses that included discussion of sexual orientation. In Biology, Psychology, Philosophy, Religious Studies, History, and various areas of literary study the gaps that the 1986 survey had found were being addressed. Meanwhile the curriculum was transformed in a number of relevant ways. New courses on AIDS and epidemiology were created in the medical school, courses on the literary representation of sexuality in most of the literature departments, and courses on sexuality and the body in Religious Studies and Judaic Studies. Even more important were the transformations of existing courses, as new scholarship was increasingly integrated into regular curricular offerings. Courses on ancient Greek history, literature, and philosophy began to devote more time to the study of the culture's sexual norms and practices. Courses in constitutional law, in moral philosophy, in many periods of history, in anthropology all began to show more awareness about issues of sexuality, both homosexuality and sexuality generally.

As yet, however, there was no formal integration among the course offerings, no interdisciplinary program that would link the different facets of the topic of sexuality and promote a more sophisticated awareness of approaches and methods. Such interdisciplinary programs had proved valuable in many different areas of the curriculum. Brown's World Hunger Program integrates the insights of history, climatology, geology, economics, anthropology, and ethics. Its Taubman Public Policy Center brings political science together with sociology, statistics, and economics. The Thomas Watson Center for International Relations pursues the integrated study of culture and politics that is necessary to think well about relations between developed and developing countries in the modern world. A Center for Old World Art and Archaeology pursues the comparative study of ancient Mediterranean cultures. Such programs are a ubiquitous feature of modern scholarship and teaching, in an era in which knowledge is undergoing rapid transformations. They encourage scholars to learn from one another in an interdisciplinary setting and to organize cross-disciplinary courses.

A formal center or program in sexuality studies or in lesbian and gay studies would, it seemed, be helpful in some respects but counterproductive in others. Such a program would be likely to generate some valuable research and teaching. But it could also draw scholars away from their departments, ultimately undercutting the effort to integrate these studies, where appropriate, into the curriculum as a whole.

A more integrated result, it was felt, could be achieved by creating an interdisciplinary undergraduate concentration that would allow students to focus on sexuality as a field of study, without creating a separate program. Sexuality is an interdisciplinary field with a burgeoning scholarly literature. It has at least as much claim to scholarly unity as environmental studies, or women's studies, or many types of area studies. Many of the most familiar academic disciplines are methodologically heterogeneous, and were brought together on account of the social concerns of a particular era in history. Classics—which combines the Greek and Latin languages, history, literature, archaeology, philosophy, religion, linguistics, and much more—is one obvious example of such a field. Although the reasons for establishing classics as a discipline were far more political than scholarly in the first place—the central motivation being the commitment of Renaissance humanists to assail church-dominated scholasticism—by now the combination of disciplines is familiar. Sometimes methodological heterogeneity is a handicap to learning; in some classics departments there is little communication between historians and literary scholars, philosophers and archaeologists. At its best, however, the field profits by its heterogeneity, generating work that pools disciplinary resources.

It seemed that Brown now had enough expert faculty to serve a specialized concentration, drawing together the diverse disciplines in an integrated seminar for concentrators in their third year of study, and providing a core of required basic courses. Over a semester, an interdisciplinary faculty group met to design the proposal; members of the group came from Medicine, History, English, Judaic Studies, Religious Studies, American Civilization, Philosophy, and Classics.

The proposal that emerged was informed by the following decisions.

1. *Inclusive definition.* Brown's program would be a comprehensive program in "Sexuality and Society," not one narrowly devoted to "lesbian and gay studies." Understanding would be best served, it was felt, by the more inclusive definition: any good study of homosexuality should be grounded in a more inclusive grasp of sexuality as a whole. Another reason for this choice was historical awareness that the categories "heterosexual" and "homosexual" are nonuniversal, in their modern form, and are not universally considered salient as sources of human identity. Scholars did not want to prejudice historical inquiry by defining the subject matter in terms of a single set of disputed categories.

A more pragmatic argument was that students in our society still need to worry about the likely effect on their careers of evidence that they have studied homosexuality. Unfortunately, in some quarters to want to know still is to be tainted; courses on gay and lesbian themes frequently have to announce that theme in a subtitle that will not appear on student transcripts, so that students of diverse sexual inclinations may enroll without prejudice to their career plans.

2. *Interdisciplinary conception.* The study of human sexuality is by its nature an interdisciplinary enterprise, calling for the input of all three major areas of the undergraduate curriculum: humanities, social sciences, and natural sciences. Disciplines that have made valuable contributions to this study

include medicine, evolutionary biology, genetics, sociology, anthropology, law, political science, philosophy, literatures of many types, classics, religious studies, and history. And yet many current university offerings in gay and lesbian studies are narrow in focus. They tend to be dominated by literary and cultural studies, with some input from the other humanities but relatively little from the sciences and social sciences. Brown was determined from the start that its program would seek the broadest possible understanding of its topic. Offerings were limited to some extent by faculty interest and availability, and thus there are gaps in the program that was created, especially, at present, in anthropology, sociology, and law. (Brown has no law school, and only a small number of law-related courses.) But the presence of a vital group of interdisciplinary researchers should generate interest among faculty in related areas, leading them to incorporate new scholarship into their research and teaching.

3. *Focus on scholarship and research.* In any relatively new field, especially an interdisciplinary one, there are dangers of superficiality. There is a risk that students will emerge with a smattering of knowledge about this and that, with no overall integrating methodology and no solid base of expertise. This danger is not peculiar to new disciplines. It is a standing problem, for example, in classics, where students may easily emerge with assorted bits of knowledge about the history, literature, art history, and philosophy of two cultures, in some cases spanning a period as long as twelve centuries. This knowledge is usually connected to some degree by study of Greek, Latin, or both, but that link is becoming increasingly weak in the contemporary watered-down version of the undergraduate major in classics, which in many institutions demands relatively little language study. Nor does linguistic knowledge supply methodological sophistication in the various disciplines that compose classics.

The Sexuality and Society concentration at Brown addressed this problem by insisting that all students who concentrate in the program have, as well, a substantial disciplinary expertise amounting more or less to a second major. By this requirement the program protected its future students from the charge of superficiality; more important, it guaranteed that they would have rigorous training in one established academic discipline. The program also requires that all concentrators take a group of required courses offered by the program's core faculty, one of which would be a seminar on methodologies, taken in the junior year. This seminar is addressed, each week, by faculty from the relevant disciplines, who introduce students to current research techniques.

There have been difficulties in implementing this strategy. Differences have surfaced about the relatively large role played by contemporary literary theory in the concentration. Faculty in Philosophy, Religious Studies, and Medicine have had to keep pressing for an emphasis on rigorous scholarly argument and traditional methods of inquiry, alongside approaches influenced by postmodernist literary theory. They argue that a goal of the concentration should be to make the study of these topics a respected part of the curriculum as a whole; this legitimation will occur only if program offerings are held to the highest standards of rigor and of methodological diversity. These arguments continue, but the program's broad focus, together with its rigorous exchange of ideas and arguments among the disciplines, helps to allay institutional and student fears that such programs are bound to be one-sided and ideological.

Any program in the study of sexuality is a failure if it remains isolated from the rest of the campus. Some such offerings may even serve to segregate students and faculty interested in these issues from their peers. Scott Braithwaite, reflecting about his undergraduate education at Brigham Young University, lamented the fact that his fellow students did not have the opportunity to get to know him—that is, to get to know something about gay men, their history, the variety of their choices in different places and times. This meant, he plausibly argued, that they could not have the love (and, we should add, respect) that their religion instructed them to have for all persons. University of Nevada at Reno student Eric Chalmers, by contrast, did have a chance to get to know what the life of a gay man might be like. As a future health care worker, he now has an understanding of some of his future patients that would otherwise have eluded him. We should strive to make this understanding and sympathy generally available, however we construct more specialized studies. At Brown, interdisciplinary courses on sexual topics attract a broad and diverse student following; it remains to be seen whether the specialized concentration will do the same.

Any program studying sexuality must address a common charge: that such programs are motivated by the "political agenda" of promoting the social acceptance of homosexuality as an acceptable "lifestyle," and that its faculty are not inquiring as scholars but are "proselytizing" for this lifestyle. The response should be that the primary motivation for such studies is to gain knowledge that we need if we are to think well about a crucial area of human life. An ancillary motivation is indeed one of fostering respect, tolerance, and friendship. These are fine aims for a curriculum in a democracy to have. A liberal democracy such as ours is built on mutual respect and toleration among citizens who differ deeply about basic goals and aspirations. The old curriculum that maintained silence about homosexuality was defective because it contained unjustifiable gaps in scholarship, and also because these silences implied that certain people were not worthy of serious study. To say this implicitly or explicitly about one's fellow citizens is objectionable, and the study of sexuality is in part motivated by a wish to correct that bad situation. To this extent, there is likely to be an informal link between support for such studies and support for institutional policies of nondiscrimination and social toleration. This linkage should not be seen as unacceptably ideological by people who strongly defend academic policies promoting mutual understanding, respect, and toleration among people of different religions or classes or races.

Nor was the status quo ante apolitical in its focus on majority experience. The study of heterosexual erotic love, which for centuries has been a central pillar of humanities curricula, expressed the social majority's fascination with that group of experiences, both moral and immoral, and its sense that they were at the heart of human life, whether for better or for worse. (Adultery and illegitimacy were, of course, widely studied in literature and history, in a way that lesbian and gay sexuality was not.) In general, to make something an object of study is at the very least to recognize its salience in human life, and until very recently heterosexuals claimed that privilege for their erotic lives, however disorderly, while denying it to others.

In the spring of 1989 the classical scholar John J. Winkler, one of the pioneers of the study of desire and sexuality in the ancient Greek world, came to Brown to give the major endowed lecture in the Classics Department. The lectureship was established by a donation from the living widow of a distinguished classicist in her husband's memory, and the widow was in attendance. Partly in honor of the donor, Winkler had chosen to address the topic of heterosexual marriage, speaking about the love of Penelope and Odysseus in Homer's *Odyssey*. This lecture, which eventually became the final chapter in his book *The Constraints of Desire*, argued that even in a hierarchical society in which women are unequal, an individual man and woman can create a passionate relationship of mutuality and equality.[24] To the elderly donor and the large assembled audience, Winkler—a gay man already ill with the AIDS of which he died a year later, an AZT pillbox strapped to his waist with a beeper that reminded him of his medication in the middle of the lecture—presented a surprising and eloquent defense of the possibilities of heterosexuality. He began, however, with a vivid reminder. He said: "This is my first venture in Straight Studies"—reminding the audience that what is taken to be unmarked and unremarkable has itself a political content, includes some issues and people and excludes others. "Straight Studies" did not have to be called that, since that was what the entirety of the academy was. Proponents of "gay studies" are asking to be seen as part of the world too.

This will be taken to be an insufficient reply. Don't students get taught in such courses that being gay is all right, and don't they frequently make life choices as a result of that teaching? Don't gay professors in such programs openly proselytize for their lifestyles, leading impressionable young people in that direction?

Any reply to these charges must be nuanced. It is certainly true that many, though by no means all, professors in these areas are themselves lesbian or gay. It is also true that most, though not all, who teach and do scholarship in this area favor an end to discrimination against lesbian and gay people in our society. This political judgment is probably not unconnected with what they learn when they do study the history and variety of human sexuality. It is true that these attitudes are frequently conveyed to students. It is also true that many lesbian and gay students who have experienced discrimination and intimidation find this a reassuring climate in which to "come out" and to affirm their identity. For this reason parents can get the impression that it is the course that has produced the orientation. But of course this is highly unlikely to be the case. Sexual orientation is formed very early in life; and orientations, once formed, are highly resistant to change by either social or psychological forces.

The example of an openly gay or lesbian instructor—whether in a course with that theme or in some other course—can frequently encourage a young student to affirm his or her homosexuality more openly, and perhaps even to choose sexual conduct in accordance with his or her preference, rather than either celibacy or an attempt to form, against one's preference, a heterosexual relationship. The same may be true of the influence of straight instructors who manifest toleration and respect for gay and lesbian people. Interacting with such people, the student may come to feel that a life as an openly lesbian or gay person need not be a damaged or unhappy life, and may feel able to pursue that life. In a world in which large numbers of lesbian and gay teenagers experience depression and even attempt suicide, this seems not a bad development; nor is it viewed negatively by all parents. A newfound confidence and self-esteem would not prevent the student from deciding to follow the teaching of his or her religion, where the overt expression of homosexual preference in sexual conduct is concerned—although it will undoubtedly ensure that the arguments of the religion will be scrutinized for their textual basis, their internal coherence, and their humanity. Since every major religion in America contains internal debate and plurality on this issue, this outcome is not subversive of religion as such.

Frequently the student leaders of the lesbian and gay community on a modern campus are intolerant of conservative opinion. Insofar as these students are likely to be leaders in any curricular development in this area, those intolerant views may make their way into the classroom. Intolerance of conservative thought is frequently a problem in faculty circles as well. The political right in America bears some of the blame for this situation, since its members have not always distanced themselves sufficiently from a politics of hatred and disgust; nor have they sufficiently welcomed people of diverse sexual orientations. It is not too surprising that "gay Republican" should seem to some of our students' ears something of a contradiction in terms. On the other hand, all political viewpoints ought to be respected in any discussion of these matters, and on many campuses liberals are too intolerant of conservative opinion on matters such as abortion and homosexuality. Students cannot be expected to construct a tolerant and respectful intellectual community unless faculty give a firm example, making it clear that open expression of diverse points of view on these as on other issues is an essential part of a free academic community.

This is not a simple question. There are some positions that most of us feel to be beyond the bounds of reasoned debate. The view that all Jews are by nature immoral and evil, the view that all Irish people are stupid, the view that all women are by nature depraved, amoral beings incapable of rational thought, the view that all believing Catholics are captives of a monolithic ideology that will prevent rational thought and responsible citizenship—all these views have been widely held in American society at some time, and yet we would rightly view with alarm an instructor who taught these views as if they were fact. Sometimes even to stage a debate about a proposition dignifies it inappropriately. If a university were to organize an academic conference around the question "Did the Holocaust take place?" or the question "Can Catholics think for themselves?" or the question "Can women do logic?"—offering equal time to proponents of both views on each of these questions—most members of modern academic communities would feel that the event was not a genuine scholarly event, but an excuse for ugly prejudices to parade as if they were knowledge. The very organization of the question seems suspect, as if the pro and the con have equal weight. Some scholars view debate about the morality of homosexual conduct in that light, as a challenge to the dignity of persons based on ignorance and prejudice. They believe that attacks on homosexuals as immoral and depraved have no more place in the classroom than attacks on Catholics or Irish people or Jews as immoral and depraved. That is to say, they hold that one might legitimately study such materials as examples in the sociology of prejudice, but not as if they had equal weight with the contradictory opinions.

At Brown, however, in the spring of 1995, the departments of Religious Studies, Judaic Studies, Philosophy, Classics, Political Science, and History organized a large, nationally publicized conference on the topic "Homosexuality and Human Rights in the Major Religious Traditions." The conference was sponsored in part by the National Endowment for the Humanities, through the Rhode Island State Humanities Council. One "conservative" and one "liberal" speaker were invited from each of the following denominational groups: Judaism, Roman Catholicism, mainline Protestant churches, and African-American churches. Speakers were asked to address the current state of debate in their denominations. The conference concluded with a more general roundtable discussion on the role of religion in American public discourse. Despite the legitimate concern that the plan gave a platform and hospitality to people who are committed to what many believe to be offenses against human dignity, the conference organizers argued strongly in favor of this type of reasoned dialogue. In this current political climate, any reasoned debate is better than its absence. To encourage people to confront these difficult issues calmly and with careful historical, textual, and moral arguments is already progress. It is also progress if the occasion helps to dispel the impression that all academic scholars in sexuality studies are radicals with a single agreed agenda.

With these goals in mind, organizers worked for weeks before the conference to make clear to all involved, including and especially students, the great importance of reasoned debate and dialogue in a pluralistic democracy. At the conference itself, each session was prefaced by discussion of civility and reason. (Catholic theologian John Courtney Murray's well-known statement "Civility dies with the death of dialogue" became the touchstone for these discussions.) The result was in fact a dialogue of a fascinating and remarkably civil kind, of a type that our democracy badly needs. Such efforts should be undertaken more often, especially in universities in which there is little internal debate between liberals and conservatives.

Brown's efforts are fairly typical of what is taking place on these issues in universities and liberal arts colleges of various types, especially private ones. Some institutions have been more ambitious in their efforts than others. At the University of Chicago, a Workshop on Human Sexuality led by sociologist Edward Laumann and biologist Martha McClintock and an ambitious new gender studies program generate new research, foster graduate and undergraduate courses, and bring in outside speakers, creating a rich and diverse climate of high-level scholarship. At New York University, a new interdisciplinary program is well funded and has embarked on an undergraduate concentration program much like the one at Brown, though with less emphasis on medicine and biology. At Yale, a smaller center, led by the late John Boswell, has generated opportunities for visiting scholars, integrated offerings in the current curriculum, and fostered new initiatives.

State institutions face complex pressures. The course "Struggles for Equality" at SUNY–Buffalo did not include the topic of sexual orientation, vulnerability to public opinion may have played a role. But such choices are not universal. The University of Iowa was one of the pioneers of gay studies in this country. At the University of Nevada at Reno the incorporation of material about sexual diversity has proceeded relatively smoothly and unobtrusively in courses of many kinds, from Eric Chalmers' English course to the required Western civilization course, where Deborah Achtenberg convinced her colleagues to add the poetry of Sappho, and historical readings relating to it, to the required core list. The next year, when Achtenberg was not teaching the course, the group of faculty voted that Sappho had been a great success and that they should keep her in. In neither of these cases, however, is the study of human sexuality undertaken in a very systematic or methodologically cohesive way.

Problems of several kinds arise when material on sexuality is added to the curriculum. At the University of California at Riverside, sexuality studies were initiated more or less entirely from within the humanities. The dominant approach has been linked to postmodernist literary theory. This theoretical orientation has led to controversial choices of conference topics and visiting speakers. Focusing on a 1993 conference, philosopher David Glidden argued that faddish, eye-catching topics were promoted at the expense of both substance and breadth of coverage. He pointed to an absence of philosophy and social science from the design of the conference on "queer theory," and argued that in this way scholars are cutting themselves off from the urgent concerns of a community that is debating issues of nondiscrimination and equality. Nonetheless, Glidden strongly supports the pursuit of knowledge in this area, and acknowledges the presence in the gay studies group of first-rate scholars whose work does not conform to the narrow postmodernist paradigm he criticized. He is cosponsoring a dissertation on gay studies, and deplores recent efforts by state legislators to block approval of a minor in gay studies, despite a provision in the state constitution protecting the university from political control.

Another difficulty arises when the institution itself resists the open discussion of sexual issues. At Brigham Young and Belmont, it is virtually impossible for faculty to discuss homosexuality in the classroom in an unconstrained manner. This problem is not peculiar to religious institutions. At Morehouse, neither the administration nor the student body seemed at all eager to discuss sexuality, and especially homosexuality. One Morehouse student expressed frustration with this situation, connecting the curricular issue to a climate of silence about gay issues in campus social life, and also to incidents of harassment and discrimination. He argued that the avoidance of sexual issues, especially those pertaining to homosexuality, has led to educational deficiencies, including, ironically, gaps in understanding of some of the most distinguished African-American writers (such as James Baldwin). "Sexuality," he comments, "is one of the things black men write about, and if it comes up it comes up. *You are living.* So it's an issue that will come up, and you will discuss it." Although Morehouse's neighbor Spelman encourages campus discussion of lesbian and gay issues, these efforts are opposed by conservative students, particularly those from evangelical religious groups. Posters announcing such discussions have been pulled down; students who attend are treated with hostility.

On many U.S. campuses, lesbian and gay students are targets of violent and abusive behavior. Although data in this area are not complete, it appears that antigay violence on campuses is correlated with the absence of open discussion, and that institutions like Brown and Chicago, which do a lot to educate students in this area, are less plagued by violence. At Notre Dame, which combines a long tradition of drunken partying with virtual curricular silence about sexuality, abuse of lesbian and gay students has become so severe that in 1994 a group of 276 faculty members signed a public petition protesting the administration's lack of support for these students' situation. Led by philosopher of religion Philip Quinn, the petition asked for understanding and an end to violence. To take a representative example, a study at the University of Massachusetts found that 21 percent of lesbian and gay students, compared to 5 percent of the entire student body, reported having been physically attacked.[25] Assaults on personal dignity through verbal abuse and hate speech are even more common. Our campuses should do much better than this. We should be setting a high standard of respect, toleration, and friendship for the larger society to follow. We should be preparing our students to make the larger society into a more respectful and less violent place. Education about sexuality is a very important part of that effort.

Education is changing this situation, and such overtly hostile attitudes are increasingly rare, at least on many campuses. Although it is a tough struggle, and one in which many individuals have suffered many forms of discomfort and career adversity, sexuality in general and homosexuality in particular are by now becoming accepted as legitimate topics of inquiry. There is much more to be done.

Teaching about human sexuality is a difficult and delicate task. We are approaching concerns which lie deep in many of us, and which are frequently central to the ways in which we define our identity and search for the good. The same is true of teaching about love or anger or the accumulation of wealth. But for some reason our society has proved able to tolerate research and controversy on these matters more easily, and has not felt as keenly threatened by the very fact of open inquiry or by the presence of a diversity of perspectives. Sexuality studies, by contrast, appear threatening—perhaps because they bring interdisciplinary inquiry to an area that might have been thought to be the preserve of moral and religious discourse. That this has long been so for love, or anger, or greed—and all this without causing our moral sense in these areas to evaporate—should have been seen as reassuring. It seems perfectly possible both to study economics in a scientific way and to maintain moral views about greediness and exploitation. So, too, it is possible to investigate sexuality historically and scientifically, without losing one's sense of moral urgency about one's choices.

What is the source of the resistance to knowledge? In many cases, it involves a refusal of reason itself. Many resisters seem aware, at some level, that certain pictures of human beings will survive the test of rational inquiry and that others will not—that people who have studied sexuality historically and cross-culturally are more likely to question many of the demeaning and misleading stereotypes that are frequently associated with homosexuality in our society, that those who are aware of the differences manifested by history are somewhat more likely to be tolerant of the differences they see around them. This state of affairs is threatening to some; but surely to a deliberative democracy it should not be threatening. For the sake of producing citizens who are open-minded and reflective in this important area, as well as for the sake of understanding and truth generally, we should promote rigorous interdisciplinary studies of human sexuality in the undergraduate curriculum.

CHAPTER EIGHT

Socrates in the
Religious University

To cut oneself off from the reality of difference—or, worse, to attempt
to stamp out that difference—is to cut oneself off from the possibility
of sounding the depths of the mystery of human life.

Pope John Paul II, Address to the
United Nations General Assembly, October 1995

At Brigham Young University, in Provo, Utah, on February 8, 1996, new
president Merrill Bateman issued an order that all BYU faculty and staff
who are Mormons must be certified by a bishop as "Temple worthy" (recommended as worthy to enter the Temple), a stringent standard requiring
evidence of orthodoxy in belief, regular financial support of church activities,
and conformity to a set of moral imperatives ranging from abstinence from
sex outside marriage to abstinence from coffee and tea. Faculty, students,
and alumni reacted with alarm. One recent graduate wrote, on condition of
anonymity: "When bishops determine the worthiness of someone to enter
the Temple, this should be undertaken with extreme humility, care, and
privacy. To use the recommend process as a means of assigning labels to
people that will be used by administrators at BYU is sickening. I hope a few
bishops will have the courage to mail back [the] letter with the inscription:
'None of your damn business!'"[1]

At the University of Notre Dame, in South Bend, Indiana, on May 2, 1996,
the Faculty Senate met to discuss its response to administrative actions that
have denied the campus gay and lesbian group rights and privileges accorded

to other Notre Dame student groups, such as the rights to invite speakers, to choose their own faculty advisers, to host social events, and to advertise these events. By a 21-4-2 vote, the senate passed a resolution deploring these actions as "discriminatory against a group of Notre Dame students and as compromising the University's ideals and stated mission." The Mission Statement of the University, cited in the resolution, asserts that "the intellectual interchange essential to a university requires, and is enriched by the presence and voices of diverse scholars and students" and that "the University prides itself on being an environment of teaching and learning which fosters the development in its students of those disciplined habits of mind, body and spirit which characterize educated, skilled and free human beings." Furthermore, the Mission Statement holds that "the University seeks to cultivate in its students not only an appreciation for the great achievements of human beings but also a disciplined sensibility to the poverty, injustice and oppression that burden the lives of so many." These valuable ideals, the faculty resolution asserted, require criticism of administrative actions against the student group.

We live in a deeply religious nation, a nation that has traditionally linked religion to the mission of higher education. Religious loyalties have played a large role in resistance to curricular change on college campus, as those who cherish their traditions fear their subversion by professors who do not take religion seriously. But religion has also been a major source of the imperative to curricular diversity. Deeply religious people are prominent among those who have insisted that we need to confront cultural diversity, gender, and sexuality, and who have done creative scholarship in these areas.

Religion-inspired tensions between tradition and change arise on all campuses, since on every campus students brought up in religious traditions are studying new material about human diversity. But they take an especially sharp and fascinating form in institutions that have retained a strong religious affiliation. These colleges and universities have a dual mission: advancing higher education in a pluralistic democracy, and perpetuating their specific traditions. If we can show that even in those institutions the cultivation of humanity and good citizenship requires both Socratic inquiry and curricular attention to diversity, we will have a very good argument that this holds true of the more secular schools as well. Seeing how religious universities have struggled to come to grips with these goals in the light of their own distinct traditions, we understand the goals better and see their American future more clearly.

Some thoughtful people feel that the very existence of religious institutions of higher learning is threatened by recent curricular changes, as well as by the liberal emphasis on academic freedom.[2] But we should begin by taking very seriously the Pope's warning: to shun diversity is a way of closing oneself off from a part of the mystery of human life. It seems plausible to think that a truly religious life should be open to humanity in all of its cultural forms. As the Pope stated, "Our respect for the culture of others is . . . rooted in our respect for each community's attempt to answer the question of human life . . . every culture has something to teach us about . . . that complex truth. Thus the 'difference' which some find so threatening can, through respectful dialogue, become the source of a deeper understanding of the mystery of human existence."[3] It seems plausible that a religious university can thrive only if it protects and fosters inquiry into all forms of human culture and self-expression, providing students with the mental tools they need to confront diversity in their own lives as citizens, workers, and friends. This does not entail a hands-off attitude to criticism of what one encounters; it does entail respect, and a sincere and prolonged effort at understanding.

Religious institutions have a special reason to attend to norms of respect and understanding and to instantiate these in a curriculum for world citizenship. Secular groups may found universities and colleges for all kinds of reasons; when a religious body does so, moral considerations are inevitably salient. Among these moral concerns is likely to be a desire to foster love of one's neighbor, a value rightly emphasized in every major U.S. religion. But ignorance is a great enemy of love; and an education in human diversity is a necessary weapon against ignorance.

Many of our colleges and universities had religious origins: Harvard, Yale, and Duke are only three of the most famous examples. Brown, founded in 1764, was the first college in the colonies that did not have a religious test for entrance, and even Brown retained for many years close ties to the Baptist and Quaker faiths. Although many once-religious schools have cut themselves off from those denominational roots, many have chosen to retain them. Some such schools are seminaries, which educate clergy. But many more are full-scale colleges and universities, offering a liberal arts education to undergraduates and many forms of graduate education.

These institutions have developed within a nation defined by liberal ideals of religious toleration, free exercise of religion, and nonestablishment of religion. Our liberal-democratic tradition views itself not as the enemy of religion but as its vigilant protector. It is precisely because religious faith is so important to people that our tradition makes freedom of conscience and religious exercise a nonnegotiable part of American life. Other personal commitments do not enjoy the same legal status—for example, as reasons for refusing to work on a given day, or as reasons against military service. The implicit rationale for this special treatment of religion seems to be that to ask people to go along with a religious custom for any reasons other than those given by their own conscience would be to violate their humanity at its very core. The Pope stressed this idea in his United Nations address: our respect for humanity shows us "how important it is to safeguard the fundamental right to freedom of religion and freedom of conscience, as the cornerstones of the structure of human rights and the foundation of every truly free society." When we consider what standards of pluralism, academic freedom, and nondiscrimination should obtain in a religious college or university, it is important to remember that these institutions, like others, prepare citizens for a democratic culture defined by those ideals. Religious institutions cannot select policies that subvert the very conditions of a healthy religious pluralism.

Indeed, our own constitutional traditions have fostered a far greater diversity of religious colleges and universities than exists anywhere else. No other nation in the world contains a rich plurality of faiths actively maintaining institutions of higher learning.[4] Elsewhere, either universities are purely secular or they retain (as in Britain) links to an established state church. The United States, by contrast, has a remarkable religious diversity in higher education. We have large numbers of Roman Catholic colleges and universities, with differing relations to the Vatican, sponsored by particular religious orders with their distinct philosophies of education. We have Baptist, Methodist, Lutheran, Episcopalian, evangelical, Presbyterian, Quaker, and Mennonite institutions. We have several Jewish institutions, ranging from seminaries to Brandeis, a major university with both undergraduate and graduate programs. Brigham Young, a Mormon institution, is the largest private university in the country. The United States has protected and fostered this pluralism in a manner unparalleled in the world, precisely because of its acute sensitivity to any infringement of religious liberty and its respect for diversity.

All religions are interested in religious training, but not every religious training program for young adults is part of a college or university, institutions traditionally linked with particular values of scholarship, inquiry, and argument. Religions differ in their support for higher education, as they also differ in their estimation of the role of reason, inquiry, and argument in the good human life. The Amish religion, for example, has been highly controversial in our nation for its negative attitude even toward compulsory secondary education. In a famous Supreme Court case, *Wisconsin v. Yoder,* Amish parents successfully argued that their right to free exercise of religion included the right to keep their children away from mandatory high school, fostering communal values through work (a decision that in my view underrates the importance of education to democratic citizenship).[5] The Amish faith will not, then, be likely to establish a college or university.[6] When a religious denomination does establish a university, it does so, we must assume, not simply in order to provide its members with credentials that make them more marketable in a society that prizes college degrees, but also in order to support scholarly research and to provide a higher education, fostering inquiry as a basis of citizenship and good life. Freedom of inquiry and the related academic freedoms are essential bulwarks of any institution that would like to call itself a college or university. A denomination has the option not to support higher education at all, if it does not like these values, as some religions may not. What is at issue is the proper role of guarantees of free inquiry and of curricular diversity, should it choose to support higher education.

Notre Dame and Brigham Young lie in many ways at opposite ends of a spectrum on issues relating to academic freedom, Socratic inquiry, and diversity in religious higher education. Their struggles to chart a course protecting both religious identity and academic excellence pinpoint the challenges faced by many other religious schools. Drawing on a long Roman Catholic tradition of inquiry and higher education, Notre Dame has constructed a genuinely religious education within a first-rate research university with strong guarantees of academic freedom and a commitment both to Socratic searching and to international study. Issues concerning women and sexuality continue to be deeply divisive, both in curricular matters and in campus life; but faculty feel free to state their views even where those conflict with official church doctrine. The case of BYU shows a university far more disposed to restrict scholarship and inquiry in the name of religious belief. An attitude of anti-intellectualism increasingly shapes the course of the institution. This state of affairs, rather than promoting a strong distinctively religious institution, threatens to stifle its academic spirit and thus jeopardizes its status as a religious institution of higher education.

With this topic, as with the topic of race, it is necessary to indicate one's own biographical relation to it, to alert the reader to any prejudices that may color the account. I was brought up as an Episcopalian Christian and converted to (conservative) Judaism at the age of twenty, shortly before marrying. I take my relation to Judaism very seriously, gave my daughter a religious education, and am a member of a synagogue—although I focus on religion's moral and social content and am uncertain about metaphysical belief.

Notre Dame: Diversity and the Examined Life

The University of Notre Dame sits in the middle of a peaceful and prosperous world, where cattle placidly graze in rolling green farmland. Entering the campus, a visitor sees the sun strike the gold dome of the Administration Building, topped by a statue of Our Lady. On the library wall is the mosaic known as Touchdown Jesus, a full-body Christ, hundreds of feet high, arms outstretched in benediction, positioned so as to be seen by fans through the goal posts in the football stadium. Not far away is its counterpart, Number One Moses—a towering dark sculpture of a ferocious Moses stamping on the head of the Golden Calf, breaking its neck and holding one finger aloft in triumph. This gesture is used to celebrate the victories of the basketball team, when it stamps on its opponents with appropriate ferocity. The whole campus of contradictions—with its material opulence and its tradition of missionary activism, its ferocious athletic rivalries and its renowned center for Peace Studies, its dedication to Our Lady and its mostly-male leadership, its adulation of athletes and its distinguished Philosophy Department, its Indiana pastures and its ornate, Old World–style Basilica—sits there before the visitor, like an exotic creation of the American religious mind.

It began, indeed, that way, as a most improbable thought—when, over

150 years ago, founder Rev. Edward F. Sorin built a log cabin on the shores of a lake in the Indiana wilderness. Standing in the clearing, with a wagon containing about $300 in possessions, here, he said, was "L'Université de Notre Dame du Lac." Today, using a phrase that compounds the cultural contradictions, Harold Attridge, dean of the College of Arts and Letters, called this founding gesture "an archetypal act of chutzpah."[7]

Notre Dame was founded in 1842 to provide a higher education to Catholic young men. Most of its early students were the sons of immigrants. Both as such and as Catholics they would at that time have been discriminated against in the major secular universities and colleges. The university's primary purpose was therefore twofold: to provide these young men with an education that combined intellectual development with spiritual enrichment and, in so doing, to prepare Catholics for entry into the professions and into the American middle class. Later Notre Dame inaugurated the nation's first Catholic engineering program and its first Catholic law school. Serious academic research and graduate education were not Notre Dame's focus until relatively recently; most of this transformation can be traced to the presidency of Theodore Hesburgh, whose vigilant concern for academic freedom was crucial in explaining the university's success in recruiting high-quality research faculty.[8] Meanwhile, the fame of Notre Dame's athletic programs contributed to its success in fundraising; since 1970 the university has created more than 100 endowed chairs.

Today Notre Dame enrolls about 7,600 undergraduates and 2,500 graduate students (including law and business); women were never excluded from graduate programs and were admitted as undergraduates in 1972; they now make up about 44 percent of both undergraduate and graduate enrollments. The university has a close though not always happy relationship with St. Mary's, a neighboring liberal arts college for women. In 1967 the board of trustees, which had consisted only of members of the Congregation of the Holy Cross, became a lay board. By statute, the president must still be a priest from the Indiana Province of the Congregation, a small order associated with international missionary and development work. The provost need not be a priest, and the university has recently appointed its first non-Catholic provost, a religious Protestant.

I have visited Notre Dame at different times, as the guest of the Philosophy Department (one of the university's strongest departments, and highly respected nationwide), the Program in Liberal Studies, the Gender Studies

Program, and the Law School. My primary guide to the history of diversity issues on campus is Philip Quinn, a leading philosopher of science and philosopher of religion, 1995 president of the American Philosophical Association's Central Division,[9] who left a tenured position at Brown for Notre Dame because he preferred the environment of a Catholic university. Though a critic of political liberalism for its attempts to exclude religion from the public realm, Quinn is a leading liberal on faculty issues of gender and sexuality.

To a person who makes more than a casual visit to its campus, Notre Dame feels very different from the major secular universities with which it competes. Some of these differences are on the surface. Sports dominates the imagination of the campus, and its facilities, to an unusual degree. The student body is homogeneous, racially and ethnically: Polish- and Irish-Americans predominate, and there are very few African-American or even Hispanic faces. Males predominate numerically (although numbers are rapidly converging); women seem especially quiet and unassertive. As a Jew used to finding many other Jews among my faculty colleagues, I'm struck by the small number of Jews around me and—despite Attridge's telling phrase—the relatively slight influence of Jewish culture.[10] These are some impressions.

A deeper sense of the Catholic character of Notre Dame emerges when one talks with faculty members. One quickly finds that religious and ethical concerns are straightforwardly accepted as part of academic life. Every area, from scientific research to economics to philosophy, is powerfully infused with them. Ethical concerns, even when couched in secular language, have little place in a secular university's departments of economics, applied mathematics, or computer science. Religious concerns have little place in any department of the secular university, apart from departments of religious studies, which consider such issues from a historical/comparative viewpoint. Many outstanding members of the Notre Dame faculty chose Notre Dame because they sought a climate in which their spiritual concerns could be recognized as central to their lives and work, something that seemed impossible on the campuses of Harvard, Brown, and Yale. Quinn, for example, became alienated by the way in which the secular academy marginalizes religion, studying it as a set of institutions and practices but never engaging with the perspective of religious believers. Imagine, he says, how people who love science would feel about a university that contained a Department of Science Studies, but no science departments that conducted research.[11]

Although Quinn's contrast between religious and secular universities seems too sharp—it ignores, for example, the mixed character of institutions such as Yale, Harvard, and the University of Chicago, which have excellent divinity schools that do study religion from the inside—his picture of Notre Dame is accurate. Notre Dame's intellectual culture is far from monolithic. On many specific issues, from contraception to homosexuality to women's role in society, individual faculty members may agree more with their respective allies in the non-Catholic world, liberal or conservative, than they do with one another. Nonetheless, there is a remarkable degree of agreement about which issues are important, and that these issues prominently include issues of ethical and spiritual value. It would seem odd, for example, to discuss economic questions without also reflecting about the relationship between human dignity and the accumulation of wealth. It would seem odd to do scientific research with military implications, without at the same time discussing intensively the morality of war and the prospects of a lasting peace. This convergence of focus constitutes one central aspect of Notre Dame's Catholic identity.

George Bernard Shaw once declared that a Catholic University is a contradiction in terms.[12] He meant that the concept of a university includes a freedom and openness that the authoritarian character of the Catholic church, in his view, excluded. Theodore Hesburgh, Notre Dame's distinguished president emeritus, concedes that there is not yet in the United States a Catholic university that is truly great by contemporary standards, but he insists that "a university does not cease to be free because it is Catholic." The church need not enter the world of the modern university at all: but if it does choose to do so, it must do so on the terms that this world has established, which include extremely strong protections for the freedom of inquiry—not only of the great scholar but of all members of the university. Hesburgh cites Cardinal Newman: "'Great minds need elbow room, not indeed in the domain of faith, but of thought. And so indeed do lesser minds and all minds.'"[13]

Roman Catholicism is well placed theologically to establish a religious university that is both truly religious and truly a university. Although at various times in history the Catholic church has impeded intellectual inquiry, the tradition gives learning and inquiry pride of place in its account of a worthwhile human life. Consider the poet Dante's description, in the *Paradiso,* of his encounters with models of human excellence, celebrated saints and martyrs and heroes, in circles of ascending virtue. Very high up in this elect company is his philosophical mentor St. Thomas Aquinas—who taught in the first great Catholic university in medieval Paris and encountered opposition for his interest in the pagan philosopher Aristotle.[14] Aquinas tells Dante in no uncertain terms that a good Christian life requires self-examination through reason, including the philosophical use of reason (*Paradiso* XIII.115–123):

> "He ranks very low among the fools who says 'yes' or 'no' without first making distinctions . . . since often opinion, rushing ahead, inclines to the wrong side and then passion binds the intellect. Far worse than useless . . . is the quest of a person who casts off from the shore and fishes for the truth without the art."

Of course reason should not reject the guidance of religion: Aquinas can use Aristotle and end up in Paradise, but Aristotle himself ends up in limbo, closed off from grace and its bliss. But "the art" of Socratic reflection is an essential part of a Catholic life.

Notre Dame has committed itself to this norm. Although, like all Catholic universities, Notre Dame must deal with its complex relationship to the Vatican, which has sometimes given rise to problems about academic freedom,[15] the theory embedded in the tradition supports efforts by administration and faculty to promote open inquiry and an atmosphere of free classroom debate. Addressing the Faculty of the College of Arts and Letters in 1993, Dean Harold Attridge described the identity of Notre Dame as growing out of two paradigmatic narratives: the story of Jesus, which gives the university its elusive and yet compelling vision of "a realm of peace and justice"; and the story of Socrates, which

> has defined for twenty-four centuries the essential components of the life of the mind: to wit, the ability to give a reasoned basis for belief and the quest to find the truth that lies behind appearances. His practice of asking embarrassing questions, even at the risk of personal loss, and even without hope of an immediate answer, is fundamental to what we are.

The Catholic identity of Notre Dame, Attridge concluded, "is a matter of how two such fundamental stories relate." At one level, there is tension: for at many times in history the secular quest for knowledge and the religious quest for meaning have been deadly enemies. At a more fundamental level, however, Attridge sees no conflict.

> The commitment to work for the reign of God is entirely compatible with the quest to know the truth and to live in conformity with it. Not to engage in the, oftentimes abrasive, quest for truth is, in fact, to run the risk of setting up idols. At a university, particularly a university that seeks to work for the kingdom of God, the quest of Socrates must be sacrosanct.[16]

The university's current Mission Statement, adopted in 1992–93, defines it as "a Catholic academic community of higher learning . . . dedicated to the pursuit and sharing of truth for its own sake." The opening paragraphs of this statement emphasize the centrality of values of "free inquiry," "open discussion," and the "academic freedom which makes open discussion and inquiry possible." This aim is said to require openness to "the presence and voices of diverse scholars and students," united not by "a particular creedal affiliation" but, rather, by "a respect for the objectives of Notre Dame and a willingness to enter into the conversation that gives it life and character." Its very Catholic character "presupposes that no genuine search for the truth in the human or the cosmic order is alien to the life of faith." In no uncertain terms, the Mission Statement dedicates the university to the pursuit of academic excellence: "The University should set the goal of becoming one of the premier private universities in the country, renowned for research as well as teaching."

At the same time, however, the Mission Statement emphasizes that the Catholic identity of the university "depends upon, and is nurtured by, the continuing presence of a predominant number of Catholic intellectuals." The implicit tension between the two aspects of the Notre Dame mission has therefore required delicate balancing. To what extent may departments legitimately give a job candidate's religion weight in hiring, even when this would mean hiring a less qualified person? To what extent should they do so, if they want to promote academic excellence?

The current president, Edward A. Malloy, indicated in a report to the trustees that his objective is that "dedicated and committed Catholics . . . predominate in number among the faculty." (Here he echoes language used by Pope John Paul II in *On Catholic Universities*.) A majority of the current faculty who responded to a recent questionnaire distributed by the Faculty

Senate found the talk of numerical quotas excessively rigid in a university aspiring to become a peer of the best secular universities.[17] "If the predominance doctrine is enforced," Quinn argues, "Notre Dame's ability to improve the quality of its faculty will be curtailed and its ambition to become a great university will, under currently foreseeable conditions of faculty supply and demand, be doomed to frustration." Other faculty disagree, arguing that the preponderance doctrine is crucial to a healthy Catholic university. The current policy, as reflected in the Mission Statement, is to discriminate in favor of Catholics in initial hiring, but not in tenure and promotion. Frequently, too, where Catholics cannot be found there is active recruitment of religious Christians from other denominations, many of whom are more devout and more religiously oriented than many of the Catholic faculty, and some of whom have become among the staunchest defenders of the institution's Catholic character.[18]

The Mission Statement's reference to "appropriate critical refinement" also attracts our attention. What limits on research and scholarly position-taking does it suggest? It would appear that at present tenured faculty members can say and publish anything they please, without fear of reprisal. Quinn's manuscript on the Notre Dame curriculum volunteered statements criticizing the administration on faculty hiring, and criticizing the Vatican itself on homosexuality. He has made similar statements in campus debates. He does not appear to fear reprisals. Similarly, untenured philosopher Paul Weithman—a student of John Rawls at Harvard who came to Notre Dame because he was committed to teaching in a Catholic university—has published a paper critical of the church's and the administration's official policy on the morality of homosexual relations;[19] and yet Weithman enjoys widespread respect on campus. When he organized a conference on religious discourse in a pluralistic society, Father Hesburgh himself agreed to give the opening address. Weithman and his wife, Maura Ryan, a bioethicist teaching in the Theology Department, are good examples of the sort of vigorous leadership for the next generation that Notre Dame fosters by supporting respectful dissent.

Nor are visiting speakers subject to any religious or ethical test. I have repeatedly lectured at Notre Dame taking positions on gay rights that are inconsistent with the current official position of the church, although they have much support from many believing Catholics. The faculty who have invited me, both tenured and untenured, continue to do so without reprisals, although there are other faculty who take a dim view of my position, and although the current president is the author of a book that takes a negative view of homosexual acts. Threats to the speech of visitors have generally come from outside the campus, and they have usually been vigorously opposed. For example, in 1954, when conservative theologians in Rome tried to get Father Hesburgh to withdraw a book published by the University of Notre Dame Press because of an article by liberal Jesuit John Courtney Murray on religious liberty in a pluralistic society—defending positions that are by now official positions of the church—Hesburgh fought vigorously, and even gave Murray an honorary degree to indicate the extent of his support for dissent.[20] Attridge insists that defense of faculty who take unorthodox positions is essential—not only to the recruitment of excellent Catholic faculty, but also to the further development of the church itself. "Only when such positions are presented honestly and forcefully will the teaching of the church be what it can and should be."[21]

On the other hand, candidates for new faculty appointments sometimes do encounter a critical scrutiny that compares their positions to church orthodoxy. Charles Curran, a Catholic theologian whose dissident views on contraception have been controversial for years, was voted an appointment by Notre Dame's rather liberal Theology Department; the administration did not approve the appointment, in part because of pressures from outside the university. In 1994–95, an offer of appointment in Philosophy to the distinguished Protestant philosopher Jean Hampton generated controversy because she frankly stated her pro-choice views on abortion (views consistent with her Protestant religious commitments). Although the administration did approve an offer of appointment, Hampton was not offered the endowed chair that the department had originally wished to give her; she declined the offer.

Sometimes there are reasons to think that Catholic institutions wish latitude to discriminate in hiring in accordance with Catholic moral positions. When the American Philosophical Association's National Board discussed its nondiscrimination statement in 1991, faculty from several religious institutions, both Catholic and Protestant, favored a version that exempted religious institutions from the general provisions, although the position of any particular institution as such remained unclear. Sexual orientation and religious membership were the focal points of controversy. After lengthy debate, only the latter exemption was granted. In general, too, one notices that non-Catholics who are made offers of appointment at Notre Dame are frequently more conservative—and in many cases more religiously observant—than the Catholic faculty. This phenomenon suggests that some kind of informal testing may be involved in the hiring process, even though the primary factor is probably self-selection.

Until recently, the undergraduate student body of Notre Dame was very homogeneous. Quinn describes it as "all-male, mostly white, almost entirely Catholic, predominantly middle-class, and for the most part intellectually philistine." In recent years the admission of women and concerted efforts to recruit members of racial minorities have changed the picture to some extent. But progress has been slow, even with Hispanic students who are a natural constituency on religious grounds, and even given the presence of ample resources for financial aid. In 1987 the university studied the problem of minority enrollment, proposing an ambitious set of goals. Noting that African-American students frequently feel unwelcome on campus, the Committee on Minority Students insisted that it was urgent to solve this problem—couching their argument in terms of the university's Catholic character itself: "As the nation's premier Catholic University, Notre Dame has a keen responsibility to serve church and society as a beacon against prejudice and a credible witness to the kind of harmonious cultural diversity which is the goal of these broader communities."[22] Diversity on campus, they argue, is also educationally important: one cannot educate "concerned and enlightened" citizens who will be prepared to cope with racial and ethnic diversity if one provides them for four years with a "white, homogeneous, and upper-middle class" educational home. These recommendations are gradually being implemented, although competition for talented minority students is keen and the attractions of Notre Dame for such students are not always compelling.

All Notre Dame undergraduates, in addition to other liberal arts requirements, must take two theology and two philosophy courses. One of the theology courses is an introduction to academic study of the Bible; the other is chosen from a wide range of courses focusing on particular doctrines. One of the philosophy courses is an introduction to central problems of philosophy; the other is selected from a group of courses that focus on ethics, politics, religion, or the nature of persons. The philosophy requirement is older and more traditional than the theology requirement.

These courses provide a basis of Catholic Socratism for all students. They are designed to produce a spirit of responsibility for self: students learn how to subject what they have absorbed to critical scrutiny, in order to decide how they really want their lives to go. They learn to do so, furthermore, with an adequate grasp of the history of the Catholic tradition and the alternatives it presents.

The philosophy requirement creates large demands on staff; students are not always able to get into the course of their choice. On the whole, though, the intellectual level of the classes is high—not surprising, given the quality of the department. Asked why they were required to take philosophy, students in Quinn's course "Science and Human Values" were eager to justify the requirement. Several insisted that a philosophy requirement is valuable because people's faith is important to them, and they want to be able to defend it to others. Others stressed the idea that a person's religious life cannot grow unless one are forced to think for oneself. Not all students agreed with this positive assessment. One, an economics major, said that the philosophy requirement is a diversion from his main business, which is "to get a job." This is probably the dominant view of Notre Dame students when they arrive. That so many have discovered other ways of looking at philosophy—apparently sincerely—is a considerable tribute to the faculty. Students freely exchanged dissenting opinions in class, at times criticizing policies of the university administration and the church hierarchy.

How does Notre Dame deal with the issues of diversity that most exercise secular universities? In general, its Catholic character has made it highly self-conscious about world citizenship. Issues of diversity receive prominent discussion, although curricular achievements are still uneven.

STUDY OF NON-WESTERN CULTURES

Like the Stoics, contemporary Catholics hold that the best sort of citizenship recognizes common human needs and duties all over the globe. The Pope's speech to the United Nations emphasized the urgency of the international human rights movement and the relief of poverty. A recent statement by the United States Catholic Conference asserts unequivocally that all aspects of international economic policy must "reflect basic moral principles and promote the global common good."[23]

Today the church recognizes that respect for human dignity requires learning about cultural and religious difference. Equally important, the number of Catholics in the non-Western world will soon outstrip those in Europe and the United States. The church must know its members worldwide through a study of their cultures and languages. For such reasons American Catholic universities have increasingly focused not only on the morality of international politics—for example, in Notre Dame's prestigious Joan B. Kroc Institute for International Peace Studies and its Helen Kellogg Center for International Studies—but also on the teaching of non-Western cultures.

Notre Dame has addressed the curricular issues primarily through a committee on cultural diversity in the College of Arts and Letters. Student demand for such courses continues to exceed the university's ability to supply them. Some faculty, including both Quinn and his more conservative colleague David O'Connor, would like to see more course development; Quinn expresses impatience with the pace of Notre Dame's progress. The university offers only one course in Asian philosophy, and courses on non-Western religions are oversubscribed. Occasionally, basic courses incorporate non-Western texts along with Western ones: David O'Connor once taught the *Bhagavad Gita* alongside Homer's *Odyssey*. He remarks, however, that since he himself is an expert in Western philosophy, this approach does not really yield a satisfactory understanding of the particularity of a culture: "If I teach the *Bhagavad Gita*, it sounds like Stoicism."

The catalogue confirms the thinness of Notre Dame's current offerings. There is no program or department in East Asian or South Asian studies, in Middle Eastern studies, or in Judaic studies. The oddly constituted Department of Classical and Oriental Languages and Literatures, in addition to a robust program in Greek and Latin, offers a handful of elementary- and intermediate-level courses in Arabic, Syriac, Chinese, and Japanese. Anthropology offers several non-Western courses: "Comparative Religions," "Peoples of the Mediterranean," "Peoples of Africa," "Societies and Cultures of Latin America," "Contemporary Middle East." However, there are more courses dealing with Ireland than with either China or India—an understandable focus, given Notre Dame's history, but one that does not prepare students to understand many world debates. The situation is similar in History: some basic surveys of Japanese, Chinese, Latin American, and Middle Eastern history (nothing on South Asia), but a dominant focus on Europe and America, and no apparent opportunity for advanced work in any non-Western area. No other department has significant non-Western offerings.

There are quite a few study-abroad programs, including programs in Mexico, Japan, Jerusalem, and Cairo.

Further non-Western course development has widespread faculty and student support. But progress will require hiring faculty for that purpose, something that seems not to be a high priority of the administration. To some extent this may be because most specialists in these areas are not Catholic: here is a tension between the aim to be a university that is catholic (universal) and the aim to hire a predominant number of Catholics.

ETHNIC MINORITY STUDIES

Catholics used to be an embattled minority group in America. Even though by now they are the largest religious denomination in the United States (over 20 percent of the total population), their history is intimately bound up with their earlier status. Notre Dame justly prides itself on the fact that its curriculum gives Catholics the means to understand their own history. In a sense, the entirety of the Notre Dame curriculum, and especially its theology requirement, can be seen (at least historically) as a form of minority studies. Notre Dame is more focused on the Catholic tradition than either Morehouse or Spelman is on the African-American tradition. The strong offerings in the study of Ireland and Irish Americans, as well as of Eastern European immigration, complement usefully the theological studies that acquaint students with the essence of their religion.

But that does not mean that Notre Dame can afford to ignore the plural culture in which its students live, especially since world Catholicism has become increasingly diverse. Athletic recruitment also plays a role in the push for racial and ethnic balance. Aggressively and with some success, the university has sought to diversify its ethnic makeup. Faculty recruitment and retention have proved particularly difficult, given the town's reputation as an inhospitable place for minorities; but faculty exchanges have been instituted with some predominantly black colleges in the South and with predominantly Hispanic schools in the Southwest.

Partly with a view to enhancing student recruitment, the curriculum has made considerable efforts to incorporate the experience and culture of American minorities. There is a small but respected program in African-American studies, which offers a major. Both History and Anthropology offer courses on Africa and African-Americans—including a two-semester sequence in African-American history; Anthropology also studies Native

American society, and History offers a general course on ethnic history in addition to its focus on Irish-Americans. The Romance Languages Department offers some courses in Hispanic culture. The small number of minorities on the faculty poses problems for all these efforts. As of 1996, of 677 faculty, only 75 belonged to minorities, and among these only 8 African-Americans.

WOMEN'S STUDIES

"The Catholic church is not exactly a feminist institution," said Kevin Janicki in Phil Quinn's class, as if stating the obvious. Given that starting point, he continued, there are limits to what can be done with women's issues. Quinn concurs: "As anyone familiar with the paternalistic history of the Catholic church would expect, for women things are not as good as they should be at Notre Dame." Women have been at Notre Dame since the early 1970s. Their numbers, once small, are rapidly approaching equality, and gender-blind admissions will begin once the construction of two new dorms is completed. There are many signs, however, that Notre Dame is not yet fully a place for and about them.

When one considers the history of coeducation at Notre Dame, one has to see progress. Hesburgh asserts that in 1952, 95 percent of the students would have been against coeducation; by 1972 they were overwhelmingly for it. Yet even his narrative of the happy development inspires unease:

> Coeducation has had a marvelous effect on Notre Dame. First and foremost, we had always maintained that we were in the business of educating students for leadership, and now we had broadened that commitment to include the other half of the human race. Almost as important, the women brought their great gift of femininity to our campus. During its all-male years Notre Dame tended to be a kind of rough, raunchy, macho place. Our women students brought a good measure of gentility to the campus and enhanced the family feeling of it. With women actually there, the men could stop thinking about them as a breed apart.[24]

Hesburgh's intentions are evidently of the best; and his description is plausible. Consider, however, the situation of women on a campus that expects them to civilize raunchy macho athletes, and to represent "the gift of femininity" rather than simply to go about their business of learning. Although

Hesburgh criticizes students who regard women as "a breed apart," he seems to do as much, in his own way. To be welcomed as an emblem of gentility is better than not being welcomed; but it is not as good as being welcomed as a person.

Today Notre Dame continues to experience tension over women's role on campus. The tremendous social influence of male sports gives campus life an aggressive atmosphere. Social relations between male and female students are far more tense and uneasy than at many other institutions, still governed by the twin poles of incurious avoidance and drunken partying. Nor are there many women, especially tenured women, on the faculty, although their numbers are growing. (As of 1996, 113 out of 677 faculty are women, but only 20 out of 290 full professors, and only 31 out of 202 associate professors.) The large Philosophy Department contains no tenured women, although it now has two tenure-track women. By statute, the president of the university must be a priest, and therefore, obviously, a male. While faculty may freely question the Vatican's views on women's issues, a student women's group that dispensed information about contraception and abortion was denied official recognition.

In Quinn's class of twenty-five, the three women were largely silent. They seemed tentative, depressed, lacking in the physical exuberance that the males displayed. Relations between male and female students did not appear to be good; some of the male students expressed themselves with a contemptuousness that more than explained the women's silence. During a discussion of women's studies, a male student asked why men need to sit in a class to learn about women, when they see them on campus anyway. After class, a woman who had been silent during the general discussion said quietly that the male-dominated character of the Catholic church makes it difficult for her to feel like an equal citizen.

It is not surprising, then, that Notre Dame has not been a pioneer in the curricular development of women's studies. In contrast to the situation on most university campuses of comparable size, there was for a long time no women's center, where faculty and students could gather to discuss both intellectual issues and issues of campus life. Recently, however, a small Women's Resource Center was founded, a sign of the growing status of women on campus. Recently, too, a gender studies program has been created; despite extremely slim funding, it offers an undergraduate minor and sponsors a weekly faculty discussion group. The level of enthusiasm and lively debate in this group appears very high, despite little support from a predominantly conservative student body.

Joan Aldous, William R. Kenan Jr. Professor of Sociology and former chair of the gender studies program, was the only female full professor on the faculty in 1976. Aldous, a non-Catholic, is evidently a person of enormous determination. Overcoming a severe physical handicap that prevents the normal use of her hands, she has become an eminent scholar and tough administrator, fighting resourcefully for the new program. Women, she believes, are not a favored minority at Notre Dame. She has seen considerably more support for African-American studies than for women's studies, both financially and politically. (One unspoken theme is that making African-Americans at home conduces to the success of Notre Dame's athletic recruitment, whereas making women feel at home is not big business in any sense of the word.) But the new program exists, underfunded yet undaunted. The choice to call it Gender Studies rather than Women's Studies reflects the founding group's views about what it would take to make the discipline look intellectually respectable at Notre Dame.

Aldous considers it important to title courses in nonthreatening ways. For example, she substituted the now-popular title "Today's Gender Roles" for the previous title "Changing Gender Roles" when she discovered that male students thought the course would be about sex change operations! Initially, there were virtually no men in the course; now it is one-quarter male. But even with all these efforts, it is difficult to convince people at any level in the university to care about further curricular development. Aldous notes that "most people are not prone to speak out against injustice, whether they're fifty or twenty-five."

More recently Kathy Biddick, a medieval historian who currently chairs the program, has shown resourcefulness and tenacity in making it a lively place for people from a variety of disciplinary backgrounds. The liberal Theology Department contains a number of outstanding women who have strong interests in women's issues. Young faculty who understand the backgrounds from which students are coming and their likely conceptions of gender roles are making a great effort to talk to students in a variety of settings, from independent study courses in sexual ethics to informal meetings in dorms. So one has a sense of very gradual change.

Yet there is something in the classroom and campus atmosphere that sends the message to women that this is not a place for them to be conspicuous and assertive. Notre Dame will have to work harder to become a fully inclusive university. One helpful step would surely be to give increased funding to Gender Studies so that male students would be able to learn more about the history and the lives of women.

HOMOSEXUALITY

Of all issues of diversity on the Notre Dame campus, this is the most bitterly divisive. The administration has persistently refused official recognition to the gay and lesbian student group. Early in 1995 the group, which had met unofficially in vacant space in the counseling center, was informed that it could no longer use that space. Students and faculty are uncertain what prompted this change, but they speculate that conservative alumni may have applied pressure on the administration. In response, the Faculty Senate voted overwhelmingly to support not only the use of the room by gay and lesbian students, but also official recognition of their organization. Quinn writes:

> For the most part, issues of sexual orientation are glossed over, evaded or ignored in the classroom. Free reason, or even the more limited rational capacity Christians are wont to attribute to fallen humanity, has little chance to prevail in discussions of sexual orientation at Notre Dame. Those of us who find this deplorable can try to defend the professional rights and academic freedom of gays and lesbians against the institutional oppression they suffer at Notre Dame. Beyond that, modest gestures of support are feasible.

The position of the church on homosexuality is intensely contested within the church itself. It appears reasonable not to shut off this debate on campus, and liberal faculty at Notre Dame have made a concerted effort to bring to campus speakers with diverse viewpoints. The campus itself contains a wide range of positions, ranging from the conservative views of John Finnis of the Law School to the moderate-liberal views of Quinn and fellow philosopher Paul Weithman. It seems that both sides should support the Faculty Senate in pressing for conditions in which students themselves can become full partners in this debate and the learning that is its precondition.

Catholicism and cultural diversity are allies at Notre Dame when it comes to the study of non-Western cultures and American minority experience. On women's issues, they have been antagonists in the past, although the situation seems to be slowly improving. On sexual orientation, despite the presence of diverse viewpoints on the faculty, they remain antagonists for the present. But the severe reaction of the administration has prompted the faculty to unusual solidarity in defense of the freedom to assemble, argue, and inquire. There are strong reasons to think that a real respect for "the reality of difference" entails allowing those arguments to go forward.

On the whole, Notre Dame has succeeded well in constructing a distinctively religious campus that is also a place of genuine inquiry and debate. Certainly, continued vigilance is needed to preserve a space for free argument on every topic, including those arguments that challenge orthodoxy and ask the tradition to change in order to be "all that it could be." But the dedication of the institution to the Socratic ideal is not merely cosmetic; its faculty seem unusually committed to that norm. They will need to cling to it, if they are to prove Shaw wrong and realize greatness within a Catholic university.

Brigham Young: Revelation through Reason?

Notre Dame is heir to a centuries-long tradition of Catholic higher education, whose architects included Thomas Aquinas and a long line of eminent thinkers. Brigham Young, by contrast, is the only Mormon university in the world (although it has a branch campus in Hawaii). Apart from what unfolds at BYU from day to day, there is no Mormon tradition of higher education; nor is there any clearly agreed tradition of Mormon theology that gives guidance to educational leaders.

BYU grew out of an older system of religious academies that, in turn, grew out of a system of church-related schools; the schools date back to 1847, with the first arrival of Mormon settlers in the Utah Valley. From the first, the Church of Jesus Christ of Latter-day Saints set out to distinguish itself from denominations that were anti-art and anti-education. Through its vigorous support of music and dance, the church has made Utah a famed center for choral music, orchestral music, and ballet. Through its vigorous support of education, it produced Brigham Young Academy. Founded in 1875, the academy became a university in 1903 and is now the largest private university in the United States. The church owns the university and subsidizes approximately two-thirds of its operations from the tithing fund. This gives the elders of the church great power over BYU, and many serve as members of its board of trustees. The remaining money comes from tuition, which is higher for non-Mormon ($3,300 per academic year in 1993–94) than for Mormon students ($2,200). In 1992–93 there were 27,985 fulltime students (26,266 undergraduate and 1,719 graduate and professional students), plus 2,419 part-time day students and 1,238 evening students. In 1994, a faculty report stated that actual enrollment was probably around 33,000. BYU ranks tenth in the number of National Merit Scholars enrolled, and third in the number of Advanced Placement test scores sent to the university.

Students at BYU must conform to an exacting code of dress and behavior, which includes abstinence from coffee, tea, all forms of alcohol, and sexual abstinence unless married. Profanity, the wearing of beards, and sleeveless dresses are all forbidden. Attendance at religious convocations is strongly urged—the university basically shuts down during those hours. Attendance at Sunday church services is required for certification, and each semester students must be certified as acceptable by a bishop. As might be expected, these regulations produce a relatively homogeneous student body—although BYU's low tuition makes it attractive to many who do not really like the rules. Politically, there is great homogeneity; although Democrats do indeed exist at BYU, they are frequently ridiculed and harassed.[25] BYU recruits some minority Mormon students in urban areas; because of the success of its missions abroad, it enrolls a certain number of Asian and Hispanic students; but total minority enrollment stands at 4 percent.

BYU states in no uncertain terms the religious goal of its education: students are to be taught "the truths of the gospel of Jesus Christ." "Any education is inadequate which does not emphasize that His is the only name given under heaven whereby mankind can be saved."[26] Notre Dame demands serious respect for the Roman Catholic tradition, but (in keeping with the Pope's own views) does not deny that Christians have something to learn from other traditions. BYU from the beginning stakes out a position that is likely to deter non-Christian students and faculty from attending; in both areas Mormons are given a high degree of preference.

The LDS Church is governed by a group of elders ranked in order of age. Elders, moreover, show one another great deference, frequently refusing to criticize one another's statements. This system ensures that church (and therefore, ultimately, university) governance will rest in the hands of people of very advanced age (sometimes with impaired mental competence);

aggressive statements may well go uncriticized, creating uncertainty as to how far they express church doctrine. Thus Elder Boyd Packer, who said in a speech on May 18, 1993, that the three great enemies of Mormonism were feminists, homosexuals, and intellectuals, has had a powerful influence in part because other elders have been reluctant to criticize his views. Although in 1995 Packer ceased to be a member of the Board of Trustees at BYU—in a move that was thought to signal support for academic freedom—Bateman's new policy on faculty orthodoxy suggests that Packer's views have not been marginalized.

Uncertainties are compounded by the fact that there are no general guidelines as to which statements of elders, past and present, are authoritative. Moreover, the doctrine of "continuing revelation"—conspicuously invoked on June 9, 1978 to alter long-time church policy by admitting African-American males to the priesthood—makes it perpetually unclear whether the statements that seem most authoritative today will continue to bind tomorrow.[27]

Faculty and administrators at BYU differ intensely about the role of a university education in the religious life and about the proper relation between reason and revelation. At one pole are those who take the view that Mormon higher education should offer unquestioning acculturation into Mormon traditions, while providing useful vocational skills. Adherents of this position are skeptical of graduate education at BYU. They tend to support a strong and rather nonacademic religion requirement for students, and to favor standards of religious orthodoxy both for student enrollment and for faculty hiring and retention. One theological justification offered for this view is that reason must operate within limits set by revelation. It is claimed that strong limits on criticism of church officials create a new and different type of academic freedom, more appropriate to a religious university than are the norms of the secular academy.[28]

People at the other pole want a BYU that is rather like Notre Dame: aspiring to academic excellence in both undergraduate and graduate education, preserving strong guarantees of academic freedom and inquiry, and protecting BYU's religious character not by opposing dissent, but by luring talented Mormon faculty with a commitment to scholarly open-mindedness. In theological terms, this wing can insist that freedom of inquiry is a long and deep part of the Mormon tradition. Joseph Smith—an autodidact who was extremely keen on linguistic and historical study—wrote that he wished Mormons not to be hostile to science, but to see science—and reason generally—as avenues through which divine revelation takes place. Like other aspects of early Mormonism (for example, its skepticism about private property), Smith's views on learning have been muted of late by the Mormon hierarchy.

Attacks on faculty for their scholarly views are not new at BYU: in 1911 three professors were fired for their defense of evolutionary theory and their revisionist biblical scholarship. But in recent years, after an era of relative tolerance, issues of academic freedom have become especially vexed. In 1993 Cecilia Konchar Farr of the English Department, hired specifically to teach feminist literary theory, was denied a three-year pretenure renewal.[29] Although initially claims were made about alleged defects in her scholarly publications, eventually these were withdrawn, and the grounds for dismissal focused on criticisms of her "citizenship" that referred to her feminist activism. (Farr discussed feminist issues in her teaching, worked to publicize and oppose violence against women, and once spoke at a pro-choice rally—although she stated that her own personal position opposed abortion and supported the position taken by the First Presidency of the LDS Church. She made the speech with the full support of her local ecclesiastical leaders.) The Farr case, together with the firing of another liberal faculty member, anthropologist David Knowlton (apparently for his statements in academic contexts critical of church policy and the BYU administration), led to the voluntary departures of a number of outstanding faculty, especially women, some with national reputations. Harold Miller, dean of general and honors education, also resigned over these events. Bateman's new policy will lead to more voluntary departures—and undoubtedly to more dismissals. Meanwhile, BYU graduates who are obtaining doctorates elsewhere—a standard source of future BYU faculty—are increasingly judging that a career at BYU is not for them. Phi Beta Kappa, the national student scholarly honor society, has repeatedly refused BYU's request for a campus chapter, on grounds of its restrictions on academic freedom. These are ominous signs for the future of BYU as a university.

Nor are faculty currently free to invite chosen visitors to campus. MacArthur Fellow, Pulitzer Prize winner, Harvard professor of history, and Mormon Laurel Thatcher Ulrich was declared unfit to give the keynote address at the 1993 BYU Women's Conference—with no explanation and no opportunity for discussion—and has not been allowed to speak on campus since. Other speakers have been similarly vetoed.[30]

To understand the impact of these restrictions on current faculty, consider the case of Scott Abbott. A committed Mormon, Abbott is a well-regarded scholar of German Romanticism. After getting his B.A. at BYU, he went to graduate school at Princeton, where he taught a class in Mormon beliefs to the Princeton undergraduates. On getting his Ph.D., Abbott went to teach at Vanderbilt, where he earned tenure in 1988. But his Mormon roots and family ties led him to return to BYU, with a tenured associate professorship in Germanic Languages and Literatures, moved by a "desire to work at the university that had shaped me and that would shape my fellow Mormons in years to come."[31] At first Abbott was happy with his strong department and his highly intelligent students, and confident about his role in the university. He was exactly the sort of talented, confident, and committed citizen that would strengthen BYU for the future, both an excellent scholar and a commanding speaker. To be sure, the combination of German Romanticism and a professorship at BYU is an unusual one today, indicative of potential conflict, given the currently narrowed understanding of the university's moral agenda. Nonetheless, at the time of his appointment BYU was big enough to contain his field and the view of life one might derive from it, to its advantage.

Things changed abruptly for Abbott in September 1992, when he published, in the liberal Mormon journal *Sunstone* (now off-limits to BYU faculty who want to remain in good standing), an article called "One Lord, One Faith, Two Universities: Tensions between 'Religion' and 'Thought' at BYU." This article is an extremely mild statement about the importance of academic freedom. Abbott cites a letter in which Joseph Smith declared that "the first and fundamental principle of our holy religion is, that we believe that we have a right to embrace all, and every, item of truth, without limitation or without being circumscribed or prohibited by the creeds or superstitious notions of men, or by the dominations of one another." Starting from this basis, he defends academic freedom as essential to a strong BYU. In the process, he politely criticizes statements of several church leaders, especially Elder Boyd Packer, on the limitations of reason, and on the need to ensure the board of trustees control over standards of faculty excellence and conduct. Abbott denies that academic excellence is subversive of religious loyalty, and questions Packer's strong opposition between reason and "the workings of the spirit." Abbott argues that it is through an aggressive assertion of the connections between reason and faith that BYU can best retain a distinctive identity in a secular world. In particular, he questions the intense scrutiny that faculty encounter when they want to write on Mormon history or on contemporary Mormon life.

For this statement—which resembles the orthodox Roman Catholic line on academic freedom—Abbott's "Temple recommend" (official certification of worthiness to enter the Temple) was removed, and his promotion from tenured associate to full professor was denied. He was ordered to apologize to the elders whom he had criticized. His situation at BYU became one of extreme jeopardy. The death of his gay brother from AIDS in 1994 added to his questions, making him think critically about many aspects of church policy and question his own happy status as his family's "good brother." In 1994 he wrote an autobiographical narrative that won first prize from the Utah State Arts Council in the category of nonfiction. Toward the end of the book Abbott describes himself taking a walk, after his brother's death, in the Utah mountains. On the trail he comes across a dead mouse. It looks like a perfect mouse, plump, with a gleaming coat—until he notices that it has no head and that insects are feeding on the remains of the neck. In this way, with a curious blend of the Utah sublime and the Germanic grotesque, Abbott portrays his own situation in a religion that seems to be asking him not to have a mind of his own.

The case of John Armstrong, a student leader at BYU, illustrates the strains of BYU's current policies on its student population. An academically excellent student, John was bound for success in his profession (the study of ancient Greek philosophy), hoping to get a Ph.D. elsewhere and to return to BYU as a faculty member. As a student leader, he was a liberal, questioning official stances of elders and university administrators on a number of issues. On the other hand, he has continually exercised meticulous courtesy to the administration and loyalty to his religion. In style of life and seriousness of commitment he is an exemplary Mormon who finds the moral demands of Mormon life comfortable and appropriate; indeed, his goal clearly has been to become a leader in the faith. Currently John is a graduate student at the University of Arizona, pursuing his studies of Plato. He has written on the topic of reason and revelation, expressing views similar to Abbott's.[32] Abbott's experience indicates that Armstrong is unlikely to be hired at BYU now, nor would he be likely to choose a job there. The university's policies thus cut it off from the most talented and vigorous of its own younger generation. The contrast with Notre Dame's good treatment of young liberals such as Paul Weithman and Maura Ryan is instructive.

Faculty are currently protesting this narrowing of limits on speech and behavior. On March 21, 1996, the BYU chapter of the American Association of University Professors submitted a statement to BYU's accreditation team detailing events that appear to compromise academic freedom, including the following general conclusion:

> As things now stand, the administration can, on an *ad hoc* basis and without accountability, take action on any faculty member it wishes simply by saying that the faculty member's teaching or writing is contrary to the interests of the church. Few, if any, of us want to harm the church. And, guided by our religious convictions, most of us exercise self-restraint in what we profess. Still, if we are to flourish, we must have the freedom to think, to probe, to question. When we take steps seriously to limit that inquiry we cease to be a university. And when faculty members must constantly second-guess whether their work will pass administrative muster, they cease to be scholars.[33]

The authors of the AAUP report stress that what they are after is "the kind of open and productive criticism and argumentation that foster good thinking and moral decision making." This, they argue, must include the freedom to discuss policies without constant fear of being branded "advocates of the adversary."

Given these restraints on faculty and student intellectual life, it would be surprising if the BYU curriculum showed dedication to the goals of Socratic inquiry and world citizenship. Indeed, those goals are not well supported. Universitywide requirements are two: religious education and physical education. Students are required to take seven religion courses, each worth two credit-hours. Religion courses, taught for the most part by faculty without advanced degrees, are deliberately nonscholarly in character. Students are assessed by multiple-choice tests that give no opportunity to develop a line of argument or to express a doubt. The emphasis is on imparting orthodoxy rather than on teaching students to reflect. Thoughtful faculty both liberal and conservative feel dissatisfied with this narrow approach to religious education.

BYU has no philosophy requirement, nor is there the slightest chance that it would have one. According to the *Encyclopedia of Mormonism*, which presents thoughtful mainstream accounts of issues, "Contemporary analytic and existential movements in philosophy have had little impact on [Mormon] thought, not because it is not aware of them, but because it has different answers to the questions they pose . . . Answers to the questions How may I know? What is the seen world? What is the unseen world? and How shall I be wise? are all answered personally for every fully participating Latter-day Saint." Mormon culture, the entry summarizes, "does not encourage philosophizing."

Nonetheless, BYU does have a reasonably good philosophy department, some of whose faculty have national reputations—particularly in the history of philosophy, which is perhaps less controversial on campus than contemporary issues. BYU has sent talented undergraduates on to good graduate programs elsewhere. Student majors emphasize that they feel free to study authors who ask uncomfortable questions: for example, a Nietzsche course taught by philosopher Jim Faulconer focused on his critique of Christianity. Dan Graham, a conservative Mormon and internationally respected expert on Socrates and Aristotle, holds that there are ways to introduce philosophical questioning that are consistent with the Mormon way of life. Teaching the skills of Socratic argument, he urges, is fully consistent with indicating that some conclusions are more strongly supported than others and with pointing out that reason is not the only guide to human life.

Despite such valuable efforts, the impact of Socratic questioning is not felt in the student body as a whole. No BYU administrator would describe the institution's allegiance the way Attridge described that of Notre Dame, saying that the two founding narratives are the story of Socrates and the story of Jesus. In general, BYU is far from realizing Socrates' goal of the examined life.

To what extent has Brigham Young University, like Notre Dame, attempted to build a curriculum for world citizenship? BYU has vast resources; its potential for exciting offerings in the various areas of human diversity is large. For the most part, however, this potential is untapped—because the study of diversity is not valued by those who control the direction of the university.

STUDY OF NON-WESTERN CULTURES

Because the church maintains missions all over the world, and because many BYU undergraduates are on their way either to or from such missions, the university has, in one sense, a markedly cosmopolitan atmosphere. No university in this country offers more foreign languages—including rarely taught languages of Australasia and the South Pacific, Persian Farsi, Haitian Creole, some Native American and some African languages. Many BYU students are proficient in a non-Western language. (John Armstrong, who did his missionary work in China, is fluent in Mandarin as well as in ancient Greek and Latin.) Seven hundred are currently enrolled in courses in Japanese, and a large number also study Korean—probably larger than on any other U.S. campus. Nor does instruction stop with formal language instruction: there are rich programs in Near Eastern studies, Latin American studies, Canadian studies, Asian studies, and international relations.

Nonetheless, the fact that these rich resources are all deployed toward missionary activity poses problems. In any religious institution, students will tend to approach a foreign culture from the vantage point of their own convictions. And yet, as the Pope emphasized, good Christians in a plural world may, and should, strive for a genuine openness to the other culture's understanding, thinking that they may learn something from the way in which a different group of people has puzzled about the mysteries of existence. On the whole, this is not the case at BYU. The basic aim of foreign instruction is to produce converts abroad—and this means producing students who can operate abroad with courtesy and tact, but without being touched or changed by what they encounter. The kind of openness described by the Pope might be risky in a young missionary, and BYU does not, on the whole, seek such openness. As one faculty member observed, "The 'world citizen' is not the conception here—this is a church of apostles. The question it asks is, What people do we want representing the truth?"

Some faculty strive for more curricular coverage of foreign cultures; these, however, find the students hard to reach. Valerie Hudson, a young professor of political science working on women's roles in developing countries, reports that her students enter class with the conviction that American culture already contains everything good. She believes that faculty have a responsibility to encourage greater respect for other nations' traditions. Other faculty, however, sense institutional pressure not to expand coverage of non-Western cultures; chairs are urged to assign interested faculty to other, more traditional courses.

ETHNIC AND RACIAL MINORITIES

The entire curriculum of BYU, with a commitment to Mormonism at its core, is a form of minority study; and yet this study is not thriving. Whereas

Notre Dame encourages the scholarly study of Roman Catholic history and theology, BYU shies away from similar scholarship about Mormonism. Faculty pursuing such inquiries are subject to an unusual degree of surveillance and pressure. Students have few opportunities to learn about their own tradition and its debates. Many faculty deplore this situation.

About other minorities there are some course offerings: an honors program dealing with African-American and Native American experience, an American studies major, and off-campus service learning projects of various types. On the whole, though, homogeneity of perspective is prized, and there is no serious interest in urging students to understand the situation of other groups and religions within their own culture. Only one faculty member, a specialist in Native American studies, is formally trained in an ethnic minority literature; other courses are offered on a self-taught, ad hoc basis.

A serious obstacle to learning about minority experiences is the existence of rules governing exposure to disturbing materials. Mormons are not supposed to see an R-rated movie, no matter what the reason for the R rating. Consequently, faculty who wanted to urge students to see *Schindler's List* in order to gain an understanding of the Holocaust were unable to do so. The Utah Arts Council offered a grant so that all high school students in the state could see it without charge, but this was no use to students who wanted to remain in good standing in or for BYU. One faculty member remarked, "This culture tries to provide childhood." In a world with a history of ethnic brutality, childhood may be a bad state for a citizen to be in.

WOMEN'S STUDIES

Women may not hold the Mormon priesthood, a status widely distributed among men and a *sine qua non* of advancement. This situation has increasingly been challenged by younger scholars. A growing contingent of feminist Mormons has been advancing interpretations of scripture that stress the role of the "Mother in Heaven," in order to defend a larger role for women in the church hierarchy.[34] They have also produced historical evidence (disputed) that Joseph Smith and Brigham Young actually did extend the priesthood to women.[35] Many hope, furthermore, that even if the historical argument is not accepted, a future revelation may bring change. The history of women within Mormonism is a lively topic of research, as are contemporary issues involving women's role.[36]

Unfortunately, virtually none of this new work is now carried on at BYU. In the early 1990s there was a lively feminist community that considered itself free to investigate all areas of Mormon history and thought—although they already had experienced difficulty securing approval to publish the results of their research into controversial areas of Mormon history. In the wake of Farr's dismissal, however, many of these faculty left the university. Some dedicated scholars remain, and are working hard to sustain the Women's Research Institute that was founded in 1978.

Nonetheless, women teaching women's issues at BYU do so under heavy constraint. Some, like Farr, have been attacked for politicizing the classroom. Others have been urged to drop certain authors from their syllabi. Male faculty may have more freedom to teach feminist writers than do female faculty. Philosopher Jim Faulconer taught a seminar on feminism, which included writers such as Catharine MacKinnon and Drucilla Cornell. But males are not exempt from criticism: one in the English Department was refused a tenure-track slot after a conservative parent, a church official, complained about his assignment of a Margaret Atwood novel.

Recently opposition to feminist scholarship has intensified. The AAUP chapter, along with its general report, submitted a separate document titled "Limitations on the Academic Freedom of Women at Brigham Young University." It described numerous cases of refusal to hire new faculty put forward by departments (four such cases from the English Department), termination of employment, vetoing of speakers, and interference with faculty speech and publication. In 1995, to give a representative case, Professors Karen E. Gerdes and Martha N. Beck were forbidden to publish the results of their study of the experiences of Mormon women survivors of childhood sexual abuse and the alleged indifference of Mormon leaders when they asked for help. Both professors have since left the university.[37] For several years now, female candidates for faculty employment have been asked by the academic vice-president whether they would agree not to publish their research if a church leader asked them not to. It has been suggested to the candidates that they must agree not to publish in such a case.[38]

In the spring of 1996, English professor and feminist Gail Turley Houston was fired despite a positive recommendation for tenure from her department and high teaching ratings. The administration made no attempt to discredit Houston's professional work, alleging instead an absence of "gospel insights" and "spiritual inspiration" in her teaching, and charging her with "contradicting fundamental church doctrine" in a statement that she prayed to the Heavenly Mother as well as the Heavenly Father. They also cited a statement praising "free agency" as an appropriate goal for women. Houston, who has accepted a tenure-track position at the University of New Mexico at Albuquerque, states that her Mormon beliefs are "at the center of my life . . . But I feel peaceful and calm because I've tried to speak the truth as I see it about issues vital to the church and university community."[39]

So long as feminist scholarship about Mormon history and contemporary Mormon life is forced outside BYU, the university will not have a women's studies program worthy of the name. The constraints encountered by female faculty are so invasive, and so unequal, that a BYU job is currently an unattractive option for loyal Mormon women.

HOMOSEXUALITY

There is little clarity about the reasons for Mormon strictures against homosexual acts. Although marriage is a necessary condition of morally approved sex, sexual acts within marriage need not be open to procreation, as is the case in Roman Catholicism. There is no ban on contraception or on oral and anal sex acts. Homosexual acts, like premarital acts, are regarded as immoral because they occur outside marriage; but that does not explain the extreme aversion with which many Mormons regard homosexuals. Many Mormons hold that a norm of heterosexuality is a profound part of Mormon theology and its whole understanding of salvation. Others, however, disagree, insisting that we know too little about gender to infer such conclusions from the extant scriptural sources. Meanwhile, the official position of the church is similar to the official Roman Catholic position: love the sinner, hate the sin.[40] Chastity, therapy, and "repentance" are recommended.

The BYU curriculum in general avoids discussion of this troublesome issue. Scott Braithwaite writes:

As I dealt with my same-sex orientation at BYU I remember feeling very isolated . . . A church-controlled environment tends to make any nonconformist feel out of place, even when that nonconformity is beyond the person's control . . . The first mention of homosexuality in any of my BYU courses was during "Child Development" by Price. When he mentioned the topic I gave full attention—homosexuality was caused by a dominant mother and absent father . . . I halfheartedly tried to buy into the idea, but I knew so many dominant mothers that 90 percent of the population must be homosexual, and my father was in full attendance—far from absent. The one BYU course required for every student that should deal with homosexuality is biology. While I praise my biology [instructor] for talking frankly about the heterosexual human sex act, no mention was made about sexual variation that exists in nature. Not surprising—the concept of sexual variation is not well embraced by the church.

The pain of not being able to find out what has been written and experienced by others in this area creates a warping isolation that undermines self-esteem and drives the young person who wants a Mormon life into an adversarial position.

Faculty at BYU say that they do not believe there is much violence against gays and lesbians on the BYU campus. But Abbott and several others stress that silence and ignorance reinforce cultural stereotypes that do lead to violence against gays in our society. Certainly, silence is inimical to esteem and love. Whatever members of the church think about the issue, they should support knowledge rather than ignorance.

"The glory of God is intelligence": that is the motto of Brigham Young University. The institution needs to reflect about these words. Intelligence is indeed glorious, and an unintelligent conformity to rule is not. However, certain conditions are required for the flowering of intelligence in a university, and adherence to them is essential. This is the challenge facing BYU, if it wants to be an inspiration to Mormon youth and a leader of Mormon life for the future.

Notre Dame and BYU: Two Directions for Citizenship

These two cases indicate the range of positions on issues of diversity recently taken by universities with religious affiliations. Some house even fewer tensions between academic and religious missions than does Notre Dame; but these are largely more secular institutions, such as Brandeis University, which have understood the religious mission in a more restricted way from the start. Brandeis aims to support the religious life of Jewish students and to make them feel at home, but it has never sought a "preponderant number" of Jewish faculty or students. For institutions whose religious identity more centrally shapes campus life, the available choices seem to lie between these two poles. Belmont University, a Baptist institution in Nashville, imposes more restrictions on faculty conduct and speech than does Notre Dame, but far fewer than does BYU. Like BYU, it contains considerable anxiety about the study of women and sexuality, and makes little effort to study African-American culture. On the other hand, its Philosophy Department serves a large student population, promoting Socratic inquiry and teaching some effective cross-cultural courses.

The examples of Notre Dame and BYU challenge the claim that religious institutions of higher learning are in peril *because* they have followed the norms of academic freedom and merit-based promotion that are current in the secular academy. In fact, they are in peril to the extent that they do *not* do so. Hiring in accordance with religious membership seems a perfectly appropriate way to maintain a distinctive tradition; on the other hand, penalties for unorthodox speech and research cut out the very core of a university. Notre Dame is vital, and able to attract fine Catholic scholars away from secular universities, precisely because it respects their minds and gives them freedom, following both Jesus and Socrates. BYU was moving in this same direction. The current imposition of restrictions on inquiry and dissent seems little short of suicidal in an institution that retains the ambition to be a university offering undergraduate and graduate degrees, not simply a religious training program. The Mormon commitment to education and to the arts, long a great strength of the Latter-Day Saints, is in jeopardy—*precisely because* standards of freedom that are derided in some quarters as "liberal" and "secular" have not been taken seriously enough as essential elements of human respect in a democratic culture.

Nor is the new emphasis on diversity a threat to the genuinely religious identity of these campuses. It is easy to see that to be a good Catholic university one ought to follow the guidance set forth in the Pope's address, cultivating receptivity and understanding toward cultural difference. This receptivity should extend to the areas of gender and sexuality as well, where more debate and dialogue should be promoted. "Civility dies with the death of dialogue," wrote distinguished Catholic thinker John Courtney Murray— and the occasional lack of civility on sexual matters at Notre Dame reflects an absence of sufficiently respectful and pluralist dialogue. At BYU, resources and reasons exist for the development of a uniquely rich curriculum in international and minority studies—although both need to be developed independently of their narrow missionary purpose if understanding is to be promoted. In the areas of gender and sexuality, dialogue, which at present is discouraged, would considerably enhance the lives of people who suffer low self-esteem and ostracism; to encourage such dialogue seems morally essential.

Love of the neighbor is a central value in all major American religions. These religions call us to a critical examination of our own selfishness and narrowness, urging more inclusive sympathy. It is possible to love one's neighbors without knowing anything about them, without enriching one's reason by factual knowledge and one's imagination through narrative. But it is not very likely that ignorant people will direct their love in adequate practical ways; and ignorance can all too easily become twisted in the direction of prejudice and hate. All universities can and should contribute to the development of citizens who are capable of love of the neighbor. But the religious universities have this mission at their heart in a special way; and it is presumably for reasons such as these that the major religions have founded universities, believing that love at its best is intelligent and that higher education can enhance its discrimination. If they believe this, they must respect the life of the mind, its freedom, and its diversity; and they should seek a truly civil dialogue on the most pressing issues of human difference.

The "New"
Liberal Education

Fear not O Muse! truly new ways and days receive, surround you.

Walt Whitman, *Song of the Exposition*

Like Seneca, we live in a culture divided between two conceptions of a liberal education. The older one, dominant in Seneca's Rome, is the idea of an education that is *liberalis*, "fitted for freedom," in the sense that it is aimed at freeborn gentlemen of the propertied classes. This education initiated the elite into the time-honored traditions of their own society; it sought continuity and fidelity, and discouraged critical reflection. The "new" idea, favored by Seneca, interprets the word *liberalis* differently. An education is truly "fitted for freedom" only if it is such as to *produce* free citizens, citizens who are free not because of wealth or birth, but because they can call their minds their own. Male and female, slave-born and freeborn, rich and poor, they have looked into themselves and developed the ability to separate mere habit and convention from what they can defend by argument. They have ownership of their own thought and speech, and this imparts to them a dignity that is far beyond the outer dignity of class and rank.

These people, Seneca suggests, will not be uncritical moral relativists—for ownership of one's own mind usually yields the understanding that some things are good and some bad, some defensible and others indefensible. Nor will they scoff at the traditions that the older "liberal" education prizes: for

293

they know that in tradition lies much that has stood the test of time, that should command people's respect. They will start from convention and tradition when they ask what they should choose, viewing it as essential food for the mind. On the other hand, they do not confuse food with the strength in the mind that the food is supposed to produce. They know they need to use tradition to invigorate their own thought—but this benefit involves a willingness to criticize it when criticism is due. They do not prize custom just because of its longevity, nor do they equate what has been around a long time with what must be or with what is "natural." They therefore want to learn a good deal about other ways and people—both in order to establish respectful communication about matters of importance and in order to continue rethinking their own views about what is best. In this way, they hope to advance from the cultural narrowness into which we all are born toward true world citizenship.

Our country has embarked on an unparalleled experiment, inspired by these ideals of self-command and cultivated humanity. Unlike all other nations, we ask a higher education to contribute a general preparation for citizenship, not just a specialized preparation for a career. To a greater degree than all other nations, we have tried to extend the benefits of this education to all citizens, whatever their class, race, sex, ethnicity, or religion. We hope to draw citizens toward one another by complex mutual understanding and individual self-scrutiny, building a democratic culture that is truly deliberative and reflective, rather than simply the collision of unexamined preferences. And we hope in this way to justify and perpetuate our nation's claim to be a valuable member of a world community of nations that must increasingly learn how to understand, respect, and communicate, if our common human problems are to be constructively addressed.

As in Seneca's Rome, so too in our nation, this ideal of an education for freedom has its detractors. In Rome, the cultivated elite frequently resisted the Stoics' ideas about the insignificance of rank and hierarchy, their insistence on acknowledging the equal humanity and educational potential of male and female, slave and free. In our own society, traditionalists frequently resist the idea that we should cultivate our perceptions of the human through a confrontation with cultures and groups that we have traditionally regarded as unequal. Defenders of the older idea of a gentleman's education urge that our colleges and universities focus on acculturation to what is great and fine in our own tradition, rather than on Socratic and universalistic goals. Insofar as this education reaches out to new citizens, it will do so because they agree to accept time-honored gentlemanly standards. They should not expect that their own experiences and traditions will form part of the curriculum. They may enter the academy only on sufferance and in disguise. They may remain only so long as they do not allow their nongentlemanly voices to be heard, or inject their nontraditional experiences into the dignified business of liberal learning.

This way of thinking, though common enough, is foreign to what is finest in our democratic educational traditions, which have been built on ideas of equality and mutual respect. Seneca does not show us directly how to criticize such an opponent, since his time is so unlike our own. From his basic idea of the cultivation of humanity, however, we can derive our own answer. We do not fully respect the humanity of our fellow citizens—or cultivate our own—if we do not wish to learn about them, to understand their history, to appreciate the differences between their lives and ours. We must therefore construct a liberal education that is not only Socratic, emphasizing critical thought and respectful argument, but also pluralistic, imparting an understanding of the histories and contributions of groups with whom we interact, both within our nation and in the increasingly international sphere of business and politics. If we cannot teach our students everything they will need to know to be good citizens, we may at least teach them what they do not know and how they may inquire. We can acquaint them with some rudiments about the major non-Western cultures and minority groups within our own. We can show them how to inquire into the history and variety of gender and sexuality. Above all, we can teach them how to argue, rigorously and critically, so that they can call their minds their own.

It is relatively easy to construct a gentleman's education for a homogeneous elite. It is far more difficult to prepare people of highly diverse backgrounds for complex world citizenship. Curricula aiming at these ideals fit no general mold. Where they are well constructed, they are constructed resourcefully on the basis of local knowledge, knowledge of the institution's student body, its material resources, and its faculty. Socratic argument, for example, is often best advanced by a required course or courses in philosophy; in some institutions, however, a more flexible system of infusing Socratic values into courses of many types may achieve good results. An understanding of race and ethnicity is frequently best promoted by an integrated interdisciplinary course required of all students, such as the

SUNY–Buffalo course on American pluralism, or the Scripps course on Enlightenment thought and its critics. But at some institutions, for example Brown and Grinnell, students find enough course offerings in a variety of different departments to attain a comparable degree of understanding without a single common course. The diversity of institutions and students puts enormous pressure on faculty to think creatively and to invest their time in curricular development.

Such projects do not always succeed. At the University of Nevada at Reno, resources are so limited that the basically well-reasoned program in human diversity can achieve little more than an amorphous elective requirement comprised of existing courses. Many institutions face such pressures. At the University of California at Riverside, otherwise promising proposals in sexuality studies and women's studies are marred by tensions between postmodernist faculty in literature and faculty adhering to more traditional canons of rational argument, who feel, plausibly enough, that the postmodernist attack on truth threatens the very possibility of ethical and political criticism. At Riverside, too, we see tensions between an approach to ethnic studies that sees it as an important area of understanding for all students and an approach based on identity politics. Both of these tensions arise on many campuses, threatening world citizenship. Finally, some such projects are derailed by opposition from an administration unwilling to permit faculty to incorporate controversial new material into their teaching. One salient example of this kind of failure is the assault on feminist scholarship at Brigham Young University, but at many institutions these new studies are more passively discouraged by insufficient financial support.

Far more often, however, we see an astonishing variety of creative proposals that promise a rich future for our democracy if only they will continue developing and find the support they deserve. The most successful proposals include some ambitious multicourse programs, such as the Cultural Encounters Program at St. Lawrence, where a creative and tenacious faculty group has transformed many aspects of the curriculum; the Afro-American Studies program at Harvard, where Skip Gates, Anthony Appiah, Cornel West, William Julius Wilson, and others are bringing distinguished scholarship and humane ideals to a field that has too long been treated as a poor relation; and the program in Sexuality and Society at Brown, where a multidisciplinary faculty drawn from the humanities, the social sciences, and the biological and medical sciences are working to present students with an integrated understanding of this important area of personal and political life. Successes also include required basic courses, such as the American pluralism course at SUNY–Buffalo, or the Scripps course on the legacy of the Enlightenment, or required philosophy courses at Notre Dame, Bentley, Harvard, and Pittsburgh, or Spelman's course on the African diaspora. They include countless individual elective courses at the departmental level: Steve Salkever and Michael Nylan's course in comparative political philosophy at Bryn Mawr; Ronnie Littlejohn's course on comparative moral philosophy at Belmont; Susan Okin's course on women in political thought at Stanford; Marilyn Friedman's class on feminist political thought at Washington University; Amartya Sen's course on hunger and famines at Harvard; Eve Stoddard's course on the female body at St. Lawrence. Finally, campuses also foster world citizenship through noncurricular projects such as conferences and visiting lectures. Brown University's conference on Homosexuality and Human Rights in the Major Religious Traditions was an outstanding example of such a project, promoting civil dialogue across political lines on a deeply divisive issue.

The future of these projects is, however, highly uncertain. They face some peril in our time, above all the risk of being undermined by a growing interest in vocational, rather than liberal, education. It now seems to many administrators (and parents and students) too costly to indulge in the apparently useless business of learning for the enrichment of life. Many institutions that call themselves liberal arts colleges have turned increasingly to vocational studies, curtailing humanities requirements and cutting back on humanities faculty—in effect giving up on the idea of extending the benefits of a liberal education to their varied students. In a time of economic anxiety, such proposals often win support. But they sell our democracy short, preventing it from becoming as inclusive and as reflective as it ought to be. People who have never learned to use reason and imagination to enter a broader world of cultures, groups, and ideas are impoverished personally and politically, however successful their vocational preparation.

This peril to democracy is compounded by the assault on curricular diversity that has been repeatedly launched by defenders of the gentleman's model of liberal education. In principle, the gentleman's model and the world-citizen model agree on the importance of a shared humanistic education for the culture of life. Against the challenge of vocationalism, they ought to be allies rather than opponents. But this has not always been the case. By portraying today's humanities departments as faddish, insubstantial, and controlled by a radical elite, cultural conservatives—while calling for a return to a more traditional liberal arts curriculum—in practice feed the popular disdain for the humanities that has led to curtailment of departments and programs and to the rise of narrow preprofessional studies. When critics such as Allan Bloom, Roger Kimball, and George Will caricature the activities of today's humanities departments by focusing only on what can be made to look extreme or absurd, they probably do not promote their goal of increasing university support for traditional humanistic education. In practice, the state legislator or parent who reads such attacks is far more likely to develop a disdain for the humanities and to press for cuts in that entire area, often in favor of narrow vocational education. If people view the teaching that is actually going on in the humanities as incompetent and even politically dangerous, it is all too easy to feel justified in cutting off funds and turning increasingly to the safer terrain of accounting, computer science, and business education.

It is urgent, then, to say that the disdainful picture is inaccurate. The energy, goodwill, and resourcefulness of our humanities faculty should command our profound respect, whether or not we agree with every proposal that is made. (It would be impossible to agree with all proposals, since there is endless variety, disputation, and debate.) These faculty are educating citizens of widely varying types—in many case students who would not have been in college at all one or two generations ago. Wisely, instructors at both elite and more inclusive schools are not seeking to make these nontraditional (and traditional) students into little Roman gentlemen; nor are they seeking to turn them into clones of the radicals of the 1960s. Instead, they are seeking to elicit from them the best in citizenship and understanding that they can achieve, starting from where they are. At Bentley, Krishna Mallick teaches a philosophy course for people who never thought Socratic argument would be a part of their lives; by the end of the course their attitude to political debate has been transformed. At Notre Dame, faculty working in the area of gender studies start from an awareness of the cultural background of Notre Dame students and their likely stereotypes, in order to work toward a more inclusive understanding of women and their lives.

Because the world in which we live is complex, this enterprise requires learning about racial, ethnic, and religious difference. It requires learning about the history and experience of women. It requires gaining a reflective understanding of human sexuality. And it requires learning how to situate one's own tradition within a highly plural and interdependent world. These things are difficult to do, and they are not always done well. But often they are done extremely well—by men and women of highly varied religious, ethnic, and professional backgrounds, many of whom are struggling to keep their departments going, or moving from untenured adjunct job to adjunct job, in a time of economic constraint and contraction of academic programs. It is to their hope and ingenuity that we owe our future as a democracy.

In Pomona, California, Laurie Shrage, professor of philosophy from California State Polytechnic University, talks about the struggle to keep philosophy going in an institution increasingly dominated by vocational goals and increasingly indifferent to the idea that philosophy forms part of a basic liberal education. Faculty in the Cal State system have an extremely heavy teaching load, and Shrage, teaching in both philosophy and women's studies, has even more duties than many. Despite these impediments she has achieved widespread respect for her writing about legal and moral issues in the area of prostitution and women's equality and, more recently, about the role of a religious or ethnic identity in giving meaning to one's life. A petite woman in her forties, her energy and humor are contagious.

The Pomona students, says Shrage, are bound for a wide range of professions—engineering, business, computer science, high school and elementary school teaching. (Not many go for medicine or law, fields that are known to find a philosophy major highly desirable.) Most of them fear philosophy, convinced, without any prior experience, that it is too hard for them. Although the university has a "critical thinking" requirement, other humanities departments offer courses that satisfy it, usually without much emphasis on logical analysis or argument. Shrage and her colleagues have not been able to persuade the administration that philosophy's attention to logic and rigor has a distinctive contribution to make. This, Shrage feels, is a loss for the students, both as people and, ultimately, as citizens. They do not learn to argue about issues of the day with rigor, curiosity, and mutual respect. Courses in business and engineering pay lip service to the importance of ethical issues, including some attention to ethics in their regular courses; but they are not the focus of such courses and do not get covered fully; meanwhile, the existence of some ethical discussion in those courses reinforces the students' sense that they do not need philosophy.

What do Shrage and her colleagues do to keep philosophy going? Shrage says she doesn't have much hope of attracting many future engineers or even high school teachers to her courses. But she is not giving up; and now she speaks with passionate enthusiasm. In thinking how to keep the field going, she has decided to focus on the future elementary school teachers. They seem less rigidly preprofessional, more ready to get interested in what a liberal education might offer. Shrage has therefore designed a course for them, "Philosophy through Children's Literature," which explores ways in which they can use works of L. Frank Baum and other classic children's authors to awaken wonder and questioning—about space and time, about the mind, about what a human being is, about what friendship is. Shrage smiles at the thought that she has discovered a route to her goal, even when all the obvious routes were blocked.

In Cambridge, Massachusetts, Krishna Mallick talks about Bentley College, her students, and cross-cultural understanding. Mallick was born in Calcutta; although she has lived in this country for more than twenty years, she still wears a sari and speaks with a heavy Bengali accent. For years she has taught as an adjunct at Bentley and at nearby Salem State College, without a tenure-track position. Mallick has an ability our nation badly needs: the ability to generate excitement about rational debate in students who never cared about it before. She keeps awakening this eagerness in students like Billy Tucker (who in 1995–96 took his second course with her, on Indian thought). How can this cultivation of humanity continue? Few people who teach at privileged institutions would be able to hold out against the discouragement Mallick contends with. How does she go on as she does, without a decent salary, without benefits, without any job security? Mallick shrugs, as if that is a slightly strange question. I guess it is the joy of it, she says. It is because I like them. Each class, all new and different people. I just like them.

Such teachers have embarked on a project that urgently demands our support, since we all live in the nation that will be governed, for better or for worse, by people who have, or who do not have, the complex understanding they seek to impart. It would be catastrophic to become a nation of technically competent people who have lost the ability to think critically, to examine themselves, and to respect the humanity and diversity of others. And yet, unless we support these endeavors, it is in such a nation that we may well live. It is therefore very urgent right now to support curricular efforts aimed at producing citizens who can take charge of their own reasoning, who can see the different and foreign not as a threat to be resisted, but as an invitation to explore and understand, expanding their own minds and their capacity for citizenship.

"Soon we shall breathe our last," wrote Seneca at the end of his treatise on the destructive effects of anger and hatred. "Meanwhile, while we live, while we are among human beings, let us cultivate our humanity." Across the United States, colleges and universities are working to develop curricula that will meet the challenge contained in those words. Let us support them.

NOTES

INDEX

NOTES

CHAPTER ONE   Socratic Self-Examination

1. See in particular Roger Kimball, *The Tenured Radicals* (New York: Harper & Row, 1990).
2. In 1993, when I visited the campus, Belmont was affiliated with the Southern Baptist Convention, though it is so no longer.
3. Heraclitus is a possible exception, but he certainly is no democrat.
4. Aristotle, *Eudemian Ethics* 1.1216a26–39.
5. Cicero, *Tusculan Disputations* 5.4.10.
6. Plato, *Apology* 20C.
7. *Apology* 30E–31A.
8. *Apology* 38A.
9. See Gregory Vlastos, *Socrates: Ironist and Moral Philosopher* (Cambridge and Ithaca: Cambridge University Press and Cornell University Press, 1991).
10. Lysias, *Against Eratosthenes* (oration 12).
11. See Plato, *Laches, Lysis, Charmides, Euthyphro*.
12. Plato, *Republic* 352D.
13. See Vlastos, *Socrates*.
14. On "deliberative democracy" and its roots in Madison, see, for example, Cass R. Sunstein, *The Partial Constitution* (Cambridge, Mass.: Harvard University Press, 1993), pp. 133–145, 162–194.
15. *Apology* 20AB.
16. On the period, see A. A. Long, *Hellenistic Philosophy* (London: Duckworth, 1974).
17. Seneca, criticizing himself in *On Anger* 3.36.
18. See Roman Stoic Musonius Rufus, "That Women Too Should Do Philosophy."
19. Not all Stoics were democrats, although Roman Stoicism was frequently associated with republican anti-imperial movements, and Stoic ideas of freedom were frequently appealed to throughout history in justification of anti-imperial acts (not least in the American Revolution).

20. Plato, *Phaedrus* 275A–E.

21. Epictetus, *Discourses* 1.4.13–17.

22. Seneca, *Letter* 33.

23. See E. D. Hirsch, Jr., *Cultural Literacy* (Boston: Houghton Mifflin, 1987), who uses the term *cultural literacy* to denote a basic grasp of cultural information that proves necessary to decode other information.

24. For a related argument, see Randall L. Kennedy, "Racial Critiques of Legal Academia," *Harvard Law Review* 102 (1989): 1745–1819.

25. Putnam and Davidson are the closest to Kant, Quine and Goodman in the middle, Rorty at the other extreme.

26. See Louise B. Antony, "Quine as Feminist," in *A Mind of One's Own: Feminist Essays on Reason and Objectivity*, ed. Louise B. Antony and Charlotte Witt (Boulder: Westview Press, 1993).

27. See Martha C. Nussbaum, "Skepticism about Practical Reason in Literature and the Law," *Harvard Law Review* 107 (1994), 714–744; and "Sophistry about Conventions," in *Love's Knowledge: Essays in Philosophy and Literature* (New York: Oxford University Press, 1990), pp. 220–229.

28. Amartya Sen, in Steve Pyke's photographic collection *Philosophers*, 2nd ed. (London: zelda cheatle press, 1995), unpaginated.

CHAPTER TWO   Citizens of the World

1. "Anna" is a woman I interviewed in China. Her name has been changed.

2. *New York Times*, July 4, 1996, p. 1.

3. All judgments about the Cynics are tentative, given the thinness of our information. The central source is Diogenes Laertius' *Lives of the Philosophers*. See B. Branham and M.-O. Goulet-Cazé, eds., *The Cynics* (Berkeley: University of California Press, 1996).

4. Plutarch, *On the Fortunes of Alexander* 329AB = *SVF* 1.262; see also Seneca, *On Leisure* 4.l.

5. For Paine, see *The Rights of Man*, pt. 2; for Smith, see "Of Universal Benevolence," in *The Theory of Moral Sentiments* (Indianapolis: Liberty Classica, 1982), vol. 6, pt. 2, p. 3, with special reference to Marcus Aurelius; for Kant, see *Perpetual Peace*, in *Kant's Political Writings*, ed. H. Reiss, trans. H. Nisbet, 2nd ed. (Cambridge: Cambridge University Press, 1991). For a discussion of Stoic ideas in Kant's political thought, see Martha C. Nussbaum, "Kant and Stoic Cosmopolitanism," *Journal of Political Philosophy* 5 (1997): 1–25.

6. See Tagore, "Swadeshi Samaj," cited in Krishna Dutta and Andrew Robinson, *Rabindranath Tagore: The Myriad-Minded Man* (London: Bloomsbury, 1995).

7. Kwame Anthony Appiah, *In My Father's House: Africa in the Philosophy of Cultures* (New York: Oxford University Press, 1991).

8. See W. K. C. Guthrie, *History of Greek Philosophy,* vol. 3 (Cambridge: Cambridge University Press, 1969).

9. See Stephen Halliwell, *Plato: Republic V* (Warminster: Aris and Phillips, 1993).

10. The Hellenistic era is usually taken to begin at the death of Alexander the Great, 323 B.C.; Aristotle died in 322. Although Diogenes was a contemporary of Aristotle, his influence is felt in the later period. See A. A. Long, *Hellenistic Philosophy* (London: Duckworth, 1974).

11. The translation by R. D. Hicks in the Loeb Classical Library volume 2 of Diogenes Laertius is inadequate but gives the general idea. All citations here are from that *Life,* but the translations are mine.

12. Dionysius was the one-man ruler of Syracuse in Sicily whom Plato attempted, without success, to turn into a "philosopher-king."

13. The Stoic school had an extraordinarily long life and a very broad influence, extending from the late fourth century B.C. to the second century A.D. in both Athens and Rome.

14. Diogenes uses the single word *kosmopolitēs,* but Marcus Aurelius prefers the separated form.

15. See Marcus Aurelius, *Meditations,* trans. G. M. A. Grube (Indianapolis: Hackett, 1983).

16. The image is suggested in Cicero and is explicit in Hierocles, a Stoic of the first–second centuries A.D. (quoted here); it is probably older.

17. This is material from a draft written by the ANC for the new constitution; it was presented by Albie Sachs to a meeting on human rights at Harvard University in October 1993.

18. See E. D. Hirsh Jr., ed., *What Your Second Grader Needs to Know* (New York: Doubleday, 1991).

19. Charlotte Witt, *Substance and Essence in Aristotle* (Ithaca: Cornell University Press, 1989); Louise B. Antony and Charlotte Witt, eds., *A Mind of One's Own: Feminist Essays on Reason and Objectivity* (Boulder: Westview Press, 1992).

20. Grant H. Cornwell and Eve W. Stoddard, "Things Fall Together: A Critique of Multicultural Curricular Reform," *Liberal Education,* Fall 1994, pp. 40–51.

CHAPTER THREE   The Narrative Imagination

1. The issues of this chapter are treated at greater length in Martha C. Nussbaum, *Poetic Justice: The Literary Imagination in Public Life* (Boston: Beacon Press, 1996).

2. Ralph Ellison, *Invisible Man* (New York: Random House, 1992), pp. 563, 566, 3.

3. Ibid., p. 572.

4. Ibid., pp. xxiv–xxv, xxvi.

5. See Nussbaum, *Poetic Justice,* for Dickens' discussion of this case.

6. See Lionel Trilling, *The Liberal Imagination* (New York: Scribner's, 1953).

7. Jean-Jacques Rousseau, *Emile, or On Education,* trans. Allan Bloom (New York: Basic Books, 1979), p. 224.

8. On this phenomenon, see Charles Taylor, *Sources of the Self: The Making of the Modern Identity* (Cambridge, Mass.: Harvard University Press, 1989); also Ian Watt, *The Rise of the Novel* (Berkeley: University of California Press, 1957).

9. The original Stoics were critical of most literature of their time, since they believed that it usually exaggerated the importance of circumstances for human well-being. But this aspect of their view is logically independent of their interest in sympathetic perception, which naturally led them to take an interest in cultivating the imagination.

10. Walt Whitman, "By Blue Ontario's Shore."

11. Wayne Booth, *The Company We Keep: An Ethics of Fiction* (Berkeley: University of California Press, 1988).

12. See Stanley Cavell, *The Claim of Reason: Wittgenstein, Skepticism, Morality, and Tragedy* (New York: Oxford University Press, 1976).

13. See Judith Frank, "In the Waiting Room: Canons, Communities, 'Political Correctness,'" in *Wild Orchids and Trotsky: Messages from American Universities,* ed. Mark Edmundson (New York: Penguin, 1993), pp. 125–149.

14. George Will, *Newsweek,* April 22, 1991.

15. Clive Bell, *Art* (London: Chatto & Windus, 1913); Roger Fry, *Transformations* (London: Chatto & Windus, 1926).

16. Edward Bullough, "Psychical Distance as a Factor in Art and as an Aesthetic Principle," *British Journal of Psychology* 5 (1912): 87–98.

17. W. K. Wimsatt and Monroe C. Beardsley, "The Intentional Fallacy," *Sewanee Review* 54 (1946); also Cleanth Brooks, *The Well-Wrought Urn* (New York: Harcourt Brace, 1947).

18. Milton Friedman, "The Methodology of Positive Economics," reprinted in Daniel M. Hausman, ed., *The Philosophy of Economics* (Cambridge: Cambridge University Press, 1984), p. 212.

19. Ellison, *Invisible Man,* p. xxvi.

CHAPTER FOUR   The Study of Non-Western Cultures

1. R. Littlejohn, handout for "Advanced Moral Theory," fall 1993.

2. See Cruz v. Beto, 405 U.S. 319 (1972).

3. John Searle, "The Storm over the University," *New York Review of Books,* December 6, 1990, p. 39.

4. See also Martha C. Nussbaum and Amartya Sen, "Internal Criticism and Indian Rationalist Traditions," in *Relativism,* ed. Michael Krausz (Notre Dame: Notre Dame University Press, 1989).

5. For example, the philosophies of Schopenhauer and Nietzsche were deeply influenced by Buddhism. They, in turn, influenced artists such as Richard Wagner and D. H. Lawrence.

6. The current debate about the teaching of Chinese culture is especially rich and helpful: see especially Stephen Salkever and Michael Nylan, "Comparative Political Philosophy and Liberal Education: 'Looking for Friends in History,'" *Political Science and Politics*, June 1994, pp. 238–247; a longer version of this paper, titled "Teaching Comparative Political Philosophy: Rationale, Problems, Strategies," was presented at the 1991 annual meeting of the American Political Science Association and is available from the authors upon request. See also Zhang Longxi, "Knowledge, Skepticism, and Cross-Cultural Understanding" (manuscript, April 1993); idem, "Out of the Cultural Ghetto: Theory, Politics, and the Study of Chinese Literature," *Modern China* 19 (1993): 71–101; Lee Yearley, *Mencius and Aquinas: Theories of Virtue and Conceptions of Courage* (Albany: SUNY Press, 1990).

7. See Yearley, *Mencius and Aquinas*, pp. 201 ff.

8. See Henry S. Richardson, *Practical Reasoning About Final Ends* (New York: Cambridge University Press, 1994).

9. See Lydia Goehr, *The Imaginary Museum of Musical Works: An Essay in the Philosophy of Music* (Oxford: Clarendon Press, 1992).

10. Paul Ehrlich, *The Population Bomb* (New York: Ballantine, 1968), p. 15; see the critique in Amartya Sen, "Fertility and Coercion," *University of Chicago Law Review* 63 (1996): 1042.

11. See Amartya Sen, "Is Coercion a Part of Asian Values?" (manuscript, September 1995).

12. See Charles Taylor, *Sources of the Self: The Making of the Western Identity* (Cambridge, Mass.: Harvard University Press, 1989).

13. See my discussion of these issues in "The Feminist Critique of Liberalism," an Amnesty Lecture forthcoming in the volume *Women's Voices, Women's Lives*, ed. M. Forey and J. Gardner (New York: HarperCollins, 1997); and in my forthcoming book *Sex and Social Justice* (New York: Oxford University Press).

14. See S. M. Marglin and F. Appfel Marglin, eds., *Dominating Knowledge* (Oxford: Clarendon Press, 1993).

15. See Sen and Nussbaum, "Internal Criticism"; also Martha C. Nussbaum, "Human Functioning and Social Justice: A Defense of Aristotelian Essentialism," *Political Theory* 20 (1992): 204–246.

16. S. Radakrishnan and C. A. Moore, eds., *A Sourcebook in Indian Philosophy* (Princeton: Princeton University Press, 1957), p. xxiii.

17. See Bimal Matilal, *Perception: An Essay on Classical Indian Theories of Knowledge* (Oxford: Clarendon Press, 1986).

18. Ibid., pp. 4–5.

19. Daniel Bonevac, William Boon, and Stephen Phillips, eds., *Beyond the Western Tradition: Readings in Moral and Political Philosophy* (London and Toronto: Mayfield, 1992).

20. Zhang Longxi, "Knowledge, Skepticism, and Cross-Cultural Understanding," Distinguished Humanist Achievement Lecture, University of California at Riverside, 1993.

21. See Sen, "Is Coercion a Part of Asian Values?"

22. John Locke, *An Essay Concerning Human Understanding* (1690), book 2, chaps. 13, 19.

23. Matilal, *Perception*, p. 4.

24. Allan Bloom, *The Closing of the American Mind: How Higher Education Has Failed Democracy and Impoverished the Souls of Today's Students* (New York: Simon and Schuster, 1987), p. 36.

25. In the *New York Times*, March 10, 1994, Bellow states that he made the remark in a telephone interview, to illustrate the difference between preliterate and literate societies, without normative intent. He adds that he forgot that he had in fact read a Zulu novel: *Chaka*, by Thomas Mofolo.

26. Frédérique Marglin, "Smallpox in Two Systems of Knowledge," in Marglin and Marglin, *Dominating Knowledge*, pp. 102–144.

27. S. A. Marglin, "Losing Touch: The Cultural Conditions of Worker Accommodation and Resistance," in ibid., pp. 217–282.

28. See Salkever and Nylan, "Teaching Comparative Political Philosophy," p. 17.

29. Dan Sperber, "Apparently Irrational Beliefs," in *Rationality and Relativism,* ed. Martin Hollis and Steven Lukes (Oxford: Basil Blackwell, 1982), pp. 179–180.

30. Salkever and Nylan, "Teaching Comparative Political Philosophy," p. 25.

31. See Martha C. Nussbaum, "Non-Relative Virtues," in *The Quality of Life,* ed. Martha C. Nussbaum and Amartya Sen (Oxford: Clarendon Press, 1993).

32. Salkever and Nylan, "Teaching Comparative Political Philosophy," p. 19.

33. Arthur M. Schlesinger Jr., *The Disuniting of America: Reflections on a Multicultural Society* (n.p.: Whittle Direct Books, 1991), p. 76.

34. See Sen, "Is Coercion a Part of Asian Values?"

35. See Nussbaum, "The Feminist Critique of Liberalism."

36. Sen, "Is Coercion a Part of Asian Values?"

37. See M. F. Burnyeat, "Did the Ancient Greeks Have the Concept of Human Rights?" *Polis* 13 (1994): 1–11; Fred D. Miller Jr., *Nature, Justice, and Rights in Aristotle's Politics* (Oxford: Oxford University Press, 1995); and symposiums on Miller's book in *Review of Metaphysics* 49, no. 4 (1996), and *Ancient Philosophy,* Fall 1996.

38. See Sen, "Is Coercion a Part of Asian Values?"

39. Translation from D. C. Sircar, *Asokan Studies* (Calcutta: Indian Museum, 1979), pp. 34–35, edict XIII, quoted in Sen, "Is Coercion a Part of Asian Values?"

40. Sircar, *Asokan Studies,* p. 37, quoted in Sen, "Is Coercion a Part of Asian Values?"

41. *Alberuni's India,* trans. E. C. Sachau, ed. A. T. Embree (New York: W. W. Norton, 1971), p. 20, quoted in Sen, "Is Coercion a Part of Asian Values?"

CHAPTER FIVE   African-American Studies

1. Later that evening, during the speech, Muhammed was shot (not fatally) by a former member of his sect. The first doctor to treat him was Jewish.

2. Werner Sollors, Caldwell Titcomb, and Thomas A. Underwood, eds., *Blacks at Harvard: A Documentary History* (New York: NYU Press, 1993). On the odd publishing history of this volume, see Thomas Underwood, "African Americans at Harvard: The Story of a Book," delivered as a talk at the Harvard Club of New York, June 1994, under the title "Of Harvard, but Not in It: *Veritas* in Washington Square?" and forthcoming.

3. Ahead of all other institutions in many respects was Oberlin College, which produced black graduates from its inception in 1833.

4. Phillis Wheatley, "To the University of Cambridge, in New-England," in Sollors, Titcomb, and Underwood, *Blacks at Harvard,* p. 10.

5. Theodore Parsons and Eliphalet Pearson, "A Forensic Dispute on the Legality of Enslaving the Africans, Held at the Public Commencement in Cambridge, New-England," in ibid., pp. 15, 17.

6. Alexander Crummel, "The Attitude of the American Mind toward the Negro Intellect," address as president of the American Negro Academy, 1897, quoted in Henry Louis Gates Jr., *Loose Canons: Notes on the Culture Wars* (New York: Oxford University Press, 1992), pp. 72–73.

7. See Virginia Woolf, "On Not Knowing Greek," in *The Common Reader* (New York: Harcourt, Brace, 1925).

8. Richard T. Greener, "The White Problem," in Sollors, Titcomb, and Underwood, *Blacks at Harvard,* pp. 42–56.

9. Ibid., pp. 47, 49.

10. Ibid., p. 50.

11. Ibid., p. 53.

12. See David Levering Lewis, *W. E. B. Du Bois: Biography of a Race, 1868–1919* (New York: Henry Holt, 1994).

13. W. E. B. Du Bois, "A Negro Student at Harvard at the End of the Nineteenth Century," in *W. E. B. Du Bois: A Reader,* ed. David Levering Lewis (New York: Henry Holt, 1995), pp. 271–290.

14. See Sollors, Titcomb, and Underwood, *Blacks at Harvard,* pp. 195–227. Yale had already completely prohibited Negro residence in the dormitories.

15. Du Bois, quoted in ibid., p. 219; originally published in *The Crisis* (1923).

16. John Hope Franklin, "A Life of Learning," a Charles Homer Haskins Lecture

delivered in 1988 at the American Council of Learned Societies, printed in Franklin, *Race and History: Selected Essays, 1938–1988* (Lafayette: Louisiana State University Press, 1989), and reprinted in Sollors, Titcomb, and Underwood, *Blacks at Harvard,* pp. 289–295. Franklin, the first black president of the American Historical Association, received more than 100 honorary degress.

17. Frank Snowden, *Blacks in Antiquity* (Cambridge, Mass.: Harvard University Press, 1970).

18. See David Levering Lewis, ed., *The Portable Harlem Renaissance Reader* (New York: Viking, 1994).

19. Albert C. Barnes, "Negro Art and America," reprinted in ibid., pp. 128–133.

20. A. M. Jones, *African Music,* 2 vols. (Oxford: Oxford University Press, 1959); Gunther Schuller, *Early Jazz: Its Roots and Musical Development* (Oxford: Oxford University Press, 1968).

21. See Schuller, *Early Jazz,* pp. 27, 63–64.

22. Countée Cullen, "The Shroud of Color," in Sollors, Titcomb, and Underwood, *Blacks at Harvard,* pp. 242, 249.

23. Arthur A. Schomburg, "The Negro Digs Up His Past," in *Racial Integrity: A Plea for the Establishment of a Chair of Negro History in Our Schools, College, Etc.* (1913), reprinted in Lewis, *Harlem Renaissance Reader,* pp. 61–67.

24. Nathan Huggins, "Two Decades of Afro-American Studies at Harvard," in Sollors, Titcomb, and Underwood, *Blacks at Harvard,* pp. 505–511.

25. See ibid.

26. W. E. B. Du Bois, "The Negro College" (1933), reprinted in *Du Bois: A Reader,* pp. 69–70.

27. Ibid., p. 72.

28. Gates, *Loose Canons,* p. 113.

29. Walter E. Massey, remarks at Opening Convocation, Morehouse College, September 19, 1996, p. 2.

30. See Eileen Southern, "A Pioneer: Black and Female," in Sollors, Titcomb, and Underwood, *Blacks at Harvard,* pp. 499–504.

31. Schomburg, "The Negro Digs Up His Past," p. 66.

32. See Claudia Mills, "Multiculturalism and Cultural Authenticity," *Philosophy and Public Policy* 14 (1994): 1–5.

33. See Christopher Edley Jr., "The Boycott at Harvard: Should Teaching Be Colorblind?" in Sollors, Titcomb, and Underwood, *Blacks at Harvard,* pp. 462–466. For an impressively argued general account of the situation in the legal academy, see Randall L. Kennedy, "Racial Critiques of Legal Academia," *Harvard Law Review* 102 (1989): 1744–1819.

34. Huggins, "Two Decades of Afro-American Studies," pp. 505 ff.

35. Gates, *Loose Canons,* p. 127.

36. For example, Daniel Bonevac, William Boon, and Stephen Phillips, eds., *Beyond the Western Tradition* (Mountain View, Calif.: Mayfield, 1992); for more advanced students, Kwasi Wiredu's *African Philosophy* (Washington, D.C.: University Press of America, 1979).

37. W. E. B. Du Bois, "Of the Training of Black Men," in *The Souls of Black Folk* (New York: Vintage, 1990), p. 82.

38. Gates, *Loose Canons*, p. 176.

39. Syllabus, "African Diaspora and the World," Spelman College.

40. Massey, remarks at convocation, p. 2.

41. "The African-American Studies Major in the Department of History at Morehouse College," 1996.

42. Schomburg, "The Negro Digs Up His Past," p. 66.

43. See Jay H. Jasanoff and Alan Nussbaum, "Word Games: The Linguistic Evidence in *Black Athena*," in *Black Athena Revisited*, ed. Mary Lefkowitz and Guy Rogers (Chapel Hill: University of North Carolina Press, 1996).

44. Martin West, *Early Greek Philosophy and the Orient* (Cambridge: Cambridge University Press, 1971).

45. This suggestion is a problem in the argument of Mary Lefkowitz, *Not Out of Africa: How Afrocentrism Serves as an Excuse to Teach Myth as History* (New York: Basic Books, 1996).

46. See ibid.

47. See Richard King, *African Origin of Biological Psychiatry* (Germantown, Tenn.: Seymour-Smith, 1990); Carol Barnes, *Melanin* (privately published); Frances Cress Welsing, *The Isis Papers* (Chicago: Third World Press, 1991), pp. 1–16.

48. Michael Bradley, *The Iceman Inheritance* (New York: Kayode, 1978).

49. See Dyson's essay on Jeffries in *Reflecting Black* (Minneapolis: University of Minnesota Press, 1993).

50. Chinua Achebe, "An Image of Africa," in *Hopes and Impediments* (New York: Doubleday, 1988), p. 18.

51. Ibid.

52. Du Bois, "The Negro College," p. 75.

CHAPTER SIX   Women's Studies

1. See Susan Moller Okin, *Justice, Gender, and the Family* (New York: Basic Books, 1989).

2. See Amartya Sen, "More than 100 Million Women Are Missing," *New York Review of Books*, Christmas issue 1990, pp. 61–66; Martha C. Nussbaum and Jonathan Glover, eds., *Women, Culture, and Development* (Oxford: Clarendon

Press, 1995); Jean Drèze and Amartya Sen, *Hunger and Public Action* (Oxford: Clarendon Press, 1989).

3. See Anne Fausto-Sterling, *Myths of Gender,* 2nd ed. (New York: Basic Books, 1985).

4. See the United Nations' *Human Development Report* (New York: United Nations Development Programme, 1994), which estimates that if it were counted as output in national income accounts, global output would rise by 20 to 30 percent.

5. Gary Becker, *A Treatise on the Family,* rev. ed. (Cambridge, Mass.: Harvard University Press, 1991). See critical discussion in Okin, *Justice, Gender, and the Family,* and in Nussbaum and Glover, *Women, Culture, and Development.*

6. Martha Chen, lecture at Brown University, spring 1995.

7. See Amartya Sen, "Gender and Cooperative Conflicts," in *Persistent Inequalities,* ed. Irene Tinker (New York: Oxford University Press, 1990), pp. 123–149.

8. See the very end of Book VII.

9. The area of caring and family ethics, by now a major component of philosophical women's studies, developed slightly later than some of the others, although it was preceded, in the 1970s, by a general revival of interest in the topics of friendship and emotion. See, for example, Sara Ruddick, "Maternal Thinking," *Feminist Studies* 6 (1980): 342-367; Laurence Blum, *Friendship, Altruism, and Morality* (London: Routledge, 1980); Joyce Trebilcot, ed., *Mothering: Essays in Feminist Theory* (Totowa, N.J.: Rowman and Allanheld, 1984); Carol Gilligan, *In a Different Voice* (Cambridge, Mass.: Harvard University Press, 1982); Nel Noddings, *Caring* (Berkeley: University of California Press, 1984); Christina Hoff Sommers, "Filial Morality," *Journal of Philosophy* 83 (1986): 439–456.

10. See the excellent disciplinary surveys in Domna C. Stanton and Abigail J. Stewart, eds., *Feminisms in the Academy* (Ann Arbor: University of Michigan Press, 1995).

11. Jean Hampton, "Feminist Contractarianism," in *A Mind of One's Own: Feminist Essays on Reason and Objectivity,* ed. Louise B. Antony and Charlotte Witt (Boulder: Westview Press, 1992), pp. 227–255; Virginia Held, *Feminist Morality: Transforming Culture, Society, and Politics* (Chicago: University of Chicago Press, 1993); John Rawls, *A Theory of Justice* (Cambridge, Mass.: Harvard University Press, 1991) and "Political Liberalism: Women and the Family" (manuscript).

12. See Marcia Homiak, "Feminism and Aristotle's Rational Ideal," in Antony and Witt, *A Mind of One's Own;* Nancy Sherman, *The Fabric of Character: Aristotle's Theory of Virtue* (Oxford: Clarendon Press, 1989); Linda Hirshman, "The Book of 'A,'" *Texas Law Review* 70 (1992): 971–1012.

13. See Helen Longino: "To See Feelingly: Reason, Passion, and Dialogue in Feminist Philosophy," in Stewart and Stanton, *Feminisms in the Academy,* pp. 19–45.

14. See Annette Baier, "Hume: The Reflective Woman's Epistemologist?" in Antony and Witt, *A Mind of One's Own*, pp. 35–48; Helen Longino, "Essential Tensions—Phase Two: Feminist, Philosophical, and Social Studies of Science," ibid., pp. 257–272.

15. Antony and Witt, *A Mind of One's Own*, reviewed in Martha C. Nussbaum, "Feminist Philosophers," *New York Review of Books*, October 20, 1994, pp. 59–63.

16. Sarah Pomeroy, *Goddesses, Whores, Wives, and Slaves* (New York: Schocken, 1975); idem, *Xenophon's Oeconomicus* (Oxford: Oxford University Press, 1994).

17. See Sarah Pomeroy, "The Contribution of Women to the Greek Domestic Economy," in Stewart and Stanton, *Feminisms in the Academy*, pp. 180–195.

18. See especially Catherine Lutz, *Unnatural Emotions: Everyday Sentiments on a Micronesian Atoll and Their Challenge to Western Theory* (Chicago: University of Chicago Press, 1988).

19. See ibid. and Michelle Z. Rosaldo, *Knowledge and Passion: Ilongot Notions of Self and Social Life* (Cambridge: Cambridge University Press, 1980)..

20. Sarah Blaffer Hrdy, "Empathy, Polyandry, and the Myth of the Coy Female," in *Feminist Approaches to Science*, ed. Ruth Bleier (New York: Teachers College Press, 1991), 119–146, with bibliography; quotations on pp. 124, 125.

21. Ibid., pp. 134, 137.

22. Frans de Waal, "Bonobo Sex and Society," *Scientific American*, March 1995, p. 88.

23. Christina Hoff Sommers, *Who Stole Feminism?* (New York: Simon & Schuster, 1994), p. 89.

24. Daphne Patai and Noretta Kortge, *Professing Feminism* (New York: Basic Books, 1994).

25. Here Hoff Sommers cites philosopher Roger Scruton and colleagues in *Education and Indoctrination* (London: Sherwood Press, 1985), p. 96.

26. Sanford H. Kadish and Stephen J. Schulhofer, *Criminal Law and Its Processes: Cases and Materials*, 6th ed. (Boston: Little, Brown, 1995), chap. 4. See also Schulhofer, "Taking Sexual Autonomy Seriously: Rape Law and Beyond," *Law and Philosophy* 11 (1992): 35 ff., which won the American Philosophical Association's Fred Berger Prize in 1994 for the best article on philosophy and law.

27. Aristotle, *Nicomachean Ethics* 1095a5, 1103b26 ff., 1143b18 ff., 1179b35 ff.; *Eudemian Ethics* 1214b12 ff., 1215a8 ff.

28. Eve Stoddard, "The Politics of Autonomy: Wordsworth, Kant, and Moral Practices," manuscript in progress.

29. Barbara Herman, *The Practice of Moral Judgment* (Cambridge, Mass.: Harvard University Press, 1993); Onora O'Neill, *Acting on Principle* (New York: Columbia University Press, 1975) and *Constructions of Reason* (Cambridge: Cambridge University Press, 1989).

30. Marilyn Friedman, *What Are Friends For? Feminist Perspectives on Personal Relationships and Moral Theory* (Ithaca: Cornell University Press, 1993).

31. Iris Young, *Justice and the Politics of Difference* (Princeton: Princeton University Press, 1990).

32. See John Searle, "The Storm over the University," *New York Review of Books,* December 6, 1990.

33. Susan Moller Okin, *Women in Western Political Thought* (Princeton: Princeton University Press, 1979).

34. John Stuart Mill, *The Subjection of Women,* ed. Susan M. Okin (Indianapolis: Hackett, 1988); Okin, *Justice, Gender, and the Family.*

35. Hoff Sommers, *Who Stole Feminism?* p. 258.

36. Marilyn Friedman, "Does Sommers Like Women? More on Liberalism, Gender Hierarchy, and Scarlett O'Hara," *Journal of Social Philosophy* 21 (1990): 83, cited in Hoff Sommers, *Who Stole Feminism?* p. 258.

37. Hoff Sommers, *Who Stole Feminism?* pp. 258–259.

38. Ibid., pp. 259, 260.

39. John Harsanyi, "Morality and the Theory of Rational Behaviour," in *Utilitarianism and Beyond,* ed. Amartya Sen and Bernard Williams (Cambridge: Cambridge University Press, 1992), pp. 39–62.

40. Catharine MacKinnon, *Feminism Unmodified* (Cambridge, Mass.: Harvard University Press, 1987).

41. See especially Amartya Sen, "Gender Inequality and Theories of Justice," in Nussbaum and Glover, *Women, Culture, and Development,* pp. 259–273.

42. See Gary Becker, "The Economic Way of Looking at Life," in *The Essence of Becker,* ed. Ramón Febrero and Pedro S. Schwartz (Stanford, Calif.: Hoover Institution Press, 1995), pp. 633–658.

43. See Amartya Sen, "Freedoms and Needs," *New Republic,* January 10–17, 1994.

44. See Barbara Herman, "Could It Be Worth Thinking with Kant about Sex and Marriage?" in Antony and Witt, *A Mind of One's Own,* pp. 49–67.

45. Christina Hoff Sommers, "Should the Academy Support Academic Feminism?" *Public Affairs Quarterly* 2 (1988): 97–120.

CHAPTER SEVEN   The Study of Human Sexuality

1. Richard A. Posner, *Sex and Reason* (Cambridge, Mass.: Harvard University Press, 1992), p. 2.

2. Ibid., pp. 347, 346, 4.

3. U.S. v. Lallemand, 989 F.2d 936 (7th Cir. 1993).

4. Robert T. Michael, John H. Gagnon, Edward O. Laumann, and Gina Kolata, *Sex*

in America: A Definitive Survey (Boston: Little, Brown, 1994); Edward O. Laumann, John H. Gagnon, Robert T. Michael, and Stuart Michaels, *The Social Organization of Sexuality* (Chicago: University of Chicago Press, 1994).

5. Michael et al., *Sex in America*, p. 27.

6. Ibid.

7. Ibid., p. 29.

8. On changing norms, see Daniel M. Kahan and Martha C. Nussbaum, "Two Concepts of Emotion in Criminal Law," *Columbia Law Review* 96 (1996): 269–374.

9. Jean Briggs, *Never in Anger* (Cambridge, Mass.: Harvard University Press, 1981).

10. See Anne Fausto-Sterling, *Myths of Gender* (New York: Basic Books, 1992).

11. This example is based on the case of an MIT undergraduate who was expelled from ROTC after he discovered his sexual orientation.

12. Kenneth Dover, *Greek Homosexuality*, 2nd ed. (Cambridge, Mass.: Harvard University Press, 1986).

13. See David M. Halperin, *One Hundred Years of Homosexuality and Other Essays on Greek Love* (New York: Routledge, 1990); John J. Winkler, *The Constraints of Desire: The Anthropology of Sex and Gender in Ancient Greece* (New York: Routledge, 1990); Maud Gleason, *Making Men* (Princeton: Princeton University Press, 1995). For my work on this topic, see Martha C. Nussbaum, "Platonic Love and Colorado Law," *Virginia Law Review* 80 (1994): 1515–1651, with an appendix coauthored by me and Dover; and Nussbaum, "*Erōs* and the Wise: The Stoic Response to a Cultural Dilemma," *Oxford Studies in Ancient Philosophy* 13 (1995): 231–267.

14. See, e.g., Dover, *Greek Homosexuality*, p. vii: "A combination of love of Athens with hatred of homosexuality underlies the judgments that homosexual relations were 'a Dorian sin, cultivated by a tiny minority at Athens'" (Dover quotes scholar J. A. K. Thomson, whose view he is disputing).

15. Kenneth Dover, personal communication, February 11, 1994, on file with the *Virginia Law Review*.

16. C. J. Fordyce, *Catullus: A Commentary* (Oxford: Clarendon Press, 1961), p. v.

17. Both entries are from Charlton T. Lewis and Charles Short, *A Latin Dictionary* (1879). The 1968 *Oxford Latin Dictionary* is better, but not good: *pedicare* is defined as "to commit sodomy with," despite the fact that "sodomy" can designate both oral and anal sex acts, as the Latin verb cannot. As for the *irrumator*, he now is "one who submits to *fellatio*," which is not really the way the Romans saw things; for the *irrumator* is clearly thought to be the active, penetrative party, not one who passively "submits" to anything. The 1970 edition of Catullus by Kenneth Quinn gives precise definitions, but in Latin: "Literally, *pedicare* =

mentulam in podicem inserere and *irrumare* = *mentulam in os inserere*"; note to poem 16. See J. N. Adams, *The Latin Sexual Vocabulary* (Baltimore: Johns Hopkins University Press, 1982).

18. Roth v. U.S, 354 U.S. 476 (1957).

19. Kenneth Dover, *Marginal Comment* (London: Duckworth, 1994), p. 111.

20. See also Michel Foucault, *The Use of Pleasure*, vol. 2 of *The History of Sexuality*, trans. Robert Hurley (New York: Pantheon, 1985).

21. For the slimmer evidence on female homosexuality, see Dover, *Greek Homosexuality*, pp. 171–188.

22. Michael et al., *Sex in America*, p. 44; Laumann et al., *The Social Organization of Sexuality*, p. 543.

23. Laumann et al., *The Social Organization of Sexuality*, p. 548.

24. Winkler, *The Constraints of Desire*.

25. See Gary D. Comstock, *Violence against Lesbians and Gay Men* (New York: Columbia University Press, 1991).

CHAPTER EIGHT   Socrates in the Religious University

1. My source is John Armstrong, a BYU alumnus currently completing a Ph.D. at the University of Arizona.

2. See, for example, "The Death of Religious Higher Education," editorial, *First Things*, January 1991; and, in the same issue, George Marsden, "The Soul of the American University." See also Douglas Laycock, "The Rights of Religious Academic Communities," *Journal of College and University Law* 20 (1993): 15–42.

3. Pope John Paul II, Address to the United Nations General Assembly, October 5, 1995.

4. In the Republic of Ireland, formerly Catholic and Protestant institutions are all secular; anxiety about religious establishment is so strong that the study of Catholic theology is permitted only at Trinity College, the former Protestant institution.

5. Wisconsin v. Yoder, 406 U.S. 205 (1972).

6. In the late nineteenth century, however, Amish communities played a role in the creation of what are now known as Mennonite colleges.

7. Harold. W. Attridge, "Reflections on the Mission of a Catholic University," in *The Challenge and Promise of a Catholic University*, ed. Theodore M. Hesburgh (Notre Dame: Notre Dame University Press, 1994), p. 22.

8. See Theodore M. Hesburgh, "Academic Freedom," in *God, Country, Notre Dame: The Autobiography of Theodore M. Hesburgh* (New York: Doubleday, 1990), pp. 223–245.

9. Quinn's presidential address, "Political Liberalisms and Their Exclusions of the

Religious," is published in *Proceedings and Addresses of the American Philosophical Association* 69 (1995): 35–56.

10. Recently, however, the Theology Department appointed Rabbi Michael Signer to the Abrams Chair in Judaic Studies.

11. Philip Quinn, "Cultural Diversity and Catholicism in the University: Allies or Antagonists?" (manuscript, 1994).

12. See Theodore M. Hesburgh, "The Challenge and Promise of a Catholic University," in Hesburgh, *The Challenge and Promise,* p. 4.

13. Ibid., pp. 3, 5.

14. See ibid, p. xiv.

15. See Hesburgh, "Academic Freedom."

16. Attridge, "Reflections," pp. 17–18, quoting his own earlier speech.

17. Quinn, "Cultural Diversity," pp. 8–9.

18. See, for example, Alvin Plantinga, "On Christian Scholarship," in Hesburgh, *The Challenge and Promise,* pp. 267–295. Plantinga is a widely respected philosopher of religion from the Dutch Reformed Protestant tradition.

19. Paul Weithman, "Natural Law, Morality, and Sexual Complementarity," in *Shaping Sex, Preference, and Family: Essays on Law and Nature,* ed. David Estlund and Martha C. Nussbaum (Oxford: Oxford University Press, 1997), pp. 227–246.

20. See Hesburgh, "Academic Freedom."

21. Attridge, "Reflections," p. 24

22. Report of the Committee on Minority Students, 1987.

23. Administrative Board of the U.S. Catholic Conference, *Political Responsibility* (Washington, D.C, 1995).

24. Hesburgh, *God, Country, Notre Dame,* p. 182.

25. See Paul C. Richards, "Satan's Foot in the Door: Democrats at BYU" (manuscript, August 1993).

26. "The Mission of Brigham Young University," *Brigham Young University Bulletin,* 1993–94, p. 1.

27. On "continuing revelation," see Joseph Smith's "Wentworth Letter," March 1842, reprinted in *Encyclopedia of Mormonism,* ed. Daniel Ludlow (New York: Macmillan, 1992).

28. See BYU's current policy on academic freedom, cited in Laycock, "Rights of Religious Academic Communities."

29. Documents in Farr's case are cited in Brian Kagel and Bryan Waterman, "BYU, Crisis on Campus: The Farr/Knowlton Case" (manuscript, July 1994).

30. BYU Chapter of the American Association of University Professors, "Report on Issues of Academic Freedom at BYU," March 21, 1996.

31. Scott Abbott, "One Lord, One Faith, Two Universities: Tensions between 'Religion' and 'Thought' at BYU," *Sunstone,* September 1992, p. 15.

32. John Armstrong, "A Mormon Response to the Reason/Revelation Dichotomy" (manuscript, 1994).

33. BYU Chapter of AAUP, "Report on Issues."

34. See "Mother in Heaven," in *Encyclopedia of Mormonism*. See also Linda P. Wilcox, "The Mormon Conception of a Mother in Heaven," in *Women and Authority: Re-Emerging Mormon Feminism*, ed. Maxine Hanks (Salt Lake City: Signature Books, 1992), pp. 3–21.

35. See Michael Quinn, "Mormon Women Have Had the Priesthood since 1843," in Hanks, *Women and Authority*, pp. 365–409.

36. For two recent collections, see Maureen Beecher and Lavinia Fielding Anderson, eds., *Sisters in Spirit: Mormon Women in Historical and Cultural Perspective* (Urbana: University of Illinois Press, 1992); and George D. Smith, ed., *Religion, Feminism, and Freedom of Conscience: A Mormon Humanist Dialogue* (Buffalo: Prometheus Books, 1994).

37. Their research was published in *Affilia: Journal of Women and Social Work* 11 (1996).

38. BYU Chapter of the American Association of University Professors, "Limitations on the Academic Freedom of Women at Brigham Young University," March 21, 1996.

39. Peggy Fletcher Stack, "Feminist Fired by BYU for Beliefs," *Salt Lake City Tribune*, June 8, 1996.

40. See the pamphlet *Understanding and Helping Those Who Have Homosexual Problems* (Salt Lake City: LDS Church, 1992); also Boyd K. Packer, "The Father and the Family," *Ensign* 5 (1994): 19–21. A sophisticated and interesting discussion is in Dallin Oaks, "Same-Gender Attraction," in *Ensign* 23 (1995): 7 ff. See also BYU's *Student Review*, no. 6 (1991).

I would like to thank Ross Davies for his assistance in preparing the index.